The Rorschach: A Comprehensive System, in two volumes
 by John E. Exner, Jr.
Theory and Practice in Behavior Therapy
 by Aubrey J. Yates
Principles of Psychotherapy
 by Irving B. Weiner
Psychoactive Drugs and Social Judgment: Theory and Research
 edited by Kenneth Hammond and C. R. B. Joyce
Clinical Methods in Psychology
 edited by Irving B. Weiner
Human Resources for Troubled Children
 by Werner I. Halpern and Stanley Kissel
Hyperactivity
 by Dorothea M. Ross and Sheila A. Ross
Heroin Addiction: Theory, Research and Treatment
 by Jerome J. Platt and Christina Labate
Children's Rights and the Mental Health Profession
 edited by Gerald P. Koocher
The Role of the Father in Child Development
 edited by Michael E. Lamb
Handbook of Behavioral Assessment
 edited by Anthony R. Ciminero, Karen S. Calhoun, and Henry E. Adams
Counseling and Psychotherapy: A Behavioral Approach
 by E. Lakin Phillips
Dimensions of Personality
 edited by Harvey London and John E. Exner, Jr.
The Mental Health Industry: A Cultural Phenomenon
 by Peter A. Magaro, Robert Gripp, David McDowell, and Ivan W. Miller III
Nonverbal Communication: The State of the Art
 by Robert G. Harper, Arthur N. Wiens, and Joseph D. Matarazzo
Alcoholism and Treatment
 by David J. Armor, J. Michael Polich, and Harriet B. Stambul
A Biodevelopmental Approach to Clinical Child Psychology: Cognitive Controls and
Cognitive Control Theory
 by Sebastiano Santostefano
Handbook of Infant Development
 edited by Joy D. Osofsky
Understanding the Rape Victim: A Synthesis of Research Findings
 by Sedelle Katz and Mary Ann Mazur
Childhood Pathology and Later Adjustment: The Question of Prediction
 by Loretta K. Cass and Carolyn B. Thomas
Intelligent Testing with the WISC-R
 by Alan S. Kaufman
Adaptation in Schizophrenia: The Theory of Segmental Set
 by David Shakow
Psychotherapy: An Eclectic Approach
 by Sol L. Garfield
Handbook of Minimal Brain Dysfunctions
 edited by Herbert E. Rie and Ellen D. Rie
Handbook of Behavioral Interventions: A Clinical Guide
 edited by Alan Goldstein and Edna B. Foa
Art Psychotherapy
 by Harriet Wadeson
Handbook of Adolescent Psychology
 edited by Joseph Adelson
Psychotherapy Supervision: Theory, Research and Practice
 edited by Allen K. Hess

Continued on back

THE COURSE OF
ALCOHOLISM

THE COURSE OF ALCOHOLISM

FOUR YEARS AFTER TREATMENT

J. MICHAEL POLICH

DAVID J. ARMOR

HARRIET B. BRAIKER

A WILEY-INTERSCIENCE PUBLICATION

JOHN WILEY & SONS, New York • Chichester • Brisbane • Toronto

Published by John Wiley & Sons, Inc.

This publication is designed to provide accurate and
authoritative information in regard to the subject
matter covered. It is sold with the understanding that
the publisher is not engaged in rendering legal, accounting,
or other professional service. If legal advice or other
expert assistance is required, the services of a competent
professional person should be sought. *From a Declaration
of Principles jointly adopted by a Committee of the
American Bar Association and a Committee of Publishers.*

Library of Congress Cataloging in Publication Data
Polich, J. Michael.
    The course of alcoholism.

    (Wiley series on personality processes ISSN 0195-4008)
    Continues: Alcoholism and treatment, by D. J. Armor.
    "A Wiley-Interscience publication."
    Includes index.
    1. Alcoholism—Treatment—Longitudinal studies.
2. Psychotherapy—Evaluation. I. Armor, David J.,
joint author. II. Braiker, Harriet B., 1948- joint
author. III. Title. [DNLM: 1. Alcoholism. 2. Al-
coholism—Therapy. 3. Behavior. 4. Longitudinal studies.   WM274 P766c]
RC565.P619   616.86'106   80-24316
ISBN 0-471-08682-7

Printed in the United States of America
10 9 8 7 6 5 4 3 2 1

Series Preface

This series of books is addressed to behavioral scientists interested in the nature of human personality. Its scope should prove pertinent to personality theorists and researchers as well as to clinicians concerned with applying an understanding of personality processes to the amelioration of emotional difficulties in living. To this end, the series provides a scholarly integration of theoretical formulations, empirical data, and practical recommendations.

Six major aspects of studying and learning about human personality can be designated: personality theory, personality structure and dynamics, personality development, personality assessment, personality change, and personality adjustment. In exploring these aspects of personality, the books in the series discuss a number of distinct but related subject areas: the nature and implications of various theories of personality; personality characteristics that account for consistencies and variations in human behavior; the emergence of personality processes in children and adolescents; the use of interviewing and testing procedures to evaluate individual differences in personality; effects to modify personality styles through psychotherapy, counseling, behavior therapy, and other methods of influence; and patterns of abnormal personality functioning that impair individual competence.

IRVING B. WEINER

University of Denver
Denver, Colorado

Preface

This book describes a scientific research study of the course of alcoholism among patients who were followed over a four-year period after treatment. The study results were originally published as a report of The Rand Corporation, supported by Contract ADM-281-76-0006 of the National Institute on Alcohol Abuse and Alcoholism, U.S. Department of Health, Education and Welfare.* With support from The Rand Corporation, this volume was expanded to include more extensive discussion of the theoretical implications of the research, but otherwise the text is essentially the same as that in the original report.

The study is concerned with the natural history of alcoholism, particularly with the stability of alcoholic remission. Our purpose is to improve general understanding of alcoholism by tracing patterns of change in alcoholic behavior. We stress that our findings represent observations of the behavior of alcoholics; they are *not* prescriptive statements about how alcoholics should behave or how treatment should be conducted. This study does not recommend any particular treatment approach and does not recommend either controlled drinking or abstention as the more appropriate goal for alcoholics.

The present study is a sequel to our earlier work in which we reported on the same group of alcoholics 18 months after treatment.†* Rand research on alcoholism is continuing with further longitudinal studies of treated and untreated alcoholics.

J. Michael Polich
David J. Armor
Harriet B. Braiker

Santa Monica, California
January 1981

*J. Michael Polich, David J. Armor, and Harriet B. Braiker, *The Course of Alcoholism: Four Years After Treatment,* R-2433-NIAAA, Santa Monica, The Rand Corporation, 1980.
†*David J. Armor, J. Michael Polich, and Harriet B. Stambul, *Alcoholism and Treatment,* New York, John Wiley & Sons, 1978.

Acknowledgments

This study would not have been possible without the support and encouragement provided by several officials of the National Institute on Alcohol Abuse and Alcoholism. In particular, useful aid and advice have been given throughout the study by Leland Towle, Donald Patterson, and David Promisel, all of the NIAAA Office of Program Development and Analysis.

Valuable advice and comment were given by several research colleagues, including Dr. Samuel Guze, Department of Psychiatry, Washington University, St. Louis; Dr. Richard Jessor, Department of Psychology, University of Colorado; Dr. Sol Levine, Department of Sociology, Boston University; Dr. Charles Lieber, Mt. Sinai Medical School, New York; Dr. Robin Room, Social Research Group, University of California, Berkeley; Dr. Griffith Edwards, Institute of Psychiatry, University of London; Dr. David Kanouse, Social Science Department, Rand; and Dr. John Rolph, Statistics Group, Rand.

Considerable credit for the successful execution of the study goes to Dr. Henry Becker and Shirley Blumberg, who supervised the fieldwork conducted by the Johns Hopkins University. Overall organization of data collection and coding was handled by Jan Meshkoff, and computer programming was done by Kathryn Bers. Dr. Lee Ruggels and Ann Mothershead of SRI International assisted in the study design and arrangements with individual Alcoholism Treatment Centers. Expert secretarial support for the entire project was provided by Marjorie Schubert of Rand. Finally, special thanks go to the energetic Johns Hopkins interviewing staff, and especially to the subjects who gave their time and cooperation for research on the nature of alcoholism.

J. M. P.
D. J. A.
H. B. B.

Contents

ONE INTRODUCTION   1

Objectives and Research Questions, 2
Research Background, 4

Implications of the Classical Conception of Alcoholism, 4
Alternative Conceptions of Alcoholism, 6
Evidence on Change in Alcoholism, 7
Methodological Issues, 9

Context of This Study, 11
Plan of the Book, 14

TWO STUDY DESIGN AND METHODS   15

Background of the Cohort, 15
The NIAAA Monitoring System, 15
Origination of the Cohort, 16
Representativeness of the Study Cohort, 18

Four-Year Followup Sampling, 20

Defining the Sampling Frame, 20
Basic Sampling Results, 23

Data Collection Procedures, 25

Chronology, 25
Subject Interviews, 26
Validity Procedures, 27
Mortality Data Collection, 31

Assessing Potential Bias Due to Nonfollowup, 31

THREE DRINKING PATTERNS AT FOUR YEARS   35

Length of Abstention, 36
Quantity of Alcohol Consumption, 39

Alcohol Dependence Symptoms, 46
Adverse Consequences of Drinking, 50
Risk Patterns of Drinking Behaviors, 53
Assessment of Status at Four Years, 60

The Measure of Status at Four Years, 60
Adequacy of the Status Assessment, 61
Characteristics of the Status Groups, 64

Validity of the Status Classification, 67

BAC Measures and Consumption, 67
Collateral Measures, 68

Status at Four Years and Drinking at Admission to Treatment, 71
Alternative Definitions of Followup Status, 75
Assessing Group Changes Over Time, 77

FOUR   PSYCHOSOCIAL FUNCTIONING AT FOUR YEARS   80

Social Adjustment, 81

Social Adjustment at Four Years, 82
Time Trends in Social Adjustment, 85

Life Satisfaction and Stressful Events, 86

Life Satisfaction, 86
Stressful Life Events, 87

Emotional Adjustment and Personality, 89

Psychiatric Symptomatology, 91
Emotional Stability and Personal Resources, 93

Beliefs About Alcoholism, 97
Traditional Disease Concept, 97
Alcoholic Self-Concept, 99

Overall Psychosocial Profile of Drinking Categories, 100

Discriminant Function Coefficients, 101
Status Category Discrimination, 103

FIVE   MORTALITY   105

Mortality Data, 106
Underlying Cause of Death, 107
Actual and Expected Mortality, 111

Mortality by Age Group, 115
Mortality After the 18-Month Followup, 115

Alcohol-Related Mortality, 117
Correlates of Alcohol-Related Mortality, 121

Mortality Following Admission to Treatment, 121
Mortality After the 18-Month Followup, 123
An Alternative Method for Determining Alcohol-Related
Mortality, 125
Drinking Status at 18 Months, 127

SIX TREATMENT AND DRINKING BEHAVIOR   129

Effects of Subject Characteristics, 131
Measuring Treatment Patterns, 135
Assessing Amount and Type of Treatment, 137

Followup Status and Amount of Treatment, 137
Followup Status in Contact and Admission Samples, 139
Followup Status and Setting of Treatment, 140

Reentry to ATC Treatment, 141
Non-ATC Treatment and Assistance, 146

Formal Treatment from Non-ATC Sources, 147
AA Participation, 148

Models of Treatment and Drinking Behavior, 152

SEVEN STABILITY AND CHANGE IN DRINKING PATTERNS 159

Relapse, 160

Relapse: Definitions of Status at Four Years, 163
The "Remission" Definition, 172
Correlates of Relapse, 175
Theoretical Implications, 182

Stability of Status, 183

Definition of Stable Groups, 184
Correlates of Stable Status, 186

Long-Term Pattern of Drinking, 189

Amount of Abstention Over Four Years, 190
Long-Term Consumption Patterns, 192
Alcohol Incidents Over Four Years, 194
Definition of Long-Term Pattern of Alcohol Behavior, 196
Relationship Between Long-Term Pattern and Status at
Four Years, 196

EIGHT   CONCLUSIONS   201

    Drinking Behavior at Four Years, 202

      Basis of the Classification of Drinking Status, 204
      Comparisons With the 18-Month Study, 206

    Methodological Analysis, 207
    Mortality, 209
    Psychosocial Functioning, 209
    Treatment, 211
    Relapse and Stability, 214
    Implications for Policy and Research, 217

Appendix

  A.   FOLLOWUP RATES AND POTENTIAL BIAS
      ANALYSIS   222

  B.   VALIDITY OF SELF-REPORTED DRINKING
      BEHAVIORS   233

  C.   SUPPLEMENTAL ANALYSES   257

  D.   INDEX CONSTRUCTION   269

  E.   CLIENT INTERVIEW FORM   275

      REFERENCES   312

INDEX   325

ONE

Introduction

By all accounts, alcoholism is a persistent and chronic disorder. In fact, the most prominent feature of the condition is its apparent intractability. In medical definitions, chronicity is the essential characteristic that distinguishes alcoholism from more transient conditions. And in common parlance, a person labelled as "alcoholic" is one who has a history of repeated uncontrolled drinking, usually resulting in serious impairment. Accordingly, the future prospects for the chronically impaired alcoholic are very uncertain. Lay groups such as Alcoholics Anonymous contend the disorder is a lifelong disease that may be contained, but never cured. The prevailing view among physicians is similarly pessimistic. The consensus seems to be that alcoholism is persistent, difficult to treat, and apt to follow a dangerous course without strong intervention (Pattison, 1976).

Yet, the scientific evidence documenting positive change among alcoholics is widespread. Numerous clinical followup studies have shown that persons diagnosed as alcoholics, however serious their condition, can show considerable improvement after treatment. Research suggests that significant rates of remission may exist even without intervention. General population surveys have uncovered many cases of former problem drinkers whose problems have abated within a short period. Close experimental study has revealed that the drinking behavior of alcoholics is highly variable and apparently malleable by external influences. In short, the prevailing image of monolithic alcoholism, highly resistant to change, is discrepant with a great deal of modern evidence (Clark, 1975).

The way in which this discrepancy is reconciled is crucial to our understanding of alcoholism and to our policies for combating it. The key question is this: How alterable or unalterable is alcoholic behavior? If the disorder proves intractable, even small amounts of headway made against it will appear important. But if its course proves highly variable and subject to substantial remission, our expectations will be appropriately higher. Calculations of what constitutes a success in treatment clearly depend on the frequency of remission, and on the degree to which remission can be expected to continue without relapse. Plainly, all of these issues are germane to decisions about where to place societal resources—i.e., should they be devoted to treatment or to prevention. Evaluation and policy making depend on an empirically verified model of the process of change in alcoholism.

At this point, our understanding of that process is highly tentative. As we will show in our examination of the scientific literature, many issues about the course of alcoholism remain unresolved and are informed only by very limited data. The purpose of this study is to build a better empirical basis for understanding alcoholism by tracing its course over several years within a large national cohort of alcoholics. The analysis reported here concerns a randomly selected group of 922 subjects who contacted treatment centers funded by the National Institute on Alcohol Abuse and Alcoholism (NIAAA) during a baseline period in 1973. These subjects have been followed in a longitudinal design over a period of about 4 years; repeated assessments have been made at initial contact, 18 months, and 4 years, with more than 85 percent of the treatment admissions located at 4 years. The resultant data thus constitute both a series of point assessments and a longitudinal history of the cohort. In addition, we have obtained longitudinal treatment reports from the participating facilities. The data are broad in scope: they cover drinking and drinking problems, psychosocial functioning, physical functioning, and external assessments obtained from blood alcohol measurements as well as from collaterals. Together the various sources of information on this cohort make up a useful data base for tracing the course of alcoholism after treatment.

OBJECTIVES AND RESEARCH QUESTIONS

One immediate objective of this study is to describe the functioning of former patients of the NIAAA facilities. We accept the fact that these patients were admitted to clinical treatment for alcoholism as prima facie evidence that they suffered from the disorder. Fortunately, our baseline data on treatment admissions may be used to confirm this evidence. One of our first tasks will be to describe the cohort's drinking and social characteristics at admission to treatment, and then compare our sample with other groups identified as alcoholic. As we will show, the typical subject was highly impaired by alcohol at the baseline point, and most of the sample showed unmistakable signs of alcoholism, such as symptoms of alcohol dependence and extremely high levels of alcohol consumption.

The fact that this cohort is drawn from treatment centers means, of course, that the results apply principally to alcoholics who have, in one way or another, reached the point of contacting a treatment facility. Inferences to the "general" population of all alcoholics, including the untreated, may be hazardous. However, the scope of the study is considerably broader than a simple assessment of the condition of former patients. We intend to document, in quantitative detail, the nature and patterns of behavioral functioning among alcoholics. We will examine, in addition to alcohol use, symptoms of alcohol dependence and the adverse social consequences directly linked to alcohol consumption. Our purview also embraces psychological, social, and physical functioning, including morbidity and mortality.

Our central interest lies with the patterns of change in alcoholism. Most importantly, we will isolate the types of alcoholic remission and will examine their stability over time. We will also trace the varieties of treatment in which the subjects have been involved over a 4-year period and will examine the linkages of such treatment to alcoholic behavior. Finally, we will bring data to bear on several methdological issues that affect alcohol research, including the validity of self-reports, the generalizability of samples, and the effect of nonresponse or nonlocation rates on overall assessments at followup.

Because these issues are diverse, it may be useful to outline briefly the main research questions to be addressed. These can be grouped under four broad headings as follows:

Posttreatment Assessments. What are the characteristic patterns of posttreatment functioning among alcoholics? How much improvement may we expect to find relative to initial condition, in what forms, and along what dimensions? In particular, what types of drinking patterns are observed? What physical and medical problems are prominent? Are particular types of psychological or social functioning intimately associated with specific drinking or abstinence patterns? Do the various dimensions of drinking fit together with psychological, social, and physical conditions into identifiable clusters or do the dimensions crosscut each other significantly?

Stability and Change. What is the direction and extent of change in alcoholic condition over time? Do successive followups show a progressive worsening of conditions? Do problems remain "chronic," or do many individuals exhibit patterns of alcoholic remission? How stable is such remission when it occurs—is it lasting or transient? Does a patient's level of functioning at one point presage a particular course or prospect for future points?

Prognosis and Intervention. How do initial subject characteristics and types of intervention relate to subsequent functioning? How important are such factors as the presence of dependence symptoms, severity of impairment, amount of consumption, and social adjustment? What is the extent and role of treatment in the history of these alcoholics? How common is reentry to treatment or utilization of less formal treatment resources such as Alcoholics Anonymous? Is there significant change in alcoholism even with little or no intervention?

Methodology.   How representative is this cohort with respect to other known populations of alcoholics? What is the impact of the small group of nonresponding cases on the results? How likely are the findings to be affected by errors or underreporting in our self-report data?

These research questions are not novel in the field of alcoholism research; rather, they constitute a catalog of significant issues that students of alcoholism face. Our approach, however, grows out of the particular features of recent research and the circumstances surrounding the development of the NIAAA followup cohort. It is worthwhile, therefore, to consider the background of this research.

RESEARCH BACKGROUND

The literature documenting previous alcoholism research is so vast that a detailed review here is beyond our scope. Several comprehensive reviews focusing on treated populations have been done recently (Baekeland et al., 1975; Pomerleau et al., 1976; Emrick, 1974, 1975), and our own view of the general state of alcoholism research is available (Armor et al., 1978). Below we will simply outline some of the more salient aspects of thought and research on alcoholism that bear directly on an attempt to trace alcoholic behavior over time.

Implications of the Classical Conception of Alcoholism

Any consideration of the course of alcoholism is conditioned in large part by the conceptual scheme inspired by Jellinek (1946, 1960). This traditional model informs and directs much thinking and practice concerned with the treatment of alcoholism. Jellinek himself proposed an inclusive definition of "alcoholism"; his view encompassed any and all forms of adverse effects due to alcohol. Nevertheless, his emphasis was clearly placed on those "species," particularly the *gamma* species, that appeared to represent a disease process. In this view, addiction to the drug ethanol is a disease whose criterion is "loss of control." According to the classical formulation, a person suffering from the disease has been incapable of controlling his use of ethanol; the presence of ethanol in his body sets off a "chain reaction" leading to continued consumption despite his wishes. Physical dependence, manifested by withdrawal symptoms when alcohol ingestion is interrupted, represents the mechanism underlying this reaction.

Jellinek posited the existence of other forms of addiction as well. For example, he isolated as *delta* alcoholism the behavior of continuous drinking throughout the day, where the problem is inability to abstain rather than inability to stop. He also described nonaddictive forms of alcoholism, such as psychological dependence without physical dependence. Although Jellinek explicitly recognized that these disorders did not exhaust all phenomena called "alcoholism," his interpreters have tended to equate alcoholism with the gamma subtype as Jellinek defined it (Mann, 1958).

A particularly important aspect of the traditional conception of alcoholism is the assumption that the disease typically progresses through a series of definite stages. As outlined in Jellinek's classic articles on this subject (1946, 1952b), the addictive process begins with heavy drinking for relief of stress; passes into a "prodromal" phase marked by the onset of blackouts; proceeds thence into a "crucial" phase marked by the appearance of loss of control and morning drinking; and finally goes into a "chronic" phase indicated by binges, anxieties, cognitive impairment, tremors, and the accumulation of adverse social and physical consequences.

These phases of addiction were derived from retrospective accounts of AA members in the 1940s. Replication studies have called into question the invariance of the presumed order of phases and the existence of any particular order at all (Park, 1973; Trice and Wahl, 1958). As Clark has noted (1975), the dissemination of this theory among alcoholism organizations has been so wide that nowadays self-reports of crucial events in the sequence may, to some extent, reflect acceptance of the theory rather than occurrence of the events. Clearly a prospective study is needed to establish the typicality of any such progressive sequence, but none has been conducted in clinical populations. It has also been documented that an AA population is measurably different from other alcoholic groups on many characteristics, so that the universality of the progression is as yet unestablished (Trice and Roman, 1970).

It is obvious that clinical data alone are insufficient to establish a progression, because a retrospective analysis of alcoholics cannot determine the transition probability from one phase to the next—i.e., the probability that a person showing symptoms of one stage will actually go on to develop the symptoms of the successive stages. Nonetheless, the progressive model outlined by Jellinek remains the only widely known paradigm for change in alcoholism over time, and its validity is frequently assumed.

As a recent World Health Organization committee on definitions has recognized, there is no doubt that these events, particularly loss of control, reflect an important component in the experience of many alcoholics (Edwards et al., 1977b). Nevertheless, many elements of the traditional model have been challenged by an accumulation of empirical evidence. Both experimental and nonexperimental studies have failed to find support for the loss of control hypothesis (Paredes et al., 1973), and several other constructs associated with the model have been called into question by recent evidence (Pomerleau et al., 1976). Keller (1972) has suggested that a reformulation of the basic loss-of-control mechanism is in order, noting that uncontrolled drinking does not occur at all times among addicted drinkers but rather only with a certain nonzero probability. As Clark has pointed out (1975), this gives the notion of alcoholism a certain on-again, off-again quality, but perhaps that changeability represents the empirical reality of the disorder. A view that treats alcoholic symptomatology as variable over time rather than as lifelong and immutable would certainly be in better accord with the limited evidence from general-population surveys of problem drinkers (Clark and Cahalan, 1976).

Alternative Conceptions of Alcoholism

Other approaches to the definition and conceptualization of alcoholism have emphasized different criteria. The widely cited World Health Organization definition (1952) uses the criterion of "dependence" when it appears in conjunction with excessive drinking and "interference with bodily and mental health." Psychiatric research has sometimes fastened on the co-occurrence of several disparate indicators to reach a diagnosis (such as liver damage, inability to stop drinking, social adverse effects, and guilt because of drinking, as in Goodwin et al., 1971, or in Barchha et al., 1968). The diagnostic scheme proposed by the National Council on Alcoholism (1972) similarly relies on an eclectic list of "hints" of alcoholism while attempting to weight more heavily those factors that have played a central role in the traditional conception, such as withdrawal symptoms and tolerance. There is some empirical basis for questioning whether these wide-ranging sets of indicators hold together, but at least among clinical samples the relatively close relationship among the central alcoholism symptoms (blackouts, morning drinking, "shakes," inability to stop drinking) seems to be confirmed (Horn and Wanberg, 1969; Armor et al., 1978).

The physical sequelae of prolonged heavy drinking have always attracted attention and have sometimes been utilized as if they indicated alcoholism directly. For example, cirrhosis mortality rates have long been used as a measure of the rate of long-term heavy drinking and, by implication, of "alcoholism" in a population (Keller, 1962). The direct link between prolonged heavy drinking and liver disease has been well established clinically (Lelbach, 1974), and the aggregate correlation between a population's cirrhosis mortality rate and its alcohol consumption has been shown to be very strong across many different cultures and time periods (Bruun et al.,

1975). This has led one group, loosely known as the "single-distribution" school, to focus attention on amount of consumption rather than on symptoms as a direct indication of alcoholism (Schmidt and Popham, 1978). Indeed, these investigators have proposed a limit of 150 milliliters of ethanol per day as the standard for assessing "alcoholism," interpreted as a behavior exhibiting such high consumption as to entail extreme risk of organic pathology (De Lint and Schmidt, 1971).

Several elements from these diverse formulations have been brought together by a recent working group assembled by the World Health Organization. This group, charged with reviewing definitions and measures related to "alcohol-related disabilities," suggested that the persistence of abnormal drinking commonly found in alcoholics is often linked to the alcohol dependence syndrome (Edwards et al., 1977b). In this view, a subjective feeling of impaired control over drinking is one element useful for clinical diagnosis of the syndrome, along with such other elements as the amount of consumption, deviance in setting or style of drinking, and the appearance of withdrawal symptoms. In another context, Edwards (1974) has suggested that drug dependence needs to be conceptualized as a matter of degree rather than as an all-or-nothing attribute. The degree of drug dependence may be indicated by the extent to which use of the drug shows a lack of "plasticity," i.e., the capability of being molded or changed by external forces. Such a conception, of course, is 180 degrees different from the traditional notion of inability to control drinking; if the ability to drink or not to drink can be altered or conditioned by external circumstances, the conditions for the traditional model would appear to be unfulfilled. In fact, in most modern views, the extent to which symptoms such as uncontrolled drinking may progress, remit, or abate over time remains an empirical question.

Evidence on Change in Alcoholism

A great deal of the existing evidence on the extent of change in alcoholism comes from followup studies of clinical populations. This literature, which is now so extensive that careful review of it has almost become a profession in itself, does not readily lend itself to generalization (Emrick, 1974). Comparison across studies is perilous because of the lack of explicit measurement procedures and the frequent use of broad clinical judgments of what is "improved," "unimproved," etc. Added to this are the numerous methodological deficiencies to which applied research is usually subject, such as the use of convenient samples rather than random ones, failure to measure all sample members at followup, and lack of randomization or statistical control in analysis (Hill and Blane, 1967). Nevertheless, certain broad patterns of findings from clinical research appear frequently enough to suggest the degree to which empirical reality fits the theoretical models of alcoholism.

The most obvious of such findings is the substantial evidence of improvement that occurs in many alcoholics between admission to treatment and various points of followup. Emrick (1974) found a mean rate of 67 percent "improved" in a review of 265 studies. In one of the best-designed experimental studies to date, Edwards et al. (1977a) recently reported a rate of 63 percent. At least one long-term study (5 years from admission to followup) discerned an 80-percent rate of favorable outcomes among those located (Fitzgerald et al., 1971), while Clare (1976) suggested that a rate of 50 percent is closer to the truth. However, there is a general feeling among methodological critics that all such rates are potentially inflated by the presumed high proportion of "failures" among those not followed up (Hill and Blane, 1967; Baekeland et al., 1975). Moreover, the clinical impression that success is fleeting appears unaffected by positive followup data. Finding that 40 percent of alcoholic felons were in remission at the time of an 8-year followup, Goodwin et al. (1971) characterized this rate as "rather high" and speculated that alcoholic felons may suffer from less serious problems than clinical alcoholics even though their apparent symptomatology may be equally severe.

In light of traditional conceptions of the chronicity of alcoholism, what has been even more suprising is the *nature* of followup behavior observed among alcoholics. Complete abstinence characterizes only a minority of patients even at fairly short followup intervals (Emrick, 1974). Long-term abstinence is even less frequent, and the proportion of patients remaining abstinent declines dramatically within the first 2 years (Orford et al., 1976); only 10 to 15 percent of patients may be found abstaining continuously from initial treatment to a 1- or 2-year followup (Fitzgerald et al., 1971; Gerard and Saenger, 1966; Armor et al., 1978). Yet among the drinkers, varying proportions at any one time show strong evidence of remission. Literally dozens of independent studies have observed abatement of symptoms despite continued drinking (Pattison, 1976; Lloyd and Salzberg, 1975). The stability of this abatement, however, has rarely been subject to empirical test. Armor et al. (1978) found that roughly half of remitted drinkers at one point were similarly classified at a later point, a finding consistent with those of Orford et al. (1976). An additional complexity is introduced by the observation, noted by Gerard and Saenger (1966), that neither abstinence nor remission of symptoms may be assumed to imply a general improvement in nondrinking domains (i.e., psychological adjustment or social functioning). About the best that can be concluded at present is that the progressive deterioration posited by the traditional model of alcoholism is not observed in aggregate assessments of treated groups.

Additional evidence supporting the notion that alcoholism is not necessarily chronic comes from studies of "untreated" problem groups. Imber et al. (1976) found significant improvement among minimally treated alcoholics at both 1-year and 3-year followups, although long-term abstinence rates reached a mere 10 percent. Kendell and Staton (1966) found 16 percent abstention and 36 percent nonproblem drinking among untreated clinic referrals at long-term followup (although in fact many of these referrals received some help in the meantime). As mentioned above, Goodwin et al. (1971) discerned remission of problems among 40 percent of alcoholic felons at an 8-year followup. Reviewing retrospective life histories of alcoholics gleaned from relatives' reports, Lemere (1953) estimated that 11 percent stopped drinking altogether in the absence of serious illness requiring it, and another 10 percent experienced gradual attenuation of problems. Drew (1968) has argued that, based on the age distribution of treatment admissions, alcoholism must gradually abate over time, being a "self-limiting disease."

In reviewing these and other bits of evidence on "spontaneous recovery," Smart (1975) has concluded that while the phenomenon undoubtedly occurs, it may well be limited to only a few percent per year of an original cohort of alcoholics. Roughly similar conclusions may be drawn from survey studies that have identified problem drinkers at one point in time and reinterviewed the same persons later (Clark and Cahalan, 1976; Roizen et al., 1978). Such remission rates have also been observed even among problem groups identified by classical alcoholism symptoms (Clark and Cahalan, 1976). The paucity of studies dealing with untreated alcoholics or problem drinkers is remarkable, however, and it must be concluded that very little is definitely known about the course of alcoholism in the absence of treatment.

Methodological Issues

No examination of the alcoholism literature can avoid the thorny methodological issues that surround the substantive conclusions of even the best-designed studies. A vital issue is the adequacy of sampling and population definitions. By taking clinic admissions as the defined population of alcoholics, many studies avoid the difficulties of defining alcoholism but wind up by simply accepting the definitions of admissions personnel, with whatever vagaries they may contain, and whatever selective factors may induce alcoholics to be presented for treatment in the first place (Clark, 1975; Miller et al., 1970). Thus, even the elementary specification of the sampling universe is often omitted. In sampling, consecutive admissions or random selection may be used, but frequently exclusions are made on the basis of sex, mental competence, physical disorders, or even social stability (Baekeland et al., 1975; Pittman and Tate, 1969). In addition, subjects may exclude themselves by refusing treatment or by failure to show up, a factor sometimes compounded by the evaluator's decision to include in the study only persons completing a specified period of treatment (Miller et al., 1970). All of these exclusions imply restrictions on generalizability; hence methodological critics have repeatedly urged that exclusions be avoided or at least reported with acknowledgement of their effect on representativeness.

A much more difficult methodological issue crops up in the frequent inability of followup studies to obtain data on the entire sample. Of course, nonfollowup can result from a variety of sources (inability to locate, refusal, death, incapacitation), not all of which are necessarily indicators of bias in the obtained sample. This general problem of nonresponse by targeted sample members is a common issue in all types of survey studies, where response rates of 80 percent are generally accepted as adequate. In the alcohol and drug fields, however, nonresponse is often taken as an indication of unfavorable status or treatment failure; indeed, Baekeland et al. (1975) went so far as to suggest that nearly every case lost to followup might be considered a failure. Similarly, Pittman and Tate (1969), after finding 12 out of 13 nonfollowup cases "functioning poorly," suggested that followup rates of at least 90 percent should be required for definitive results. The questionableness of such extreme assumptions of nonfollowup bias is demonstrated by the recent data of Moos and Bliss (1978). However, these authors did find a tendency for nonfollowup cases, especially noncooperators, to be worse on a number of dimensions than those successfully followed. The importance of this issue suggests that a close examination of the potential for bias among nonfollowups is in order, no matter how high the followup rate.

A third important methodological issue, and a most difficult one, is the question of the validity of self-reports relating to alcohol. The view is widespread that denial and minimization distort such self-reports, despite the results of a few studies suggesting that self-reports may not be very inaccurate after all (Gerard and Saenger, 1966; Guze et al., 1963; Sobell and Sobell, 1975). Clinical followup studies seem especially vulnerable to such problems because the alcoholic may wish to present himself in the best light to avoid shame or pressure for further treatment. Certainly the incentives for distortion are reduced to the extent that the followup organization is nonthreatening (e.g., not associated with police or welfare agencies) and nonclinical (e.g., not reporting back to the original treatment or identification agency).

Research on the validity question is, unfortunately, in a primitive state. One of the problems is that for many phenomena (e.g., symptoms) only the subject is in a position to observe the event. This makes the subject's self-report imperative, yet it also makes any sort of corroboration difficult. The result is paradoxical. Where outsiders (collaterals) are used to corroborate self-reports, it is found that many of them are in a poor position to give corroboration; they just do not know the requisite facts (Guze et al., 1963). This situation may seem less problematic where official records are used for corroboration (as in Sobell, Sobell, and Samuels, 1974), but even records can be faulty—as is well known in studies of police records—and the events measured are usually restricted to very serious adverse drinking consequences, omitting alcoholic symptomatology or consumption. Numerous other methodological issues exist, such as the value of quantitative measures versus global judgments and the optimum period of followup (Hill and Blane, 1967). However, the three issues just enumerated appear to pose the most serious threats to the ultimate validity of assessments of alcoholic history. In our discussion of study design (Chapter 2), we will explain how this study has attempted to evaluate the impact of such methodological problems.

CONTEXT OF THIS STUDY

The development of this study occurred against the general research background just described, but within a special context formed by the history of the NIAAA evaluation system and research growing out of that system. A brief sketch of this special context will help to place the present study in perspective.

The development process began in 1970 when NIAAA was first established by the U.S. Congress with a mandate for conducting treatment and rehabilitation efforts (Public Law 91-616). In 1971, NIAAA began to fund a network of comprehensive alcoholism treatment centers along with a monitoring system for collecting data on every client served. Under the monitoring system, individual data were collected at the time of a client's initial contact with the center (called "contact"). More data were obtained at the time of formal admission to treatment (called "admission") and 6 months after admission ("6-month followup"). In addition, each center filed a monthly treatment report with the monitoring system, detailing the types of treatment and number of days, hours, or visits of each type provided to each client. These data were to be used for evaluation of programs as well as for general research. Gradually, information on a large cohort of alcoholics began to accumulate, reaching a total of 11,000 admissions by 1974.

It soon became evident that additional information would be desirable. The admission and followup forms provided fairly detailed information on drinking, symptoms, and social circumstances (see Armor et al., 1978).

However, the 6-month followup reports were completed on only 25 percent of persons admitted, leading to the possibility of bias due to nonfollowup. Also, doubts arose about the adequacy of a followup as early as 6 months, even though the median length of treatment was only about 3 months. In response, NIAAA commissioned an 18-month followup study based on a random sample of admissions and contacts from eight selected treatment centers. The eight centers themselves constituted a purposive sample of all centers, although the characteristics of the individual persons selected were very close to those in the entire system of 44 treatment centers (Armor et al., 1978). The overall study design and data analysis were accomplished by the Stanford Research Institute and published in an SRI report (Ruggels et al., 1975). Slightly later, the same data were further analyzed and compared with the 6-month followup reports in a more comprehensive study by the present authors (Armor et al., 1976). This study, often referred to as the "Rand Report" (Hingson et al., 1977), was later expanded into a book with documentation of the extensive debate that followed the original publication (Armor et al., 1978).

The 18-month studies documented several significant facts that, by and large, are in accord with the modern literature on alcoholism. First, they showed that the aggregate outcome rates from the 6-month followup were nearly the same as those from the 18-month followup, even though considerable amounts of individual shifting from one status to another could be observed among individuals measured at both points. Second, they showed that substantial rates of remission among drinkers could be found within the periods before followups. A large group of alcoholics, termed "normal drinkers" in the Rand study, reported low-to-moderate levels of drinking but little or no symptomatology. Because these persons exhibited behavior that is commonly found among nonproblem drinkers in general population surveys, they were included among remissions. Third, the data showed that subjects who received significant amounts of treatment (about five outpatient visits or 3 weeks of intermediate care) fared somewhat better than those who received minimal amounts of treatment or only a single "contact." Because the treatment groups were not randomly assigned, some of these findings were only suggestive rather than definitive. However, the fact that the results held up under controls for a wide range of variables (severity of alcoholism, social stability, socioeconomic status, etc.) appeared to strengthen the implications.

As is usual in research, these results stimulated further questions as soon as they were reported. Many of the questions thus brought to the fore have become essential items on the agenda for the present study. In particular, methodological issues regarding the adequacy of followup and the validity of self-reports were pointedly raised by some of the limitations in the 18-month study.

First, there were the perennial doubts about self-reports. As in most studies, there was no opportunity at the 18-month followup to collect external validating data against which the subject self-reports could be compared. At the time, very little information on this issue was available although we did include some data from other sources in our study (Armor et al., 1978). Second, the presence of substantial nonresponse constituted a weakness. Only about 60 percent of the intended sample was interviewed, leaving open the question of possible nonfollowup biases. The 18-month studies demonstrated that the obtained sample was equivalent to the target sample on numerous characteristics at admission and adduced other arguments suggesting relatively small bias, but the only decisive condition for resolving the issue—a very high followup rate—was absent. Third, the adequacy of the term of followup (18 months after admission) could be questioned. Although most studies have conducted their followups at 6 months or 1 year, the possibility remained that the rates of remission might later decline. Associated with this possibility was the fact that the 18-month study focused on very recent drinking behavior, covering 30 days before the followup interview. This made it necessary to classify any persons not drinking in the past 30 days as "abstaining," even if a drinking bout had just occurred in the previous month. It also led to the possibility that the observation of moderate drinking could, during the 30-day period, be masking a short-term oscillation involving moderate-drinking phases mixed with heavy-drinking phases.

The present study was designed against the backdrop of these methodological considerations. Indeed, in many respects the most important reasons for undertaking a 4-year followup of this cohort arose from the motivation to surmount these methodological obstacles and to retest the findings of the 18-month and 6-month followups. In the meantime, certain advances have been made that also influenced this study. One of them is the increasing recognition in the scientific literature that many alcoholics, whether treated or not, go back to drinking after periods of abstinence without experiencing alcohol-related problems to the same degree as they previously had (Pomerleau et al., 1976; Smart, 1975; Saunders and Kershaw, 1979; Pattison, 1976). The stability of this nonproblem drinking is therefore an important issue.

A second advance is the trend toward more specific differentiation between the alcohol dependence syndrome and other alcohol-related problems, exemplified by the recent World Health Organization report (Edwards et al., 1977b). When the dependence syndrome is seen in the WHO framework, the centrality of dependence is clear and the need to test its empirical importance becomes even more obvious. At least one study of a heterogeneous population has documented the importance and measurability of dependence symptoms (Polich and Orvis, 1979), but specific use of the concept in followup studies has been limited. It has long been our hypothesis that dependence symptoms—

not just loss of control but a broader set of indicators—could well constitute a useful set of empirical criteria for establishing a threshold of high-risk, problem-prone drinking behavior. This study therefore set out to isolate and test the value of dependence symptoms, broadly defined, in tracing the history of a clinical population.

PLAN OF THE BOOK

The remainder of this book is divided into seven chapters. Chapter 2 describes in detail the design of the followup study and its methods, including the results of the fieldwork and our attempts to address methodological questions. In Chapter 3, we describe the basic results of measuring drinking behavior and alcohol-related problems in the followup cohort. In Chapter 4, we examine psychosocial functioning through interview responses and self-descriptions at the 4-year followup point. Chapter 5 deals with rates of mortality, causes of mortality, and the extent to which alcohol appears to be involved in the excess mortality that is apparent. Chapter 6 reports on the extent of treatment that has occurred in this population over 4 years and the relation of that treatment to drinking status at followup. Chapter 7 analyzes long-term patterns of stability and change over the 4-year period, including relapse. Finally, Chapter 8 provides a summary of the results and general conclusions about the nature and course of alcoholism.

TWO

Study Design and Methods

This study was designed to trace the history of alcohol-related problems among a cohort of individuals who contacted NIAAA Alcoholism Treatment Centers (ATCs) as prospective clients during a baseline period in 1973. Data were collected from the cohort at initial contact, at admission (if admitted to treatment), and at several subsequent followup points, including 6 months, 18 months, and 4 years after contact (Fig. 2.1). In this chapter we describe 'he details of the design and the methods of carrying it out. Our topics include the background of the cohort; the 4-year followup sampling; the procedures of other data collection; and an assessment of the potential bias due to nonfollowup.

BACKGROUND OF THE COHORT

The NIAAA Monitoring System

As described in Chapter 1, data on the subject cohort grew out of the monitoring system covering all NIAAA-funded Alcoholism Treatment Centers (ATCs). In early 1973, when the baseline measurements on the cohort

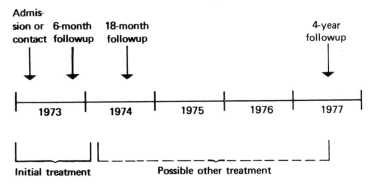

Figure 2.1 Time framework of the research.

were initiated, there were 44 ATCs operating in the system. From 1971 until that time, several thousand patients had been admitted to formal treatement. The monitoring system collected very limited data from each prospective client at initial contact: primarily race, sex, referral source, treatment disposition, and whether the referral was related to an arrest for driving while intoxicated (DWI). If the prospective client was admitted to formal treatment (either inpatient or outpatient), a much longer and more detailed form was filled out by an ATC staff member in the course of an admission interview.[1] Whether or not the individual was ever admitted to the ATC, the center assigned the person an identifying number and maintained records on every treatment service provided to that person (e.g., hours of detoxification, days of hospital stay, number of outpatient counseling sessions, etc.). The ATCs delivered contact records, admission records, and monthly treatment reports for each case to a central computer system that maintained files for each individual. These files constitute the baseline and initial treatment data for the present study.[2]

Origination of the Cohort

In late 1973, NIAAA initiated an 18-month followup study covering a subset of the 44 ATCs then in operation. Eight such ATCs participated in the study. The ATCs were selected by judgment rather than at random, the principal objective being diversity based on the geographical location of the facility, its size, and the nature of its program.[3] All admissions who made initial contact with these centers between January 1 and April 30 1973 were included in the 18-month study sample (N = 1340). In addition, a random sample was drawn from prospective clients who made contact during that period but who were not admitted (N = 976). This latter sample was intended to represent a minimally treated "contact only" comparison group. Between July and October 1974, these target samples were followed up via personal interview. Slightly more than two-thirds of the total target sample were actually located, including approximately 60 percent interviewed and 5 percent deceased.

---

[1]These forms are reproduced in Armor et al. (1978).

[2]Treatment centers were also expected to attempt a followup interview at 6 months after admission, as well as certain shorter-term followups. However, only about 25 percent of such followups were actually filed, and this study does not use them for analysis.

[3]The ATCs were those located in Baltimore, Md.; Orlando, Fla.; Fort Dodge, Iowa; Pine Bluff, Ark.; Fort Worth, Texas; San Antonio, Texas; Phoenix, Ariz.; and San Jose, Calif. Basic statistics on individual ATCs may be found in Appendix C. Overall, variations associated with individual centers (e.g., region of the country) appear not to affect the results in a signficant way.

Further details on the 18-month procedures may be found in Armor et al. (1978) and Ruggels et al. (1975).

The determination of whether a given alcoholic would become an admission or a "contact only" (or, indeed, whether a particular alcoholic in the community would present himself even as a contact) was not a random one. The treatment centers by and large have facilities for treating most types of patients; but in the nature of the treatment admission process, many prospective admissions are referred elsewhere, or refuse to enter treatment. The centers had a policy of not filing an initial contact report for nonproblem drinkers, and each center had a data coordinator to monitor reporting practices. Therefore, the nonadmission (contact) group should not contain any significant number of persons without alcohol problems. However, the precise nature of the nonadmissions' alcohol problems was not ascertained at baseline because no detailed data were collected for them. An indication that their problems were substantial can be seen in the fact that 47 percent of the "contact only" sample had heavy consumption or alcoholic symptoms at the 18-month followup, a rate that was 14 percentage points higher than that for the admissions (Armor et al., 1978, p. 117). However, we do not have detailed statistical data on their behavior at the baseline. The nonadmission group remains a useful comparison group, then, but not a definitive one of the sort used in the study by Edwards et al. (1977a).

Analysis of admission data on the ATC population showed clearly that individuals admitted to these programs for DWI violations were a much less impaired population than the other alcoholics at the centers (Armor et al., 1978). Also, DWIs were attending outpatient sessions under court order, in contrast to the voluntary presence of the other patients. Therefore, DWIs, who constituted about 15 percent of admissions, were excluded from consideration for the 4-year followup. Similarly, females were excluded from consideration because of their less-impaired condition and their small numbers (also about 15 percent of the total). Since the 4-year followup was designed to concentrate on a smaller random sample with more intensive procedures and detailed data, to include these groups would have produced very small samples for analysis (perhaps 50 of each). Rather than use valuable resources to follow such small groups at 4 years, we omitted them from the 4-year sampling frame. (These groups were followed up at 18 months but not included in most analyses in the 18-month study.) No other exclusions were made from the 4-year study sample of patients admitted to treatment. Patients who received an admission form but never returned, those who dropped out of treatment, or those with physical or mental disorders were all included in our target sample. In the 18-month study, a small number of cases ($N = 47$) were excluded from the followup procedures because of their wishes to remain anonymous at that time, but these persons were retained in the target sample for the 4-year followup.

Representativeness of the Study Cohort

A common problem in comparing studies of alcoholism treatment stems from the differing compositions of clinic populations. In many instances, it is difficult to determine the representativeness of a sample vis-à-vis a conceptual population of "all treated alcoholics" (Miller et al., 1970). Hence generalizability may be restricted. One might well ask, How representative is the ATC population? Being publicly supported, the ATCs could be suspected of reaching alcoholics with lower socioeconomic status or perhaps of serving a disproportionate number of public inebriates. The latter possibility appears not to have happened. Analysis of the admission data showed that only about 15 percent of the ATC admissions could be classified as public inebriates (using the criteria of living in group quarters, being unmarrried, and being unemployed). To further address these issues, we have compared the ATC admissions with those in a representative national sample of all U.S. alcoholism treatment facilities.[4] These facilities were randomly drawn from the 1973 directory of the Alcohol and Drug Problems Association of North America stratified by geographical region (northeast, midwest, south, and west) and by setting of treatment offered (hospital inpatient, intermediate, and outpatient). Baseline data were collected through personal interviews at time of admission by outside researchers (not affiliated with the facilities), using consecutive admissions in the spring of 1976.

Table 2.1 compares the entire ATC population, the sampling frame for the eight ATCs, and the national representative facility sample in terms of characteristics at admission to treatment. By and large it may be seen that for each characteristic, the subjects in the sample of eight ATCs are very close to the full ATC population. (There are some statistically significant differences appearing by virtue of the very large sample sizes, but the estimated underlying population parameters are obviously very close together.) Perhaps more surprising, the patients of NIAAA treatment centers are not very different from the national sample of patients at admission. If anything, the ATC groups appear to be slightly better off at admission in terms of prognostic factors such as marital status and behavioral impairment. In our judgment, the modest size of these differences suggests that the ATC population is broadly similar to the general population of persons who enter

---

[4]We are following up patients of these facilities in a separate study under NIAAA Grant No. 3 R01 AA01203-4. Full details will be contained in later reports. The facilities include private and public organizations ranging from hospitals with coordinated outpatient programs to short-term residential units.

Table 2.1   Characteristics of Admissions at NIAAA Treatment Centers and National Sample of U.S. Facilities[a]

Characteristic	Percent with the Characteristic		
	NIAAA ATCs, 1973		U.S. Facilities, 1976 (representative sample of all alcoholism facilities)
	44 ATCs	8 ATCs	
Alcohol consumption 5 oz. or more[b]	58	61	59
Behavioral impairment score (mean)[c]	13.9	13.9	14.6
Previously treated for alcoholism	44	43	(d)
Ever attended AA	57	58	(d)
Employed currently	36	36	40
Separated/divorced	36	36	50
Nonwhite, Spanish	27	22	23
Non-high-school graduate	53	49	52
Years in community (under 4)	50	52	51
Age 50 or over	31	42	29
(N)	(3117)	(1423)	(821)

[a]Male non-DWI admissions only.
[b]Consumption measured by the NIAAA quantity-frequency index representing ounces of ethanol per day over a 30-day period. For computation methods, see Appendix D.
[c]Score, ranging from 0 to 30, derived from the mean of 12 impairment items representing alcoholism symptoms and problems (tremors, morning drinking, difficulty sleeping, missing work because of drinking, etc.). For computation methods, see Appendix D.
[d]Not available.

formal treatment at recognized alcoholism facilities in the United States. Certainly the ATC population is not radically different. For example, it does not include only one socioeconomic group or only a particular range of symptom severity.

It should be noted that both the subject population and the treatment centers are highly diverse in character. Impressionistically, the centers appeared to follow a policy of serving all comers within their "catchment area," but the nature of the programs, as well as the local populations, varied in a number of ways that would influence the types of referrals and admissions. A description of the particular programs and their individual treatment modalities is beyond our scope here, but clearly the centers are varied in organization, scope, and setting. In Fort Dodge, Iowa, for instance, the ATC staff was intimately familiar with most aspects of the surrounding rural community and its population, whereas in the decentralized units of the large San Jose facility, the center interacted with a much more differentiated and mobile patient population in a metropolitan setting. In our view, these variations among sampling sites are desirable because they provide coverage of the wide diversities that exist among the nation's treatment facilities.

FOUR-YEAR FOLLOWUP SAMPLING

Defining the Sampling Frame

In the execution of the 18-month study, it was apparent that the size of the followup rate was depressed somewhat by the dilution of resources in tracking down so many subjects (N = 2316), many of whom turned out to be less than optimally suited for analysis. Both DWI and female subjects appeared to represent special populations that were simply not present in sufficient proportions to support detailed analysis in a representative sample. Then, too, we questioned whether the relatively few such persons, even if followed up, might constitute a highly select subset of their parent populations. For different reasons, the nonadmissions possessed certain disadvantages for analysis, not being randomly equivalent to the admissions and not having a baseline measurement of alcohol problems. Accordingly, the sample design for the 4-year followup excluded females and DWIs entirely and targeted only a random sample of nonadmissions for followup activities. The steps followed in establishing the sampling frame for the 4-year study are shown in Fig. 2.2.

The top of Fig. 2.2 shows the very beginning of the sampling process, in which the population is defined as those persons contacting one of eight ATCs during the baseline period (January through April 1973). From that population was drawn the target sample for the 18-month study; 100 percent of admissions during that period were included, but for nonadmissions, a random probability sample was drawn. (Only 60 percent of this sample was interviewed, but both 18-month followup and nonfollowup cases were retained in the 4-year sampling frame.) We then selected only male non-DWI cases and subdivided them into admissions and nonadmissions. Our primary interest lay in the admissions because detailed baseline data were available for them. We were especially interested in those admissions who had been successfully followed up at 18 months because they had been given a posttreatment assessment.

To ensure representation of all admissions regardless of whether they had been located at 18 months, we included both types: (I) those interviewed at 18 months; and (II) those not interviewed for whatever reason. Group II thus contained people who were unlocatable at 18 months, those who refused, those who had died, and all other noninterviewees. In order to concentrate resources on those with the most data, all members of Group I were included

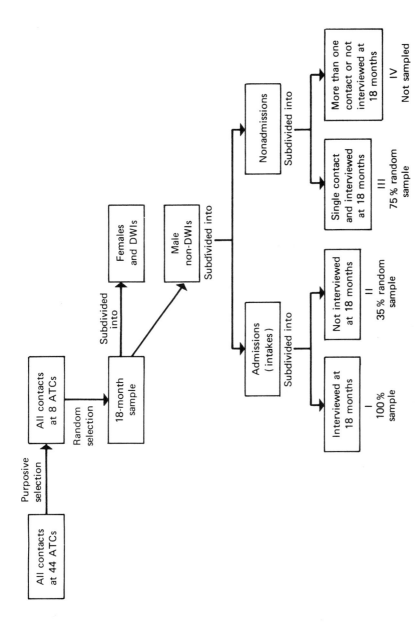

Figure 2.2 Sampling frame definition.

All contacts at 44 ATCs → Purposive selection → **All contacts at 8 ATCs** → Random selection → **18-month sample**

Subdivided into → **Females and DWIs**

→ **Male non-DWIs** → Subdivided into

Admissions (intakes) → Subdivided into
- **Interviewed at 18 months** — I — 100% sample
- **Not interviewed at 18 months** — II — 35% random sample

Nonadmissions → Subdivided into
- **Single contact and interviewed at 18 months** — III — 75% random sample
- **More than one contact or not interviewed at 18 months** — IV — Not sampled

21

in the 4-year target sample; members of Group II were randomly selected at a 35-percent rate. The resulting 4-year target sample of admissions thus constituted a stratified disproportionate *random sample of all male non-DWI individuals who had been admitted to treatment* at the designated treatment centers.[5]

The procedures for sampling nonadmissions were quite different. Because they represent a convenient "minimally treated" group (in many cases entirely untreated), our interest was in restricting selection to those with the lowest amounts of treatment. The monitoring system files included all records of ATC treatment for these people even though they were not formally admitted to treatment. Most had very short-term detoxification or a single outpatient visit at the time of initial contact. To concentrate our effort on those who had received the least intervention and for whom previously recorded data were available, we subdivided all nonadmissions into: (III) those who had made only a single contact with the treatment center *and* had been interviewed in the 18-month study; and (IV) all others, including all of those who had made more than one contact or who were not interviewed at 18 months.[6]

Only Group III was sampled for followup (75 percent were randomly drawn); locating Group IV would have been quite difficult and extremely expensive, because most of them had not been traced in over 4 years and many were essentially "treatment refusals" or very early "dropouts." Thus, Group III became our best available set of "untreated" alcoholics (i.e., untreated by the ATC). To ensure that they had actually experienced serious alcohol problems, our field team examined ATC records of those individuals whenever their history obtained at the 18-month followup failed to show significant alcohol problems. (These were cases in which the subject denied ever having had a "drinking problem"; reported no tremors, blackouts, morning drinking, or missing meals because of drinking; and reported abstaining or consuming less than 3 ounces of ethanol per day in the 30 days before the 18-month interview.) In all but two cases, such individuals showed indications of alcohol problems in the clinical files; these two cases were omitted from the sample on grounds that they did not show evidence of alcoholism of any sort.

---

[5]The use of disproportionate sampling implies that weighting might be needed to project the sample results back to the original admission population, but our analysis (Appendix A) has shown that weighting has little effect, except for mortality analysis where Group II, by definition, contains all of those subjects who were deceased within the first 18 months. We have computed the weighted results for most of the analyses, but in this report, for statistical simplicity, we show unweighted results where the weighted results are very close.

[6]Technically, the "single contact" criterion was that the individual received at most one day of inpatient treatment and at most one outpatient visit between January 1973 and April 1974. (The outpatient visit usually represented the original screening interview.)

Table 2.2   Sample Design

	Interview Status at 18 Months	
Admission Status	Cases Interviewed	Cases Not Interviewed
Admission	593 (I)	165 (II)
Contact	164 (III)	— (IV)

NOTE: Numerals in parentheses refer to groups shown in Fig. 2.2.

The resulting sample for the 4-year followup was composed of the three groups shown in Table 2.2. After the above sampling procedures were carried out, the target sample consisted of 922 cases. The intent during the fieldwork was to concentrate on the 593 cases that had been admitted to treatment and interviewed at 18 months, since only these people could be traced over 4 years at three time points (admission, 18 months, and 4 years). If any substantial biases in 4-year status were present in this group by virtue of failure to follow up at 18 months, the bias would be apparent from Group II and we could compensate for it through weighting. Finally, information about persons not treated by the ATCs could be found by examining Group III.

Basic Sampling Results

The attempts to relocate the 922 individuals at the 4-year followup were quite successful. The completion rates for each of the three sampling strata are shown in Table 2.3.[7] Interviews with survivors and reports of deaths (with cause of death) both constitute followup "outcomes," and therefore both events are treated as completed cases. All other fieldwork outcomes (refused, not located, unable to interview, etc.) are treated as noncompletions. Overall, 85 percent of the target sample was completed, a very respectable rate.[8] This fact in itself creates a strong presumption that the obtained sample will be representative of the total target sample. Suppose, for example, that 50 percent of the obtained sample have a given characteristic (say, abstention). Even if only 25 percent of the nonfollowup cases have the same characteristic—an extreme degree of bias, as we shall see in our examination of bias estimates—the total target sample rate would be 46 percent (.85 × .50 +

---

[7]Basic frequency distributions of the sample characteristics may be found in Appendix C.

[8]If attention is restricted to completions among the living (presuming that all cases not known dead were still living), the interview rate would be $668/809 = 82$ percent.

Table 2.3   Completion Rates for Three Sampling Strata

Item	Sampling Strata			Total
	I	II	III	
	Admissions, Interviewed at 18 Months	Admissions, Not Interviewed at 18 Months	Contacts, Interviewed at 18 Months	
Number of names drawn	593	165	164	922
Number of cases interviewed	478	70	120	668
Number of cases known deceased	62	35	16	113
Total number of cases completed	540	105	136	781
Completion rate (%)	91	64	83	85

$.15 \times 25 = .4625$), and thus the true rate would be only a few points off from the apparent rate in the obtained sample. Therefore, whatever reasonable assumption about bias may be imposed, the results from a followup with this level of response are not likely to be heavily influenced by nonfollowup bias. It is notable that the completion rate for Group II is much lower than that of the other three groups. This is to be anticipated, of course, because almost all of these individuals were not located in the previous followup. Hence, they had already passed through a screen that guarantees difficulty in following up.

A detailed distribution of our fieldwork results is shown in Table 2.4. Among the cases not completed, those not located constitute the largest group. Despite a nationwide search and the use of a 6-month interview period, those cases could not be traced. The state death records of all sampling sites and neighboring states were checked; thus, it appears unlikely that very many of the unlocateds were undetermined deaths, although a few could have moved out of the state before death. We found few survivors who had moved more than 200 miles. The *local* mobility of this population is considerable, however, and this factor probably accounts for the unlocateds. The refusal rate was quite low (4 percent), perhaps because a fee of $10 was paid for consenting to the interview. Other causes of nonresponse included only five cases in which the survivors were living outside the United States (less than 1 percent) and seven cases in which they were physically or mentally incapacitated to the point where interview was impossible (1 percent).

Table 2.4 Fieldwork Results

Field Result	Percent Distribution of Field Result				
	I Treated, Interviewed at 18 Months	II Treated, Not Interviewed at 18 Months	III Untreated, Interviewed at 18 Months	All Groups	(N)
Interviewed	81	42	73	73	(668)
Deceased	10	21	10	12	(113)
Refused	4	7	4	4	(40)
Incapacitated[a]	1	0	2	1	(7)
Outside U.S.	1	1	1	1	(5)
Not located	4	29	10	10	(88)
Lost in transit[b]	0	0	1	(c)	(1)
Total number of names drawn[d]	(593)	(165)	(164)	(922)	

[a]Unable to speak; mentally incompetent; in prison with no access allowed.
[b]Interviewed but form destroyed.
[c]Less than .5 percent.
[d]Does not necessarily add to 100 percent because of rounding.

DATA COLLECTION PROCEDURES

The data elements to be collected during the 4-year followup period were diverse, corresponding to our intention of gathering not only self-report interview data, but also psychometric data, blood alcohol levels, corroboration from collaterals, and mortality information. The main subject interview form is reproduced in Appendix E; other interview forms and data collection instruments may be obtained from the authors. The rationale for their content may best be explained when the results are discussed in later chapters. Here we simply indicate how the instruments were used and the sequence of events in the field data collection phase.

Chronology

Activities connected with field data collection began in early March 1977, when government approval of the study was obtained. The approval process, primarily intended to ensure the protection of human subjects in research, imposed a number of conditions, such as the use of special written consent forms (discussed below); these will be duly noted.

Johns Hopkins University conducted the fieldwork as a subcontractor under the general direction of The Rand Corporation.[9] During March, April, and May, the Johns Hopkins team visited each of the eight sampling sites and established a local field office headed by a local supervisor. The supervisor recruited interviewers and office staff, for the most part using experienced personnel who had worked on interviewing assignments for national survey organizations. No abstainers, ATC staff members, or persons with strong beliefs on alcohol (pro or con) were employed. The most diverse locating tools were used, including the following: admission records from the ATC; information obtained from interviewees in the 18-month study ("Who will know where you are in the next few years?" etc.); postcards with forwarding addresses; personal calls to the subject's address and to the addresses of relatives; police records; social welfare department records; and contacts with community agencies. In speaking with such persons and agencies, interviewers did not disclose that the study concerned alcoholism or that the subject was associated with the ATC; such information was disclosed only to the subject in private in order to protect confidentiality. Actual interviewing began in late May 1977 and continued through the early weeks of December, thus covering about 6 months. The flow of results showed that the last month's output was very meager, so that the field period could probably have been limited to 5 months with little adverse effect on the completion rate.

Subject Interviews

The principal source of 4-year followup information was the main subject interview (see Appendix E). This 37-page instrument took about 75 minutes to administer, usually in the subject's home; in all cases the interview was conducted in private (no other family members were allowed). Before beginning the interview, the interviewer read an opening statement and obtained the subject's oral consent for the interview. A payment of $10 was promised for his cooperation. The interview covered several dimensions of the subject's history and status: current social and economic status; interpersonal relationships; recent drinking behavior; recent alcohol dependence symptoms and adverse effects of alcohol; variations in drinking ("binges," etc.) over the past year; alcohol-related attitudes and self-concept; physical health, psychiatric symptoms, and medical conditions; significant alcohol-related events occurring in the subject's life during the past 4 years; history of abstention and heavy drinking; and experiences with treatment, AA, or other assistance for alcohol problems.

[9]The John Hopkins fieldwork was directed by Dr. Henry Becker and Ms. Shirley Blumberg, to whom we express our gratitude for a high degree of success.

At the end of the interview, the subject was asked to fill out the self-administered psychological assessment form. About 20 percent of the interviewees did not complete the form because of difficulty with language or reading. Outright refusals to fill out the forms were rare. The self-administered form provided assessments of several standard psychological scales, including impulsivity, autonomy/dependency, emotional stability, and internal-external locus of control (see Chapter 4 for more details). This form typically required 15 minutes to complete.

Validity Procedures

Types of Procedures. At the conclusion of the main interview, each subject was asked to participate in additional procedures that would produce data on the validity of the self-reports he had just given in the interview. As discussed in Chapter 1, the validity issue is a difficult problem that faces all clinical research, and, indeed, even general population studies (Pernanen, 1974). The design encompassed two separate types of externally collected data bearing on self-report validity:

1. *BAC Measurements.* Each subject was asked to take a breath test that would result in a reliable measurement of blood alcohol concentration (BAC) after laboratory analysis. This BAC reading could then be compared with the subject's interview reports of alcohol consumption during the 24 hours preceding the breath test.

2. *Collateral Interview.* Certain randomly selected subjects were asked to permit a subsequent interview with a collateral (a person who knows the subject well), whose responses concerning the subject's alcohol-related behavior (e.g., symptoms and adverse effects) could be compared with the subject's own account.

These data were collected in the following way. After the Self-Administered Form had been completed, the subject was paid his $10 fee. From this point on, one of three procedures was followed for groups labeled A, B, and C. Each procedure dealt with issues of self-report validity.

- Group A was asked to take a breath test at that time only, with $5 additional compensation for the test.
- Group B was asked to take a breath test immediately and also to consent to a second short interview within a week or two, to be immediately followed by a second breath test. $5 was offered for each test.
- Group C was asked to take a breath test immediately and also to give the name of a collateral who could be interviewed by Johns Hopkins about the subject. Compensation of $5 was offered to Group C members.

Each subject was randomly assigned before the fieldwork to one group only (A, B, or C) and was given a request/consent form for that group. The standard procedure was for the interviewer to read or paraphrase the consent form and then to ask the respondent to read it and sign it.

Prior Subject Knowledge. It is important to bear in mind that the subject was not apprised before or during the interview that a breath test would be requested. Therefore the information obtained during the interview from Groups A and B was given in the absence of any expectation that the interviewer would "check up" on the subject.

The situation was less clear-cut for Group C because the use of the collateral imposed several requirements relating to human-subject protection. For Group C, an alternative form of the opening statement was required by the federal Office of Management and Budget. In this alternative statement (given before the interview to Group C subjects *only*), the subject was informed that at the end of the interview he would be asked "to allow us to contact a close friend or relative to obtain additional information." No mention of a breath test was made. Analysis of important 4-year followup variables showed only minor differences between Group C subjects and those of the other groups; therefore, we assume that this "warning" did not affect interview behavior.

Another requirement concerns the timing of interviews with collaterals. To properly inform the subject of possible risks growing out of the collateral interview, we had to obtain written consent from the subject giving Johns Hopkins permission to approach the collateral. (Only one subject refused permission for the collateral interview.) A 48-hour waiting period was imposed to allow subjects to reconsider if they had any reservations about allowing Johns Hopkins to interview the collateral, and each subject was given a business card with a telephone number that he could call to rescind permission (none did so). After 48 hours, the interviewer approached the collateral, explained the procedure, and obtained written consent from the collateral before conducting that interview. (No collaterals refused.) In these circumstances, there is the possibility that some conversations between the subject and collateral could have taken place in the interim, leading to changes in the collateral's responses. Given the results of the collateral interview and our reading of the fieldwork experience, we doubt that such an effect was very significant, but the possibility cannot be entirely discounted. Obviously, no collateral interview can attain the certainty and accuracy of a breath test; but on the other hand, the range of behaviors that can be assessed via collateral report goes well beyond the highly restricted measure of current blood alcohol concentration (BAC).

BAC Instruments. The breath test instrument used was the Luckey Laboratories SM-7 device, consisting of a glass tube attached to a balloon and a volumetric plastic bag. The apparatus is packed in a small box (5 cm by 12 cm), is lightweight, and is easily portable. The subject blows up the balloon, from which exhaled breath passes through the glass tube into the volumetric bag fastened to the other end of the tube. Exactly 2100 cc of breath passes through the tube, which is packed with silica gel. The silica gel retains alcohol for several months. No immediate reading is possible; the gel must be unpacked and analyzed in the laboratory to determine the alcohol concentration.

It is well established that the resulting concentration is very highly correlated with blood alcohol concentration. Before using this method, we obtained experimental data from nine subjects, including blood alcohol concentration measured by both blood test and SM-7 readings. The subjects were inexperienced in the use of such devices but were trained in the same way as our interviewers. Consistent with the findings of other researchers (Glendening et al., 1971), our results showed that the correlation between blood readings and SM-7 readings was over .99, with a very small downward bias in the SM-7. During the fieldwork, the glass tubes were shipped by air to our laboratory for analysis.[10] Two samples from each tube were independently analyzed by gas chromatograph, and the results almost always agreed within a small deviation. The laboratory procedure also included simultaneous analysis of a standard with each tube to ensure proper calibration.

Second Subject Interview. Because the SM-7 indicates only instantaneous blood alcohol readings, we arranged for members of Group B to undergo a second interview and breath test. The intent here was to obtain a second sample of the subject's BAC to expand the period of behavior measured. The second interview was restricted to recent drinking behavior to provide a self-report against which the second BAC reading could be compared.

Validity Samples and Fieldwork Results. All subjects in sampling Groups II and III were classified as Group A for the validity procedures; i.e., they received only the single breath test. Group I, for which we wanted the most complete information, was randomly divided into three groups (A, B, and C) in proportions of one-sixth, one-half, and one-third. (These proportions were dictated by cost constraints; it would have been impossible to conduct all procedures with all subjects.) Of course, the validity procedures were inapplicable to subjects not interviewed. In addition, we designated those few subjects who were interviewed at a location more than 100 miles from the sampling point as inappropriate for the Group B and Group C procedures. This was done to avoid the considerable cost of sending an interviewer back

[10]Analysis was conducted by Valley Toxicology of Davis, California, a forensic laboratory licensed by the State of California.

Table 2.5 Completion Rates for Validity Procedures

Sample Groups and Procedure Designated	Number of Names Drawn	Number of Interviews	Number Eligible for Validity Procedure[a]	Number of Validity Completions	Percent Completed
I: *Admissions Interviewed at 18 Months*					
A. Main interview plus BAC 1	100	79	79	75	95
B. Main interview plus BAC 1; then second interview plus BAC 2	297	235	209	193	92
C. Main interview plus BAC 1; collateral named by subject, then interviewed	196	164	148	128	86
II: *Admissions Not Interviewed at 18 Months*					
A. Main interview plus BAC 1	165	70	70	67	96
III: *Single Contact Nonadmissions*					
A. Main interview plus BAC 1	164	120	120	115	96

[a]Number of interviews less the number of cases residing over 100 miles from the sampling point.

over 100 miles for a second interview or a collateral interview. As shown in Table 2.5, this exclusion affected only a small number of cases, and these proved not to be substantially different from the others. Among those persons who were eligible for the validity procedures after this exclusion, the cooperation rates were quite high. We obtained breath tests from 95 percent of those eligible in Group A, and from over 85 percent for Groups B and C. We attribute this high rate of success partly to the payments offered but also partly to the rapport and confidence developed by the Johns Hopkins interviewers during the main interview.

Mortality Data Collection

The local county and state death records were examined to verify reported deaths. Altogether 113 deaths were reported. Official death certificates were obtained for almost all of them (106). When certificates could not be obtained, local informants verified the deaths. Further information on mortality is given in Chapter 5.

Because ambiguities on death certificates are well known, we also conducted supplemental "collateral" interviews with local informants when the role of alcohol in the cause of death was uncertain. Such interviews were not conducted when the death certificate indicated an obvious alcohol-related disease (e.g., cirrhosis of the liver or chronic alcoholism). For deaths due to accidents, on the other hand, collateral information could be valuable in establishing the circumstances of death. (Was he intoxicated? Had he been drinking? Was alcohol a factor in the death?) It became clear during the fieldwork that the circumstances of death would be very important in analyzing mortality because many deaths were due to accidents or suicides and the mortality rate was quite high. Supplemental interviews were therefore conducted with as many local informants as could be found.

ASSESSING POTENTIAL BIAS DUE TO NONFOLLOWUP

It was emphasized in Chapter 1 that the issue of possible biases arising from failure to follow up all sample members is a recurrent problem in treatment research. The present study contains two rather unusual features that permit us to explore the extent of nonfollowup bias. First, the fact that we have data from three time points enables us to examine persons who were not followed up at a given time point in terms of their characteristics at another time point. Second, our data collection procedures included a measurement of elapsed time and effort expended in locating each case, so that we can plot the features of the samples that would have been obtained had we spent less time or effort, resulting in a lower followup rate. This permits us, in effect, to specify the relationship between sample results and effective response rates. The discussion here summarizes some of the more significant points of our analysis of these issues; supporting documentation may be found in Appendix A.

Because the monitoring system collected baseline data on all admissions, these data may be used to compare the characteristics of the subjects successfully followed up with those not followed up. Several admission characteristics that relate either to prognosis or to nonfollowup are given in Table 2.6. Because such a high rate of response was obtained, the completed cases (followups, including successful interviews and verified death reports) are very close to the original target sample. There is a hint that nonfollowup cases tended to have slightly less favorable prognostic characteristics; for example, they were slightly more likely to be socially unstable, to show higher consumption levels, and to show higher rates of alcoholic symptomatology at admission. However, these differences are very small. The only substantial difference is the one associated with geographical mobility (less than 4 years in the community before admission), and this variable has proved insignificant as a predictor of followup status in both the present study and the 18-month study. The implication seems to be that the principal unique characteristic of

Table 2.6 Characteristics of Four-Year Followup Groups at Admission to Treatment

Characteristic at Admission	Percent with the Characteristic		
	Drawn Sample	Completed Cases	Noncompleted Cases
Age 50 or over	44	43	46
Less than 4 years in community	44	42	56
Low socioeconomic status	45	45	50
Low social stability	45	44	50
Alcohol consumption over 5 oz. per day[a]	59	58	65
High symptomatology[b]	78	79	87
Previously treated for alcoholism	42	42	46
(N)	(758)	(645)	(113)

[a]Quantity-frequency index of total consumption, past 30 days (see Appendix D for calculation methods).
[b]At least one instance of two or more of the following symptoms: tremors, morning drinking, blackouts, missing meals, and continuous drinking over 12 hours at a time (see Appendix D for item definitions).

nonfollowups is their history of moving about, a behavior that obviously makes them more difficult to locate but does not imply a bias in prognosis.

Admission variables constitute the only information available on nonfollowup cases. Unfortunately, because admission variables are so weakly related to followup statuses (Armor et al., 1978), it is not entirely satisfying to know simply that the groups were equivalent at admission. Even if the groups were equivalent at the beginning of treatment, it is still possible that the "successes" become more easily traceable at followup as a concomitant of their improvement. If this were so, one should find that the most easily located cases show the best followup improvement. Thus, the general relationship between an individual's followup functioning and the degree of effort expended to locate him is a question of considerable interest.

We have investigated this issue in detail by stratifying our obtained sample for Group I according to the amount of fieldwork required to obtain each completed interview. As shown in Appendix A, several stratifying variables are available, such as hours of locating time, number of contacts required to complete a case, and elapsed time between the assignment of a case and its completion. A result that is representative of most of these analyses is shown in Fig. 2.3 The abscissa represents "effective response rate" for a given level of effort (in this case, number of persons and agencies contacted). Different

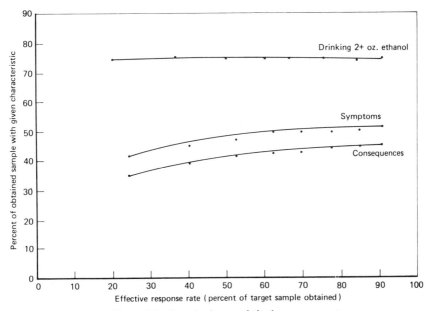

Figure 2.3   Sample characteristics by response rate.

points on the abscissa represent the percentage of the target sample that would be obtained if only a given level of effort were expended. (Since there is only a discrete number of persons/ agencies contacted for each case, there are only a few points to be plotted, but the trend is regular.) The ordinate axis represents the characteristic of the sample that would have been reached for a given level of effort. Clearly there is some relationship between effective response rate and the characteristics of the sample; the trends are upward for drinking, symptoms, and the occurrence of adverse drinking consequences. For example, if we had stopped followup work at a level of effort producing only a 40 percent response rate, 36 percent of the sample would show adverse consequences; whereas with a 91 percent response rate, 42 percent of the sample showed consequences. However, the rate of increase is notably gradual; in particular, the difference made by moving from a response rate of 60 or 70 percent to one of 90 percent is quite small.

For maximal accuracy of the sample, of course, the highest possible response is desirable. However, because the marginal cost of increasing response rates is very high (in 1977, several hundred dollars per case to go beyond 80 percent), it is questionable whether extremely high response rates are cost-effective for most studies, particularly since we observe no discontinuity or nonlinearity in the trends. The absence of any discontinuity also suggests that it is reasonable to project the lines out to the 100 percent mark on the abscissa to estimate the composition of the entire drawn sample. Obviously such a projection would be very close to the results of our obtained sample.

It is still *possible,* as some observers argue, that the subjects not located actually have characteristics that differ sharply from those of the obtained sample. However, such an assumption is not supported by our data, and it would be a most unusual result in any survey study of bias. We conclude, therefore, that there is no evidence here that followup studies are significantly affected by nonresponse, provided that at least 60 to 70 percent are followed up.

THREE

Drinking Patterns at Four Years

A central objective of this study is to assess the condition of an alcoholic cohort 4 years after diagnosis. Such an assessment can focus on a number of different aspects of alcoholic behavior and can cover a variety of time periods. In this chapter, we will concentrate on drinking patterns, i.e., on alcohol consumption, symptoms, and the immediate adverse consequences of the excessive use of alcohol. From them, we will derive an overall classification of the individual's drinking status, or *status at 4 years;* in other words, we will derive a basic assessment of his condition during the period approximately 4 years after admission or contact.

The measurement period for assessing drinking status within the framework of the 4-year followup is shown in Fig. 3.1. Our present interest lies in looking carefully at the behavior of survivors during the segment of time at the extreme right of the figure, namely, during the 6 months before the followup point. Since most individuals were followed up during the summer of 1977, this means that "status at 4 years" refers roughly to the first half of 1977. There is also another period, lasting about 4 years, between admission and the followup assessment. This latter 4-year period we will reserve for an examination of *long-term* patterns, which we will discuss in Chapters 6 and 7. In this chapter, we carry out a detailed investigation of the types of alcohol-related behavior that are relevant in determining the status of alcoholics 4 years after treatment.

First, we examine the frequency and nature of abstention during the 6 months before followup. It turns out that this task is not as simple as the apparent dichotomy between drinking and abstention might seem to suggest, since shifts between drinking and abstention are quite common. We then take up the topic of quantity of alcohol consumption, followed by an analysis of symptoms of alcohol dependence and the adverse consequences of drinking, such as problems with health, law enforcement, and interpersonal relationships. Then, we assemble the above elements into our overall typology of a subject's condition: his status at 4 years. Finally, we investigate the characteristics of groups defined by the typology.

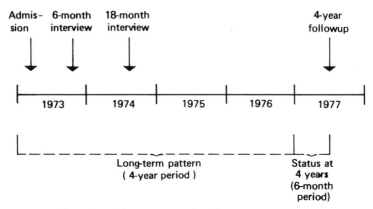

Figure 3.1   Measurement periods for status assessments.

LENGTH OF ABSTENTION

The 4-year followup interview (Appendix E) enquired, in detail, into the subject's drinking over the past few months, beginning with his specifying the last day on which he drank an alcoholic beverage. Even if it occurred some time ago, this "date of last drink" is obviously a salient event for an abstaining alcoholic, and therefore it is usually very easy to determine. Table 3.1 shows the distribution of the length of abstention from alcohol, determined from the date of the subject's last drink. The table shows that 28 percent of the

Table 3.1   Distribution of the Length of Abstention

	Percent Distribution		
Length of Abstention[a]	4-Year Followup,[b] 1977	18-Month Followup, 1974	Admission to Treatment,[b] 1973
Abstained 1 year or more	22 ⎱ 28	24	0
Abstained 6 to 11 months	6 ⎰		
Abstained 3 to 5 months	6 ⎱ 15	21	7
Abstained 1 to 2 months	9 ⎰		
Drank past month	57	55	93
(N)	(474)	(474)	(474)

[a]Length of time abstained prior to interview.
[b]Tabulation limited to only those assessed in 18-month followup to show time trend within a cohort. Total 4-year followup interviews (N = 548) have a virtually identical distribution.

admissions had abstained throughout the past 6-month period; most of them had been abstaining even longer. For those who had abstained, the measurement of drinking behavior is obviously very simple because there was none. (This does not imply that their overall psychological or social adjustment was favorable, as we shall see in Chapter 4.) However, most of the sample—72 percent—reported consuming at least some alcohol during the 6-month period. These proportions seem to have remained quite stable since the 18-month followup, and naturally, they represent a great "improvement" since the period of admission, when almost no one was abstaining.

Among subjects who drank at all in the past 6 months, most were currently drinking (within the past 30 days) at the time of the interview. A modest-sized group (15 percent) reported that although they had drunk some alcohol during the 6 months, they had abstained for at least 1 month preceding the interview. This "short-term abstainer" group bears special examination, because the experience of shifting back and forth between heavy drinking and total abstention is a familiar pattern from both clinical and everyday experience with alcoholics. A priori, one might argue that such a pattern indicates a continuing problem rather than a remission. In the 18-month studies, there was no provision for obtaining information about any drinking before the "past 30 days," so these short-term abstainers were perforce treated as remissions. The 4-year followup interview questioned respondents much more carefully about their behavior over the past 6 months. One interesting result is the pattern shown in Table 3.2 describing the *number of months* in which the subject abstained for the entire calendar month. Here we find that drinking every month—i.e., drinking on at least 1 day during each of the past 6 months—is actually a minority behavior pattern. A large number of alcoholics shift back and forth between drinking for a time and then abstaining for a time within the relatively short period of 6 months. The table shows that this pattern is similarly prominent among our sample of "contact

Table 3.2 Distribution of Abstention During Past Six Months

	Percent Distribution	
Abstention Pattern	Admissions	Contacts
Continuous abstention (abstained all 6 months)	28	16
Abstention with drinking interludes (abstained 4 or 5 months)	11	8
Predominant drinking, some abstention (abstained 1 to 3 months)	20	26
Drinking every month (drank all 6 months)	41	49
(N)	(548)	(120)

only" cases. It is also notable that most of the shifting back and forth involves more than an occasional "slip" (represented by those who abstained for 4 or 5 calendar months of the 6). Most alcoholics who are not continuously abstaining are drinking during much, if not all, of the time over a 6-month period.

This presents a difficult conceptual and measurement problem. In the presence of a great deal of change, how is the overall pattern of drinking to be measured? As noted above, this problem was avoided in the 18-month study and in the NIAAA monitoring system by simply enquiring into only very recent drinking. To explore the characteristics of less recent drinking, we have adopted the procedure exemplified in Fig. 3.2. This diagram shows two

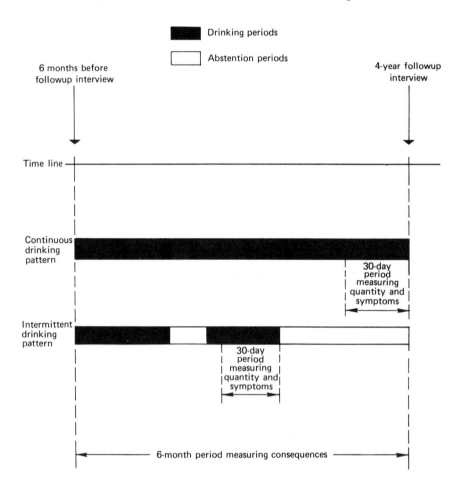

Figure 3.2   Measurement periods for two patterns of drinking (4-year followup status).

patterns of drinking that were very common in our sample over the 6 months before the interview. The first, represented by a solid bar, presents no measurement problem because the drinking is continuous. The second bar represents a pattern of intermittent drinking interspersed with periods of abstention, including abstention over the past 30 days or more.

The 4-year followup interview measured both of these patterns by asking the subject about his drinking during the *30 days before his last drink*. Our experience has convinced us that drinking is so variable and recall so complicated that a fairly short period is best for assessing the complexities of alcohol consumption. For that reason, instead of trying to measure the entire 6-month period in detail, we have concentrated on this 30-day period. As shown later in this chapter, the 30-day period proves to be very representative when compared with the results for the entire 6-month period. The one area in which it is not representative is the area of adverse consequences of drinking, such as law enforcement incidents, hospitalization, or health problems. These consequences often take the form of gross events that are relatively infrequent but highly salient to the subject. Hence, in assessing consequences, we have relied primarily on assessments of the entire 6 months.

A detailed distribution of the periods when the last drink occurred is given in Table 3.3. The subjects reporting in the top panel drank within the past 6 months; hence their recent alcohol problems (high consumption, symptoms, or consequences) will be assessed. Those in the bottom panel were abstaining throughout the 6-month period, and so their drinking will not be assessed.

QUANTITY OF ALCOHOL CONSUMPTION

As a measure of posttreatment functioning, quantity of alcohol consumption occupies a paradoxical status. Obviously, quantity of consumption is a highly significant factor in the etiology of alcoholism. In particular, the onset of physical dependence and organic pathology, such as liver damage, is directly related to the amount of ethanol consumed (Gross, 1977; Lelbach, 1974). The Jellinek model of alcoholism has tended to inhibit consideration of quantity by suggesting that quantity is unimportant after addiction is established. Nevertheless, sustained high consumption rates and episodes of heavy drinking are clearly associated with increased risks even in general populations (Polich and Orvis, 1979). Therefore, they ought to be taken into account in an assessment of alcohol-related problems.

The 4-year followup interview asked the subject to give a detailed account of his drinking during the 30-day period before his last drink. For each type of beverage, he was asked how much he consumed on a *typical* day when he drank during that period. In addition, he was asked on how many days he reached or exceeded certain fairly high levels. For example, the interview

Table 3.3 Period of Last Drink and Alcohol Problem Assessment

Approximate Period When Last Drink Occurred	Point of Last Drink, in Days Before Interview	Percent Reporting Last Drink at That Point	Alcohol Problem Assessment
Past week	0-6	47	
Past month, but not past week	7-29	10	
1 month ago	30-59	6	Recent Problems Assessed[a]
2 months ago	60-89	3	
3 months ago	90-119	3	
4-5 months ago	120-182	3	
6-11 months ago	183-364	7	
1 year ago	365-729	4	
2 years ago	730-1094	5	Problems Not Assessed
3 years ago	1095-1459	5	(Abstaining)
4 years ago or more	1460 or more	7	
(N)		(548)	

[a]Quantity of consumption and symptoms assessed over the 30 days before last drink. Adverse consequences assessed over the 6 months before the interview.

enquired: On how many days did you drink as many as 10 cans of beer or more? And, on how many days did you drink between 6 and 9 cans of beer? The wine and liquor question sequences asked about similar critical levels of wine and liquor consumption. The intention was to describe first the subject's typical drinking, and then to obtain a means of determining how much *atypical,* heavy drinking had occurred, as has been done in a number of survey studies (e.g., Cahalan and Cisin, 1968). The typical-amount responses were combined across beverages to estimate the quantity of ethanol consumed on a typical day. The responses concerning frequency of atypical amounts were combined to estimate the number of days on which the individual exceeded limits of approximately 3 ounces of ethanol (e.g., 6 cans of beer) and 5 ounces of ethanol (e.g., 10 cans of beer). Details are given in Appendix D.

The frequency distribution of our measure of the typical quantity of alcohol consumed is shown in Table 3.4. The actual answer categories allowed the respondent to use any convenient volume measures he chose, such as beer cans, wine glasses, fifths, or quarts. These volume units were then converted into ethanol equivalents by applying the container size (obtained from the respondent) and the ethanol content for the particular type of beverage consumed (e.g., sherry, Chablis, malt liquor, etc.). For ease of interpretation, we also show in this table the approximate number of average-sized drinks that would be required to reach a particular ethanol quantity. Clearly many of

Table 3.4 Frequency Distribution of Typical Quantity[a] of Alcohol Consumed (30 Days Before Last Drink)

Typical Quantity Consumed	Equivalent Number of Drinks (approximate)	Percent Distribution	
		Among Persons Drinking in Past 6 Months[b]	Among All Cases[c]
0.1-1.0 oz.	1-2	10	7
1.1-2.0 oz.	3-4	14	10
2.1-3.0 oz.	5-6	14	10
3.1-4.0 oz.	7-8	10	7
4.1-5.0 oz.	9-10	7	5
5.1-7.0 oz.	11-14	13	9
7.1-10.0 oz.	15-20	12	9
Over 10.0 oz.	Over 20	20	14
Abstained past 6 months	None	—	28
(N)		(389)	(548)

[a]Amount of ethanol consumed on a typical drinking day. 1 ounce = 29.57 milliliters.
[b]Excluding abstainers.
[c]Including abstainers.

these subjects are still consuming very large amounts when they drink. If we adopted the 150-milliliter cutoff proposed by the single distribution researchers (Schmidt, 1976), 45 percent of the drinkers would fall above that amount (approximately 5 ounces). Another substantial group, 31 percent of the drinkers, consumes less than 5 ounces but more than 2 ounces on a typical drinking day. These amounts, while not above the 150-milliliter cutoff, may still imply substantial risk (Pequignot et al., 1978; Lieber, 1979). We have tentatively imposed the 2-ounce cutoff point as the upper limit of a fairly modest level of drinking, recognizing that any such standard is essentially arbitrary.

A notable property of these drinking quantities is shown in Table 3.5. Here typical quantity is classified according to the date of the subject's last drink. This allows us to compare the typical drinking behavior of current drinkers with the behavior of subjects who abstained during the past month but drank earlier. The latter were people classified as "short-term abstainers" in the 18-month studies for lack of any information about their recent drinking behavior. Table 3.5 shows that the quantities consumed by the short-term abstainers, particularly those who drank just 1 or 2 months ago, are much larger than those consumed by current drinkers. Fully 71 percent of the 1-to-2-month abstainers had been consuming more than 5 ounces per day, a rate that if prolonged implies a high risk of liver damage (Wallgren and Barry, 1970). This pattern of extreme behavior among short-term abstainers is replicated throughout our data, not only for consumption but also for symptoms and other alcohol problems. It suggests that many short-term abstainers are in a very short period of remission, possibly between heavy-drinking episodes or binges. We will return to this aspect of abstention several times in our analysis as we examine the evidence on the recent history and prognosis for short-term abstention patterns.

Table 3.5   Distribution of Typical Quantity of Alcohol Consumed, by Point of Last Drink[a]

Typical Quantity Consumed	Percent Distribution, by Point of Last Drink			
	Past Month	1-2 Months Ago	3-5 Months Ago	6-11 Months Ago
0-1 oz.	10	10	6	10
1-2 oz.	15	10	10	10
2-3 oz.	16	6	10	8
3-4 oz.	12	2	6	10
4-5 oz.	8	2	6	3
Over 5 oz.	40	71	61	59
(N)	(307)	(51)	(31)	(39)

[a]Ounces of ethanol consumed on a typical drinking day.

Table 3.6   Drinking Quantity and Frequency (30 Days Before Last Drink)

Typical Quantity on a Drinking Day	Percent Reporting Designated Number of Days Over 3 oz.[a]		Percent Reporting Designated Number of Days Over 5 oz.[b]		(N)
	1-2 Days	3 or More Days	1-2 Days	3 or More Days	
0-1 oz. (1-2 drinks)	10	3	3	3	(39)
1-2 oz. (3-4 drinks)	14	26	6	6	(55)
2-3 oz. (5-6 drinks)	18	60	16	22	(55)
3-5 oz. (7-10 drinks)	(c)	(c)	17	33	(65)
Over 5 oz. (over 10 drinks)	(c)	(c)	(c)	(c)	(175)

[a]Percentage of each typical-quantity category who reported consuming 3 ounces or more during the given number of days, within the 30-day period. (Includes all days reported in questions 20D, 20E, 21F, 21G, 22E, and 22F, Appendix E.)

[b]Percentage of each typical-quantity category who reported consuming 5 ounces or more during the given number of days, within the 30-day period. (Includes all days reported in questions 20D, 21F, and 22E, Appendix E.)

[c]100 percent by definition.

One reason for marking the boundary of our typical-quantity measure at 2 ounces is shown in Table 3.6. This table shows the relationship between the typical quantity during the 30-day period and the number of days when the subject consumed higher amounts of ethanol. We view the occurrence of any days when the 5-ounce limit was exceeded as a serious sign of dangerous drinking behavior for an alcoholic sample. This table shows that many of those respondents who describe their drinking as fairly moderate (i.e., 2 to 3 ounces per day) also admit to at least some days *during a 1-month period* when their drinking far exceeded that moderate level. It is thus arguable that a "typical-day" report of 2 to 3 ounces may be masking the occurrence of several atypical but very high drinking days in the same general period of time. We believe it is prudent to recognize only those individuals who report very low quantities of typical drinking as having a generally "low" level of consumption, since the occurrence of some heavy-drinking days during a 30-day period calls into question the typicality and significance of the moderate-drinking days. For example, of the 55 cases reporting a typical level of 1 to 2 ounces, many reported at least 1 day when their drinking exceeded 3 ounces. This leads us to adopt a fairly conservative approach in classifying overall drinking behavior.

The logic of our consumption ("Q") classification is shown in Table 3.7. We propose to designate a case as one of definite low consumption ("Low Q")

Table 3.7   Consumption ("Q") Classification

Typical Q	No Days 3 oz. or More	1+ Days 3 oz. or More	
		No Days 5 oz. or More	1+ Days 5 oz. or More
Under 2 oz.	Low Q	High Q	Very High Q
2-5 oz.	High Q[a]	High Q	Very High Q
5 oz. or more	Vacant (by definition)	Vacant (by definition)	Very High Q

[a]Includes only subjects reporting typical Q between 2 and 3 ounces who also report no days of 3 ounces or more.

only if the typical Q is less than 2 ounces and there are no days in the 30-day period when consumption exceeded 3 ounces. If there is an indication that drinking on any day passed into the level of 2 to 5 ounces, the case is designated as "High Q." This could happen either by an individual's reporting that he typically drank between 2 and 5 ounces or by reporting that his typical consumption was less than 2 ounces but that on at least 1 day his consumption was greater (i.e., some days more than 3 ounces but no days more than 5 ounces). Finally, if on any occasion the consumption level exceeded the 5-ounce cutoff, the case is designated "Very High Q." This group includes both those reporting typical consumption of more than 5 ounces *and* those reporting typical consumption of less than 5 ounces when at least 1 day's consumption was more than 5 ounces. These limits are thus quite conservative.

The percentage distribution of these consumption patterns is shown in Table 3.8. Using the criteria just described, 17 percent of the persons drinking in the 6 months before the interview can be described as Low Q drinkers. Twenty-two percent are in the High Q category. Most of them are placed in this category because of their typical consumption reports, although a few are so classified because of their reports of some high-consumption days combined with a typical quantity consumed of less than 2 ounces. Most of the drinkers are in the Very High Q category. Of these, about three-fourths reported that on their typical drinking days they consumed more than 5 ounces of ethanol; the remainder are classified as Very High Q because on 1 or more days they consumed more than 5 ounces, although they did not have a typical consumption rate of more than 5 ounces. The overall picture is that most sample members who drink at all drink fairly large amounts.

This does not necessarily mean, however, that their total ethanol intake is extremely high. As shown in Table 3.9, some members of the sample who reported high consumption *on drinking days* nonetheless had a fairly low reading on the quantity-frequency index of total alcohol consumption (QF). This index measures the total ethanol intake of the individual over the 30-day

Table 3.8 Distribution of Consumption Patterns

		Percent Distribution	
Consumption Pattern	Definition	Among Drinkers[a]	Among All Cases
Low Q	Typical Q under 2 oz. and no days over 3 oz.	17	12
High Q (atypical)	Typical Q under 2 oz. and 1+ days 3-5 oz.	5	4
High Q (typical)	Typical Q 2-5 oz. and no days 5 oz. or more	17	12
Very High Q (atypical)	Typical Q under 5 oz. and 1+ days 5 oz. or more	16	11
Very High Q (typical)	Typical Q 5 oz. or more	45	32
Abstention	Abstained throughout past 6 months	—	28
(N)		(389)	(548)

[a]All persons drinking in the past 6 months.

Table 3.9 Average Daily Consumption, by Consumption Pattern (Percent of Total Drinkers)[a]

Consumption Pattern	Average Daily Consumption (QF)						Total
	0-1 oz.	1-2 oz.	2-3 oz.	3-4 oz.	4-5 oz.	Over 5 oz.	
Low Q	15	2	0	0	0	0	17
High Q (atypical)	3	2	0	0	0	0	5
High Q (typical)	11	3	2	1	0	0	17
Very High Q (atypical)	4	3	4	4	1	0	16
Very High Q (typical)	8	4	3	2	3	25	45
Total	41	14	9	7	4	25	100

[a]Base N = 389 (all persons who drank in the past 6 months).

period, divided by the 30 calendar days in the period.[1] It thus reflects the total amount of ethanol to which the body is exposed, the factor that is most intimately associated with liver disease and other organic problems. The data suggest that although the QF is a highly important risk factor for organic complications, it is not fully descriptive of the heavy drinking patterns of alcoholics. To consider the implications of this fact for analysis, one need only calculate the characteristics of a group that appears to be low in consumption

[1]For computation methods, see Appendix D.

on the basis of QF. Suppose, for example, we had defined a "moderate" consumption level by using a QF-based criterion of 1 ounce or less. In such a classsification, 41 percent of the drinkers would fall in the "moderate" consumption category. However, only about one-third of those so identified would actually be Low Q cases, i.e., consistent low-quantity drinkers (15 out of 41 percent). Many, in fact, would have reported at least some days when they consumed more than 5 ounces. It is for this reason that both the 18-month study and the present study placed constraints on typical quantity *on a drinking day* rather than relying strictly on a measurement of total ethanol consumption.

ALCOHOL DEPENDENCE SYMPTOMS

Alcohol consumption is only one factor in a large number of behavioral problems that typically manifest themselves in alcoholism. As explained in Chapter 1, traditional models suggest that alcohol dependence is a fundamental condition underlying alcoholism. Indeed, some approaches would suggest that high alcohol consumption in itself need not indicate dependence, since many persons in the general population drink heavily without developing the other elements of the alcohol dependence syndrome and without experiencing the social and behavioral problems of clinical alcoholics. Of course, the people under study here had previously been diagnosed as alcoholic. That fact alone places them apart from others and suggests concern about any indication of an alcohol problem that they might manifest. Therefore, in looking for the reemergence of alcoholism, it is reasonable to impose less stringent criteria than would be used in making an initial diagnostic classification. The appearance of alcohol dependence symptomatology in this population may well be viewed as a very grave indication of continuing alcohol problems, and the level of such symptoms need not be very high to warrant concern.

Several symptoms that may be interpreted as indicators of alcohol dependence are shown in Table 3.10. All are commonly found in alcoholic samples and frequently used for diagnosis of alcoholism (Filstead et al., 1976; National Council on Alcoholism, 1972). As Table 3.10 makes clear, the proportion of drinkers affected ranges from 29 percent to 42 percent, depending on the symptom selected; and 64 percent of the drinkers are affected by one or more symptoms. Among these reporting a given symptom, the median frequencies range from 4 days to 15 days during a 30-day period. Evidently symptoms are usually recurrent; they cannot generally be discounted as representing isolated events.

Table 3.10   Drinkers Reporting Symptoms of Alcohol Dependence[a]

Symptom	Percent Reporting Any Occurrence in 30-Day Period		Median Days Reported[b]
	Among Drinkers	Among All Cases	
Tremors (had "the shakes")	31	22	7
Morning drinking (had "a drink as soon as you woke up")	41	29	15
Loss of control ("tried to stop drinking but couldn't")	32	23	4
Blackouts ("memory lapses or 'blackouts' ")	29	20	4
Missing meals ("missed a meal because of drinking")	42	30	6
Continuous drinking (12 hours or more) ("your longest period of continuous drinking")	37	26	(c)
One or more symptoms	64	46	15
(N)	(389)	(548)	—

[a]Symptoms measured in the 30 days before the last drink among persons who drank in the past month (for measurement procedures, see Appendix D).
[b]Among those reporting at least one instance of the symptom in the 30-day period.
[c]Not available because of item wording.

Most definitive are the withdrawal symptoms: tremors and morning drinking. The item "morning drinking" specifically enquires about drinking immediately after awakening, which we interpret as drinking to forestall the reappearance of withdrawal distress after blood alcohol concentration has declined during sleep. "Loss of control" must be counted as a significant symptom even though its theoretical status has beeen recently questioned, as discussed in Chapter 1. In our view, it represents the best available subjective indication of inability to manage the use of alcohol, a classical element of most conceptions of alcoholism.

The theoretical status of blackouts is less clear. This symptom is, of course, historically important as the indicator of the onset of addiction in Jellinek's progressive scheme, and it has been prominent as a predictor for dis-criminating alcoholic versus nonalcoholic groups. Indeed, blackouts, morn-ing drinking, and tremors were the principal discriminating variables among the large set of National Council on Alcoholism diagnostic criteria employed in a recent analysis (Ringer et al., 1977).

"Missing meals" is included among the symptoms because of the special nature of this population. Ordinarily one might not consider "missing meals because of drinking" to be a reliable indicator of alcohol dependence. In an alcoholic group, however, it is likely that such an event represents a recurrence or continuation of preoccupation with alcohol, to the exclusion of other everyday activities. Hence, it may indicate dependence.

Finally, the questionnaire item on "continuous drinking" has appeared in several of our analyses as a significant correlate of the other symptoms and as a significant predictor of persistent alcohol-related problems. This item, unlike the others, does not measure the frequency of occurrence. Instead, it asks for the *longest period* in the 30 days during which the subject drank continuously. We have selected a period of 12 hours or more because it represents a highly deviant behavior, suggesting uncontrolled drinking.

Overall, then, this list includes symptoms sampling the domains of deviant drinking, withdrawal symptoms, and subjective experience of loss of control, all of which were suggested by the World Health Organization committee as indicators of the alcohol dependence syndrome (Edwards et al., 1977b). Because the elements of the syndrome are somewhat diverse, our symptom list is likewise diverse. It covers some behaviors, such as continuous drinking or missing meals, that are as much clues to an underlying problem as they are decisive proof of dependence. Our strategy has been to encompass such behaviors in our measure, if possible, to ensure that all indicators of dependence are being considered.

The test of the validity of this strategy is whether or not the individual behaviors hang together empirically. If, as we believe, all of these measures relate to the underlying construct of alcohol dependence, they ought to exhibit strong covariation. Table 3.11 shows that they are, in fact, fairly highly intercorrelated.[2] Moreover, all of the loadings on the first principal component extracted from the correlation matrix are high. The first component dominates the variance in the matrix (covering 52 percent of the total), and the first eigenvalue is the only one exceeding unity, lending further support to a unidimensional interpretation. Elsewhere it has been shown that these same symptoms form a similarly strong factor in a heterogeneous general population (Polich and Orvis, 1979).[3]

The empirical coherence of our dependence measures justifies combining them into an overall scale of alcohol dependence, as shown in Table 3.12. In constructing this scale, we summed the frequency values for each of the six symptoms, which yielded a score that may be interpreted as an intensity score

---

[2]These results are based on measures of the *frequency of occurrence* of the six symptoms rather than on measures of intensity. We recognize that intensity may be an important element of dependence (e.g., a slight tremor versus gross shaking). However, no measurement of different intensity levels seemed feasible in a standardized interview, so our scaling of dependence symptoms relies on frequency as a proxy for intensity.

[3]Further factor analytic results (Appendix C) demonstrate that the dependence symptoms and consumption measures cluster around one factor and that this factor is differentiated from factors representing such consequences as medical conditions and law enforcement incidents.

Table 3.11 Correlational Analysis of Symptoms

Symptom	Product Moment Correlation						Loading on First Two Principal Components[a]	
	Tremors	Morning Drinking	Loss of Control	Blackouts	Missing Meals	Continuous Drinking	I	II
Tremors	1.000						.750	-.229
Morning drinking	.545	1.000					.822	.062
Loss of control	.441	.408	1.000				.622	-.528
Blackouts	.452	.496	.393	1.000			.742	-.119
Missing meals	.481	.615	.343	.536	1.000		.806	.187
Continuous drinking	.251	.383	.144	.262	.413	1.000	.532	.727

[a]The first two eigenvalues = 3.11 (52 percent of variance) and 0.91 (15 percent of variance). The number of cases = 389 (all persons drinking in past 6 months).

Table 3.12   Dependence Symptoms Index

Index Value[a]	Percent Distribution	
	Among Drinkers[b]	Among All Cases
0	36	26
1-2	12	9
3-5	9	6
6-10	7	5
11-20	8	6
21-40	13	9
Over 40	15	11
Abstained, past 6 months	—	28
(N)	(389)	(548)

[a]Sum of the number of days in which a symptom was experienced, across 6 symptoms (tremors, morning drinking, loss of control, blackouts, missing meals, and continuous drinking).
[b]Persons drinking in the past 6 months.

for dependence.[4] For example, if an individual reported four instances of tremors, six of morning drinking, and three of blackouts, he would receive a scale score of 13. This could represent 13 separate days on which symptoms occurred, if all symptoms occurred on different days, but the likelihood is that the symptoms overlapped on a few heavily symptomatic days. The frequency distribution in Table 3.12 shows that multiple instances of this type are quite common. Many people in the sample reported three or more instances, whereas only 9 percent reported just one or two instances. Later in this chapter we will examine characteristics of the dependence groups to determine whether the cases reporting infrequent symptoms are engaging in high-risk behavior. For the present, it is important to note simply that the number of such cases is fairly small.

ADVERSE CONSEQUENCES OF DRINKING

As noted in Chapter 1, many accounts of alcoholism focus not on alcohol dependence, but rather on the various adverse consequences or complications

[4]A weighted scale, using the principal-component weights, could have been employed, but the simpler equal-weight sum was so highly correlated with the weighted version that the simpler version was chosen ($r = .99$). In addition, basic relationships reported in this chapter appear to be unaffected by the choice of particular items. As shown in Appendix C, a scale composed of the "classical dependence" items (tremors, morning drinking, and loss of control) produces virtually the same relationships as the six-item scale.

that arise from excessive drinking. This is true particularly of research using the Jellinek definition (1960) and the World Health Organization 1952 definition. Accordingly, the 4-year followup instrument contained a battery of questions enquiring about the recent occurrence of the most serious consequences related to alcoholism.

Basically, these consequences represent an eclectic list of concrete problems that can be directly attributed to alcohol or that are so attributed by the subject. Only subjects who had consumed alcohol during the previous 6 months were designated as experiencing "consequences." As shown in Table 3.13, among health-related consequences we included any occasion on which a physician diagnosed or treated liver disease during the 6-month period (including cirrhosis, hepatitis, or fatty liver), as well as a respondent's report of "still having" the disease if he said that a physician had diagnosed it at some time in the past. Also counted were any instances during the 6-month period when a physician advised the subject to stop drinking altogether because of medical conditions, or when the subject was hospitalized overnight because of his drinking (attribution made by the subject).

Finally, the occurrence of any other disease with a fairly definite relationship to alcoholism was treated as an adverse consequence. These

Table 3.13 Adverse Consequences of Drinking[a]

Adverse Consequence	Percent Reporting	Percent Reporting This Consequence But No Others
Health		
Liver disease diagnosed or treated by physician	13	0
Liver disease reported by subject	16	1
Medically advised to stop drinking	6	1
Hospitalized because of drinking	23	3
Alcohol-related disease episode	20	1
Any of the above	40	—
Law Enforcement		
Arrested for DWI	6	0
Jailed because of drinking	18	4
Any of the above	19	—
Work and Interpersonal Relations		
Unable to work because of drinking	6	1
Missed two or more days' work because of drinking	19	4
Got into fights or arguments two or more times because of drinking	16	5
Any of the above	34	—
Total Experiencing One or More Consequences	58	—
(N)	(393)	(393)

[a]Consequences occurring in the past 6 months, among persons drinking in the past 6 months. For measurement procedures, see Appendix D.

diseases included hepatitis or "yellow jaundice" (whether or not treated), pancreatitis, internal bleeding, and "DTs, convulsions, or hallucinations related to alcohol" occurring during the 6-month period. Obviously these are fairly serious disorders for which drinking is generally contraindicated. Although it is possible that in some cases the disorder was primarily the result of prolonged heavy drinking before the past 6 months, we judged that even in such instances the subject's continued drinking was almost certainly damaging his health. Therefore, such a person was experiencing consequences of current drinking as well as past drinking.

The law enforcement incidents include being arrested for driving while intoxicated and being jailed because of drinking, regardless of the charge. Besides these, we included three consequences from the domain of social effects (work and interpersonal problems). Such a consequence was imputed if the subject reported that he did not have a job because of his drinking problem; if he reported missing two or more days of work because of drinking during the 30-day period before his last drink; or if he reported getting into fights or arguments at least twice while drinking during the 30-day period.

The first column of Table 3.13 shows that most of the drinkers were affected by one or more of these serious consequences during the 6 months before the interview. The second column of the table shows that no single consequence from this set predominates. The consequence most commonly occurring singly is "fights or arguments while drinking"; 5 percent of the drinkers reported this consequence in the absence of any others. The definition of the "adverse consequence" group, therefore, is not especially dependent on any single consequence.

The distribution of the number of consequences reported during the past 6 months is shown in Table 3.14. Twenty-eight percent of the total sample

Table 3.14   Distribution of the Number of Adverse
Consequences

	Percent Distribution	
Number of Consequences Reported	Among Drinkers[a]	Among All Cases
0	42	30
1	20	14
2	14	10
3	9	7
4	9	7
5 or more	5	4
Abstained past 6 months	—	28
(N)	(393)	(548)

[a]Persons drinking in the past 6 months.

experienced two or more serious consequences during the 6 months before the followup. However, another 14 percent of the sample experienced just one of these consequences. Are these people to be regarded as having a less serious alcohol problem than those with multiple consequences?

In some respects, this question is an enquiry into the meaningfulness of a scale of number of consequences, i.e., into the scalability of the consequence items. One approach might be to construct a numerical scale of consequences as a continuous variable, as we did with symptoms. However, our data show that consequences, unlike symptoms, tend to be quite diverse and rather weakly intercorrelated.[5] Hence a numerical scale of consequences may not be justified as representing an underlying unidimensional continuum of severity. Moreover, we view "consequences" as having a conceptual status different from that of dependence symptoms. Whereas the symptoms reflect an underlying condition that causes other behavior and perpetuates itself over time, consequences are simply the reactions of the biological and social systems to the phenomena of drinking and dependence. Consequences are therefore useful as indicators of the damage done by drinking and alcohol dependence. In our judgment, even one of the consequences from the above list is sufficiently grave to reflect a serious problem in the precipitating behavior, particularly when the group in question has an alcoholic history. Accordingly, we tentatively treated all cases with even one consequence as cases of a continuing "alcohol problem."

RISK PATTERNS OF DRINKING BEHAVIORS

Our eventual objective in this chapter is to combine the various measures of alcohol problems into an overall classification of the subject's status at 4 years. In doing so, we face a number of difficult classification decisions. In particular, the behaviors represented by consequences, symptoms, and consumption quantity must be broken into categories representing meaningful groups that are empirically different in their patterns of alcohol use. To some extent we can be guided by conceptual considerations, as we were in deciding that all persons with consequences should be treated as a unitary category. In most cases, however, we have relied on more empirical criteria, particularly criteria reflecting better or worse prognoses attached to different behavior patterns. In this section we report some of the correlational results and prognostic data that have guided us in constructing an overall classification of status at 4 years.

An important set of results is contained in the simple relationship between dependence symptoms and consequences at the 4-year followup. This relationship is shown in Table 3.15, together with the percentages calculated in both directions. In the top panel of the table, the data are presented to show

[5]See the factor analysis of symptom, consequence, and consumption measures in Appendix C.

Table 3.15   Relationship Between Symptoms and Consequences at Four Years

Dependence Symptom Level (4 Years)	Percent Reporting Designated Level of Consequences (4 Years)					
	0	1	2	3 or More	Total, 1 or More	(N)
0	77	17	4	2	23*	(129)
1-5	51	26	10	13	49*	(79)
6-20	23	29	29	19	77	(52)
Over 20	11	21	21	47	89	(132)
Number of Consequences (4 Years)	Percent Reporting Designated Level of Symptoms (4 Years)					
	0	1-5	6-20	Over 20	Total, 1 or More	(N)
0	60	24	7	9	40*	(166)
1	26	24	17	33	74*	(86)
2	11	14	26	49	89	(57)
3 or more	2	12	12	74	98	(83)

*The difference between the percentages marked is statistically significant ($p < .001$).

the percentage of cases at each symptom level who reported adverse consequences. There is a very important threshold between those with no dependence symptoms and those with one or more. Interpreted as the risk of a serious consequence, these results suggest that such risks double as one moves from drinking without symptoms to drinking with even minimal symptoms: the rate of consequences rises from 23 to 49 percent. The fact that the absolute level is so high for persons with low-level symptoms (49 percent) suggests that it would be unwise to treat low-symptom drinkers as problem-free.

The lower panel of Table 3.15 shows that a similar relationship can be observed from the other direction. That is, as the number of consequences increases from zero to one, the probability that any symptoms have also been experienced almost doubles from 40 percent to a very high 74 percent. Moreover, this is not an artifact of setting the symptom cutoff point at zero versus one or more. As the table indicates, a threshold in the probability of symptoms exists between zero and one consequence, regardless of the symptom level that is examined. For example, the probability of experiencing 20 or more symptoms in a month—surely a serious sign of dependence—rises from 9 percent to 33 percent as the number of consequences changes from zero to one. The impression one receives is that symptoms of dependence and adverse consequences of drinking are bound together very closely; moreover, even low levels of one variable portend significant risks for the other.[6]

These data are cross-sectional, of course. One might therefore argue that the relationships could be due to subjects' tendencies toward consistency in reporting rather than to any true connection between dependence and adverse consequences. To test such an hypothesis, we also examined longitudinal relationships, in which alcohol problems are measured at 18 months and are correlated with problems measured at 4 years. Unfortunately, the 18-month interview data did not contain measures of adverse consequences, and therefore we are restricted to looking at the apparent effects of varying symptom levels on later alcohol problems. For our purposes, this limitation is not especially serious because we view dependence as the central variable in the process. We primarily wish to test the importance of dependence symptoms as potential causal factors in the perpetuation of alcohol-related problems.

Table 3.16 shows the result when dependence symptom level at 18 months is tabulated against three alcohol problems occurring later: consequences at 4 years; symptoms at 4 years; and alcohol-related deaths at 4-years. (The definition of an alcohol-related death is explored in detail in Chapter 5; here it may be described simply as a death due to an alcohol-related disease, such as cirrhosis, or due to an accident or suicide in which alcohol was judged a significant factor by a collateral.) The data strongly suggest that drinking with no symptoms at 18 months is much less risk-laden than drinking with low symptom levels. For those drinking with 1 to 5 symptoms at 18 months, the data show a 48 percent rate of consequences, a 71 percent rate of symptoms, and a 7 percent alcohol-related mortality rate. These rates may be compared with the considerably lower rates on the same three variables for people who drink but have no symptoms. Both the absolute risk levels and the patterns of relative risks suggest a threshold between those having no symptoms and those with at least one symptom. Obviously, there is a gradient corresponding to symptom level within the symptomatic drinkers; the greater the level, the higher the probabilities of later alcohol problems. The greatest part of the variance in such problems, nevertheless, is captured by the simple distinction between symptomatic and nonsymptomatic drinkers. Therefore, we decided to make that distinction in constructing a classification of status at 4 years.

[6]Analysis reported in Appendix C shows that the finding of a threshold between zero symptoms and one or more symptoms holds up under several variations of measures. For example, the threshold appears even for people reporting just one or two symptoms. In addition, the presence of symptoms raises the rate of adverse consequences even when one examines disaggregated consequence measures (health, law enforcement, or interpersonal problems considered separately) and when one includes only the "classical" dependence symptoms (tremors, morning drinking, and loss of control).

Table 3.16 Alcohol Problems at Four Years, by Symptom Level at 18 Months

Symptom Level at 18-Month Interview	Percent of Survivors Reporting Any Consequence at 4 Years	Percent of Survivors Reporting Any Symptom at 4 Years	Base Number of Cases (Survivors)	Percent Alcohol-Related Deaths, 18-Months to 4 Years[a]	Base Number of Cases (All 18-Month Interviewees)
0	30*	38**	(76)	3	(103)
1-5	48*	71**	(48)	7	(69)
6-20	74	91	(34)	7	(54)
Over 20	79	95	(63)	11	(100)

[a]Percentage of all 18-month interviewees dying from alcohol-related causes between 18 months and 4 years ("alcohol-related deaths" as defined in Chapter 5).

*Difference between percentages marked is statistically significant, $p < .05$.

**Difference between percentages marked is statistically significant, $p < .001$.

Table 3.17 Alcohol Problems at Four Years, by 18-Month Drinking Behavior

Drinking Behavior at 18-Month Interview[a]	Percent of Survivors Reporting Any Consequence at 4 Years	Percent of Survivors Reporting Any Symptom at 4 Years	Base Number of Cases (Survivors)	Percent Alcohol-Related Deaths, 18 Months to 4 Years[b]	Base Number of Case (All 18-Month Interviewees)
Abstained 6 months or more	31	23	(115)	1	(140)
Abstained 1-5 months	52	43	(99)	9	(124)
Drank, no symptoms	27	34	(85)	3	(103)
Drank, symptoms	61	71	(175)	9	(223)

[a]Association of drinking behavior categories with all column variables (consequences, symptoms, and alcohol-related deaths) is statistically significant (Chi-square test, $p < .01$).

[b]Percentage of all 18-month interviewees dying from alcohol-related causes between 18 months and 4 years ("alcohol-related death" as defined in Chapter 5).

Several notable results growing out of this decision can be seen in Table 3.17. This table compares 18-month symptomatic drinkers, nonsymptomatic drinkers, short-term abstainers, and long-term abstainers in terms of alcohol problems measured at 4 years. The data imply that the best prognosis exists for long-term abstainers and for nonsymptomatic drinkers. In contrast, the prognosis for short-term abstainers appears almost as unfavorable as that for drinkers with symptoms, particularly in terms of mortality. Compared with nonsymptomatic drinkers, the long-term abstainers have lower rates of mortality or continued symptoms, but a slightly higher rate of consequences. However, all the differences between long-term abstainers and nonsymptomatic drinkers are fairly small and they are not statistically significant.[7]

These results contain two important findings that build on our knowledge from previous followup studies. First, they indicate that the presence of alcohol dependence symptoms, even at very low levels, is a serious indication of continuing alcohol problems. It is not only that people with dependence symptoms are likely to have recently experienced adverse consequences of drinking. More than that: When examined several years later, they are more likely than others to be dependent on alcohol, to experience future adverse consequences of drinking, and to die prematurely of an alcohol-related cause. Under these circumstances, it would be imprudent to treat any alcoholic with dependence symptoms as being in a favorable condition. This represents a departure from the assumptions of the 18-month study, where certain drinkers with infrequent symptoms were included in a remission category. The 4-year data, however, clearly indicate the high risk attached to such behaviors.

The second significant finding concerns the unfavorable status of short-term abstention. Students of alcoholism have always been aware of the suspect character of such behavior, which suggests cyclical variation between heavy-drinking bouts and "drying out" periods. However, there is always a hope that a particular individual will continue abstaining—that a case of "short-term abstention" appearing at a followup will develop into a case of long-term abstention or drinking without problems. Unhappily, that development is more unusual than it is common. The data indicate that the problem rate among short-term abstainers has been high during their recent drinking periods, and they are apt to have similar problems later on.

Like the finding on nonsymptomatic drinking, this conclusion has important implications for changes in our methodology. In the previous assessments of this cohort, drinking behavior was measured only during the

---

[7]For survivors, both long-term abstainers and nonsymptomatic drinkers are significantly different from the combined other groups ($p < .01$), but they are not significantly different from each other (at the .05 level). For deaths, the test results are the same, except that the first difference reaches only the .05 level but not the .01 level.

30 days before the interview; therefore, short-term abstainers were necessarily treated only as "abstainers." As noted earlier, in the 4-year followup design, we enquired about all drinking behavior in the "30 days before your last drink," thus obtaining a measure of previous drinking for current abstainers. Because we decided on a 6-month period for assessing drinking status at this followup, it is natural to classify the drinking of all short-term abstainers, as well as current drinkers, according to the last drinking period. If a short-term abstainer's drinking is moderate and problem-free, he will then be so classified; if it is not, his unfavorable status at followup will be properly captured.

Up to this point we have said little about the risks of different *quantities* of consumption, as opposed to symptomatic drinking. The rates of current symptoms and adverse consequences, classified by the consumption patterns defined earlier, are shown in Table 3.18. Evidently there is a fairly strong correlation between heavy drinking and the other problem measures. Whereas the rates of symptoms or consequences are at approximately the 25 percent mark for Low Q drinkers, the rates are considerably higher for the other quantity levels. Nonetheless, our conceptual approach suggests that dependence symptoms are likely to be more centrally involved in the course of alcoholism. If dependence is interpreted as a "need" for large amounts of alcohol, the principal causal agent is the presence of dependence, and not the high consumption quantity. (This is true even though a nondependent person may initially develop dependence through extended heavy consumption.) Therefore, we expect that dependence should be a more reliable indicator of future alcohol problems than high consumption alone.

Table 3.19 lends support to this thesis. Here we tabulate rates of alcohol problems at 4 years according to the subject's consumption and symptom levels at the 18-month followup. For consequences at 4 years, the picture is clouded by an interaction; neither symptoms alone nor high consumption

Table 3.18   Rates of Symptoms and Adverse Consequences, by Consumption Patterns

Consumption Pattern, 4 Years[a]	Rate of Symptoms, 4 Years (Percent)	Rate of Adverse Consequences, 4 Years (Percent)	(N)
Low Q	22	25	(67)
High Q (atypical)	47	26	(19)
High Q (typical)	46	40	(67)
Very High Q (atypical)	71	58	(62)
Very High Q (typical)	87	80	(176)

[a]Association of consumption pattern with both column variables (symptoms and consequences) is statistically significant (Chi-square test, $p < .001$).

Table 3.19 Alcohol Problems at Four Years Based on 18-Month Consumption and Symptoms

Alcohol Problem at 4-Year Followup	Drinking at 18-Month Followup			
	Consumption Under 2 oz.[a]		Consumption 2 oz or More[a]	
	No Symptoms	Symptoms	No Symptoms	Symptoms
Percent reporting any consequences[b] (survivors)	25	35	29	64
Percent reporting any symptoms[b] (survivors)	35	65	32	72
Number of cases (survivors)	(55)	(20)	(31)	(153)
Percent alcohol-related deaths, 18 months to 4 years[c]	3	10	3	9
Number of cases (all interviewees at 18 months)	(66)	(30)	(37)	(191)

[a]Typical quantity of ethanol consumed on a drinking day.

[b]Tests of statistical significance for percentage differences comparing "no symptoms" with "symptoms" groups are as follows: 25 vs. 35, not significant ($p > .10$); 35 vs. 65, $p < .01$; 29 vs. 64, $p < .001$; 32 vs. 72, $p < .001$.

[c]Percentage of all 18-month interviewees dying from alcohol-related causes between 18 months and 4 years ("alcohol-related death" as defined in Chapter 5). Percentage differences comparing "no symptoms" with "symptoms" groups are not statistically significant ($p > .10$).

alone raises the consequence rate very much, but together they boost the rate precipitously. By comparison, the data for symptoms at 4 years and for alcohol-related mortality are consistent in showing that dependence symptoms have a main effect on later alcohol problems, whereas high consumption does not.[8] These results constitute a third important finding that affects our classification of drinking status. The data indicate that, in general, high levels of consumption are associated with increased numbers of alcohol problems. However, this association cannot be demonstrated to be a causal one. On the contrary, high consumption in the absence of dependence does *not* appear to increase the risk of later problems. We do not have a full explanation to offer for this finding. Nonetheless, the data are consistent with the theoretical expectation that alcohol dependence is a more serious condition than mere high consumption.

ASSESSMENT OF STATUS AT FOUR YEARS

The Measure of Status at Four Years

The foregoing analysis is the basis for constructing our composite assessment of status at 4 years. Our intent is to measure both actual drinking behavior and the problems caused by it. We therefore wish to include the subject's dependence symptoms, the adverse drinking consequences he has experienced, and his alcohol consumption pattern. As we have seen, dependence symptomatology apparently plays a highly important role in perpetuating alcohol problems. Because even low levels of such symptoms imply potential future problems, we will treat even one instance of symptoms as evidence of a significant condition. Similarly, in our judgment, the seriousness of the consequences we have identified makes the occurrence of even one of them a prima facie "alcohol problem." Added to that consideration, we have the evidence adduced in the previous section suggesting that the occurrence of even a single consequence is closely linked to other alcohol problems. Although consumption itself is more difficult to separate into problem-prone patterns versus others, the data presented above suggest that a conservative

[8]The small number of cases in the off-diagonal cells (those with symptoms and low consumption, or no symptoms and high consumption) prevents some of these comparisons from being statistically significant at the .05 level. By that standard, the mortality proportions are not significantly different from each other, whereas the 65 versus 35, 64 versus 29, and 72 versus 32 comparisons involving symptom versus nonsymptom groups are significant at the .01 level. However, estimated death rates for both "symptoms" groups are consistently about three times the rates for the "no symptoms" groups, which suggests that if we had larger samples, the survivor findings would be replicated among the deaths.

yet meaningful split could be made between those witn "low" versus "high" consumption reports. These are the distinctions underlying the 7-category classification of drinking status at 4 years, as shown in Table 3.20.

In this classification, persons abstaining for either 1 year or 6 to 11 months are treated simply as abstainers. This reflects our basic decision to rely on the 6-month period before the interview for the followup assessment. Among those who drank some alcoholic beverage during that period, the classification differentiates those *without* symptoms or consequences according to the amount of consumption (consistently low amounts versus high amounts). The remaining persons, those with immediate problems manifested as either dependence symptoms or adverse consequences, are classified according to whether they have experienced one or the other or both types of problems.

The extent of serious problems in this sample is notable. If just the symptom and consequence groups are taken as reflecting immediate problems, 54 percent of the admissions are classified as having alcohol problems at the time of the 4-year followup. Most of these problem cases report symptoms of alcohol dependence. The groups that are abstaining at the 4-year followup are smaller, together making up 28 percent of the sample. Even after imposing the fairly stringent criteria for low consumption levels, we find 8 percent reporting low to moderate consumption levels without immediate problems. Another 10 percent of the sample report higher levels of consumption without problems. These results lend support to the notion that for many alcoholics their condition is indeed chronic, in the sense that the types of problems that result in an alcoholism diagnosis are still present after a 4-year interval.

Adequacy of the Status Assessment

A number of methodological questions may be posed regarding the adequacy of the classification of status at 4 years. One issue is that of the representativeness of the 30-day assessment period. Recall that both consumption and symptoms were measured according to the 30 days before the subject's last drink, on the assumption that the last drinking period would be an accurate representation of drinking throughout the 6-month period. Is this assumption reasonable? A conclusive answer to that question is not possible without a continuous record of behavior over 6 months. However, we have some data bearing on the point from questions in the inte:view that enquired about the entire 6-month period. Table 3.21 shows these data, which relate consumption and symptoms over the 6-month period to drinking behavior classified according to status at 4 years.

Table 3.21 shows the percentage of drinkers in a given status category who reported at least 1 month of the 6 when their typical quantity exceeded 5 ounces of ethanol. These cases would thus be inconsistent with a classification

Table 3.20 Drinking Status at Four Years

Group No.	Drinking Status	Definition[a]	Percent Distribution[b]
1	1-year abstention	Abstained 1 year or more	21 ⎫ 28
2	6-11 month abstention	Abstained 6-11 months	7 ⎭
3	Low Q	Quantity consistently low, no symptoms, and no consequences	8 ⎫ 18
4	High Q	Quantity not consistently low, no symptoms, and no consequences	10 ⎭
5	Adverse consequences	Any instance of consequences without symptoms	6 ⎫
6	Dependence symptoms	Any instance of symptoms without consequences	12 ⎬ 54
7	Symptoms and consequences	Any symptoms in the presence of any consequences	36 ⎭
(N)			(548)

[a]Based on measures of consumption quantity in the 30 days before last drink; symptoms in the 30 days before last drink; and consequences in the 6 months before interview.
[b]Subjects admitted to treatment.

Table 3.21   Consistency of Drinking Status With 6-Month Drinking Patterns

Group No.	Drinking Status at 4 Years	Percent with Very Heavy Drinking (over 5 oz.), Past 6 Months[a]	Percent with Symptoms, Past 6 Months[b]	(N)
3	Low Q	5	2	(42)
4	High Q	33	7	(57)
5	Consequences	33	33	(30)
6	Symptoms	46	57	(67)
7	Symptoms and consequences	77	84	(196)

[a]Percentage reporting at least 1 month in the past 6 months when the typical quantity consumed on a drinking day was over 5 oz. of ethanol.
[b]Percentage reporting the occurrence of at least one symptom outside the 30-day assessment period during the past 6 months.

of Low Q during the 30-day period but not with other classifications. The results show that only 5 percent of the Low Q category exhibited such inconsistency. Table 3.21 also shows the percentage who reported the occurrence of at least one symptom during the past 6 months that was not included in the original 30-day period. On this measure, inconsistencies would occur for any subjects reporting such symptoms if they were also classified as Low Q, High Q, or Consequences (i.e., without symptoms at the 30-day assessment). Once again, the Low Q group appears highly consistent, as does the High Q group. An absence of symptoms and consequences as measured by the variable "status at 4 years," then, is likely to imply an absence of *any* symptoms throughout the 6-month period before the interview.

Interestingly, the group with "consequences only" is not so symptom-free; in fact, one-third of the subjects who reported no current symptoms but at least one serious consequence admitted having had some symptoms during the few months preceding the interview. Many people with consequences, then, have a history of intermittent dependence symptoms even when they are currently symptom-free. Moreover, of all the subjects in the sample who reported consequences, 87 percent (196/226) reported *concurrent* symptoms. When one considers these findings together, the condition of a person who has even one consequence appears unfavorable indeed.

In summary, the burden of these results is to suggest a fairly sharp differentiation between two classes of drinkers in the alcoholic population: those who have any type of manifest problems (symptoms or consequences) and those without problems. The latter are quite consistent in reporting the absence of any sort of problems over our entire 6-month assessment period.

The data argue strongly in favor of treating any subjects with either symptoms or consequences as cases of continuing "alcohol problems." In

Table 3.22   Distribution of Drinking Status at Four Years, by Modified Definitions

		Percent Distribution of Cases[a]		
			Modified Definitions	
Group No.	Drinking Status at 4 Years	Existing Definition[b]	Defining Symptoms as Three or More Events[c]	Defining Consequences as Two or More Events[d]
1	Abstained 1 year	21	21	21
2	Abstained 6-11 months	7	7	7
3	Low Q	8	8	9
4	High Q	10	14	13
5	Consequences	6	9	1
6	Symptoms	12	8	24
7	Symptoms and consequences	36	33	24
Problem Rate[e]		54	50	49

[a]Total N = 548 (all admissions).
[b]Any instance of symptoms counted as a "symptom" case; any instance of consequences counted as a "consequence" case.
[c]Only cases with 3 or more symptom-events counted as "symptom" cases.
[d]Only cases with 2 or more consequences counted as "consequence" cases.
[e]Percentage of sample with symptoms or consequences, as defined.

many of our multivariate analyses, we will distinguish such problem drinkers from the nonproblem drinkers and the abstainers. Before going on to other issues, however, we pause to examine the implications of our chosen cutting-off points on our basic results. Suppose, for example, we had adopted as a standard for dependence, not one symptom, but something higher. Or, suppose we had insisted on a report of not just one consequence, but two or more in order to recognize an alcohol problem. What would the distribution of "status at 4 years" be with these modifications?

Table 3.22 shows what would occur if the definitions of drinking status were modified at the margin in such ways. Although some of the percentages in the individual problem categories change, the overall problem rate is affected by only 4 or 5 percentage points. The proportions in the Low Q category are hardly changed at all. In our view, such changes would not affect the overall picture of this cohort. The impression would still be one of severe and chronic problems affecting about one-half of the cohort.

Characteristics of the Status Groups

The meaning of the classification may be explicated by considering the other alcohol-related characteristics that differentiate the status categories. Table 3.23 shows the nature of typical quantities of alcohol consumed across the five groups, by classification of drinking status at 4 years. By definition, of course,

Table 3.23   Consumption Quantity, by Drinking Status at Four Years

| Group No. | Drinking Status at 4 Years | Typical Quantity of Consumption | | | | | |
| | | Percent Distribution of Cases | | | | | |
		Under 2 oz.	2-5 oz.	Over 5 oz.	Median	Mean	(N)
3	Low Q	100	0	0	0.94	1.13	(42)
4	High Q	18	58	24	2.88	3.67	(57)
5	Consequences	43	37	20	2.57	2.97	(30)
6	Symptoms	24	43	33	3.69	4.97	(67)
7	Symptoms and consequences	7	25	68	7.58	9.73	(193)

the Low Q group is much below the others. Only the "symptoms and consequences" group shows a typical pattern of extreme consumption, such as one normally finds in admission samples. In the other categories, the average person consumes between 2.5 and 4.0 ounces on a drinking day (5 to 8 drinks). It is important to note that more than three-fourths of the High Q group consume less than 5 ounces on a drinking day, and their median Q is less than 3 ounces. Our designation of them as "High" is merely a relative term (comparing them with the group that consumes less than 2 ounces); considering their freedom from manifest problems, it should be clearly understood that they do not exhibit followup behavior similar to the typical alcoholic at admission to treatment.

Further indications of the characteristics that differentiate the status categories can be seen in the medical conditions reported at the 4-year followup, as shown in Table 3.24. Because liver impairments are the disorders most clearly linked to excessive alcohol consumption, we have tabulated separately liver conditions and other conditions whose connections to alcohol abuse are more tenuous. Indeed, we used current liver disease as a definitional criterion for the consequence categories, which accounts for the low rates in Groups 3, 4, and 6. The high rates of liver problems for Groups 5 and 7 are worth noting, nonetheless. In addition, the substantial rate among 6- to 11-month abstainers suggests that the beginning of their abstention may have been motivated by recognition of deteriorating health. In general, the rates for cirrhosis are very high (compared with those of a "normal" population), although certainly they do not imply that the disease is widespread in this population.

In contrast, other conditions that *could* be linked to alcohol are very prevalent in the sample. We have designated these others as "possibly" alcohol related because they are frequently found in clinic populations but are by no means definitive as indicators of alcoholism. Most of the subjects in the sample have at least one of these conditions, and there is a tendency toward

Table 3.24 Alcohol-Related Medical Conditions, by Drinking Status at Four Years

Group No.	Drinking Status at 4 Years	Percent Reporting Medical Conditions					(N)
		Liver Conditions		Other Possibly Alcohol-Related Conditions[c]			
		Cirrhosis (ever diagnosed)[a]	Any Liver Disease[b]	One or More, Past 6 Months	Two or More, Past 6 Months		
1	Abstained 1 year	10	10	48	28		(117)
2	Abstained 6-11 months	13	23	51	28		(39)
3	Low Q	2	2	55	14		(42)
4	High Q	0	0	51	28		(57)
5	Consequences	23	37	55	27		(30)
6	Symptoms	0	0	78	48		(67)
7	Symptoms and consequences	13	32	80	70		(196)

[a]Subject reporting that cirrhosis was diagnosed by a physician at any time in his life.
[b]Subject reporting that cirrhosis was ever diagnosed; or that he received medical treatment for any liver problem in the past 6 months; or that he had "hepatitis or yellow jaundice" in the past 6 months.
[c]Occurrence in the past 6 months of anemia, weakness in limbs, numbness in legs, dizziness, loss of balance, or fractures.

very high rates in the symptomatic categories (Groups 6 and 7). Considering the percentage of each status group with two or more such conditions, we find little variation among the first five groups except for a lower rate among Low Q subjects. Again the rates for both groups of symptomatic drinkers are highly elevated, suggesting an intimate link between the presence of dependence symptoms and general physical deterioration.

VALIDITY OF THE STATUS CLASSIFICATION

A direct method of examining the validity of the classification of status at 4 years is provided by our two supplemental measures: the BAC readings and collateral information. These measures generated external data against which the self-reports of some of our sample members may be compared. The BAC measures are directly relevant to the validity of consumption reports, i.e., to the distinction between Low Q and High Q categories of status at 4 years. The collateral interviews cover a much broader ground and can be used to judge the credibility of consequence and symptom reports. Assessment of validity is at best a matter of inference and judgment. This is especially true in the measurement of alcohol-related behaviors, because there is no easily available "true" measure (or criterion) against which other instruments may be compared. These complications are discussed in detail in Appendix B, which reports the results of our validity analysis. Here we merely summarize the import of our findings for the measurement of status at 4 years.

BAC Measures and Consumption

The data in Appendix B show that subject reports of abstention over the past 2 days before the interview are almost always consistent with the BAC (only 4 percent inconsistencies, i.e., a positive BAC with a report of abstention). Among the drinkers, however, there is a substantial amount of underreporting. About 25 percent of the recent drinkers appear to be underreporting typical quantity consumed by at least 1 ounce, judging by the BAC reading. The rates of such underreporting are shown in Table 3.25. (These data cover only persons in our sample who drank in the recent past, as these are the only ones for whom a direct BAC assessment is feasible.) In about 25 percent of both the nonsymptom groups and the symptom groups, self-reported consumption is substantially exceeded by the estimated consumption computed from the BAC reading. Interestingly, this 25 percent rate is spread fairly evenly across all the groups, with the exception of persons reporting consequences but no symptoms. As far as the drinking status classification is concerned, the only group that could be crucially affected by an error in reported consumption is the Low Q category; even if the others underreported their consumption, they would not be reclassified, because they have already reported a high consumption level, symptoms, or consequences. Such underreporters in the Low Q group constitute only 4 cases in all. Obviously, even if these people were reclassified into a higher-quantity category, the overall results would be insignificantly affected.

We have no method of calculating the underreporting rate for all members of the Low Q category, only for those 16 cases shown in Table 3.25. One conservative approach would be to assume that all members of this category underreport consumption in the same proportions. If this were done, one-fourth of the Low Q group would be moved into the High Q group. Even this assumption does not result in a very substantial alteration of the overall results. The key to understanding this, of course, lies in the relatively low rate of underreporting coupled with the small proportion of cases that fall in the Low Q category. Under ideal circumstances, it would be best to isolate such underreporters, even though they are few in number, and to reallocate them to the proper classification. However, there is no general rule for isolating such persons. Therefore, we have not attempted to correct individual cases for presumed underreporting. It appears that the classification of drinking status at 4 years is fairly robust against the effects of underreporting consumption.

Collateral Measures

As described in Chapter 2, a random subset of subjects interviewed in Group I was designated for additional interviews with collaterals, resulting in 128 cases in which both a subject and a collateral interview were obtained. These pairs of interviews afford an opportunity to assess the agreement or disagreement between the self-reports of subjects and the observations of collaterals about those same subjects. In many ways the collaterals are probably less precise than one would wish; they may not have good opportunies to observe the subject, they may not be observant, or they may themselves make errors in reporting on the subject's behavior. These problems are particularly significant for subjective phenomena such as symptoms, but they are less important for gross events that are fairly easy to observe. Data on the agreement and disagreement between subjects and collaterals are given in Table 3.26. More detailed tables on these pairs appear in Appendix B.

There seems to be very good agreement on the basic question of drinking versus abstention. Only one subject out of 128 reported abstaining for the past 6 months when his collateral reported that he drank. Notably, in 5 percent of the pairs, the subject admitted drinking during the past 6 months, whereas the collateral denied that the subject had been drinking. For abstention, then, there is a very low rate of underreporting for the subject but a slightly higher one for the collateral.

Table 3.25 Self-Report versus BAC Inconsistency, by Drinking Status at Four Years

Group No.	Drinking Status at 4 Years	Number of Recent Drinkers (drank past 24 hours)	Number Whose BAC Is Inconsistent with Self-Reported Consumption[a]	Percent Inconsistent
3	Low Q	16	4	25
4	High Q	38	9	24
5	Consequences	17	0	0
6	Symptoms	53	18	34
7	Symptoms and consequences	96	22	23
Total		220	53	24

[a]Self-reported typical quantity exceeds the quantity estimated from the BAC. See Appendix B.

Table 3.26 Agreement Between Subjects and Collaterals

Item	Percent of Subject-Collateral Pairs Giving Designated Answer Pairs					
	Subj. Yes Coll. Yes	Subj. No Coll. No	Subj. Yes Coll. No	Subj. No Coll. Yes	Collateral Unsure	(N)
Drank anything in past 6 months	63	27	5	1	4	(128)[a]
Drank over 2 oz. per day	15	36	11	12	26	(92)[b]
Jailed for drinking	11	73	6	6	4	(90)
Hospitalized due to drinking	22	60	7	4	8	(92)
Missed work 2 days or more	2	58	9	8	24	(92)
Morning drinking	10	27	16	8	39	(92)
Tremors	15	28	10	15	32	(92)
Missed meals	21	24	9	8	39	(92)

[a]Total number of subjects with collateral interview = 128.
[b]Number of subjects reporting drinking in past 6 months = 92.

In order to analyze self-reports of drinking behavior, we must exclude the cases in which the subject did not drink. This leaves us with 92 cases for analysis, as shown in Table 3.26. (We have included the 6 cases in which the subject admitted drinking but the collateral denied it. We counted such cases as an instance of the collateral's saying *No* to the item, because there was a collateral measurement; but in effect, the collateral measure does not indicate a drinking problem.) Among the items listed in Table 3.26, there were two in which the collaterals were almost always willing to venture an answer; these were questions about whether the subject was "in jail because of drinking" or "hospitalized because of drinking" during the past 6 months. For both items, collaterals and subjects agreed in more than 80 percent of the pairs, and another 10 to 15 percent of the pairs are either instances in which the collateral was unsure or the subject admitted a problem but the collateral did not. Only a small number of the pairs (4 to 6 percent) showed a pattern of subject denial of a problem but collateral endorsement.

In all the other items, the comparison is impaired by the fact that there was a great deal of collateral uncertainty: collateral "unsures" ranged from 24 to 39 percent. For the item "tremors," a classical symptom of alcoholism that should be observable to an outsider, 32 percent of the collaterals were unsure whether or not the subject had experienced the symptom in the past 6 months. In only 15 percent of the paired answers to this item were there reports that would appear to represent subject underreporting (subject said *No,* collateral said *Yes*). The tremors question, moreover, is the item with the *highest* apparent rate of underreporting.

There are a number of alternative ways in which these results could be tabulated. For example, one could omit the cases in which the collateral was unsure or in which the collateral denied that the subject drank during the 6-month period. By such methods, the subject underreporting rate would be somewhat higher, although one would then be ignoring many cases in which the subject reported significant drinking problems and the collateral either did not know about them or did not report them. The tables in Appendix B show that in most of the pairs for which the collaterals were unsure about the subjects' symptoms, the subjects had reported frequent symptoms in their interviews. We have also examined (in Appendix B) the impact of some fairly extreme assumptions of underreporting based on what direct disconfirmation of subjects we can observe in the collateral interviews. These results suggest that if one assumed the maximum amount of subject underreporting consistent with the BAC and collateral data, perhaps 4 percent of the sample would be reclassified into consequence or symptoms categories. However, such extrapolations are very tenuous.

In all, there are relatively few subjects for whom a collateral report would imply a reclassification with respect to an occurrence of a particular symptom or adverse consequence—between 8 and 15 percent for the symptoms and between 4 and 6 percent for consequences. In view of the frequency of uncertainty among collaterals and the circumstances of data collection, it does not seem that the collateral data constitute a sound basis for assessing overall self-report validity. In areas where collaterals knew the subjects' behavior, there is good agreement (i.e., for abstention and gross events such as hospitalization or imprisonment). In areas where there is some disagreement, most of it arises from collateral uncertainty; and what direct disagreement there is, runs in both directions (subjects admitting problems denied by collaterals and vice versa). Because of these considerations, we have not attempted to make an adjustment in the tabulations for this study based on the collateral interview data.

STATUS AT FOUR YEARS AND DRINKING AT ADMISSION TO TREATMENT

Our assessment of drinking status at the 4-year followup, like that of many other studies, has found that some individuals who had been admitted to treatment for alcoholism were later drinking without overt problems. Although this finding is commonly reported in the scientific literature (Pomerleau et al., 1976), it conflicts with traditional models of alcoholism, which hold that nonproblem drinking is impossible in an alcoholic population (Roizen, 1977). One explanation for this inconsistency could be that some of our sample members, such as the nonproblem drinkers, might not have been initially dependent on alcohol.

That possibility suggests that we should examine the data on drinking behavior of subjects at admission to treatment. The distribution of this drinking behavior is shown in Table 3.27. The measurements of drinking cover the 30 days before the admission interview. As the table shows, 93 percent of the sample had been drinking during that 30-day period. Seven percent were short-term abstainers at that time; we have no specific information on their levels of alcohol consumption or dependence. However, we do have information on the adverse consequences of drinking that they had recently experienced, and the table shows that 82 percent of the short-term abstainers at admission had experienced at least one such consequence during the 6 months before admission. Given the other information in this chapter indicating the problems of short-term abstainers, we would speculate that most of the abstainers at admission were considerably impaired from alcohol, and probably had been dependent during their last drinking period.

Among those who had been drinking at admission, the majority (67 percent) reported high levels of dependence symptoms (11 or more events in

Table 3.27 Drinking Behavior at Admission to Treatment

Drinking Status and Dependence Symptoms at Admission[a]	Percent in Category	Typical Quantity of Alcohol Consumption[b]		Percent with Adverse Consequences of Drinking[c]	(N)
		Median (oz.)	Percent over 5 oz.		
Abstaining 1 month or more[d]	7	—	—	82	(40)
Drinking					
No symptoms	8	3.8	25	73	(44)
1-10 symptoms	18	7.2	65	79	(99)
11 or more symptoms	67	11.4	88	93	(365)
All subjects	100	8.7[e]	78[e]	88	(548)

[a] During the 30 days before admission to treatment.
[b] Quantity per typical drinking day, during the 30 days before admission.
[c] Arrested, jailed, or hospitalized because of drinking during the 6 months before admission; or missed work or had fights because of drinking during the 30 days before admission.
[d] All but two of these cases reported some drinking in the past 6 months.
[e] Among drinkers only (N = 508).

the 30-day period). An additional 18 percent of the sample reported low levels of symptoms (1 to 10 events in a 30-day period). Only 8 percent of the sample reported drinking with no dependence symptoms. Thus, alcohol dependence was the norm in this population at admission to treatment, and only a small fraction were entirely free of dependence symptomatology.

Table 3.27 also shows that the low-symptom group (1 to 10 symptoms) had other characteristics typical of clinical alcoholics. For example, their median quantity of alcohol consumption was 7.2 ounces of ethanol (approximatly 14 drinks per day), and 79 percent of them reported adverse consequences of drinking. We found that consumption rates were uniformly high in the low-symptom group; in particular, the median consumption level for the 28 cases who reported only 1 to 3 symptoms was 6.4 ounces of ethanol per day. It is also important to remember that in the analysis reported earlier in this chapter, even low levels of symptoms were associated with high rates of later alcohol problems and high rates of mortality. For these reasons,we have interpreted a level of 1 to 10 dependence symptoms in a population treated for alcoholism as significant evidence of alcohol dependence.

The group that stands out in Table 3.27 is the category of subjects who reported no symptoms at admission. Their alcohol consumption levels were considerably lower than in other groups, averaging 3.8 ounces per day (about 7 to 8 drinks). They would therefore appear to be heavy drinkers, but not alcohol dependent at the time of admission. (We do not know, of course, whether or not they might have been alcohol dependent at other times.) It is worthwhile to investigate the relationship of 4-year drinking patterns with membership in this nonsymptomatic group.

The distribution of drinking status at 4 years by drinking behavior at admission is shown in Table 3.28. The rate of long-term abstention at 4 years is not appreciably related to admission behavior. However, both the rate of problem drinking and the rate of nonproblem drinking are significantly related to dependence level at admission. The higher the level of dependence symptoms at admission, the higher the probability that a subject will have drinking problems at 4 years, and the lower the chance that he will be classified as a nonproblem drinker. These data also indicate the impaired status of previous short-term abstainers: The problem rates at 4 years were just as high among people who had been short-term abstainers at admission as among people who had been drinking with severe levels of symptomatology.

The main question here is whether nonproblem drinkers were confined to the group of subjects who were nondependent at admission. For this sample, the answer is clearly *No*. In the total survivor sample, 18 percent were classified as nonproblem drinkers at 4 years (Table 3.20). Table 3.28 shows that nonproblem drinkers at 4 years constituted 12 percent of those who were highly dependent at admission to treatment. Among those who had low levels

Table 3.28 Drinking Status at Four Years, by Drinking Behavior at Admission to Treatment

Drinking Status and Dependence Symptoms at Admission	Percent Distribution of Drinking Status at 4 Years							
	Abstained		Nonproblem Drinking		Problem Drinking			(N)
	Abstained 1 Year	Abstained 6-11 Months	Low Q	High Q	Consequences	Symptoms	Symptoms and Consequences	
Abstaining 1 month or more	20	8	8 } 13	5	8	12	40	(40)
Drinking No symptoms	14	7	25 } 45	20	0	27	7	(44)
1-10 symptoms	20	7	11 } 30	19	6	10	26	(99)
11 or more symptoms	23	7	5 } 12	7	6	11	41	(365)

of dependence symptoms at admission, 30 percent were classified as nonproblem drinkers at 4 years. Thus, nonproblem drinking occurred even among people who previously had shown significant signs of alcohol dependence. However, there was a strong relationship between dependence and later drinking patterns. Although the data do not support a categorical distinction between "dependent" and "nondependent," they do suggest that alcohol dependence may be viewed as a continuum. The higher the person's level on the continuum of dependence, the more unlikely he is to be classified later as a nonproblem drinker.

ALTERNATIVE DEFINITIONS OF FOLLOWUP STATUS

The picture painted by these data is remarkably different from the impression given by the 18-month studies. Here about 50 percent of the cases appear to have significant problems. In the 18-month studies, it may be recalled, an overall improvement rate of about 70 percent was reported, and remission of symptoms was found in about two-thirds of the cases. What explains this discrepancy? The answer is the difference in definitions between the two studies, a difference that stems from two important findings apparent in the 4-year followup results. At 18 months, only a 30-day period was available for assessing drinking, whereas at 4 years we have data on a period six times as long. This increase in information made it possible to examine the drinking habits of short-term abstainers, who, at 18 months, were necessarily classified as remissions. In addition, the measures used at 4 years, especially the measures of symptoms, are more restrictive than those used at 18 months. This greater restrictiveness also stems from an important finding, namely, that the presence of any dependence symptoms predicts the onset or continuation of significant alcohol problems later in life.

The contribution of these various definitional changes can be seen in Table 3.29. This table shows the status of subjects at 4 years cross-classified by the category in which they would fall if the remission definition used in the 18-month study were applied to their behavior at the 4-year point. We thus have the same individuals measured at the same time (4 years after admission) classified by two different methods. This allows us to determine how the two methods differ. The most striking difference is the way in which short-term abstainers are treated. All of these persons would have been classified as "remissions" by the previous definition, yet their recent drinking behavior shows that 84 percent in fact experienced serious alcohol problems near the followup point. The overwhelming concentration of these people in the symptoms or consequences categories causes a marked shift in the marginal distribution. If only this change were made in the remission definition, the

Table 3.29   Drinking Status at Four Years Cross-Classified by Remission Definition Used in 18-Month Study

Drinking Status at 4 Years	Remission Category Measured at 4 Years[a]			
	Long-Term Abstention	Short-Term Abstention	Normal Drinking	Nonremission
Abstained 1 year	76	0	0	0
Abstained 6-11 months	24	0	0	0
Low Q	0	10	26	0
High Q	0	5	27	11
Consequences	0	8	14	3
Symptoms	0	17	18	16
Symptoms and consequences	0	59	14	70
(N)	(155)	(83)	(126)	(179)

[a]Categories represent the group into which a case would be classified at 4 years if the criteria for the 18-month study's "remission" definition were applied. These criteria were (1) long-term abstainer if subject reported no drinking in the past 6 months; (2) short-term abstainer if subject drank in the past 6 months but not in the past 30 days; (3) normal drinker if the subject (a) reported a typical quantity on a drinking day of less than 5 oz., (b) reported a quantity-frequency index (QF, measuring average ethanol consumption per calendar day) of less than 3 oz., and (c) did not report serious symptoms; (4) nonremission otherwise. Serious symptoms were defined as frequent episodes of at least three symptoms from the set: tremors, blackouts, missing meals, morning drinking, missing work, and being drunk.

reclassification of short-term abstainers would reduce the percentage of remissions from 67 percent to 54 percent.

A second factor contributing to the changed picture is the decision to increase the stringency of criteria used for determining alcohol problems at 4 years. A small part of this stringency results from the imposition of the constraint on adverse consequences at 4 years; the measures of consequences were not available in the 18-month study. However, a more important contributor is the decision to classify even a low level of symptoms as an adverse condition. In the 18-month study, the "normal drinking" category was defined less restrictively; a subject could be so classified as long as he showed only infrequent, less serious symptoms and also met certain limits on typical and total consumption. In contrast, the new definition classifies any instance of symptoms as an alcohol problem and uses a somewhat different and generally more inclusive set of symptoms. As is evident in Table 3.29, the result of this change in criteria is that nearly half of the "normal drinkers" are found in the symptoms or consequences categories in the new scheme. These observations emphasize the fact that the measure of followup status used in the present report (status at 4 years) inherently produces fewer cases classified in the lesser-problem categories. This difference is due almost entirely to our findings concerning the adverse prognoses exhibited by the short-term abstainers and drinkers with dependence symptoms.

ASSESSING GROUP CHANGES OVER TIME

The discussion above suggests that the difference between the results of the 18-month study and the assessment of the present study at 4 years may be strictly a matter of changing definitions. In fact, that is true. When the same measures are applied to the 18-month point and the 4-year point, the two followups appear quite similar. That similarity is indicated by the data in Table 3.30, which shows assessments of several important items and indices at admission, 18 months, and 4 years.

On every measure, the cohort's degree of improvement is striking between admission and 18 months, whereas there is little change between 18 months and 4 years. There is a slight hint of improvement on some measures between the two followups, but the changes are generally very modest. The one exception is the apparent reduction in median consumption amounts on drinking days. However, because the prevalence of dependence symptoms is virtually the same across the two followups, we would not judge that very much overall improvement has occurred between 18 months and 4 years.

In contrast, the differences between the characteristics of the cohort at admission and those at either followup are quite large and highly significant. The aggregate reduction in consumption rates that was observed in the 18-

Table 3.30   Drinking Assessments at Three Time Points

Drinking Characteristic[a]	Time Point		
	Admission to Treatment	18 Months	4 Years
Abstaining past 30 days (percent)	8	45	45
Typical quantity (median)[b]	8.2	5.0	3.4
Quantity-frequency index (median)[b]	6.7	1.6	1.4
Symptoms (percent reporting)[b]			
Tremors	63	18	16
Morning drinking	66	22	20
Blackouts	49	12	13
Missing meals	69	22	20
Continuous drinking	45	27	18
One or more of above symptoms	84	36	33
Median number of symptoms	29.0	3.0	2.0
(N)	(474)	(474)	(474)

[a]In the *past 30 days* before the interview (*not* necessarily the 30 days before last drink).
[b]Among persons who drank in the past 30 days.

month study (around 70 percent) is replicated at the 4-year point; for example, the typical quantity has fallen by 60 percent and the quantity-frequency index has fallen by 80 percent. Similarly, the prevalence of dependence symptoms is very much reduced at both followups compared with what it was at admission. In the *aggregate,* then, the picture is one of substantial improvement between admission and 18 months, with stability in the cohort's condition between 18 months and 4 years. We caution that this judgment of "stability" applies only to the aggregate. As we shall see in Chapter 7, individual persons may shift back and forth between remission and alcoholic behavior even though the cohort shows consistency over time.

The simplest way to judge the magnitude and stability of the improvement between admission and the followups would be to apply the same classification at admission, 18 months, and 4 years. Unfortunately, our data from admission and 18 months are not rich enough to permit the 4-year followup status measure to be replicated at those points. Both earlier assessments lack any drinking measure for the short-term abstainers, and the 18-month study lacks any significant set of consequences. Therefore, we must make do with less-than-complete overall measures to examine the trend. If that limitation is accepted, and if one is also willing to recalculate the results when all short-

Table 3.31   Aggregate Changes in Drinking Status, from Admission to Four Years

Drinking Status[a]	Percent Distribution of Cases		
	Admission	18 Months	4 Years
Abstained 1 year or more	(b)	17	22
Abstained 6-11 months	(b)	8	7
Abstained 1-5 months	7	21	15
Low quantity	2	12	7
High quantity	(b)	6	10
Consequences only	7 ⎫	(c) ⎫	4 ⎫
Symptoms only	8 ⎬ 90	(c) ⎬ 37	10 ⎬ 39
Symptoms and consequences	75 ⎭	(c) ⎭	25 ⎭
(N)	(474)	(474)	(474)

Remission Definition	Percent Distribution of Cases		
	Admission	18 Months	4 Years
Long-term abstention	1	24	29
Short-term abstention	7	21	15
Normal drinking	7	22	23
Nonremission	85	33	32
(N)	(474)	(474)	(474)

[a]Modified to show 1-5 month abstainers as a separate category for consistency across time periods.
[b]Less than 0.5 percent.
[c]Consequence measures not available at 18 months.

term abstainers are placed in a separate category for consistency across time, it is possible to produce a reasonable analogue to the 4-year status measure at all three points. In addition, the remission definition used in the 18-month study can be compared at three points, because all of its components are available over time. The results of calculating these two special-purpose typologies are shown in Table 3.31.

The picture given by the 4-year followup data is very similar to that given by the 18-month data when the same measures are applied. Table 3.31 clearly shows the very poor condition of the cohort at admission to treatment. Fully 90 percent of the cases exhibited either symptoms or consequences at admission. In addition to those cases, another 7 percent had been abstaining for 1 month or more before admission and hence are not further classifiable. We know from our followup data that the recent condition of short-term abstainers is usually unfavorable, and one would expect that the condition was even worse in the few months before admission to treatment. Hence a strong case can be made that virtually *all* the subjects were behaving alcoholically at admission. Against this baseline period, the assessments at 18 months and 4 years show a great deal of improvement. Although there is obviously a substantial group of alcoholics whose conditions are chronic, there must also exist a large group who show patterns of improvement and remission. Some of this change could be due to treatment, some to other factors, and some to the natural tendency for any extreme group to move toward a less extreme position in a longitudinal study ("regression toward the mean"). The further specification of such over-time patterns is an important task for analysis, which we will take up in Chapters 6 and 7.

FOUR

Psychosocial Functioning at Four Years

In the preceding chapter, the 4-year drinking status categories were defined by measures of alcohol consumption, behavioral and psychological dependence symptomatology, and evidence of serious adverse consequences of alcohol abuse. Since these measures constitute the core of alcoholism problems, we have given them primary emphasis as the criteria for classification at 4 years. Our definition does not imply, however, that positive change on these measures alone necessarily reflects social and psychological rehabilitation in a broader sense. Criteria for evaluating social rehabilitation include the extent to which individuals have become reintegrated into the community in terms of full employment, increased income, improved residential status, and stable interpersonal relationships. And psychological rehabilitation depends on the attainment of positive mental health and the development of personal resources and attitudes to equip these individuals to cope adaptively with stress without resorting to excessive or abusive drinking.

In this chapter, we will examine a number of variables that constitute, collectively, psychosocial correlates of the 4-year status categories. Specifically, we will examine differences in the social, psychological, and attitudinal characteristics that typify individuals in each category. We begin with a presentation of standard indices of social adjustment—marital status, employment, residential stability, and socioeconomic status. We then turn to respondents' subjective evaluations of their general life conditions, their emotional and psychiatric adjustment, and their personality characteristics. Finally, we consider attitudinal self-perceptions as alcoholics. We conclude with a discriminant function analysis, which provides a summary profile of the seven status groups differentiated across empirically defined psychosocial dimensions.

Unfortunately, limitations of the present study design preclude conclusions as to the causal status of psychosocial variables in the natural history of alcoholism. Except for a few social indices, for which we will indicate some trends, most of the variables we will discuss here were measured only at the 4-

year followup; no comparable admission or interim followup measurements are available with which to conduct valid change analyses. Consequently, the psychosocial characteristics of our respondents will be treated only as *correlates* of the followup categories. As such, their status as etiological factors in alcoholism, as prognostic indicators of treatment outcomes, or simply as consequences of drinking or abstention must remain ambiguous pending further research.

Notwithstanding these caveats, examination of psychosocial variables as correlates of drinking status does permit an assessment of the extent to which this cohort and its subgroups have achieved rehabilitation from their level of functioning at admission in the more general sense. Moreover, the psychosocial correlates provide a kind of dimensionality or "humanness" to the status categories—they show what the *people* are like in terms of characteristics other than their drinking and immediately related behavior. Finally, our attempt to develop profiles of different followup groups by using psychosocial variables has the heuristic value of determining characteristics that differentiate between those respondents who abstain as opposed to those who drink without overt problems.

SOCIAL ADJUSTMENT

Despite intense controversy over the precise definition of alcoholism in the literature, most writers agree as to the basic characteristics of the disorder once it is established. Almost all of them mention the chronic damage to social standing that often results from sustained alcohol abuse. Manifestations of social impairment typically include loss of employment, marital instability or dissolution, loss of family and friends, and alienation from the community. Clearly, such social impairment factors may also play a causal role in the excessive use of alcohol. Multivariate approaches to the etiology of alcoholism recognize that cultural stress factors, familial patterns, and, particularly, social instability and crises are precipitating conditions for problem drinking as they interact with other predisposing physiological and psychological determinants.

Many treatment approaches to alcoholism, including those exemplified by NIAAA's treatment programs, take into consideration the cyclical nature of the relationship between social instability and abusive drinking. Heavy drinking may occur in response to changes in one's social environment that create stress; in turn, the heavy drinking may lead to continued deterioriation of social adjustment, thereby exacerbating the stress and perpetuating the self-destructive alcoholic process. Therefore, treatment interventions for alco-

Table 4.1 Social Stability, by Drinking Status at Four Years

Group No.	Drinking Status at 4 Years	Percent of Respondents Reporting Each Social Stability Measure			(N)
		(1) Married	(2) Not Living in Group Quarters[a]	(3) Employed Full Time	
1	Abstained 1 year	54	91	58	(117)
2	Abstained 6-11 months	56	80	59	(39)
3	Low Q	48	93	52	(42)
4	High Q	56	91	61	(57)
5	Consequences	45	77	27	(30)
6	Symptoms	49	90	48	(67)
7	Symptoms and Consequences	30	76	29	(196)

[a]Living in an apartment, private house, or trailer as opposed to hotel, rooming house, halfway house, street, or other.

holics who have experienced gross social deterioration as a result of long alcoholic histories emphasize restructuring the subject's environmental milieu (e.g., through placement in halfway houses) and providing vocational and/or interpersonal guidance counseling, with the aim of returning the alcoholic to a productive role in the community. Given the considerable costs of alcoholism in losses to the labor force and economic productivity, social adjustment criteria are of major concern to policymakers evaluating alcoholism treatment.

Social adjustment measures at admission to treatment are widely reported in the literature as prognostic indicators of treatment outcome. Social stability, in the form of steady employment, stable residency, and familial relationships, has been consistently documented as a positive prognostic factor in both inpatient and outpatient treatment (Smart et al., 1969; Baekeland et al., 1973; Armor et al., 1978; Ogborne, 1978). Socioeconomic status (usually related to social stability) has also been found to relate to favorable outcome (Trice et al., 1969; Gillis and Keet, 1969; Armor et al., 1978).

Social Adjustment at Four Years

Three measures of social stability for the seven drinking status categories are shown in Table 4.1. Column (1) shows the percentage that reported being married at the time of the 4-year followup. Only 30 percent of the most impaired group (Group 7) reported being married at the time of the interview, and only slightly over half of the abstainers and drinkers without manifest problems were married at that time. Moreover, drinkers in the symptoms and consequences category have a high divorce rate (see Appendix C), thus supporting the relationship between alcoholism and marital disintegration.[1] Since we recognized the possibility of stable conjugal living arrangements outside the formal structure of marriage, we also asked each respondent if he had a steady girl friend with whom he lived. Across the total sample, however, only 13 percent of the respondents reported having girl friends at all, and only 4 percent reported living with a woman. Together these data indicate that stable heterosexual relationships characterize only a minority of the total sample, with very modest rates of current marital stability even in the nonproblem drinking groups.

Column (2) of Table 4.1 shows the measure of residential stability among drinkers. Many socially impaired alcoholics live in group quarters (e.g., hotels, rooming houses, halfway houses, missions) or in otherwise transient conditions (e.g., on the street.) At the 4-year followup, only a few of the respondents reported living in group quarters. The data did indicate, however, that relative to the other categories, drinkers with consequences (Groups 5 and 7) and the relatively short-term abstainers (Group 2) are more likely to be living in unstable residential conditions.

Column (3) of Table 4.1 shows the rate of full-time employment for the seven categories. Drinkers in the consequences categories (Groups 5 and 7) report substantially lower rates of full employment than do those in other categories. These depressed rates may reflect definitional criteria, since one serious consequence of alcohol abuse is loss of employment. Even among the abstainers and the drinkers without problems, however, the percentage of those holding full-time jobs does not exceed 61 percent. Among males in the general U.S. population between the ages of 45 and 54 years, the 1977 indices show 91 percent participating in the labor force, 88 percent employed, and only 3 percent unemployed (U.S. Bureau of the Census, 1978b). The relatively low full-time employment rates among our respondents at the 4-year followup clearly mitigate any interpretation that this cohort has achieved major social reintegration despite whatever gains may have been made in overcoming their problems with alcohol. (A detailed breakdown on employment status for the seven groups is presented in Appendix C.)

Two income measures—the respondent's own total income in 1976 and total household income for 1976—are shown in Table 4.2 by drinking status at 4 years. The measure of respondent's own income clearly shows the financially adverse effect for the serious consequence groups (Groups 5 and 7).[2] A similar pattern is apparent in the distribution of household income, although the latter also reflects differences observed earlier in employment and marital

[1]The rate of divorce or separation in the general population averages 8 percent among males between the ages of 45 and 54. (U.S. Bureau of the Census, August, 1977), compared with 37 percent in the followup sample at 4 years.
[2]Median income in 1977 for males in the general U.S. population was $10,123 (U.S. Bureau of the Census, July, 1978b).

Table 4.2   Income and Occupational Level, by Drinking Status at Four Years

Group No.	Drinking Status at 4 Years	Median Own Income[a] ($/year)	Median Household Income[b] ($/year)	White Collar[c] (%)	(N)
1	Abstained 1 year	6,000	9,800	38	(117)
2	Abstained 6-11 months	5,000	10,500	31	(39)
3	Low Q	4,500	10,500	33	(42)
4	High Q	7,500	11,000	25	(57)
5	Consequences	1,000	4,800	27	(30)
6	Symptoms	4,100	6,100	31	(67)
7	Symptoms and consequences	1,200	3,700	21	(196)

[a]Respondent's own total income, 1976.
[b]Total household income, 1976.
[c]Includes professional/technical, proprietors/administrators, sales personnel, and clerical.

status.[3,4] The data on occupational level in Table 4.2 reflect the overall low socioeconomic status of the sample, with Group 7 again at the low end of the occupational distribution.

In summary, respondents in 4-year-status categories who have experienced at least one serious consequence of alcohol abuse tend to evidence poor social adjustment on a range of measures. The causal relationship between abusive drinking and social impairment is particularly ambiguous: Does excessive drinking produce social instability and a drop in socioeconomic status, or, alternatively, is such drinking a reaction to the stress of social instability and financial pressures? As stated earlier, the nature of the relationship between alcoholism, once established, and parallel social deterioration is probably interactive. Drinkers who have not experienced adverse consequences but who have experienced physical or behavioral dependence symptomatology (Group 6) do not appear to have suffered as much social deterioration, both by definition and as measured by the social correlates presented above. Interestingly, even the most favorable categories (i.e., abstainers and light drinkers without manifest problems) do not present a very positive picture of social adjustment relative to general population norms. This is not surprising, however, in light of (a) the overall instability that we have observed in drinking patterns over time and (b) the rather gross social deterioration that characterized the total sample at admission to treatment.

[3]Median household income in 1977 for the general population was $16,009 (U.S. Bureau of the Census, July, 1978b).

[4]See Appendix C for detailed distributions of income by drinking status at 4 years.

Table 4.3 Social Adjustment at Three Time Points (Percent)

Measures of Social Adjustment	1973 Admission to Treatment	1974 18-Month Followup	1977 4-Year Followup
Married	41	41	45
Divorced/separated	37	38	36
Living in group quarters	13	6	5
Employed	40	58	52
Earnings over $500/month[a]	30	36	40
(N)	(478)	(478)	(478)

[a]Constant 1977 dollars.

Time Trends in Social Adjustment

Although the absolute level of social adjustment at the 4-year point is far less than optimal, questions remain about whether and how the cohort has improved socially since admission to treatment in 1973. Table 4.3 shows five measures of social adjustment measured on a consistent cohort at three time points: admission to treatment (1973), 18-month followup (1974), and 4-year followup (1977). As can readily be seen from these data, no significant changes in marital status or in divorce rates have occurred since admission to treatment. A small drop in percentage of those living in group quarters did occur between admission to treatment and the 18-month followup point, with the percentage remaining about constant to the 4-year followup. A slight increase in percentage employed is also observed, from 40 percent employed full or part time at admission, to 58 and 52 percent at the subsequent followup points, respectively. The percentage change in those exceeding $500 in monthly earnings is, however, quite modest.

Because the phenomena underlying the employment rate are fairly complex, a more detailed breakdown of employment status over the three time points is shown in Table 4.4. These data reveal a modest decrease in the proportion unemployed between admission and the followup points. However, there is also an increase in the number of subjects not working because of illness or institutionalization. Thus, we see a slight trend over time toward increased employment among those actively seeking jobs, but this is counterbalanced by a trend toward lower rates of participation in the labor force.

In summary, positive changes in employment, income, and residential stability have occurred in the sample as a whole since admission to treatment

Table 4.4 Employment Status at Three Time Points (Percent)

Employment Status	1973 Admission to Treatment	1974 18-Month Followup	1977 4-Year Followup
Employed full time	37	49	45
Employed part time	3	9	7
Unemployed[a]	24	19	14
Ill or institutionalized[b]	10	18	22
Retired, student	6	3	7
Drinking problem[c]	20	2	5
(N)	(478)	(478)	(478)

[a]Not working because no job is available, subject is looking for a job, or subject is "temporarily laid off."
[b]Not working because of current illness or institutionalization.
[c]Not working because of a drinking problem.

in 1973. The overall degree of improvement, however, remains modest, with greatest change occurring between admission and the 18-month followup, and a subsequent leveling off thereafter to the 1977 followup point.

LIFE SATISFACTION AND STRESSFUL EVENTS

The relationship between social instability and excessive drinking observed in these data and a host of other studies is obviously subject to many interpretations. One possible explanation is that excessive drinking so debilitates the individual as to eventually preclude the maintenance of stable relationships and employment, resulting in a downward spiral of progressive social deterioration and alcoholic behavior. However, as we have seen in the preceding section, the relationship between objective social stability measures and drinking status at 4 years is far from perfect; this observation suggests the possibility that subjective dissatisfaction or unhappiness with one's life circumstances mediates the relationship. According to this latter model, the subjective experience of unhappiness may be the precipitating link to heavy drinking, where the latter serves, albeit maladaptively, as a mechanism for coping with an uncomfortable psychological state.

Life Satisfaction

To examine the relationship between subjective dissatisfaction and drinking status at 4 years, we asked respondents to rate their overall happiness or

Table 4.5   Overall Life Satisfaction,[a] by Drinking Status at Four Years

Group No.	Drinking Status at 4 Years	Percent Distribution of Cases			(N)
		Very Satisfied	Satisfied	Dissatisfied	
1	Abstained 1 year	50	38	12	(117)
2	Abstained 6-11 months	47	32	21	(38)
3	Low Q	43	48	9	(42)
4	High Q	44	38	18	(57)
5	Consequences	25	43	32	(28)
6	Symptoms	29	46	25	(67)
7	Symptoms and consequences	12	43	45	(196)
All respondents		31	41	28	(545)
1972 nationwide probability sample[b]		22	68	10	(947)

[a]Question 12, Client Interview form, Appendix E.
[b]Data reported in Campbell et al., *The Quality of American Life* (Russell Sage Foundation, New York 1976), p. 26, based on University of Michigan surveys.

satisfaction with their life circumstances. The percentage distribution of responses to that inteview question is shown in Table 4.5; a comparable distribution of responses to the same question obtained from a nationwide probability sample collected in 1972 is shown in the bottom row of the table.[5] Compared with the general population, respondents in our sample tended to give more extreme responses both ways, i.e., "very happy" or "very unhappy."

Examination of the percentage distributions among the drinking status categories reveals some important patterns. The elevated marginal proportion of respondents in our sample who rate themselves as very satisfied appears to be due primarily to the responses of individuals in Groups 1 through 4. Note the especially low percentage of Group 7 respondents (12 percent) who rate themselves as very satisfied. Fully 45 percent of this same group of highly impaired drinkers rate themselves as dissatisfied with their life circumstances. Not surprisingly, the distribution of responses to this question for drinkers who have suffered manifest consequences (Groups 5 and 7) is skewed toward the negative end; the distribution for abstainers and nonproblem drinkers is positively skewed, and that for drinkers experiencing symptoms but not adverse consequences is intermediate among the drinking status categories.

Stressful Life Events

The data in Table 4.5 are consistent with the general notion that an interactive relationship exists between excessive drinking and social impairment, at least as mediated by the subjective experience of dissatisfaction or unhappiness

[5]See question 12, Client Interview form (Appendix E).

Table 4.6 Stressful Life Events[a] Occurring During Past Four Years, by Drinking Status at Four Years

Group No.	Drinking Status at 4 Years	Percent of Respondents Reporting Each Stressful Event					(6) Percent Reporting One or More Events	(N)
		(1) Divorced or Separated	(2) Widowed	(3) Death in Family/Friend	(4) Serious Illness	(5) Out of Work		
1	Abstained 1 year	13	2	33	4	22	59	(117)
2	Abstained 6-11 months	15	—	39	—	18	59	(38)
3	Low Q	12	—	52	7	17	62	(42)
4	High Q	33	4	39	2	21	67	(57)
5	Consequences	20	—	33	7	20	60	(28)
6	Symptoms	15	2	34	—	15	48	(67)
7	Symptoms and consequences	17	—	36	3	18	55	(197)

[a]Question 60, Client Interview form, Appendix E.

with life conditions among abusive drinkers. A more formal statement of the relationship between heavy alcohol consumption and general dissatisfaction is contained in the model of stressful life events. According to this view, alcoholism (or a marked increase in alcohol consumption) may devleop during "crisis periods" when significant changes in an individual's life situation or social role lead to feelings of instability, confusion, and stress (Coleman, 1972). These crisis periods, characterized by the occurrence of one or more major life events that induce heightened stress, include, for example, death of a spouse, divorce, loss of employment, or serious personal illness. During such periods of increased stress, an individual's normal coping methods may prove inadequate, and he may resort to more extreme means of alleviating tension. The actual sedative effect of ethanol further increases the likelihood that some individuals may react to stressful life events through heavy consumption of alcohol.

To examine this notion, we asked our respondents to recall the occurrence of specific stressful life events during the 4 years preceding the interview. The percentage of respondents reporting each of five major stressful life events is shown in Table 4.6. The data are presented only for descriptive purposes, however, since the low base rates for single events and the absence of significant variation among the status categories preclude any formal test of the stressful life events model.

Column (6) of Table 4.6 shows the percentage of respondents who indicated that at least one of the five stressful life events had occurred during the period from 1973 to 1977. Although major stressful events appear to have occurred in the lives of most of our respondents (about 59 percent across the sample), there does not appear to be a systematic relationship between this occurrence and drinking status at 4 years. The lack of a relationship in these data between the objective occurrence of stressful events and problematic drinking behavior is further underscored by the data in Table 4.7. The percentages of respondents who reported symptoms or consequences at 4 years are shown in Table 4.7 according to whether or not they had experienced stressful life events, and as a function of their subjective life satisfaction. As can be seen from the data, the percentage of problematic drinkers increases markedly as a function of subjective dissatisfaction and remains largely unaffected by the occurrence of life stress.

EMOTIONAL ADJUSTMENT AND PERSONALITY

A substantial body of research has focused on identifying a consistent set of characteristics from the domains of personality and psychopathology that correlates with the development of and prognosis for alcoholism. Despite

Table 4.7   Drinking Problem Rate as a Function of Stress and Life Satisfaction

	Subjective Satisfaction[a]		Subjective Dissatisfaction	
Item	No Stressful Events	One or More Stressful Events	No Stressful Events	One or More Stressful Events
Problem Rate[b]	49	42	82	72
(N)	(167)	(227)	(66)	(85)

[a]From Question 12, Client Interview form, Appendix E; satisfaction defined as very happy or happy.
[b]Percent of group reporting symptoms or consequences at 4 years.

substantial and careful efforts, however, most writers agree that no unique, premorbid alcoholic personality has been discovered. Indeed, given the multitude of factors that impinge on the alcoholism process, few current researchers still expect to find a unitary type of alcoholic personality (Orford, 1976). Moreover, personality research with alcoholic populations is often confounded by ambiguities surrounding the etiological status of observed traits: Do certain personality and/or psychopathological features, in fact, precede the development of alcoholic behavior? Or are they merely a consequence of the addiction that already exists?

A few general findings about the relationship between personality and alcoholism do emerge from the research literature. First, longitudinal studies, although relatively rare, seem to converge on a set of high-risk personality traits that may function as predisposing factors in alcoholic behavior. This "high risk" personality is profiled as unrestrained, impulsive, aggressive, and antiauthoritarian (Williams, 1976). Empirical evidence also suggests that alcoholics show a particular cluster of personality traits once their drinking has become established. Included in this cluster are low stress tolerance (Lisansky, 1960), dependency (Blane, 1968), perceptual dependence (Witkin et al., 1959), negative self-image, and feelings of isolation, insecurity, and depression (Irwin, 1968; Wood and Duffy, 1966). And, consistent with Jessor's (et al., 1968) view of alcoholism as a form of deviant behavior, Cahalan and Room (1974) found intrapunitiveness, impulsivity, and tolerance of deviant behavior other than drinking to be personality trait correlates of problem drinkers. Interestingly, the latter authors demonstrated that personality variables were the major determinants of tangible, adverse consequences from drinking, whereas sociocultural variables were better predictors of actual heavy consumption.

Several measures of psychiatric and emotional adjustment, as well as personality traits, are reviewed in the section below as correlates of the 4-year status categories. Although the causal relationships are ambiguous, certain consistent features of emotional functioning and mental health do appear to be distinguishable among the 4-year followup groups.

Psychiatric Symptomatology

In a psychiatric sense, alcoholism is viewed as symptomatic behavior indicative of underlying pathological processes. The broad symptom complex of pathological personality traits associated with alcoholic behavior describes people with depressive, neurotic-depressive, sociopathic, and anxiety features (Hoffman, 1976). Because of its sedative effects, beverage alcohol may be used as a form of self-medication for particularly anxious individuals. Again, a mutual cause and effect relationship probably exists between alcohol consumption and psychiatric symptomatology, since prolonged drinking itself is known to produce feelings of anxiety and depression (Davis, 1971) and these feelings, in turn, precipitate further consumption. In advanced cases, heavy and continuous alcohol consumption may even result in chronic brain syndromes reflected by cognitive impairment, including disruptions in concentration and memory deficits.

The percentages of respondents, in each of the seven status categories, who reported relatively frequent occurrences of psychiatric symptoms during the 6-month period preceding the followup contact are given in Columns (1) to (5) of Table 4.8. Two measures of depression were obtained: The first, labeled "Depression" in the table, consists of frequent experiences of feeling "downhearted, blue, or depressed." As can readily be seen, Group 7 respondents were far more likely than others to report frequent depression symptomatology. The second indicator of depression, shown in Column (2) of Table 4.8, reflects "anhedonia," or the inability to experience satisfaction, pleasure, or enjoyment in daily experience; drinkers with symptoms and/or consequences were more likely to report frequent feelings of anhedonia.

Columns (3) and (4) of the table indicate, respectively, measures of general emotional stress or tension, and anxiety. The patterns here are similar, though not fully consistent. Drinkers experiencing adverse consequences (Groups 5 and 7) appear to be most affected by frequent tension or stress. Anxiety symptomatology (frequent occurrence of feeling "anxious, worried, or upset") was reported by 32 percent of Group 7 individuals, compared with more modest rates for the other status groups.

The fifth psychiatric symptom in the table is cognitive impairment, marked by problems in concentrating or remembering. The occurrence pattern is similar to those of the other symptoms, with Group 7 again significantly higher than the other groups. The absolute rates across the sample, however, are somewhat lower than for the other symptoms.

Table 4.8 Psychiatric Symptoms[a] at Four Years, by Drinking Status at Four Years

Group No.	Drinking Status at 4 Years	Percent of Respondents Reporting Symptom as Occurring "All or Most of the Time"						
		(1) Depression	(2) Anhedonia (lack of enjoyment)	(3) Tension/ Stress	(4) Anxiety	(5) Cognitive Impairment	(6) Frequent[b] "Escape" Drinking	(N)
1	Abstained 1 year	9	14	14	10	4	—	(117)
2	Abstained 6-11 months	5	23	10	10	5	59	(38)
3	Low Q	5	12	10	7	2	10	(42)
4	High Q	12	18	21	9	2	23	(57)
5	Consequences	10	43	47	10	7	47	(28)
6	Symptoms	18	31	25	18	11	49	(67)
7	Symptoms and consequences	31	52	34	32	22	73	(196)
	All respondents	24	18	32	11	19	42	(545)
	General population[c]	2	4	4	(d)	(d)	(d)	(2235)

[a] Questions 55, 52, 53, 56, 54, respectively, Client Interview form, Appendix E.

[b] Refers to "escape" reasons for drinking in past year: "I drink to forget my worries; I drink to relax; a drink helps cheer me up when I'm in a bad mood; a drink helps me when I'm depressed or nervous; I drink when I'm bored and have nothing to do; I drink to increase my self-confidence."

[c] From Rand's National Health Insurance Study data collected on a general population (N = 2235) of males and females (mean age = 35) in Seattle, Washington.

[d] Not available.

The bottom row of the table gives normative data from a general population with which to compare the present study sample. As can be seen, all groups in the present study report substantially higher incidences of psychiatric symptoms than do normals. The most striking comparison, however, is between normals and Groups 5, 6, and 7, who show rates of frequent psychiatric symptomatology on the order of 10 to 15 times the magnitude of those occurring in the general population.

When the overall pattern is examined, Table 4.8 suggests that drinkers with symptoms and/or consequences present a psychiatric picture of depression and anxiety over prolonged periods (i.e., 6 months). The relationship between such symptomatology and drinking behavior can, of course, be constructed both ways: feelings of depression and anxiety arouse the motivation to drink for symptomatic relief, or excessive drinking, which results in serious consequences and/or physiological dependence, also produces reactive depression and anxiety. In reality, the causal arrows probably point in both directions.

A measure of "escape" drinking in response to dysphoric psychological states was obtained by asking respondents how often they drank during the past year for each of the reasons listed in the footnote to Table 4.8. Column (6) in Table 4.8 shows the percentage of individuals in each of the seven categories who reported that when they drank in the past year, escape reasons were frequently important motivations. It is interesting to note the elevated proportion (59 percent) of 6- to 11-month abstainers who reported escape motivation for drinking. The elevated rates in Groups 5, 6, and 7, relative to those for drinkers without problems, parallel the trends in frequency of psychiatric symptomatology observed in other parts of the table.

In summary, the measures of psychiatric functioning (specifically, depression and anxiety) suggest that drinkers with symptoms and/or consequences are relatively less well adjusted psychiatrically than are the abstainers and drinkers without manifest problems. The data on escape reasons for drinking further support an interpretation that dysphoric psychiatric symptoms may motivate heavy drinking as a means of alleviating or mitigating the unpleasant experiences of psychological stress and flattened or depressed affect.

Emotional Stability and Personal Resources

In addition to the face-to-face interview, respondents in our followup sample also completed a self-administered form containing measures of several psychological domains. Table 4.9 presents data on four personality traits measured in that form: emotional stability,[6] impulse control[7], autonomy[7], and

[6]From the Comrey Personality Scales (Comrey, 1970).
[7]From the Personality Research Form E (Jackson, 1974).

Table 4.9 Psychological Traits, by Drinking Status at Four Years

| Group No. | Drinking Status at 4 Years | Percent of Respondents Scoring High[a] on a Scale Measuring Each Trait | | | | |
		(1) Emotional Stability[b]	(2) Impulse Control	(3) Autonomy[c]	(4) Internal Locus of Control	(N)
1	Abstained 1 year	57	52	26	51	(101)
2	Abstained 6-11 months	53	44	31	42	(32)
3	Low Q	54	40	34	43	(35)
4	High Q	49	52	32	50	(52)
5	Consequences	44	46	38	30	(26)
6	Symptoms	29	44	23	28	(52)
7	Symptoms and consequences	36	19	39	22	(173)
	All respondents	62	37	33	35	
	General population[d]	(e)	23	44	(e)	(2141)

[a]Percentage within approximate upper one-third of distribution.
[b]Cell entries are percentages occurring within approximate upper one-third of the scale distribution, representing relative absence of neurotic personality traits.
[c]Mean scores not significantly different across drinking status groups at .05 level. All other scales are significantly different.
[d]Norms established on Jackson scales using a sample of Canadian enlisted military personnel (Jackson, 1974).
[e]Normative data unavailable.

internal locus of control[8] (i.e., the extent to which a person believes that what happens to him is under his own control rather than contingent on external forces, such as fate or chance).

Column (1) of Table 4.9 shows the percentages of individuals within each status category who score relatively high on a scale measuring the general trait of emotional stability. The 20-item scale, obtained from the Comrey Personality Scales (Comrey, 1970) contains five subscales: (1) depression; (2) pessimism; (3) agitation; (4) mood instability; and (5) inferiority. The total emotional stability scale measures a personality style or trait characterized by relative freedom from each of these five indices of neuroticism. Consistent with the trends observed in psychiatric symptomatology, the proportion of individuals who are relatively free from neurotic traits declines across the seven categories, dropping particularly for Groups 6 and 7. With some minor exceptions, drinkers with symptoms and/or consequences (especially those with both) also tend to have neurotic personality traits. In summary, our measures of psychiatric symptomatology and of emotional stability as a personality trait both offer support for the widely cited assertion that individuals suffering from alcoholism exhibit personality styles marked by depression and anxiety—each of which is theoretically related to the onset and continuation of problem drinking and empirically related to unfavorable therapeutic outcome (Ogborne, 1978).

The other columns of Table 4.9 show the percentages of individuals who can be characterized as having each of three important personality traits: impulse control, autonomy, and internal locus of control. Together these traits form a core set of personal resources widely regarded by experienced clinicians as relating to the capacity for therapeutic change and the maintenance of psychological health. Moreover, these traits are associated with three major personality theories of alcoholic behavior (Williams, 1976): (1) the power theory, formulated by McClelland et al. (1972); (2) the dependency theory, variously formulated by McCord et al. (1960), Blane (1968), and Bacon et al. (1965), among others; and (3) the social psychological theory of deviance, formulated by Jessor et al. (1968). Obviously, the available data are too sparse to constitute a valid test of any theory. Rather, the theories are discussed briefly below as contexts for interpreting the data.

Before making comparisons among the followup groups, it is instructive to note how our respondents' scores compare across categories with those of a normative sample. The general population norms on the nonimpulsivity and autonomy scales are presented in the bottom row of Table 4.9. These norms have been published by Jackson (1974), based on a sample of Canadian enlisted military personnel. Contrary to our expectation, respondents in our sample reported greater impulse control (37 percent) than did the general

[8]Adapted from Rotter's (1966) short-form instrument.

population sample (23 percent), although this difference may be partially attributable to special characteristics of the normative population. As we expected, however, fewer of our respondents (33 percent) scored high on the autonomy trait measure, compared with the normative group (44 percent).

The Power Theory. This model posits that men who drink excessively do so because they have accentuated needs for personalized power. The power concern is essentially compensatory in nature; power is vigorously expressed, often through fantasy, under conditions of high alcohol consumption, in order to suppress feelings of weakness and overcome doubts about potency. According to the model, an association should exist between alcoholic drinking and personality styles characterized by poor impulse control, autonomy, and an external locus of control. The external control orientation is suggested by the notion that drinking is a compensatory drive to overcome feelings of powerlessness.

The data in Table 4.9 provide marginal support for two of the predicted relationships. The most impaired group of drinkers (i.e., Group 7) markedly differs from the others on the measure of impulse control. Only 19 percent of Group 7 respondents are scored as having strong impulse control, i.e., having the ability to inhibit activity and immediate gratification. Respondents in Groups 5 and 6, however, do not significantly differ on the impulse control trait from those whose actual drinking behavior (i.e., abstention or drinking without problems) is a testimony to impulse control almost by definition. No significant differences were found among the groups on the autonomy scale, however, thereby failing to confirm the expected association between excessive drinking and an underlying personality trait characterized by self-reliance. Finally, on the measure of control orientation, drinkers with symptoms or consequences (Groups 5, 6, and 7) do show a tendency toward a more externalized locus of control as compared with the other groups.

The Dependency Theory. According to this second model, excessive drinking represents a reaction formation against underlying unmet dependency needs. Heavy drinking, regarded as a masculine activity, is thought to serve a twofold psychological function: Drinking promotes an outward facade of independence and self-reliance, while simultaneously satisfying dependency needs by providing feelings of warmth and comfort (Williams, 1976). The theory, then, suggests a personality profile of the excessive drinker marked by regressive and immature tendencies. In the present context, these characteristics should be manifested by poor impulse control, lack of autonomy, and an external locus of control. Thus, the data in Table 4.9 seem also to provide marginal support for the dependency theory. The fact that these data, along with those of several other studies, can be interpreted to support either model—power or dependency—raises questions as to the usefulness of the theories as explanatory constructs. (See Williams, 1976, for a discussion of this problem.)

The Social Psychological Theory of Deviance. Jessor's model subsumes abusive drinking under a more complex social psychological theory of deviance. According to this view, the personality system is treated as being composed of a motivational instigation structure, a belief structure, and a personal control structure. Of the three traits considered here, the individual's locus of control orientation is most relevant to Jessor's model. Jessor et al. specifically posit that individuals who engage in excessive drinking and experience adverse consequences (i.e., deviant behavior) have an external locus of control orientation. The pattern of data in Table 4.9 provides some support for this view. In addition to having an external control orientation, the fact that Group 7 individuals are also characterized by poorer impulse control, relative to the other groups, provides further support for the general model of deviant behavior.

BELIEFS ABOUT ALCOHOLISM

Many treatment approaches to alcoholism, most prominently that of Alcoholics Anonymous, focus on individuals' attitudes and beliefs about the nature of alcoholism, and on their adoption of an alcoholic self-concept as primary levers to effect behavioral change. We included several relevant attitudinal and self-concept items in the interview to assess the relationship between respondents' beliefs about alcoholism and their status at 4 years.

Traditional Disease Concept

The percentage of respondents within each followup category that indicated endorsement of or agreement with certain beliefs about the nature of alcoholism is shown in Table 4.10. Essentially, these beliefs represent the basic tenets of the traditional disease model of alcoholism (Jellinek, 1960): (1) Alcoholism is an irreversible, progressive disease from which an individual can never completely recover (popularized with the slogan, "once an alcoholic, always an alcoholic"); (2) The disease can only be arrested through total abstinence.

The pattern in these data offers an interesting contrast to that observed in most of the preceding tables. That is, in the attitudinal domain, abstainers (Groups 1 and 2) appear most similar to the drinkers experiencing adverse consequences (Groups 5 and 7). All four groups tend to embrace the tenets of

Table 4.10 Beliefs About Alcoholism, by Drinking Status at Four Years

Group No.	Drinking Status at 4 Years	Percent of Respondents Agreeing with Traditional Beliefs			
		"Alcoholism Is an Irreversible Disease"	"Once an Alcoholic, Always an Alcoholic"	Alcoholics Cannot Resume Moderate Drinking	(N)
1	Abstained 1 year	65	77	85	(117)
2	Abstained 6-11 months	50	68	74	(38)
3	Low Q	33	33	41	(42)
4	High Q	30	38	51	(57)
5	Consequences	63	53	59	(28)
6	Symptoms	44	47	59	(67)
7	Symptoms and consequences	64	76	74	(196)

Table 4.11 "Alcoholic" Self-Concept, by Drinking Status at Four Years

Group No.	Drinking Status at 4 Years	Percent of Respondents Agreeing with "Alcoholic" Self-Concept Measure					
		Ever Alcoholic	Alcoholic[a] Now	Can Control Amount Now	Harm from Future Drinking	Death from Future Drinking	(N)
1	Abstained 1 year	92	77	(b)	91	31	(117)
2	Abstained 6-11 months	87	74	(b)	95	18	(38)
3	Low Q	52	18	95	25	0	(42)
4	High Q	55	55	89	32	0	(57)
5	Consequences	73	68	82	55	10	(28)
6	Symptoms	66	64	83	43	14	(67)
7	Symptoms and consequences	89	86	34	78	18	(196)

[a] As a percentage of respondents who agree to "ever being an alcoholic."
[b] Question not asked of current abstainers.

the traditional model. Not surprisingly, those respondents who were drinking without manifest problems at the 4-year followup (Groups 3 and 4) were much less likely to endorse these beliefs. The intermediate position of Group 5 on these attitudinal measures may reflect the clinical observation that alcoholics must "hit bottom" (i.e., suffer debilitating social, legal, and/or physical consequences) before they are ready to accept the traditional ideology.

Alcoholic Self-Concept

Another series of questions tapped respondents' self-concepts as alcoholics, and the extent to which they anticipated or acknowledged the possibility of harmful effects from future drinking.

The first column in Table 4.11 indicates the percentage of respondents in each 4-year status category who agreed with the question, "Have you ever been an alcoholic?" Here again, the abstaining groups are more similar in their responses to the drinkers with symptoms or consequences than to the drinkers without problems. A similar pattern is observed in responses to the question, "Are you an alcoholic now?" Note the low proportion of respondents in Group 3 who have a current "alcoholic" self-concept.

All respondents who did not abstain during the 6 months prior to the followup interview were also asked whether they can control their consumption when they drink or whether, in contrast, they usually lose control. Interestingly, only group 7 respondents acknowledged loss of control; the remaining groups reported being able to control their consumption.

Finally, all respondents were asked how much it would be likely to hurt them if they drink in the future. The percentage of respondents who indicated that drinking in the future would hurt them very much is also shown in Table 4.11. On this measure, the abstainers were almost unanimous in anticipating substantial harm from future drinking, with almost one-third of those in the 1-year abstention category indicating that future drinking would probably be fatal. As expected, the drinkers without problems (Groups 3 and 4) tended to deny that future drinking would be very harmful. Among Group 7 respondents, fully 78 percent indicated that drinking in the future would hurt them very much, with 18 percent acknowledging that death would result from continued drinking.

Although it is often asserted that alcoholics use denial as their principal defense mechansim, these data often fail to support this position. On the contrary, drinkers in our sample who are suffering both consequences and symptoms do not differ substantially from abstainers in acknowledging that they are alcoholic and that drinking in the future will be very harmful to them, perhaps even fatal. Moreover, Group 7 respondents tend to endorse the position that alcoholism is irreversible and that abstention is the only valid mode of recovery. These data suggest that an important personality feature of some alcoholics may be the tendency to perpetuate self-destructive behavior in the face of incongruent attitudes and beliefs. In short, a model that stresses breaking the denial defense as a necessary condition for motivating abstention may be overly simplistic.

OVERALL PSYCHOSOCIAL
PROFILE OF DRINKING CATEGORIES

Throughout this chapter, we have examined similarities and differences among respondents in the 4-year drinking status categories with respect to a number of social, psychological, and attitudinal variables. These comparisons have been based on univariate distributions on selected indices across the followup categories. Patterns or trends in the data on each psychosocial variable have been discussed separately. In this concluding section, we present the results of a discriminant function analysis that was used to empirically identify psychosocial dimensions differentiating the seven followup groups. Simply stated, a discriminant function analysis is a method for addressing a key question of the present study: At the 4-year followup, how do groups of individuals, whom we have classified according to their drinking and drinking-related behavior, differ most with respect to their social, psychological, and attitudinal characteristics?

The mathematical objective of the discriminant function technique is to construct a weighted function of a selected set of discriminating variables. One or more functions may be constructed in such a way that the groups are forced to be as statistically distinct as possible in terms of the function values (Tatsuoka, 1971). The weighting or relative size of the discriminant co-efficients can be interpreted much as in multiple regression or factor analysis; i.e., the coefficients serve to identify the variables that contribute most to differentiation along each respective function or dimension. Inasmuch as the discriminant functions can be thought of as the axes of a geometric space, they can be used as spatial analogues to study the relationships among the groups.

In performing a discriminant function analysis, one must first select discriminating variables that measure characteristics on which the groups are expected to differ. Table 4.12 lists the variables used.[9] Two summary variables on the list were constructed on both conceptual and empirical grounds. The first is a summary mental health index composed of the overall life satisfaction measure, the sum of the five psychiatric symptom items, and the emotional

---

[9]A separate discriminant analysis was performed by using just the life stress mental health scale and the personality trait scales. The results yielded just one statistically significant function dominated by mental health.

Table 4.12 Variables Selected for the Discriminant Analysis

Variable Name	Definition
Age	Mean age in years
Social stability index[a]	Unstable = living in group quarters, *or* unmarried and unemployed
Socioeconomic status index[a]	Mean of income and occupation, standardized
Mental health scale	Sum of three components (where each is standardized to have mean = 0, variance = 1): 1. Overall life satisfaction 2. Psychiatric adjustment scale (sum of five items) 3. Emotional stability scale
Impulse control score	Mean on impulse control scale
Autonomy score	Mean on autonomy scale
Locus of control	Mean on locus of control scale
Traditional beliefs scale	Sum of three traditional beliefs items
Alcoholic self-concept	"I am alcoholic now" vs. "never was," or "used to be alcoholic, but not now"
Future harm	Three-point score derived from "how much will it hurt you if you drink in the future": 1 = none, 2 = a little, 3 = a lot

[a]See Appendix D for details of index construction.

stability scale score.[10] To provide a mental health score, the three components were equally weighted, standard scored, and summed. The second summary index, the traditional beliefs score, is simply the sum of the three attitudinal items shown in Table 4.10.

Discriminant Function Coefficients

The coefficients for two discriminant functions extracted from the analysis are shown in Table 4.13, together with their accompanying eigenvalues and significance levels. The analysis yielded only two functions with significant eigenvalues. Thus, a two-dimensional solution appears sufficient to maximize discrimination among the seven groups. The two functions obtained were then rotated in the two-dimensional space to maximize interpretability.

Examination of the coefficients suggests that the first function is defined principally by the dimension of perception of harm from future drinking and, less strongly, by the alcoholic self-concept item. The second function is essentially a mental health dimension. Figure 4.1 shows a plot of the rotated discriminant coefficients in the space defined by the two functions.

[10]Cronbach's alpha = .795 for the five psychiatric symptom items.

Table 4.13 Discriminant Coefficients for Two Extracted Functions

Function Characteristics[a]	Function 1	Function 2
Lambda (eigenvalue)	.686	.370
Cannonical correlation	.638	.520
Significance level[b]	<.001	<.001

	Standardized Discriminant Coefficients[c]	
Variables	Function 1	Function 2
Age	.071	.060
Social stability	−.006	.247
Socioeconomic status	.057	.169
Life stress scale	.019	.171
Mental health scale	−.153	.634
Impulsivity	.033	−.176
Autonomy	−.024	.020
Locus of control	−.088	.198
Traditional beliefs scale	.037	−.090
Alcoholic self-concept	−.398	−.227
Future harm	−.784	.196

[a]Before rotation.
[b]Other eigenvalues not significant at the .05 level.
[c]Coefficients of variables after rotation of the axes by $\Theta = -25°$.

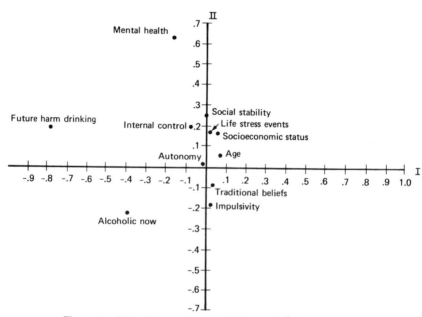

Figure 4.1 Plot of discriminant variables in discriminant space.

Status Category Discrimination

Figure 4.2 shows a plot of the centroids for the seven status groups, i.e., the location of the mean for each group on the discriminant function axes. The vertical axis in the figure represents the mental health function, with positive scores indicating emotional stability, a positive life-outlook, and relative freedom from psychiatric disturbance. The horizontal axis represents the attitudinal dimension, with negative scores indicating perception of harm from future drinking and, to a lesser extent, acknowledgment of an alcoholic self-concept. The spatial location of the group centroids shown in Fig. 4.2 graphically represents the similarities and differences among the status categories on these two dimensions. The centroids of both groups of abstainers (Groups 1 and 2) and the drinkers without symptoms or consequences (Groups 3 and 4) lie toward the positive end of the mental health dimension. In contrast to the drinkers without problems, however, the abstainers tend to perceive greater harm from drinking in the future—an attitudinal orientation for which abstention is a congruent behavioral response. The nonproblem drinkers, consistent with their behavior, tend to deny that continued drinking will have harmful effects.

The drinkers experiencing either consequences (Group 5) or symptoms (Group 6) are differentiated in the discriminant space from drinkers suffering

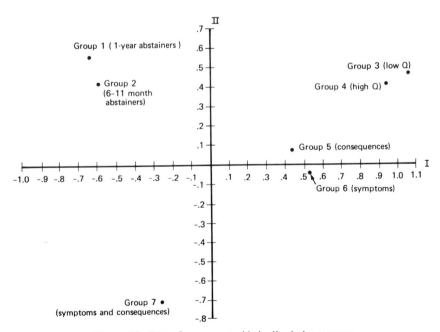

Figure 4.2   Plot of group centroids in discriminant space.

both consequences and symptoms (Group 7). The centroids of Groups 5 and 6 lie close together, on the center of the mental heath dimension and toward denial of future harm on the attitudinal dimension. In effect, these groups correspond to the clinical description of the alcoholic who has not yet "hit bottom." That is, he is not suffering sufficient social and physical consequences from drinking to break down the denial that is used as the principal defense mechanism to support continued drinking.

Drinkers with both symptoms and consequences (Group 7) lie toward the extreme negative pole of the mental health continuum. In contrast to Groups 5 and 6, however, Group 7 drinkers are closer to the abstainers on the attitudinal dimension than they are to less-impaired drinkers. Thus, respondents in Group 7 tend to acknowledge that they are alcoholic, and, furthermore, that future drinking will result in harmful effects. These drinkers are also emotionally unstable, relatively pessimistic in life-outlook, and display rather strong pathological psychiatric features. The location of Group 7 respondents in the discriminant space seems to capture the essence of alcohol addiction: Despite the fact that they have "hit bottom" and have dropped their denial with respect to their problem, these alcoholics remain mired in a self-perpetuating syndrome of emotional and behavioral pathology.

FIVE

Mortality

It has been firmly established that clinically identified alcoholics, as a group, suffer higher mortality rates than the general population, taking sex, age, and race into account (NIAAA, 1974; de Lint and Schmidt, 1976). Although the precise mechanisms causing these elevated rates are not known in detail, much research evidence suggests rather strongly that alcohol consumption itself, and its direct physiological and psychological effects, are responsible for a substantial portion of the elevated mortality. This evidence points to liver disease, accidents, and suicide as the prime causes of alcohol-induced deaths. These three causes usually show the highest elevated rates (other than alcoholism itself) in longitudinal studies of alcoholics (Brenner, 1967; Sundby, 1967; Schmidt and de Lint, 1972; Pell and D'Alonzo, 1973; Nicholls et al., 1974). Moreover, other research has established reasonable causal linkages that implicate excessive alcohol consumption in these types of death, including liver damage (e.g., Lelbach, 1974), impaired judgment and psycho-motor responses, and increased depression (e.g., NIAAA, 1978).

It was noted in Chapter 2 that the field survey efforts yielded 113 reports of death among patients selected for the 4-year followup study: these patients constitute about 12 percent of the total sample. This appears to be a high rate of mortality for a 4-year time span, and if previous research is a valid guide, it is probably higher than what would be observed for a nonalcoholic sample over the same period of time. Accordingly, a complete analysis of 4-year followup status requires a detailed assessment of mortality.

The investigation of mortality in this chapter has three objectives. First, we wish to determine the degree to which the mortality rate of our sample is elevated, if at all, compared with age- and race-adjusted mortality rates for the general male population. In addition, we will attempt to determine those causes of death that are elevated for our sample; this will help us to identify those diseases or other conditions that are responsible for the high mortality of alcoholics. The determination of elevated mortality rates for alcoholics requires the use of national death statistics for the general population as developed by the National Center for Health Statistics (NCHS). In order to have comparable statistics for our alcoholic sample, we must also classify death certificates according to NCHS's definition of "underlying cause of death." This procedure will be explained in detail below.

Second, it would be desirable if the observed deaths could be classified into those that are alcohol related and those that are not. By alcohol related, we do not necessarily mean that the immediate cause of death was due to the direct action of alcohol, but rather that drinking behavior was at least a contributing factor. The usefulness of such a classification is that it enables us to evaluate the drinking-behavior status of the nonsurvivors, at or near time of death, to supplement the drinking-behavior status of survivors presented in Chapter 3. To carry out this classification, the NCHS coding of underlying cause of death has to be augmented by other information from the death certificate and from collateral sources.

Third, one of the questions that has received scant attention in other mortality investigations is the relationship between mortality and patient characteristics, especially changes in drinking behavior following treatment. This study has the unique advantage of possessing both admission-to-treatment and 18-month-followup data on drinking status and alcohol-related impairment. Such data permit examination of the predictive association between drinking characteristics at admission or at the 18-month followup and subsequent alcohol-related mortality. In effect, this examination constitutes a type of relapse analysis analogous to that which will be carried out for survivors in later chapters. Taken together with the results of the survivor analysis, this information is useful for suggesting the relative stability of various drinking statuses at an earlier followup period and their relative prognoses for alcoholic relapse.

MORTALITY DATA

The data to be used in this chapter are derived from several sources, some collected directly by the followup survey field teams and some from secondary sources. A brief description of these data sources and their limitations will be helpful to the reader in evaluating the results in this chapter.

The initial indication of the death of a cohort member usually came from our contact with the treatment center or from the collateral source used to locate the subject. A death was considered verified if either of two criteria was met: (1) receipt of an official death certificate, or (2) confirmation of death by two independent sources, such as a treatment center staff member and a relative. For one subject, we had only a single report of death, and so he was not counted as a verified death. Verified death reports were obtained for 112 subjects (106 by means of a death certificate) out of the 922 persons in the total sample. One of the verified deaths was that of a patient whose age was unknown; therefore the analysis presented in the following sections is based on a total of 111 verified deaths.

The death certificates normally contain the following specific information as to the cause of death, typically organized in four parts of a "cause of death" section: "immediate cause of death"; two "as a consequence of" entries; and an entry for "other significant conditions" contributing to the death but not related to the immediate cause. The two "as a consequence of" entries, which are to be used for describing antecedent diseases or conditions leading up to the death, are usually not filled in when the immediate cause is fully descriptive. In addition, the death is normally classified as an accident, suicide, homicide, unknown, or in some cases as "natural." This information can be used to determine and code NCHS's underlying cause of death (NCHS, 1976).

In addition to the death certificate, in many cases a brief structured interview was conducted with a collateral source familiar with the circumstances surrounding the subject's death. These interviews were attempted only when the death certificate was ambiguous as to whether the death was alcohol related. The interview covered the respondent's understanding of the cause of death; whether the subject was drinking, drinking heavily, or not drinking in the few months before his death; and whether, in the opinion of the collateral, the drinking was a factor in his death.

To establish the expected level of mortality, by cause, we relied upon published materials from the NCHS for the U.S. general population. The primary publications used are the *United States Life Tables: 1969-1971* (NCHS, 1978), and *United States Life Tables by Causes of Death: 1969-1971* (NCHS, 1975). These documents make it possible to compute the age-, sex-, and race-specific mortality rates for selected causes for any arbitrary length of time. These life-table data do not provide information on expected suicide death rates, a cause that has figured prominently in the literature on alcohol-induced deaths, or on expected alcoholism death rates. Therefore, we derived our own tables in conjunction with suicide and alcoholism deaths published in *U.S. Vital Statistics, 1971* (NCHS, 1975).

It must be stressed that these national mortality statistics do not offer information to enable standardization on background variables other than sex, age, and race. Of particular concern is our inability to standardize for socioeconomic status (SES) and marital status, since it is quite likely that low SES persons and unmarried persons have higher than average mortality rates once their alcohol consumption is taken into account. This limitation must be borne in mind as we present the mortality analysis.

UNDERLYING CAUSE OF DEATH

The need for a well-defined procedure for classifying the cause of death arises not only from the inherent complexity of the information appearing on a death certificate, but also from the inevitable recording vagaries introduced by examining medical officers who fill out the certificate. The procedures used by NCHS to solve these problems conform to World Health Organization rules for selecting the underlying cause of death.

Basically, the underlying cause of death is "the disease or injury which initiated the train of morbid events leading directly or indirectly to death or the circumstances of the accident or violence which produced the fatal injury" (NCHS, 1976). When filling out a death certificate, a medical officer is instructed to record the immediate cause on the first line and the antecedent causes, if any, on the two "as a consequence" lines, entering the underlying cause last. Any condition that contributes to death by influencing the morbid process, but which is not related to the immediate cause, is supposed to be recorded on the "other significant conditions" line.

Unfortunately, many medical officers do not follow these instructions precisely, a fact that has necessitated a series of rules and special instructions for selecting the underlying cause. The general rule, which applies if the certificate has been completed properly, is to select the *last-mentioned* condition in the "immediate cause" or "consequence" entries unless it is highly unlikely that the last condition could have led to all conditions preceding it. There are several additional rules that cover cases in which the certificate is not filled out properly. If there are two or more unrelated conditions or causal sequences in these entries, the first-mentioned condition or sequence is selected. If the condition so selected can be considered a direct sequel of another condition in any other entry, including "other significant conditions," then this latter condition is selected as the underlying cause. Finally, there are other special rules for selecting more specific causes and for making "linkages," whereby certain combinations of causes have preferred coding of one particular condition (e.g., cirrhosis is always coded whenever it appears with alcoholism, regardless of order). The reason for mentioning these rules is that, as we shall see, the coding of NCHS's underlying cause of death omits useful information that has bearing on whether a given death is alcohol related.

For the purpose of coding and tabulation, NCHS makes use of the *International Classification of Diseases, Adapted for the United States,* or ICDA (World Health Organization, 1967). Disease and injury conditions are first given ICDA codes, and then one of these codes is chosen as the underlying cause of death.

Examples of the coding of underlying cause of death are shown in Table 5.1. Six actual cases drawn from our verified deaths are shown in the table, along with the selected underlying cause and the final ICDA code. In Case 1, alcoholism is the underlying cause since it is the last-named condition in a probable causal sequence; likewise, lung cancer is the underlying cause in Case 2. In Case 3, myocardial infarction is coded as the underlying cause rather

Table 5.1 Illustration of Coding of Underlying Cause of Death

| Case No. | Death Certificate Information | | | | Underlying Cause | (ICDA Code) |
	Immediate Cause	As a Consequence of (1)	As a Consequence of (2)	Other Significant Conditions		
1	Gastrointestinal hemorrhage	Alcohol abuse			Alcoholism	(303)
2	Cardiopulmonary arrest	Lung cancer			Cancer—lung	(162)
3	Acute myocardial infarction	Arteriosclerotic heart	Chronic atrial fibrillation	Chronic alcoholism	Ischemic heart disease— myocardial infarction	(410)
4	Pulmonary edema	Congestive heart failure	Emphysema		Respiratory—emphysema	(492)
5	Acute coronary insufficiency			Acute alcoholism	Ischemic heart disease— coronary insufficiency	(411)
6	Drowning			Cirrhosis; chronic alcoholism	Accident—drowning	(E910)

than chronic arterial fibrillation or arteriosclerotic heart because of special linkage rules. Chronic alcoholism is not the underlying cause here because it is not a recognized direct cause of ischemic heart disease. Similarly, in Case 5, coronary insufficiency is selected because acute alcoholism is not a cause of ischemic heart disease.

It must be pointed out that although four of the six cases include mention of alcoholism or alcohol abuse on the death certificate, under the NCHS rules only Case 1 has alcoholism coded as the underlying cause of death. The reason is that in the other three cases the alcohol condition is mentioned only as a contributing factor rather than as the main antecedent condition in the first causal sequence leading to death. It is apparent, then, that national health statistics may seriously underestimate the number of deaths in which alcoholism is a factor. This is one of the reasons why we will develop the concept of "alcohol-related death" in a subsequent section.

The results of the underlying-cause-of-death coding are tabulated separately in Table 5.2 for each major study group: admissions interviewed at 18 months (Group I), admissions not interviewed at 18 months (Group II), and nonadmissions interviewed at 18 months (Group III or contacts only). For the sample as a whole, the major causes of death are heart disease, accidents, and cancer, among them accounting for over half of all deaths. Suicide, nonmalignant respiratory illness, and cirrhosis are the other major causes of

Table 5.2 Distribution of Deaths, by Selected Underlying Causes of Death

Cause of Death (ICDA Codes)	Percent Distribution			
	Group I	Group II	Group III	All Groups
Cancer (140-239)	14	12	25	15
Heart disease (410-429)	21	18	31	21
Other circulatory (430-458)	2	0	0	1
Pneumonia (480-486)	3	3	0	3
Other respiratory (460-474, 490-519)	10	6	12	9
Cirrhosis (571)	8	12	0	8
Other digestive (520-570, 572-577)	2	0	6	2
Alcoholism (303)	2	6	6	4
Accident[a] (800-949, 980-989)	22	18	19	21
Suicide (950-959)	11	18	0	12
Homicide (960-969)	2	3	0	2
Other (11,580)[b] and ill-defined (796)	3	3	0	3
Deaths from all causes[c]	(62)	(33)	(16)	(111)

[a]Includes cases of undetermined suicide or accident.
[b]One tuberculosis death and one renal failure death.
[c]Number of cases.

death. All but suicide and cirrhosis are among the major causes of death in the general adult population.

The distributions of causes of death are fairly uniform across the three groups, including the known alcohol-related conditions of cirrhosis and alcoholism. Of course, the small number of cases in Groups II and III virtually precludes any significant differences from arising in these comparisons. Nonetheless, there is no evidence to lead one to conclude that these three samples represent drastically different populations.

ACTUAL AND EXPECTED MORTALITY

Determining the degree to which these mortality rates are elevated (if at all) requires a comparison of the observed rates in our sample with national rates for males, adjusted for age and race. The unique nature of our followup data allows us to carry out two distinct analyses. First, elevated total and cause-specific rates can be determined over the full 4-year period covered by this followup study for the initial sample of admissions. This analysis will answer the question of relative long-term mortality of an alcoholic sample. Second, for those alive at the 18-month followup, elevated mortality rates can be determined for the period between the 18-month followup interview and the 4-year followup. If the post 18-month followup mortality rates show the same magnitude and patterning as the postadmission rates, the stage will be set for analyzing the impact of 18-month followup status on subsequent mortality.

The 4-year analysis must be accomplished by combining deaths in Group I (admissions interviewed at 18 months) with deaths in Group II (admissions not interviewed at 18 months) and weighting them according to their true population proportions. The reason the two groups must be combined and weighted, of course, is that the 18-month followup managed to locate and interview only about 60 percent of the original admissions sample. Group II includes the noninterviewees at 18 months, some of whom were not interviewed because they had died. The expected mortality is computed for each subject according to his age (or, in the case of specific causes, his 5-year age group) and race (white versus nonwhite) by using life tables. For mortality rates given over 5-year periods, interpolation is used assuming that all 4-year followup interviews occurred 4.33 years after admission.

A comparison of actual and expected mortality, total and cause specific, is given in Table 5.3. Examining total mortality first, we can see that the expected rate of deaths among a general male population with our admission sample's age and race distribution is about 59 per thousand, or approximately 6 percent, over the 4-year period from admission to followup. The actual mortality rate observed for our sample, however, is about 145 per thousand,

Table 5.3 Actual and Expected Mortality Rates, by Underlying Cause, from Admission to Four-Year Followup

Underlying Cause of Death (ICDA Codes)	Rate of Deaths per 1000 Subjects Alive at Time of Admission to Treatment[a]		
	Actual	Expected[b]	Ratio, Actual to Expected[c]
Deaths from all causes	145	59	2.5
Cancer (140-209)	19*	12	1.7
Gastrointestinal (150-159)	1	3	0.3
Respiratory (160-163)	12*	4	2.8
Heart disease (410-429)[d]	28	24	1.2
Ischemic (410-414)	24	22	1.1
Cerebrovascular (430-438)	1*	4	0.2
Arteriosclerosis (440)	0	0	0.0
Respiratory disease (460-519)	16*	4	4.5
Influenza, pneumonia (480-486)[e]	5*	2	3.1
Cirrhosis (571)	16*	2	8.2
Alcoholism (303)	6*	0[f]	21.0
Accidental (800-807, 810-823, 825-949)	20*	4	5.0
Suicide (950-959)	23*	1[f]	20.6
(N)	(755)		

[a]Number of deaths divided by target sample size, multiplied by 1000. Groups I and II are combined and weighted to represent their true population proportions. The followup period is assumed to cover 4.33 years for all subjects.

[b]Expected death rate is based on age- and race-specific rates for the general male population as tabulated by the National Center for Health Statistics (NCHS, 1975).

[c]Ratios are computed from rates with three-place accuracy.

[d]No cases of death in this sample with codes 390-404.

[e]All are pneumonia; no cases of death by influenza in this sample (470-474).

[f]Derived from U.S. Vital Statistics, 1971 (NCHS, 1975), using methods parallel with NCHS procedures.

*Actual versus expected difference is significant at $p < .05$ or better.

or 14.5 percent. In other words, the actual death rate is about two and one-half times the rate that would be observed in the general male population, once adjustments are made for age and race to match our sample. We must remind the reader, again, that no adjustments have been made to make our low-SES sample comparable to the SES levels in the general population.

The cause-specific comparisons in the remainder of the table identify some of the sources of these elevated rates. The death rate from cancer is significantly higher than expected, and much of this increase is explained by respiratory cancer; in our sample, all respiratory cancer deaths are lung cancer. Given the well-established correlation between drinking and smoking, and the fact that smoking is widely accepted as a causal agent in lung cancer whereas alcohol is not, it is likely that this elevated lung-cancer death rate can be attributed to smoking rather than to alcohol. A similar explanation can be ventured for deaths due to noncancer respiratory diseases, which are also significantly elevated by a factor of about 4.5 in our sample. Most of the nonpneumonia deaths are due to emphysema, but there is one case of asthma and two cases of other chronic lung disease. Again, smoking is more likely than alcohol to be the causal agent in these diseases. Note that the mortality rate for pneumonia, which has been shown to be elevated in some other studies of alcoholic mortality, is also elevated in this sample by a factor of 3. This elevated rate is more likely to be due to alcoholism than to smoking.

It is noteworthy that the major circulatory diseases are not significantly elevated in this sample. The major cause of death in the general male population, ischemic heart disease, which includes acute coronaries or heart attacks, occurs in our sample at about the expected rate, or about 24 per thousand. Moreover, there were significantly fewer cases of cerebral vascular deaths (strokes) than expected. These results are consistent with those of other recent research, suggesting that alcohol per se is not a direct causal agent in arteriosclerosis and coronary heart disease (NIAAA, 1974).

Quite a different story emerges for cirrhosis mortality, where the observed rate of 16 deaths per thousand is over 8 times greater than it is for the general male population. This finding is not only consistent with the findings of other alcoholic mortality studies, but with a great body of research that finds alcohol to be the main causal agent in cirrhosis of the liver. Alcoholism per se accounts for an additional 6 deaths per thousand; not surprisingly, this rate is elevated by a factor of 21, the highest ratio in the table. In should be noted that according to NCHS rules, deaths by alcohol overdose or poisoning are classed and counted as accidental deaths, even though the examiner may have cited alcoholism as the underlying antecedent condition.

The rates for accidental and suicidal deaths are also elevated by a considerable amount, especially suicide. The suicide rate of 23 per thousand is elevated by a factor of more than 20—the second highest ratio among all causes of death. Of course, although alcohol is undoubtedly the causal agent in many of these accidental and suicidal deaths, it is also possible that a chronic alcoholic sample is affected by problems such as unemployment, social isolation, psychoneurotic disorders, or other life-style maladjustments that raise the risk of accidental or suicidal death.

The elevated cause-specific rates are fairly close to those of other studies in most respects (e.g., NIAAA, 1974). In one of the few alcoholic mortality studies showing expected versus actual rates for males, Schmidt and de Lint (1972) found that overall mortality was elevated by a factor of 2 in a sample of Canadian alcoholics. As in the present study, substantially elevated rates were found for respiratory cancer, cirrhosis, alcoholism, pneumonia, accidents, and suicide. Unlike the present study, the Schmidt and de Lint study found somewhat elevated rates for heart disease (by a factor of 1.7). They also found elevated rates for gastrointestinal ulcers, which are not tabulated here because national data were not readily available. It should be expected, of course, that some differences between the Schmidt and de Lint study and our study may arise because of the different nationalities involved, as well as from other unmeasured differences between the two samples.

Table 5.4 Actual and Expected Mortality Rates for Selected Causes, by Age Group, from Admission to Four-Year Followup[a]

Underlying Causes	Age at Admission to Treatment			
	Under 40	40-49	50-59	60+
Deaths from All Causes				
Actual	80	107	175	307
Expected	18	34	72	172
Ratio[b]	4.4	3.2	2.4	1.8
Respiratory Cancer				
Actual	0	0	15	58
Expected	0	2	6	12
Ratio	0.0	0.0	2.3	4.8
Ischemic Heart Disease				
Actual	3	18	39	51
Expected	2	11	29	73
Ratio	1.5	1.6	1.3	0.7
Respiratory Disease				
Actual	6	14	15	43
Expected	1	2	4	13
Ratio	8.9	9.5	3.6	3.4
Cirrhosis				
Actual	18	0	21	28
Expected	1	2	3	3
Ratio	19.4	0.0	7.9	10.9
Accident				
Actual	9	25	21	7
Expected	4	3	4	5
Ratio	2.4	7.4	5.6	1.5
Suicide				
Actual	12	28	12	63
Expected	1	1	1	1
Ratio	14.9	25.7	9.2	48.3
(N)	(230)	(193)	(229)	(96)

[a]Deaths per 1000 alive at admission to treatment.
[b]Ratios are computed from rates with three-place accuracy.

Mortality by Age Group

Some studies have shown that elevated mortality for alcoholics is not uniform for all age groups, and that the death rates for younger alcoholics are elevated to a higher degree than for older ones (Schmidt and de Lint, 1972). This possibility is tested for our sample in Table 5.4.

Although both expected and observed mortality rates increase with age, the rate of increase for the observed rate is less than for the expected rate. As a result, elevated mortality is greater for the younger cohorts. Alcoholics in our sample who are under 40 at admission are about 4.4 times more likely to die during the 4-year followup period than men under 40 in the general population. By contrast, the actual-expected ratio is only 1.8 for men over 60 at admission. Intermediate ages have correspondingly intermediate ratios.

With the possible exception of respiratory diseases, there is no consistent relationship between cause of death and age. It must be emphasized, of course, that because of the relatively small number of cases in each group, the cause-specific comparisons are subject to rather large random variation.

Mortality After the 18-Month Followup

A second analysis of mortality rates can be carried out for those subjects who survived and were interviewed at the 18-month followup. As shown in Table 5.2, by the time of the 4-year followup a substantial number of deaths had also occurred among these subjects, who can be divided into admissions (Group I) and nonadmissions with a single ATC contact (Group III). If these subjects are shown to have elevated alcohol-induced mortality, especially the admissions, then it will be possible to study the relationship between excess mortality and drinking status as of the 18-month evaluation.

Actual and expected mortality rates for these groups are shown in Table 5.5. Focusing on the admission sample first, it is apparent that the mortality rate is elevated by about the same degree as that shown in Table 5.3 for the total admission sample. The actual-expected ratio is 2.4 for admissions interviewed at 18 months compared with 2.5 for the total admission sample (Table 5.3). Moreover, the patterning of cause-specific rates is similar to the full admission sample in most respects. Substantially elevated rates are shown for respiratory diseases, which include lung cancer, emphysema, other lung disorders, and pneumonia. No significantly elevated rates occur for the circulatory diseases, including ischemic heart disease. Finally, the most elevated mortality rates are observed for cirrhosis, alcoholism, accidents, and suicide.

The rates for the nonadmission sample (Group III) show a somewhat different pattern, although the small sample size dictates caution in inter-

Table 5.5   Actual and Expected Mortality Rates, by Underlying Cause, from the 18-Month Followup to the Four-Year Followup[a]

| | Rate of Deaths per 1000 Subjects Alive at 18 Months | | | | | |
| | Admissions Alive at 18 Months (Group I) | | | Nonadmissions Alive at 18 Months (Group III) | | |
Underlying Cause of Death	Actual	Expected[b]	Ratio[c]	Actual	Expected[b]	Ratio[c]
Deaths from all causes	105	43	2.4	98	44	2.2
Cancer	15	8	1.8	24	8	3.1
Gastrointestinal	2	2	.7	1	2	0.3
Respiratory	7	3	2.3	0	3	0.0
Heart disease	22	17	1.3	30	15	2.0
Ischemic	19	16	1.2	24	14	1.7
Cerebrovascular	2	3	0.5	0	4	0.0
Arteriosclerosis	0	0	0.0	0	0	0.0
Respiratory disease	14	3	5.2	12	3	4.5
Influenza and pneumonia[d]	3	1	3.1	0	1	0.0
Cirrhosis	8	1	6.5	0	1	0.0
Alcoholism	2	0[e]	8.5	6	0[e]	30.5
Accidental	20	3	7.5	18	3	5.7
Suicide	12	1[e]	16.9	0	1[e]	0.0
(N)	(593)			(164)		

[a]Number of deaths divided by target sample size, multiplied by 1000. The interval between the 18-month and 4-year followups is assumed to be 2.83 years for all subjects.
[b]Expected death rate is based on age- and race-specific rates for the general male population as tabulated by the National Center for Health Statistics (NCHS, 1975).
[c]Ratios are computed from rates with three-place accuracy.
[d]All are pneumonia; no cases of death by influenza in this sample.
[e]Derived from *U.S. Vital Statistics, 1971* (NCHS, 1975).

preting the differences. Overall mortality is elevated by about the same degree with an actual-expected ratio of 2.2, but the cause-specific rates are different in several respects. The total cancer death rate is elevated but respiratory cancer is not; other respiratory disease is elevated but pneumonia is not. Also, heart disease is elevated to a greater extent than for the admission sample. Of the four causes of death that are consistently elevated in alcoholic populations, alcoholism and accidental death are elevated in our nonadmission sample but cirrhosis and suicide are not.

The fact that the pattern of alcohol-related mortality differs somewhat between the admission and the nonadmission samples raises the possibility that the two samples had a different degree or pattern of alcohol impairment at the time of initial contact with the ATC. However, the small sample sizes are such that none of the differences is statistically significant, so we could be simply observing random variation.

ALCOHOL-RELATED MORTALITY

It was pointed out early in this discussion that NCHS's operational definition of underlying cause of death, which parallels international conventions, is not necessarily the most useful approach for studying alcoholic mortality. The reason is that the NCHS cause of death is not designed to capture fully the concept of an alcohol-related death.

There are at least three analytically distinct ways in which alcohol can be a contributing cause of death. First, alcohol consumption can be the direct cause of a disease condition that is responsible for the death. The condition of alcoholic cirrhosis is the classic example; bleeding ulcers or cancer of the liver are other possibilities. The main distinction here is that the chemical properties of alcohol itself (or its metabolic byproducts) are intrinsically involved in a disease that later becomes the underlying cause of death. Second, alcohol consumption can have immediate physiological or psychological effects that lead directly to a fatal injury, whether accidental, suicidal, or homicidal. Examples would be ethanol poisoning from an alcohol overdose, an automobile or pedestrian accident while intoxicated, or suicide during an episode of depression brought on by drinking. Third, excessive alcohol consumption can lead to diseases or conditions that, while not the primary cause of death, can produce a weakened state and increase the alcoholic's vulnerability to other nonalcohol-related conditions. Examples might be a heart attack that becomes fatal because of a state of chronic alcoholism, or a serious accidental injury in which acute ethanol intoxication prevents recovery. These specific alcohol-related conditions might be considered secondary factors in a death and, as a result, might be listed as "other significant conditions" on a death certificate, or they might not be listed at all.

Of the various ways in which alcohol is implicated in a death, only the first type of causal connection (direct cause of a disease responsible for death) is captured in the NCHS classification of the underlying cause of death. As shown by the examples in Table 5.1, some information on a death certificate may implicate the second and third types of alcohol-related death, but unless it is the antecedent condition of the first-listed causal sequence, the condition will not be reflected by the NCHS code. For our purposes, then, it will be useful to have a second classification of death that focuses specifically on whether the death was alcohol related according to any one of the three causal possibilities presented above.

There are two sources of information that can help us determine whether a death was alcohol related. First, we can use supplemental information from the death certificate about alcohol-related conditions, such as cirrhosis or chronic alcoholism, that is not used in the coding of the underlying cause of death. Second, we have formal interviews with collaterals for many deceased subjects, and, in some instances, there is additional information from ATC staff members familiar with the subject. The data collected from collaterals include observations about the subject's drinking or state of intoxication before death, as well as judgments about whether alcohol was or was not a factor in the death. The information is especially important for classifying accidental and suicidal deaths. Collateral or death certificate data on alcohol-related conditions are available for 30 out of 36 deaths arising from accidents or suicides.

The nature of the information available led us to distinguish between *alcohol-related* and *probably alcohol-related* deaths. We consider a death to be *alcohol related* if either of the following conditions applies:

1. A death from diseases for which alcoholism, alcohol toxicity, liver disease (cirrhosis, fatty liver, alcohol hepatitis, and hepatoma), or gastrointestinal bleeding are listed as causes or contributing factors; or
2. A death from an accident, suicide, or homicide for which any of the diseases in Condition 1 are listed as causes or with collateral information indicating that subject was drinking before death *and* that drinking was a factor in death.

It is recognized, of course, that in some instances both liver disease and gastrointestinal bleeding might be caused by conditions other than alcohol. They are counted here as alcohol related primarily because we are dealing with an alcoholic sample, for which the chances are very high that alcohol was responsible for the condition. We also note that both cases of gastrointestinal bleeding in our sample had collateral reports that confirmed the involvement of alcohol.

A death is considered *probably alcohol related* if it is caused by disease conditions other than those listed in Condition 1 above *and* collateral information exists that the subject was drinking before death and that drinking was a factor. There are two reasons for this judgment. First, it is widely believed that medical examiners are sometimes reluctant to record alcohol-related conditions on a certificate unless those conditions inescapably caused the death; a collateral source may be more willing to give such information. Second, and perhaps more important, all but two of the thirteen cases that fall in this category have collateral sources who reported that the deceased were not only drinking but drinking *heavily* prior to death or were intoxicated at the time of death. Hence, whatever the exact physiological connections between alcohol and death, the fact that we are dealing with an alcoholic sample leads us to judge that subjects falling in this category are highly likely to be in an alcoholic state at the time of death. Under such conditions a causal connection between alcohol and death seems at least probable, regardless of the collateral's opinion.

We must emphasize that the validity of our method of classifying alcohol-related deaths naturally depends on the quality of the information we obtain from death certificates and from collateral interviews. Although the quality of death certificate information has been criticized on numerous grounds, in the case of alcoholic mortality the problems are more likely to be errors of omission rather than of commission (Medical Services Study Group, 1978). That is, given the possible stigma of death from alcoholism, alcohol-related conditions are sometimes omitted from a death certificate even when the medical examiner is aware of them. For the same reason, if an alcoholism condition *is* listed on a certificate, it is likely that the condition is present.

The collateral information is less definitive, since a lay person may not be in a good position to evaluate the role of alcohol in a death. This is probably not too serious in the cases of accidental or suicidal death, where the mere existence of drinking or intoxication can be the deciding factor. Collateral opinions are probably less meaningful when death results from disease and there is no mention of alcoholism on the death certificate; but even in this case, our classification can at least indicate the likelihood of an alcoholic relapse.

Having offered these caveats, we show, in Table 5.6, the number of alcohol-related deaths for each underlying cause of death. By definition, all deaths in which the underlying cause is cirrhosis or alcoholism are alcohol related. The two "other digestive" deaths are both by gastrointestinal bleeding, so they are also alcohol related. Less than a third of the cancer deaths are related or probably related to alcohol, but two of the three pneumonia deaths are probably related. Interestingly, about half of the heart and respiratory deaths are related or probably related to alcohol. Finally, two-thirds of the accidental deaths and one-half of the suicide deaths are judged to be alcohol related based on death certificate or collateral data. It should be noted that of the thirteen accidental and suicidal deaths classified as unrelated to alcohol, six did not have any collateral information at all. Hence, it is possible that some of these cases were also alcohol related.

Overall, it is significant that a little over half of all deaths are classified as alcohol related, which is approximately equal to the number of unexpected deaths shown in Table 5.3 (i.e., the actual rate minus the expected rate). For the sample as a whole, then, our classification does seem to account for most of the unexpected or elevated mortality that is presumably due to—or at least associated with—alcoholic behaviors. Of course, this aggregate statistic says nothing about whether persons have been classified correctly, but we shall present more information bearing on this issue in the next section.

The alcohol-related classification is important for taking us beyond a simple comparison of actual and expected mortality rates. By classifying deceased subjects according to whether their deaths were alcohol related or not, in effect we have a measure of status at some point following admission to treatment or after the 18-month followup. That is, a person whose death is

Table 5.6 Alcohol-Related Deaths, by Underlying Cause

Underlying Cause of Death (NCHS)	Number of Deaths			Total Number	Percent Related or Probably Related to Alcohol
	Alcohol Related	Probably Alcohol Related	Nonalcohol Related		
Deaths from all causes	50	13	48	111	57
Cancer	3	2	12	17	29
Heart disease	9	2	13	24	46
Other circulatory	—	1	—	1	100
Pneumonia	—	2	1	3	67
Other respiratory	1	4	5	10	50
Cirrhosis	9	—	—	9	100
Other digestive	2	—	—	—	100
Alcoholism	4	—	—	4	100
Accidents	16	—	7	23	70
Suicide	7	—	6	13	54
Homicide	—	—	2	2	0
Other and ill-defined	1	—	2	3	33

classified as alcohol related is highly likely to have been engaged in alcoholic behavior either at the time of his death or shortly before. For persons who were doing well during treatment or at the 18-month followup, then, an alcohol-related death signifies a relapse. This measure of relapse makes it possible to investigate the background characteristics of subjects at admission or at the 18-month followup that are associated with relapse among the deceased sample. Together with similar investigations among the survivor sample, this analysis can uncover characteristics that might influence future treatment strategies.

CORRELATES OF ALCOHOL-RELATED MORTALITY

As expected, the results in Table 5.6 show considerable alcohol-related mortality, accounting for over half of all deaths. Is alcohol-related mortality uniform across all types of former patients? or is it influenced by social or drinking behaviors? If certain characteristics are prognostic of alcohol-related mortality, then these characteristics might have to be taken into account when deciding or planning a course of treatment.

We will distinguish two types of prognostic analyses. First, we will examine the relationship between alcohol-related mortality and characteristics evident at admission to treatment, using the full admission sample (Groups I and II combined). Second, for Group I, we will investigate the relationships among alcohol-related mortality, 18-month drinking status, and background characteristics, as well as possible interactions. The issue being addressed in this second analysis in the impact of drinking status, measured at one followup point, on subsequent relapse in the form of an alcohol-related death.

Mortality Following Admission to Treatment

Certain patient characteristics have been shown to have some prognostic value for treatment outcomes, although the relationships are frequently fairly weak. Emphasis is generally placed on social background characteristics, such as marital and job stability, socioeconomic status (SES), age, race, and prior history of alcoholism treatment. In addition, attention is often given to drinking status and alcohol impairment at the time of admission, such as the amount of alcohol consumed and patterns of symptomatology. These variables will be examined for their impact on alcohol-related mortality.

Four-year mortality rates for six patient characteristics assessed at admission are shown in Table 5.7. Four out of the six variables—marital and job status, SES, and prior treatment—show virtually no relationship to alcohol-related mortality. The percentage dying from alcohol-related condi-

Table 5.7   Alcohol-Related Mortality, by Background Characteristics at Admission

| Background Characteristic | Percent of Category Dying Between Admission and Four-Year Followup[a] | | | Ratio[c] | (N) |
	Alcohol-related Deaths[b]	Total Actual Deaths	Expected Deaths		
Married	8	16	6	2.5	(284)
Not married	8	14	6	2.4	(472)
Working, retired	9	14	6	2.3	(514)
Not working, problem[d]	7	16	6	2.6	(241)
Lower SES	9	14	7	2.1	(342)
Higher SES	7	15	5	2.7	(414)
Under age 40	6	10	2	5.0	(288)
Age 40 or over	9	18	8	2.1	(466)
White	10*	17	6	2.9	(588)
Nonwhite	2*	6	6	0.9	(167)
No prior treatment	8	13	6	2.3	(434)
Prior treatment	9	16	6	2.7	(317)

[a]Groups I and II combined and weighted (N's are unweighted).
[b]Alcohol related or probably alcohol related (see text).
[c]Ratios are computed from rates with three-place accuracy.
[d]Not working due to illness, institutionalization, or drinking problem.
*Indicates difference significant at $p < .05$.

tions varies from 7 to 9 percent across all categories of these variables (the overall rate of alcohol-related deaths is 8 percent for the entire sample).

There is a significant relationship for race: the alcohol-related mortality for whites appears to be about four times greater than that for nonwhites. The other interesting relationship occurs for age, although the difference is not statistically significant. Younger persons have more elevated mortality than older persons, as shown by the ratio, but older persons are somewhat more likely to die of an alcohol-related condition.

There seems to be only a weak relationship between drinking status at admission to treatment and subsequent mortality, as can be seen from Table 5.8. The symptomatology measure comprises five of the six indicators of alcohol dependence described in Chapter 3.[1] It is noteworthy that there does not seem to be any relationship between the number of serious symptoms and either excess mortality or alcohol-related mortality. Although patients with only 1 to 5 symptoms show lower alcohol-related mortality than those with

[1]The five are blackouts, shakes, morning drinking, missing meals, and continuous drinking. The loss of control item was not assessed at admission.

Table 5.8   Alcohol-Related Mortality, by Drinking and Symptomatology at Admission

Drinking and Symptomatology at Admission[b]	Percent of Category Dying Between Admission and Four-Year Followup[a]			Ratio[d]	(N)
	Alcohol-Related Deaths[c]	Total Actual Deaths	Expected Deaths		
Abstained 1-5 months	4	14	6	2.3	(44)
Drinking, no symptoms	8	12	6	1.8	(52)
1-5 symptoms	1	9	6	1.6	(59)
6-20 symptoms	8	15	5	2.7	(136)
21-40 symptoms	11	18	7	2.7	(150)
41+ symptoms	9	14	6	2.5	(302)
Total	8	14	6	2.5	(748)

[a]Groups I and II combined and weighted (N's are unweighted).
[b]Number of occurrences of dependence symptoms (days, times, etc.) during 30 days before admission interview (see Chapter 3).
[c]Alcohol related or probably alcohol related (see text).
[d]Ratios are computed from rates with three-place accuracy.

higher symptom scores, persons who were drinking without symptoms have even higher alcohol-related mortality. Moreover, even though short-term abstainers have fairly low rates of alcohol-related mortality, their actual-expected mortality ratio is nonetheless well over 2. It should be pointed out that three-fourths of the drinkers without symptoms had experienced some type of adverse consequence, as defined in Chapter 3, in the year prior to admission. Therefore, the no-symptom drinkers should not necessarily be viewed as a group with less impairment than other groups.

It appears, then, that degree of impairment measured at the start of treatment is not prognostic of alcohol-related mortality during the subsequent 4 years. It is emphasized, of course, that the number of cases is quite small for the abstaining, low-symptom, and no-symptom groups. Almost 90 percent of the sample were drinking and had experienced some alcohol-dependence symptoms in the 30 days prior to starting treatment for alcoholism, and most of the others had experienced adverse consequences. Virtually everyone in the sample entered treatment with serious impairment from alcohol.

Mortality After the 18-Month Followup

When persons enter a formal treatment center for alcoholism, it is reasonable to assume that most of them will be in relatively poor condition, although, of course, some variations in impairment will exist. It is not too surprising, then, to find that a person's drinking status at the time of admission does not have a great impact on subsequent alcohol-related mortality, since persons cannot be effectively differentiated at the beginning of treatment.

A somewhat different situation exists by the time of a followup 18 months later. We know that many former patients have improved considerably, whereas others have remained unchanged by treatment. Among those who have improved, there are different modes of improvement: some have been abstaining for varying periods; others are drinking without symptomatology. A central question, then, is whether and to what extent these attained drinking statuses are prognostic of continued stability, further improvement, or relapse back to alcoholic behavior. By examining the impact of the 18-month drinking status on alcohol-related mortality, we are in effect examining its impact on relapse for the nonsurviving sample.

The relationship between drinking status at 18 months and subsequent alcohol-related mortality is shown in Table 5.9. Unlike the analysis of alcohol-related mortality and drinking status at admission, significant differences are revealed in the 18-month analysis. First, it is noteworthy that, for persons with dependence symptoms, neither alcohol-related nor elevated mortality is influenced by the *number* of symptom events. A person with 1 to 5 events is just about as likely to suffer an alcohol-related death as a person with 6 to 20 or over 40 symptom events. This finding is consistent with our conception that a threshold may exist for alcohol dependence, with 1 or 2 symptom events being just as indicative of dependence as numerous events.

For persons without symptoms, however, there are substantial differences in their chances for alcohol-related mortality. Persons who have abstained for more than 1 month but less than 6 months experience both alcohol-related mortality and elevated mortality at about the same rate as persons who still

Table 5.9   Alcohol-Related Mortality after 18-Month Followup, by Drinking and Symptomatology at 18 Months[a]

Drinking and Symptomatology at 18 Months[b]	Percent of Category Dying after 18-Month Followup			Ratio[c]	(N)
	Alcohol-Related Deaths	Total Deaths	Expected Deaths		
Abstained 1+ years	2	6	5	1.3	(98)
Abstained 6-11 months	0	2	4	0.7	(42)
Abstained 1-5 months	9	15	5	3.0	(124)
Drinking, no symptoms	3	9	5	1.8	(103)
1-5 symptoms	7	8	4	2.4	(69)
6-20 symptoms	7	13	4	3.2	(54)
21-40 symptoms	16	20	4	5.5	(51)
41+ symptoms	6	8	3	2.4	(49)
Total	6	10	4	2.4	(590)

[a]For persons alive at 18 month followup; Group I only.
[b]Number of occurrences of dependence symptoms (days, times, etc.) during 30 days before the 18-month followup (see Chapter 3).
[c]Ratios are calculated from rates with three-place accuracy.

have dependence symptoms by the 18-month followup. This is consistent with our finding in Chapter 3 that most short-term abstainers reported serious symptomatology when they last drank. These results suggest, once again, that short-term abstention is not prognostic of a stable positive status.

The picture is brighter for long-term abstainers (6 months or more) and for drinkers without dependence symptoms. These two groups, combined, have significantly lower rates of alcohol-related mortality than all other groups combined (significant at the .05 level). The long-term abstainers appear to have a slightly better prognosis than the nonproblem drinkers, since their alcohol-related mortality seems to be lower, but the difference is not statistically significant. Drinkers without symptoms do show somewhat higher overall mortality than persons who have abstained 1 year or more (9 percent versus 6 percent, respectively), but the difference is not statistically significant. We must emphasize, moreover, that the long-term abstainers and the nonsymptomatic drinkers may differ with respect to other life-style characteristics that may influence general mortality, quite apart from drinking behavior. What we can say is that the alcohol-related mortality rate was not found to be significant for either group, at least compared with the rate for short-term abstainers and symptomatic drinkers.

A multivariate regression analysis was carried out to test whether the differences in Table 5.9 are affected by various background characteristics measured at admission to treatment or at 18 months. Basically, the difference between long-term abstainers and nonsymptomatic drinkers versus short-term abstainers and symptomatic drinkers continues to be significant not only when background variables are entered into the regression equation, but also when terms representing the interaction between 18-month drinking and background status are entered. The only additional significant effects of interest occurred for race and employment status: controlling for all other background variables, whites are more likely to suffer alcohol-related mortality than nonwhites, and persons unemployed because of a drinking problem have higher rates than the employed or retired. No significant main or interaction effects were found for marital status, socioeconomic status, age, or prior treatment for alcoholism.

An Alternative Method for Determining Alcohol-Related Mortality

The way we have defined alcohol-related mortality is only one of several approaches that might be used. We would like to consider briefly one additional approach for determining alcohol-related deaths. Alcohol-related deaths could be judged as either those resulting from disease in which alcohol is inherently involved, such as cirrhosis, or those that show an elevated mortality of nearly 100 percent (i.e., virtually no cases would be observed in a

Table 5.10 Alcohol-Related Mortality from Five Selected Causes, by Drinking and Symptomatology at 18 Months

Drinking and Symptomatology at 18 Months	Percent of Category Dying after 18-Month Followup				
	Cirrhosis or Alcoholism	Accident, Suicide, Homicide	Other	Expected	(N)
Abstained 1+ years	—	2	4	5	(98)
Abstained 6-11 months	—	—	2	4	(42)
Abstained 1-5 months	1	5	10	5	(124)
Drinking, no symptoms	1	4	4	5	(103)
1-5 symptoms	3	1	4	4	(69)
6-20 symptoms	2	6	6	4	(54)
21-40 symptoms	2	10	8	4	(51)
41+ symptoms	—	2	6	3	(49)

general male population) and that are known to be caused mainly by alcohol conditions. By this approach, alcohol-related deaths would include all deaths caused by cirrhosis, alcoholism, accident, homicide, and suicide, the latter three because the expected number of deaths from accidents, homicides, and suicide in the general male population are near zero for our sample size. Respiratory deaths such as lung cancer and emphysema would be excluded because smoking, which is correlated with drinking, is the more likely causal factor.

A tabulation of these causes of death by 18-month drinking status is shown in Table 5.10. If we count only these five causes of death as alcohol related, the results clearly do not agree with those shown in Table 5.9. The most serious differences are that short-term abstainers, as well as persons experiencing more than 40 symptom events, would have much lower alcohol-related mortality, whereas that for nonsymptomatic drinkers would be somewhat higher.

Is there a way to evaluate the adequacy of the two methods? Aside from conceptual arguments, one empirical approach is to determine the accuracy with which each method accounts for the elevated mortality of each category. Since it is reasonable to assume that the elevated mortality within each category is due mostly to alcohol-related conditions, the method that most consistently explains the elevation in terms of alcohol-related conditions might be the most defensible method.

The difference between elevated mortality and alcohol-related mortality for the two methods is shown in Table 5.11. It is fairly clear that since the first method has only one discrepancy over 2 percent whereas the second method has three, the first method offers a better explanation of elevated mortality. Our conclusion is that by using collateral data and the additional data on the death certificate, one can derive a reasonably satisfactory account of elevated

Table 5.11 Comparison of Two Methods for Determining Alcohol-Related Deaths, by Drinking and Symptomatology at 18 Months

Drinking and Symptomatology at 18 Months	Elevated Death Rate Less Alcohol-Related Death Rate[a]	
	Table 5.9 Definition of Alcohol-Related Deaths	Table 5.10 Definition of Alcohol-Related Deaths
Abstained 1+ years	- 0.7	- 0.7
Abstained 6-11 months	- 1.2	- 1.2
Abstained 1-5 months	1.4	4.7
Drinking, no symptoms	1.0	- 0.9
1-5 symptoms	- 2.2	0.7
6-20 symptoms	1.4	1.5
21-40 symptoms	0.4	4.2
41+ symptoms	- 1.3	2.8
Total (weighted)	0.1	1.4

[a]Percentage of category classified as "elevated deaths," less percentage of category classified as "alcohol-related deaths." Percentage of "elevated deaths" is defined as the percentage of the category dying from any cause, less the percentage expected to die based on life tables for the general population, adjusted for age and race.

mortality due to alcohol-related conditions, not only for the sample as a whole, but for important subgroupings as well.

Drinking Status at 18 Months

In Chapter 3, a general measure was developed for assessing drinking status at 4 years. In addition, a parallel measure was described for the 18-month followup. For reasons already given, the 18-month measure is not exactly comparable to the 4-year measure (because of the different methodologies used to collect the data in the two followups). Nonetheless, it is the best available assessment of drinking status of 18 months, based on what we know of the critical interrelationships among consumption, symptomatology, and serious consequences. We will conclude the analysis in this chapter with a table showing the relationship between alcohol-related mortality and drinking status at 18 months. These results will set the stage for a discussion of the issues raised by the relationship between various abstention statuses at 18 months and subsequent mortality.

Table 5.12 shows the relationship between drinking status at 18 months and alcohol-related mortality. Since most of the rates have already been presented in Table 5.9, we show here only certain broad groups, with a breakdown between heavier and lighter drinkers and an aggregate figure for those abstaining for 6 months or more. Interestingly, the heavier, nonsymptomatic drinkers are no more likely to experience alcohol-related mortality than the

Table 5.12   Alcohol-Related Mortality, by Drinking Status at 18 Months

Drinking Status at 18 Months	Number of Alcohol-Related Deaths	Alcohol-Related Death Rate (Percent of Sample)	Ratio of Total Deaths to Expected Deaths	(N)
Abstaining 6+ months	2	1*	1.1	(140)
Abstaining 1-5 months	11	9*	3.0	(124)
Drinking, no symptoms				
0-2 oz.	2	3	2.1	(66)
Over 2 oz.	1	3	1.3	(36)
Symptoms	20	9	3.3	(223)

*The difference between abstaining 6+ months and 1-5 months is significant at $p < .05$.

lighter drinkers, although the number of cases is too small to permit a definitive conclusion.

The most important results in Table 5.12 are (a) that short-term abstainers have significantly higher alcohol-related mortality than long-term abstainers and (b) that drinkers without symptoms—even those drinking more than 2 ounces of ethanol per day—do not have significantly higher alcohol-related mortality than the long-term abstainers. Basically, the prognosis for alcohol-related mortality is just as unfavorable for short-term abstainers as it is for drinkers who show serious symptomatology. For both long-term abstainers and drinkers without symptoms, however, the prognosis is relatively good.

This difference between short- and long-term abstention creates a complication in evaluating the relative risks of abstention versus nonproblem drinking for future alcoholic relapse. Although the long-term abstainers show an excellent prognosis for avoiding alcohol-related death, one cannot reach this status without first passing through an early stage of abstention, during which the probability of a relapse leading to death may be different. This raises the question of whether the high relapse rate for the short-term abstainers at 18 months represents all early-stage abstainers in our sample, or whether the short-term abstainers differ in some fundamental way (other than length of abstention) from those who attained long-term abstention. If the latter case is true, then the low relapse rate for the long-term abstainers would be explained by these other characteristics, rather than by the length of abstention. If the first possibility is true, then the chance of an alcohol-related death for all abstainers would be somewhat higher than the rate shown in Table 5.12 for long-term abstainers. Unfortunately, our data cannot distinguish these two possibilities.[2] Clearly, further investigations of this issue should be carried out.

[2]See Chapter 7 for a fuller discussion of the issue of long- and short-term abstention.

SIX

Treatment and Drinking Behavior

Up to this point we have discussed the study cohort as though it were simply a representative group of alcoholics whose natural history was conveniently measured. However, the cohort members have a very important attribute in common: originally all of them came into contact with a publicly funded treatment program. The role played by that treatment is therefore of considerable interest. The experience of treatment studies suggests that the long-term results of treatment are likely to be limited; no brief intervention may be expected to undo entirely the considerable damage wrought by years of heavy drinking and dependence on alcohol. The results of the 18-month study confirmed this by showing that ATC treatment was only one of many factors involved in the process of remission. In fact, the patient's condition at admission and his social surroundings were more significant than treatment as correlates of 18-month outcome (Armor et al., 1978). Naturally, one may wonder whether these same patterns persist to the 4-year point. The association of treatment and followup status could well have decayed in the face of passing time and intervening events.

But assessing the role of ATC treatment is not the only reason for taking a careful look at the treatment experience of this cohort. As time passes and the occurrence of initial ATC treatment becomes just one of many previous events of potential significance, the behavior of this cohort assumes the character of a "natural" history. We have conducted much of our analysis as if the special status of the sample members as former patients were no hindrance to generalizations about the nature and course of alcoholism. Fortunately, we have certain data that allow us to examine these assumptions. For one thing, we have detailed data on the types and amounts of treatment given by the ATCs to these alcoholics. From the 4-year followup interviews, we have retrospective self-reports of other treatment or assistance they may have received. We also have a group of "contacts," whose possible benefit from exposure to the ATC was extremely small, since it consisted at most of 1 or 2 days' worth of contact out of a period of 4 to 5 years. Taking all of these data together, we can trace this history of treatment from both ATC and the non-ATC sources; we can determine whether greater or lesser amounts of treatment are associated with an alcoholic's functioning at a long-term followup; and we can assemble suggestive evidence about whether the "natural" course of alcoholism is markedly dependent on degree of involvement with treatment.

The design and purpose of this study should be borne in mind when considering the results of our treatment analyses. Our sample is a large one, and it is representative of a much larger population of alcoholics in treatment. These facts make it possible to draw generalizations from our data that would be more tenuous in a smaller-scale study. Moreover, the history of this cohort derives from the experiences of people in real treatment institutions, not in artificial experimental settings. These are significant advantages over the usual research studies dealing with a small group of subjects in one treatment environment. However, this study is not a randomized experiment. Subjects were not randomly assigned to planned treatment conditions, and the objective was not to evaluate rigorously two or more competing experimental methods. This implies important caveats about our results.

Although this study will report correlations between desired outcomes and treatment, these correlations should not be interpreted as implying *prescriptive* statements. For example, receipt of a particular form of treatment may be correlated with more favorable drinking status at the followup. However, this descriptive statement does not necessarily imply that if that particular treatment is applied to a different group, the same desired outcomes will be observed. In a natural environment, individuals in different treatment categories may be self-selected, or they may have other characteristics that differ across treatment groups. The nature of the treatment itself may also vary when treatments come about through natural processes and not as a result of deliberate intervention. Therefore, extrapolation from natural histories to treatment strategies should be done with caution. Although the present study can *suggest* possible treatment strategies, it does not indicate what the outcomes of such strategies would be. To determine such outcomes, a study designed to evaluate specific alternative treatments should be conducted.

An important aspect of nonexperimental studies is the possibility that effects of other variables could be confounded (associated) with treatment variables. Because the treatment groups we will examine were not randomly equivalent at admission, correlations of followup status with treatment group could arise from nontreatment variables. Therefore, comparisons across treatment groups should be made by using statistical controls for any such characteristics that can be measured. It is important to establish at the outset the most important subject characteristics that may affect the individual's later functioning. Accordingly, our analysis of treatment begins by examining the relationship between status at 4 years and those subject background factors that have been found significant in other research.

EFFECTS OF SUBJECT CHARACTERISTICS

As noted in Chapter 1, followup studies have almost always found that the characteristics of a subject at admission figure prominently in predicting his status at a later followup. The 18-month study was no exception in this respect; in that investigation it was concluded that such subject factors as drinking history and social surroundings had more effect on outcomes than did any measured treatment factors. In particular, results from the 18-month followup and numerous other studies have suggested that disadvantaged social surroundings, level of chronicity in drinking history, and symptomatic severity at admission betoken a poorer prognosis.

Table 6.1 shows the drinking status of the cohort at 4 years against several background characteristics measured in the admission interview. As noted in Chapter 3, level of dependence symptoms at admission shows a statistically significant correlation with status at 4 years. Persons who were previously treated for alcoholism also show a poorer prognosis than others. This probably occurs because previous treatment reflects a chronic, intractable condition, as indicated by the fact that the subject has relapsed after previous treatment. Both socioeconomic status and social stability have similarly modest relationships with drinking status at 4 years. Interestingly, neither age nor ethnicity have appreciable correlations with status at 4 years among survivors, although many observers believe that alcoholism processes differ within different age levels and ethnic groups. Considering the total rate of alcohol problems (either symptoms or consequences), one can see that, in general, these relationships are fairly weak; the problem rates do not in any case differ by more than 24 percentage points as a function of these background characteristics.

In order to test a broader set of such factors simultaneously, we conducted several analyses in which we entered various sets of background variables into multiple regression equations predicting the presence or absence of alcohol problems at 4 years. The results are shown in Table 6.2. The table presents linear regressions predicting two separate dependent variables: one indicator variable representing alcohol problems at 4 years (symptoms or consequences) versus lack of problems; and a second indicator reflecting 6 months or more of abstention versus drinking in the past 6 months.[1] Two models are

---

[1] The dependent variable for these regressions was always a zero-one dummy variable. Ordinary least-squares linear models with such measures used as the dependent variable have a number of undesirable statistical properties, such as the possibility of producing estimates not bounded by the interval from zero to one. In some circumstances a preferable alternative model is one following the logit model, i.e., $1/[1 + \exp(-bx)]$, where x is a vector of independent variables and b is a vector of coefficients fitted to the data (Cox, 1970). All the regressions in which dummy

Table 6.1 Drinking Status at Four Years, by Subject Characteristics at Admission

Subject Characteristics at Admission	Status at 4 Years: Percent Distribution of Cases							Problem Rate[a]	(N)
	Abstained 1 Year	Abstained 6-11 Months	Low Q	High Q	Consequences	Symptoms	Symptoms and Consequences		
Level of dependence symptoms[b]									
None	14	7	25	20	0	27	7	34	(44)
Low	20	7	11	19	6	10	26	42	(99)
High	22	7	5	7	6	11	41	58	(405)
Age									
Under 40	17	6	8	15	6	11	37	54	(182)
40 or older	24	8	8	8	5	13	35	53	(360)
Social stability									
Unstable	21	6	6	5	6	9	47	62	(233)
Stable	22	8	10	14	6	15	26	47	(306)
Socioeconomic status									
Lower	17	6	8	7	6	15	41	62	(241)
Higher	24	8	7	13	5	10	32	47	(307)
Previous alcoholism treatment[c]									
Yes	22	6	4	4	5	8	51	64	(302)
No	21	8	11	15	6	15	25	46	(221)
Ethnicity									
Nonwhite	21	8	8	9	3	15	36	54	(151)
White	22	7	8	11	6	11	35	52	(397)

[a]Percent with symptoms or consequences.
[b]Low = 1-10 symptoms; high = 11 or more symptoms.
[c]Before admission.

Table 6.2 Regression Models of Drinking Status at Four Years, Using Subject Characteristics at Admission as Independent Variables

| | Predicting Lack of Problems[b] | | | | Predicting 6–Month Abstention[c] | | | |
| | Model I | | Model II | | Model I | | Model II | |
Independent Variable[a]	Coefficient	t[d]	Coefficient	t	Coefficient	t	Coefficient	t
Level of Dependence Symptoms								
None	.203	2.57	.196	2.45	-.091	(-1.24)	-.105	(-1.46)
Low	.112	2.00	.112	1.99	-.019	(-0.36)	-.023	(-0.44)
Drinking History								
Previous treatment for alcoholism	-.132	-2.73	-.135	-3.02	-.017	(-0.39)	-.006	(-0.15)
History of 15 years or more of "heavy drinking"	-.059	(-1.25)	—	—	-.028	(-0.65)	—	—
Previous AA attendance	.013	(0.27)	—	—	.041	(0.89)	—	—
Background								
Nonwhite ethnicity	.044	(0.84)	.041	(0.80)	.067	(1.39)	.062	(1.30)
Age 40 or older	.073	(1.48)	.047	(1.04)	.102	2.24	.094	2.24
Socioeconomic status (high)	.121	2.66	.123	2.71	.093	2.21	.095	2.27
Social stability (high)	.086	1.87	.079	1.74	.041	(0.97)	.034	(0.83)
Years in present community (2 or more)	-.034	(-0.74)	—	—	-.013	(-0.29)	—	—
R^2	.078	(F = 4.54, p < .001)	.074	(F = 6.18, p < .001)	.026	(F = 1.45, p > .10)	.024	(F = 1.91, p < .10)

[a]Binary variables (condition named scored as 1, otherwise 0), linear regression. Logit regression models produced virtually the same statistical results (see footnote 1 of text).

[b]Binary variable (absence of symptoms or consequences = 1, otherwise 0).

[c]Binary variable (abstained 6 months or more = 1, otherwise 0).

[d]Values shown in parentheses are not significant at the .10 level. Number of cases = 548 (all admissions).

133

shown for each dependent variable. The results for the Model I regressions show coefficients when all available independent variables are included. These independent variables include all the admission measures that were suitable as possible predictors of drinking status at 4 years.[2] The list includes, in addition to the variables shown in Table 6.1, the subject's report of the number of years that he had been drinking "heavily," whether or not he had ever attended AA before admission, and the number of years that he had resided in the community. The Model II columns show coefficients when we omit the variables that in our judgment are least important. For ease of interpretability, all independent variables are scored as binary indicator variables; therefore the coefficients can be loosely interpreted as indicating the increase or decrease in the probability of the subject's possessing the dependent attribute if he possesses the independent attribute.

The Model I results for both dependent variables demonstrate that years of heavy drinking, previous AA involvement, and number of years in the community have very little effect on drinking status at 4 years. None of the coefficients for these variables reach even a marginal level of significance, nor have they been significant in any other models that we have constructed. The variables representing symptom level, previous treatment, and social status are all confirmed as having a significant effect on drinking status. Neither ethnicity nor age reach the .10 level of significance in the Model I regression predicting lack of problems, but we have retained them in later analyses nonetheless. They were retained partly because in some models age is a significant factor, and partly because we wanted to have firm documentation of whether or not these factors, which are often viewed as fundamental, exercise any apparent influence in the presence of other variables. We are particularly interested in the possibility that alcoholism processes could differ between younger persons and older persons because of the differing levels of chronicity represented by age. In our later analyses, therefore, we have

---

dependent variables were used have been run using both the linear model and the logit model (with maximum likelihood estimation of coefficients). In no case have the t-statistics for the coefficients varied substantially between the two models. Because the linear model is simpler and more widely used, we have reported its results in most places, except where display of predicted values is of prime importance.

[2] Several of the background variables included in these models could be represented either as continuous variables or as one or more classes indicated by binary variables. In the models shown, we have dichotomized all variables that were not originally dichotomous so that each can be interpreted in a similar way. The cutoffs were chosen at points judged to be conceptually meaningful, but in such a way that any underlying relationships with drinking status at 4 years were preserved. Other regression analyses have shown that the basic patterns of the results (i.e., the variables that are important according to significance tests) are not substantially changed whether one uses the dichotomous forms or the more detailed forms.

included the variables representing symptom level, previous treatment, ethnicity, age, socioeconomic status, and social stability.

One important result is apparent in these models. Long-term abstention is only marginally predictable on the basis of background characteristics. Neither of the abstention models has an F value that is statistically significant at the .05 level. With the exception of socioeconomic status and age, none of the variables measured at admission have a substantial apparent effect on later abstention.

MEASURING TREATMENT PATTERNS

The most detailed and reliable information we have on treatment comes from the monthly treatment records maintained for each patient by the ATC monitoring system. These records specify month-by-month treatment according to type and amount over the entire period from initial contact until the present. Such records reveal a fundamental difference between experimental treatment studies and naturalistic studies such as this one. Whereas the "treatment" in an experimental study is expected to be unitary, well defined, and bounded in time, the real world of treatment, as it naturally occurs, possesses none of these attributes. The ATC records from the 18-month study showed that most patients get treatment at irregular intervals (Armor et al., 1978). The most recent data assembled for the present study show, in addition, that many patients continue to get treatment for a considerable period; or more often, they come back to the treatment center later for second or third treatment "episodes." These facts are well known to treatment evaluators, of course, and in recognition some evaluators have relaxed the traditional experimental criteria that followups should always take place at a specified period after treatment has "ended" (Emrick, 1978). In truth, the end of treatment is not easy to define or measure.

Table 6.3 shows ten representative patterns of monthly treatment that illustrate conceptual and measurement complexities, and the steps we have taken to deal with them. The upper panel shows four cases for which there is a fairly clear period of initial treatment. The appearance of an "H" signifies that hospital treatment was given during the month, an "O" that outpatient treatment was given, and a "—" that no treatment was given. (For this purpose we assume that intermediate care may be combined with outpatient treatment.) Cases 2 and 4 show that only 1 month went by without any treatment, so a reasonable definition may include the successive outpatient months in the same treatment "episode." The second panel (Cases 5-7) shows something quite different. In these cases, the subjects were absent from treatment and later came back to an inpatient ward. By examining more detailed records of a

Table 6.3   Sample Monthly Treatment Patterns and Reentry Types

Case No.	Monthly Pattern[a]										Type of Reentry
	1	2	3	4	5	6	7	8	9	10	
1	H	H	O	O	O	—	—	—	—	—	None
2	H	H	O	O	—	O	O	—	—	—	None
3	O	O	O	—	—	—	—	—	—	—	None
4	H	O	H	O	—	O	—	O	—	—	None
5	H	H	—	H	H	H	—	—	—	—	Hospital
6	O	O	—	O	—	H	O	O	O	O	Hospital
7	H	O	O	—	—	—	H	H	—	—	Hospital
8	O	O	O	—	—	—	O	O	O	—	Outpatient
9	O	—	—	—	—	—	—	—	O	—	Outpatient
10	H	H	O	O	O	—	—	—	O	O	Outpatient

[a]H = hospital treatment; O = outpatient treatment; — = no treatment.

number of cases such as this one, we verified that in more than half of them the resumed hospital treatment was medical detoxification. This we do not see as a continuation of an initial treatment episode, but rather as a relapse, or in treatment terms, a "reentry." The lower panel shows other anomalous cases, where the patient was absent for 3 or more months before he reentered the outpatient modality. This pattern we define as an "outpatient reentry," although we recognize that the case is not as clear here, since it could be a continuing pattern of supportive or followup care.

Such reentry patterns are *very* common in the ATC data base, particularly when one looks over a 4-year period. Altogether, 51 percent of the admissions in our sample reentered treatment according to such a definition, and 28 percent reentered the hospital setting.[3] This is not a serious methodological problem for short-term followup because the likelihood of reentry over short periods is fairly low. Over a period of 4 years, however, a substantial amount of treatment occurs *after* reentries. This creates a methodological problem in measuring amount of treatment as an independent variable. If one simply added the total amount of treatment over 4 years and correlated it with status at 4 years, the independent and dependent variables would become con-founded because some of the independent variable (treatment) is really a response to an outcome of relapse. In the extreme case, the subjects with the worst outcomes could reenter treatment repeatedly; they would eventually receive more treatment than those who were "successes" after a short initial treatment; and a negative correlation between outcome and amount of treatment would result.[4] Since we have no data on the condition of these

[3]The technical definition used is (1) an inpatient reentry occurs wherever there is a month with recorded hospital treatment preceded by a month with no treatment; (2) an outpatient reentry occurs if a month of outpatient treatment is immediately preceded by 3 months of no treatment of any type.

[4]This did not actually occur in its extreme form in the ATC data, but it is a logical possibility.

reentries at the time they reentered treatment, there is no way to evaluate the totality of treatment or the role of reentry treatment.

Our solution will be to examine only the *initial* treatment episode as a possible factor in status at 4 years. Restricting the measurement of treatment to an initial episode means that all treatment occurring naturally is counted up to the point where the first reentry (if any) occurs. For practical purposes, our initial episode time frame will be further restricted to the period approximating the first year after admission. Thus, our definition of amount of ATC treatment is the number of inpatient days or outpatient visits occurring within the first year after admission or up to the occurrence of the first reentry, whichever comes first.

ASSESSING AMOUNT AND TYPE OF TREATMENT

Followup Status and Amount of Treatment

The median amounts of treatment received by ATC patients in each setting are shown in Table 6.4. These amounts are not very different from those recorded at the time of the 18-month followup, because relatively few subjects reentered treatment during the first year. In the 18-month study, a distinction was made between "low" and "high" amounts of treatment in each setting (using boundaries of 7 hospital days, 21 intermediate days, or 5 outpatient visits as the upper limit of low treatment). We will continue to use that distinction in this analysis.

In point of fact, the omission of postreentry treatment from the initial treatment assessment has a very limited effect on relationships involving status at 4 years, as is shown in Table 6.5. This table shows drinking status at 4 years classified by amount of treatment, using three different definitions of "amount." The top panel omits from first-year treatment any treatment occurring after either a hospital reentry or an outpatient reentry. The second panel omits only treatment provided after a hospital reentry, making the

Table 6.4   Amount of Initial ATC Treatment, by Treatment Setting

Treatment Setting	Median Amount of Treatment			(N)
	Hospital Days	Intermediate Days	Outpatient Visits	
Hospital setting	11	—	—	(58)
Intermediate setting	—	24	—	(107)
Outpatient setting	—	—	8	(163)
Combination inpatient-outpatient settings	7	12	3	(213)

Table 6.5 Drinking Status at Four Years, by Amount of Initial Treatment

Amount of Initial Treatment (First Year)[a]	Status at 4 Years: Percent Distribution of Cases								
	Abstained 1 Year	Abstained 6-11 Months	Low Q	High Q	Consequences	Symptoms	Symptoms and Consequences	Problem Rate[b]	(N)
Treatment in first year, excluding all readmissions[c]									
Low	17	8	7	9	6	13	39	58*	283
High	26	6	8	12	4	11	32	47	265
Treatment in first year, excluding hospital readmissions[d]									
Low	17	7	7	9	6	14	39	59*	275
High	26	7	8	12	4	11	33	48	273
Any treatment in first year									
Low	18	6	6	10	5	13	41	59*	223
High	24	8	9	10	6	12	32	50	325

[a]Low amount of treatment is defined as not exceeding 7 days of hospital treatment, 21 days of intermediate treatment, or 5 outpatient visits.

[b]Percent with symptoms or consequences.

[c]Excluding any first-year treatment provided after a hospital readmission; or after a resumption of outpatient treatment, provided 3 months of non-treatment have intervened.

[d]Excluding any first-year treatment provided after a hospital readmission.

*Significantly different from the problem rate for high amount of treatment ($p < .05$).

138

assumption that the "outpatient reentry" might have been followup care or otherwise not a true relapse. The lower panel makes no omissions, simply using any recorded treatment during the period. The marginals for amount of treatment are affected by these alternative definitions, but the relation of amount of treatment to followup status is not. By all three definitions, the status of patients receiving a "high" amount of treatment appears slightly more favorable at followup; the difference in the problem rate ranges between 9 and 11 percentage points. The percentage difference for the definition of amount of treatment in the top panel, which appears to be the most defensible one, is statistically significant ($p < .05$), but the size of the difference is modest.

Followup Status in Contact and Admission Samples

Some additional evidence on the correlation of amount of treatment with followup status can be found by examining the "contact only" sample. Table 6.6 shows distribution of status at 4 years and at 18 months for the same two low-treatment and high-treatment groups (as defined in the top panel of the previous table), together with the contact group. For both followups, the contact-only group, which received only the most minimal ATC treatment, has a less favorable followup status than the group receiving high amounts of treatment. The results are thus consistent with those of the 18-month study, although the correlation with amount of treatment is not as great as at 18 months.

These results also suggest that there has been a considerable degree of improvement between admission and the 4-year followup, regardless of amount of treatment. If the contact group were equivalent to the low- and high-treatment groups at the baseline (an assumption that appears plausible but cannot be tested with the available data), one might conclude that substantial rates of improvement occurred even with minimal intervention. Such an improvement could indicate that a simple referral to treatment, or the brief intervention of a single contact with treatment, might be sufficient to start the improvement process.

However, alternative explanations could also be advanced to account for the widespread improvement in this sample. An alternative explanation of particular interest here is the possibility of "regression toward the mean," the phenomenon by which any group selected because of its extreme condition at one time-point is likely to be less extreme at a later time-point. One could argue that the time of admission to treatment is probably a period of extreme stress and difficulty in an alcoholic's life. If alcoholics naturally undergo periods of improvement or remission, alternating with periods of problem drinking, it would be expected that any followup would find substantial

Table 6.6   Distribution of Drinking Status at Four Years and at 18 Months for Contacts and Admissions

Drinking Status	Percent Distribution of Cases		
	Contacts	Admissions, Low Amount of Treatment[a]	Admissions, High Amount of Treatment[a]
Status at Four Years			
Abstained 1 year	12	17	26
Abstained 6-11 months	4	8	6
Low Q	8	7	8
High Q	8	9	12
Consequences	8	6	4
Symptoms	18	13	11
Symptoms and consequences	42	39	32
Problem Rate[b]	68	58	47
(N)	(120)	(283)	(265)
Status at 18 Months			
Abstained 1 Year	8	14	19
Abstained 6-11 months	4	5	11
Abstained 1-5 months	15	21	21
Low Q, no symptoms	9	9	14
High Q, no symptoms	9	5	7
Symptoms[c]	54	46	28
(N)	(120)	(238)	(236)

[a]ATC treatment during the first year, excluding any first-year treatment provided after a hospital readmission or after a resumption of outpatient treatment, provided 3 months of nontreatment have intervened.

[b]Percentage of cases with symptoms or consequences. The percentage of "contacts" with problems is significantly different from the corresponding percentage of "admissions with high treatment" ($p < .001$), but it is only marginally different from the percentage of "admissions with low treatment" ($p < .10$).

[c]The percentage of "contacts" with symptoms is significantly different from the corresponding percentage of "admissions with high treatment" ($p < .001$), but it is not significantly different from the percentage of "admissions with low treatment" ($p > .10$).

improvement, in comparison with the time of admission to treatment. We do not know whether such a phenomenon is operating here. If we had a control group of "noncontacts," equivalent to the contacts and admissions in all respects except for treatment experience, the possible regression effect could be tested. Without such a control group, however, the possible importance of regression to the mean is unknown. In our judgment, a considerable portion of the apparent improvement between admission and followup could be due to such a phenomenon.

Followup Status and Setting of Treatment

It is also important to examine possible correlations involving the setting of treatment, although the 18-month study did not show any substantial differences between settings. A cross-classification of drinking status at 4 years, by treatment amount and treatment setting, is shown in Table 6.7. The results suggest that the correlation of followup status with amount of treatment appears only for subjects treated in outpatient or combined inpatient-outpatient settings. As shown in the lower panel, that pattern is only slightly changed by an adjustment for admission characteristics (using analysis of covariance). Moreover, Table 6.8 shows that at the 18-month followup, the same pattern can be observed: followup status is more highly correlated with amount of treatment in outpatient settings than in inpatient settings.

These results could mean that extended inpatient care is only marginally relevant to the long-term course of alcoholism, whereas extended outpatient care has some positive effect (though modest in size). However, it must be borne in mind that selection phenomena could be associated with the receipt of higher amounts of outpatient treatment. For example, the better-motivated patients may continue in treatment whereas others drop out. Or, the treatment environment might encourage the more promising patients to remain in contact with the institution and hence receive more treatment. Our data are not sufficient to show whether these possible selection effects have actually occurred. Therefore, we conclude that although the correlation could represent a treatment effect, the possibility that it reflects selection cannot be rejected.

REENTRY TO ATC TREATMENT

Initial treatment at the ATC is only a part of the total treatment picture for both the admission and the contact groups. Indeed, the ubiquity of treatment among these groups has been one of the more surprising results of this study. Table 6.9 shows one aspect of the pervasiveness of treatment: the extent of treatment reentries at the ATCs. Here the subjects are classified according to the type of reentry, i.e., the number of reentries and the setting in which they were experienced. The percentage distribution of reentries is notable. Among subjects admitted to treatment, 49 percent never reentered. This leaves 51 percent who reentered treatment at the same ATC during the 4-year period. Twenty-three percent of the reentries were recorded as "outpatient only"; these could be instances of continuing or supportive treatment rather than instances of relapse. However, another 28 percent of the sample were "inpatient" reentries (readmission to detoxification or to a hospital). These are unambiguous cases of relapse.

Table 6.10 shows that the amount of treatment given to these reentry patients was not trivial. The left-hand set of columns shows the percentage of patients of each reentry type who received any reentry treatment. About two-

Table 6.7 Distribution of Drinking Status at Four Years, by Setting and Amount of Initial Treatment

| | Percent Distribution of Cases, by Setting and Amount of Treatment[a] | | | | | | | |
| | H | | I | | O | | Combinations | |
Drinking Status at 4 Years	Low Amount	High Amount	Low Amount	High Amount	Low Amount	High Amount	Low Amount	High Amount
Abstained 1 year	12	38	26	26	14	21	13	26
Abstained 6-11 months	17	3	7	8	7	7	7	6
Low Q	4	3	2	2	9	12	10	9
High Q	12	3	7	6	9	16	10	14
Consequences	8	3	5	6	6	4	7	5
Symptoms	8	12	9	8	14	15	17	8
Symptoms and consequences	38	38	44	44	41	24	37	32
Problem rate, unadjusted[b]	54	53	58	58	61	44	66	45
Problem rate, adjusted for admission characteristics[c]	55	59	52	50	64	48	60	45
(N)	(24)	(34)	(57)	(50)	(69)	(94)	(126)	(87)

[a]H = hospital only; I = intermediate only or intermediate combined with hospital; O = outpatient only; Combinations = hospital or intermediate combined with oupatient.

[b]Percentage with symptoms or consequences.

[c]Problem rate, represented by the mean of a binary variable for problems versus lack of problems in an analysis of covariance, after adjustment for covariates (typical quantity, symptoms, previous treatment, social stability, socioeconomic status, ethnicity, and age).

Table 6.8 Distribution of Drinking Status at 18 Months, by Setting and Amount of Initial Treatment

| | Percent Distribution of Cases, by Setting and Amount of Treatment[a] | | | | | | | |
| | H | | I | | O | | Combinations | |
Drinking Status at 18 months	Low Amount	High Amount	Low Amount	High Amount	Low Amount	High Amount	Low Amount	High Amount
Abstained 1 year	18	29	10	10	9	20	17	21
Abstained 6-11 months	0	7	4	5	9	8	3	18
Abstained 1-5 months	35	25	26	32	19	18	18	18
Low Q, no symptoms	12	11	6	5	14	24	7	9
High Q, no symptoms	0	4	4	2	7	6	7	12
Symptoms	35	25	50	46	43	24	49	22
(N)	(17)	(28)	(50)	(41)	(58)	(87)	(106)	(80)

[a]H = hospital only; I = intermediate only or intermediate and hospital; O = outpatient only; Combinations = hospital or intermediate combined with outpatient.

143

Table 6.9   Reentry to ATC Treatment

Type of Reentry Recorded[a]	Number of Episodes Recorded	Percent of Sample	(N)
None	None	49	(270)
Outpatient only[b]	1	16 ⎫	(87)
	2	5 ⎬ 23	(27)
	3 or more	2 ⎭	(10)
Inpatient[c]	1	17 ⎫	(95)
	2	6 ⎬ 28	(34)
	3 or more	5 ⎭	(25)

[a]Reentry episodes that began at any time from July 1973 through December 1976. A reentry episode is defined as the occurrence of a month with recorded ATC hospital or detoxification treatment preceded by a month with no ATC treatment (inpatient reentry); or a month with recorded ATC outpatient or intermediate treatment preceded by 3 months with no ATC treatment (outpatient reentry).
[b]Includes cases with at least one outpatient reentry episode, provided they had no inpatient reentry episodes.
[c]Includes cases with at least one inpatient reentry episode. "Number of episodes" represents the number of *inpatient* reentries; outpatient reentries are disregarded.

thirds to three-fourths of the inpatient reentries received at least some recorded outpatient treatment during the reentry episode. Therefore these are not generally cases of in-and-out detoxification. On the contrary, the median amounts of reentry treatment are substantial, as shown in the right-hand set of columns. For example, of those who experienced one inpatient reentry, 38 percent received some intermediate care, averaging 13 days each; and 65 percent received some outpatient care, averaging 6.5 visits each. Evidently, substantial amounts of ATC treatment resources are being invested in the retreatment of patients who return to the center for more help after a significant period of absence.

The fact that inpatient reentry may be indicative of a chronic relapse pattern is given partial support by the data in Table 6.11, which shows the distribution of drinking status at 4 years by the number and type of reentries. The occurrence of outpatient reentries appears not to be linked to adverse conditions at a later followup; nor does a single ATC reentry appear to be so linked. If two or more reentries occur, however, the prognosis is much worse. Of course, this should not be taken as an indication that additional reentry treatment harmed the patient. It is merely a manifestation of the over-time correlation between treatment and illness: those who relapse get more treatment.

Table 6.10 Amount of Reentry Treatment, by Type of Reentry and Setting

Type of Reentry	Amount of Reentry Treatment[a]							
	Percent Receiving Any Reentry Treatment in Given Setting			Median Amount of Reentry Treatment in Given Setting[b]				(N)[c]
	H	I	O	H	I	O	Total	
None	0	0	0	0	0	0	0	(270)
Outpatient only[d]								
1 episode	0	25	89	0	26.0	1.5	2.9	(87)
2 episode	0	33	93	0	18.0	7.0	13.5	(27)
3 or more episodes	0	40	90	0	52.0	10.5	44.5	(10)
Inpatient[e]								
1 episode	100	38	65	2.0	13.0	6.5	16.2	(95)
2 episodes	100	44	71	4.5	26.0	11.0	28.5	(34)
3 or more episodes	100	60	76	8.8	22.0	11.5	33.5	(25)

[a]Treatment received from ATC during any reentry episode between July 1973 and December 1976. H = hospital only; I = intermediate; O = outpatient (admissions only; contacts excluded).

[b]Among persons receiving any treatment in that setting. Amount measured by number of days (hospital and intermediate care) or number of visits (outpatient care).

[c]Number of cases classified as the designated reentry type.

[d]Includes cases with at least one outpatient reentry episode, provided they had no inpatient reentry episodes.

[e]Includes cases with at least one inpatient reentry episode. "Number of episodes" represents the number of inpatient reentries; outpatient reentries are disregarded.

Table 6.11   Distribution of Drinking Status at Four Years, by Number of Reentries to Treatment

Drinking Status at 4 Years	No Reentries	Outpatient Only		Inpatient	
		1 Reentry	2 or More Reentries	1 Reentry	2 or More Reentries
Abstained 1 year	22	25	22	20	15
Abstained 6-11 months	5	5	14	13	7
Low Q	7	12	8	8	2
High Q	12	10	14	8	5
Consequences	6	3	0	12	2
Symptoms	14	13	11	7	10
Symptoms and consequences	34	32	32	32	59
Problem rate	54	48	43	51	71
(N)	(270)	(87)	(37)	(95)	(59)

Percent Distribution of Cases, by Number of Reentries to Treatment

NON-ATC TREATMENT AND ASSISTANCE

The high frequency of treatment in alcoholic populations is only suggested by the data on reentry to treatment. Table 6.12 shows another facet of this phenomenon. About a fourth of our sample reported receiving some other formal treatment during the 4-year period, aside from that received at the ATC. This was true even of the contact sample. Of course, some of these people overlap with those who reentered the ATC. Although the third entry of the table shows that the majority of both admissions and contacts (56 percent of admissions, 61 percent of contacts) neither reentered treatment at the ATC nor received any other formal treatment, this implies that a large minority did enter some additional formal treatment after their initial encounter with the ATC.

The second panel of Table 6.12 shows a form of assistance that is even more commonly encountered: involvement with Alcoholics Anonymous. Almost three-fourths of the admissions and about half of the contacts attended AA during the 4-year period. When this type of assistance is included, the "treatment-free" proportion of the cohort shrinks substantially; in fact, only 20 percent of the admissions and 33 percent of the contacts received none of these types of assistance. Perhaps this is not surprising for the admission sample, but it is remarkable for the contact sample. It implies that being "untreated" by a particular treatment facility or at a particular time is far different from being untreated in any absolute sense. We have seen that fairly high problem rates and substantial rates of retreatment occur in both the contact and admission samples. In light of these patterns, the distinction between them is beginning to fade. These facts suggest that the course of

Table 6.12   Percentage of Sample Receiving Assistance Other Than Initial ATC Treatment

Type of Assistance Other Than Initial ATC Treatment[a]	Percent Receiving Other Assistance	
	Contacts	Admissions
Reentry to ATC[b]	24	28
Other formal treatment (facility other than ATC)[c]	24	24
None: no reentry and no other formal treatment	61	56
AA attendance	53	71
None: no AA, no reentry, and no other formal treatment	33	20
(N)	(120)	(548)

[a]Assistance occurring since initial ATC contact.

[b]Reentry to *inpatient* ATC treatment, defined as the occurrence of a month with recorded ATC hospital or detoxification treatment preceded by a month with no ATC treatment.

[c]Treatment for alcoholism from a non-ATC "hospital, mental health clinic, or alcohol counseling center" since initial ATC contact in early 1973 (reported by subject, question 73, Client Interview form, Appendix E).

alcoholism in a treated population may be fundamentally similar to the course in a so-called "untreated" population, provided the untreated population has come in contact with a treatment institution at some time.

Formal Treatment from Non-ATC Sources

At first glance one might expect the presence of other formal treatment to constitute a positive factor for prognosis. However, other treatment probably represents another form of the reentry/relapse phenomenon that we have already seen. Table 6.13 shows that the problem rates at followup are a little greater among ATC admissions if they have received other formal treatment than if they have not. Also, the probability of being in the least favorable, most chronic category (both symptoms and consequences) was much greater among both admissions and contacts when they had had other formal treatment. Again, this may well reflect a selection effect; the most relapse-prone cases select themselves, or are selected, for further treatment after a preceding treatment fails. This phenomenon is also probably the reason why treatment before admission is a negative prognostic factor.

Table 6.13   Distribution of Drinking Status at Four Years for Contacts and Admissions, by Type of Treatment

Drinking Status at 4 Years	Percent Distribution of Cases, by Type of Treatment			
	Contacts to ATC		Admissions to ATC	
	No Other Formal Treatment	Other Formal Treatment	No Other Formal Treatment	Other Formal Treatment
Abstained 1 year	10	15	22	19
Abstained 6-11 months	2	9	6	11
Low Q	10	3	9	3
High Q	10	3	12	4
Consequences	9	3	6	5
Symptoms	22	9	15	4
Symptoms and consequences	36	58	30	53
Problem rate	67	70	51	62
(N)	(87)	(33)	(416)	(132)

AA Participation

As noted above, one of the most frequently encountered forms of assistance is that of Alcoholics Anonymous. Most of our sample members attended AA between the time of initial ATC contact and the 4-year followup. The present study was not designed as a study of AA and the available data on participation in AA are limited. In particular, we do not have detailed time-series data on a subject's attendance at AA, as we do for ATC treatment; and, of course, we have no means of accounting for possible selection effects associated with AA attendance. A specific test of the causal effect of AA participation is therefore impractical with this data base. However, the subjects' reports of their AA participation at the two followup points provide us with some insight into phenomena related to AA.

At the time of the 4-year followup, subjects were asked to report the date on which they last attended AA and to characterize that attendance as "regular" or "occasional." In the 18-month study, the regular AA attenders had a much higher rate of abstinence than occasional attenders or past attenders, but their overall remission rate was not much different from that of the rest of the sample. Table 6.14 shows the results obtained at the 4-year point by classifying drinking status at 4 years according to recency and regularity of AA attendance. The problem rate at 4 years for current, regular AA attenders is slightly lower than the rate for those who never attended AA, but the difference is not statistically significant ($p > .10$). Those subjects who attended AA irregularly or attended in the past generally had higher problem rates.

Table 6.i4 Distribution of Drinking Status at Four Years, by Recency and Regularity of AA Attendance

Drinking Status at 4 Years	Did Not Attend AA	Attended AA Over 1 Year Ago		Attended AA 1-11 Months Ago		Attended AA in Past Month	
		Occasional	Regular	Occasional	Regular	Occasional	Regular
Abstained 1 year	13 ⎫ 18	17 ⎫ 22	26 ⎫ 30	14 ⎫ 28	15 ⎫ 25	19 ⎫ 24	45 ⎫ 57
Abstained 6-11 months	5 ⎭	5 ⎭	4 ⎭	14 ⎭	10 ⎭	5 ⎭	12 ⎭
Low Q	16	5	6	10	8	5	0
High Q	17	9	16	4	5	0	1
Consequences	8	3	3	8	12	5	3
Symptoms	16	25	11	10	5	0	4
Symptoms and consequences	26	35	35	42	45	67	35
Problem rate[a]	50	63	49	60	62	72	42
(N)	(129)	(75)	(127)	(52)	(40)	(21)	(74)
Percent of total sample	25	14	25	10	8	4	14

[a]Percentage with dependence symptoms or adverse consequences of drinking at 4 years.

149

Of course, the doctrine of AA stresses lifelong abstinence, and therefore the rates of abstention are especially relevant for this particular form of assistance. Among current regular AA attenders, rates of 6-month abstention are fairly high (57 percent, as shown in the rightmost column of Table 6.14). Abstinence rates for occasional AA attenders are much lower. Indeed, even regular AA attenders who stopped attending as recently as a few months ago have abstinence rates confined to the 20 to 30 percent range. The abstinence rate for current regular AA attenders is significantly higher than that for any of the other groups ($p < .05$). Obviously, current and regular attendance at AA is strongly linked to current abstinence.

Whether this correlation arises from a causal effect of regular AA attendance or from some other factor is a question that our data are not well suited to answer. Other explanations readily come to mind. For example, it is possible that people who originally intended to abstain were more likely than others to attend AA regularly, or that those who tried but failed to abstain dropped out of AA more frequently. Either of these explanations, which appear plausible in light of the literature on AA, would represent a selection artifact. Such an artifact could explain at least part of the correlation between current abstention and current regular AA attendance. In this case, it appears that some selection is probable. This is suggested by the last entry of Table 6.14, which shows that although three-fourths of the sample attended AA at some time, only 14 percent were regularly attending at 4 years.

Our data from the 18-month followup enable us to probe this issue a little further by examining longitudinal relationships involving AA attendance. Table 6.15 shows measures of the subject's condition at 4 years classified according to his pattern of AA attendance *at the time of the 18-month followup*. Because AA attendance here was measured before the 4-year point, it cannot be the result of the drinking behavior at 4 years. The results show, as before, that irregular or past AA attenders had somewhat less favorable prognoses than others, as represented by their problem rates. Those who never attended AA and those who attended AA regularly had almost identical rates of drinking problems at 4 years. Whereas previous nonattenders were more likely than regular AA attenders to be drinking without problems at 4 years, previous regular AA attenders were more likely than the nonattenders to be abstaining for 6 months or more at 4 years. (Both comparisons are statistically significant; $p < .01$).

It is important to observe that long-term abstention does not mean permanent abstention. The third panel of Table 6.15 shows abstinence rates from the 18-month followup to the 4-year followup, making it clear that such abstention was fairly infrequent, even for regular AA attenders. Twenty-two percent of the people attending AA regularly at 18 months abstained throughout the period from the 18 month point to the 4-year point. Among

Table 6.15 Distribution of Drinking Status at Four Years, by AA Attendance at 18 Months

Drinking Status at 4 Years	Percent Distribution of Cases at 4 Years, by AA Attendance at 18 Months			
	Never Attended AA	Attended AA in Past	Currently Attending AA, Occasionally	Currently Attending AA, Regularly
Abstained 1 year	16 ⎱ 24	19 ⎱ 25	19 ⎱ 29	42 ⎱ 45
Abstained 6-11 months	8	6	10	3
Low Q	15	8	4	5
High Q	13	11	6	5
Consequences	5	8	2	3
Symptoms	20	12	8	9
Symptoms and consequences	23	36	50	33
Problem rate at 4 years[a]	48	56	60	45
Rate of abstinence since 18-month followup[b]	11	12	12	22
(N)	(107)	(235)	(48)	(86)
Percent of total sample	22	49	10	18

[a]Percentage with dependence symptoms or adverse consequences of drinking at 4 years.
[b]Percentage abstaining from the 18-month followup to the 4-year followup.

151

people who were not attending AA regularly at 18 months, this percentage dropped to between 11 and 12 percent. The difference is statistically significant ($p < .05$), but the small size of the percentages indicates that continuous abstention is uncommon in any group.

Is AA responsible for the increased rates of abstention among regular attenders? We cannot be certain, because the data are not sufficient to allow us to determine the causal relationships involved. The data show that alcoholics who regularly attend AA are not more likely than others to be free of serious alcohol problems later, but they are more likely to be abstaining as opposed to drinking without problems. We have tested these correlations using a variety of multivariate models (such as linear and logit regression analysis), and the results show no evidence that the behavior patterns of the two groups are due to other subject background or drinking characteristics that were measured. This could be taken as showing that regular AA attendance has a causal effect on later abstention. However, there is the possibility that abstainers select themselves to be regular attenders of AA. Because such a selection effect cannot be ruled out, we suggest that a more confident answer to the question of AA's effects will require a study with more control over the treatments and more information on the process of individuals' association with AA.

MODELS OF TREATMENT AND DRINKING BEHAVIOR

The data on non-ATC treatment and AA do not lend themselves to any sort of modeling. In neither case do we have adequate baseline measures of the subject's status before he entered the non-ATC assistance program. Moreover, the occurrence of non-ATC treatment is inevitably confounded with the actual outcome of ATC treatment. Such confounding can work in two different ways. In the case of a subject who received subsequent formal treatment at a facility other than the ATC, the fact of entry into that facility probably indicates a relapse after ATC discharge. In the case of AA, the fact that a subject continues to attend AA (or that he drops out) may well reflect the effect or noneffect of ATC treatment in promoting AA attendance. Therefore it is not feasible to disentangle the different effects of these non-ATC treatments in the present study.[5] Instead, we will concentrate on examining possible effects of initial ATC treatment on drinking status at 4 years.

---

[5]Despite this problem with causal order, we have experimented with including terms for non-ATC treatment and AA participation in our regression models. In every case, the size and statistical significance of the subject background and ATC treatment coefficients have remained virtually unaffected by the inclusion of such terms.

As noted above, our data base includes a set of detailed baseline measures taken just before admission to ATC treatment and at least some quantitative information about the nature of the treatment. We have observed in Table 6.7 that more favorable status at 4 years is associated with the receipt of greater amounts of treatment—in particular, greater amounts of outpatient treatment, either in outpatient-only settings or as followup outpatient care after inpatient care. This correlation is further supported by the fact that the least favorable 4-year status is shown by the most minimally treated group, the "contact" subsample. Do these relationships mean that greater amounts of treatments are responsible for better conditions 4 years later?

Although the previous results might seem to suggest an affirmative answer to the question, there is at least one obvious way in which the apparent result could be misleading, namely, if the different treatment groups were unequal at the start of treatment. This is a very real possibility because the groups were *not* randomly assigned at admission. Some aspects of human behavior, of course, cannot be assigned at random or otherwise controlled even in experiments; the amount of treatment that an outpatient receives is a notable example. Therefore, if we wish to say something about the factors that influence the course of alcoholism over time, we must examine such factors in a naturalistic study while doing all that is possible to control post hoc for intergroup differences on important variables. We have attempted to do this by formulating several multivariate models of posttreatment functioning, incorporating those subject and treatment factors that have appeared to exercise significant effects in the previous analyses.

The results of three linear regression analyses predicting various types of drinking behavior after treatment are shown in Table 6.16. The independent variables include all the factors that appeared important in the earlier part of this chapter plus three indicator variables for aspects of initial ATC treatment. We experimented with several formulations of treatment variables, searching for possible main effects and interactions among treatment settings and amounts of treatment. The treatment variables included in Table 6.16 represent all of those that have shown significant effects in any formulations. The first is an indicator variable representing the setting of treatment (outpatient setting only, or combined outpatient-inpatient settings, as opposed to inpatient-only settings). The second represents receipt of a "high" amount of treatment as opposed to a "low" amount. The third treatment variable represents the interaction of outpatient setting and high amount.

The first model, predicting lack of problems at 4 years, confirms our most important findings regarding ATC treatment. Although the amount of variance explained is small, the overall F-test is highly significant. The coefficients confirm that previous treatment is a negative prognostic factor, and that an absence of symptoms or a low level of symptoms at admission

Table 6.16   Linear Regression Models Predicting Drinking and Problem Status at Four Years[a]

Independent Variable	Predicting Lack of Problems[b]		Predicting Abstention[c]		Predicting Lack of Serious Incidents[d]	
	Coefficient	t	Coefficient	t	Coefficient	t
Drinking at Admission						
No dependence symptoms[e]	.184	2.38	−.095	(−1.32)	.200	2.72
Low dependence symptoms	.114	2.04	−.023	(−.44)	.145	2.75
Previous treatment (before admission)	−.140	−3.14	−.018	(−.43)	−.084	−1.97
Background						
Nonwhite ethnicity	.038	(.75)	.065	(1.37)	−.047	(−.97)
Age 40 or over	.049	(1.09)	.090	2.16	.052	(1.22)
Socioeconomic status (high)	.115	2.55	.086	2.05	−.054	(−1.25)
Social stability (high)	.076	1.70	.042	(1.01)	.054	(1.28)
ATC Treatment						
Outpatient settings[f]	−.112	−1.81	−.134	−2.33	.019	(.32)
High amount of treatment	−.031	(−.41)	.020	(.28)	−.097	(−1.37)
Outpatient and high amount of treatment	.187	2.09	.076	(.92)	.053	(.63)
Constant	.214		.062		.229	
R^2	.092 (F = 5.41, p <.001)		.042 (F = 2.34, p <.05)		.058 (F = 3.32, p <.001)	

[a]Linear regressions predicting binary dependent variables from binary independent variables. N = 548 cases. T-values shown in parentheses are not significant at the .10 level; all others are significant at that level. Logit regression models produce virtually the same statistical results (see footnote 1 of the text).
[b]Dependent variable = 1 if status at 4 years = abstaining, Low Q, or High Q; 0 otherwise.
[c]Dependent variable = 1 if status at 4 years = abstained 6 months or more; 0 otherwise.
[d]Dependent variable = 1 if number of incidents = 0 or 1 (including treatment reentry at the ATC, other formal treatment, or serious incidents after the first year of treatment); dependent variable = 0 if number of incidents is 2 or more.
[e]Binary variable representing level of symptoms at admission.
[f]Binary variable (outpatient or combination setting = 1; otherwise 0).

(compared with a high level) is a positive prognostic factor. This reinforces our interpretation that the severity of dependence and chronicity of the alcoholic condition are fundamental variables in the alcoholic process, independent of treatment. Subjects with higher socioeconomic status and social stability also exhibit a more favorable prognosis, regardless of treatment.

The treatment variables reconfirm what was seen in the earlier simple cross-tabulations. There is a statistically significant coefficient for higher amounts of treatment in outpatient settings, as shown by the interaction term. Although the negative coefficient for outpatient setting is only marginally significant (at the .10 level), its sign indicates that being in an outpatient setting *without* higher amounts of treatment is associated with slightly worse results at the 4-year followup. All of these results are thoroughly consistent with the cross-tabulations shown earlier. This shows that the background and drinking variables considered here are not responsible for the correlation of treatment and followup status. Even after controlling for the effects of background characteristics on which we have data, we find that the correlation remains.

The fact that inclusion of baseline variables does not attenuate the apparent effect of treatment does not necessarily mean that the association of treatment and status at 4 years is a causal one. As noted earlier, it is possible that the correlation arises from selection effects, such that the better motivated or more successful patients continue in treatment, whereas the more intractable cases drop out. Such a pattern could result from subject self-selection, or from the operation of the treatment environment in encouraging continued participation for more responsive patients. If so, the patients who were already moving toward more favorable status would ultimately receive the most treatment, and a correlation not necessarily arising from the causal operation of treatment would result. Note that this interpretation represents a situation opposite from that suggested in the argument explaining treatment reentries. There it was argued that amount of reentry treatment might be correlated with illness, whereas here the selection hypothesis asserts that treatment is correlated with health. Our data do not permit a test of the hypothesis, and it is difficult to judge how much of the actual positive correlation could be due to such a selection effect. Studies designed explicitly to evaluate alternative treatment regimens should be conducted to resolve this point.

The second and third models shown in Table 6.16 report the results when one attempts to predict (1) abstention at 4 years, and (2) a lack of serious incidents over the period from the end of initial treatment of the 4-year followup. In both of these models, the proportion of explained variance is much smaller and the coefficients are generally weaker. Aside from two background variables (age and socioeconomic status), the only significant correlate of abstention is outpatient treatment (a negative coefficient). We do not interpret this as meaning that inpatient treatment per se promotes abstention. It seems likely that subjects with the most impaired physical condition were hospitalized at admission, and we have seen elsewhere that medical problems are common among abstainers. Therefore, this result could reflect the presence of greater physical problems among hospital patients coupled with the tendency for the physically ill to abstain. However, lacking baseline data on physical condition, we cannot confirm the existence of such a phenomenon.

In the third model, we have attempted to predict the presence of two or more serious incidents over the whole time period after initial treatment. The results are notably weak, showing no significant coefficients for treatment or social background. All that appears is the tendency for people with more severe dependence and previous treatment to continue to experience alcohol-related difficulties. Once again, this suggests that it is the subject's initial characteristics, rather than the treatment he receives, that exercise the greatest influence on the course of alcoholism. This result also reemphasizes the chronic character of the alcoholic condition. It appears that even high amounts of treatment do not "inoculate" a patient against future ill effects of drinking. Looking over a long time frame, one sees an accumulation of drinking problems that may have been averted, or in remission, within a narrower 6-month period.

The models just presented could be used to provide predicted problem rates for various background and treatment groups. However, as we have noted earlier, linear regression models with dummy dependent variables have certain statistical disadvantages for such purposes. Instead, we have re-formulated the first model (predicting abstention or nonproblem drinking as

Table 6.17   Logit Model Predicting Lack of Problems at Four Years[a]

Independent Variable[b]	Coefficient[c]	t
Drinking at Admission		
No dependence symptoms	.820	2.34
Low dependence symptoms	.485	2.00
Previous treatment	-.614	-3.14
Background		
Social stability	.330	1.70
Socioeconomic status	.507	2.56
Age 40 and over	.217	(1.10)
Nonwhite ethnicity	.169	(.76)
ATC Treatment		
Outpatient settings	-.499	-1.83
High amount of treatment	-.133	(-.41)
Outpatient settings and high amount of treatment	.817	2.09
Constant	-1.251	

[a]Logit regression predicting a binary dependent variable (1 if status at 4 years = abstaining, Low Q, or High Q; 0 otherwise) from binary independent variables. N = 548 cases. The model is of the form $Y = 1/[1 + \exp(-b'x)]$, where x is a vector of independent variables and b is a vector of logit regression coefficients. T-values shown in parentheses are not significant at the .10 level; all others are significant at that level. Log likelihood ratio = 26.1, $p < .001$.

[b]All independent variables are binary indicator variables (1 = condition named, 0 = others).

[c]The coefficient of a particular independent variable (b_i) in the model $Y = 1/[1 + \exp(-b'x)]$, where b_i is an element of the vector b.

Table 6.18   Estimated Problem Rates at Four Years, by Treatment and Characteristics at Admission

| Characteristics at Admission | Percent of Cases with Problems at 4 Years[a] | | | |
| | ATC Treatment, Inpatient[b] | | ATC Treatment, Outpatient[c] | |
	Low Amount	High Amount	Low Amount	High Amount
No Dependence Symptoms				
No previous treatment	29	32	40	25
Previous treatment	43	46	55	38
Low Dependence Symptoms				
No previous treatment	36	39	48	32
Previous treatment	51	54	63	47
High Dependence Symptoms				
No previous treatment	48	51	60	43
Previous treatment	63	66	74	59

[a]Estimated from logit model, where independent variables include dependence level, previous treatment, treatment setting, amount of treatment, socioeconomic status, social stability, race, and age.
[b]Hospital or intermediate settings only.
[c]Outpatient or combined inpatient-outpatient settings.

opposed to problem drinking), using the statistically preferable logit regression method. That method has several desirable properties, the most important of which, for our purpose, is its ability to provide usable predictions of probabilities among various groups. Table 6.17 shows the coefficients and t-statistics from a logit specification using the same independent variables as those just discussed. Although the values of the coefficients are not directly interpretable, their t-statistics are very close to the similar statistics in the previous linear model. In particular, the logit results confirm again that the variables with the most significant effects are dependence symptom level, previous treatment, socioeconomic status, and the interaction of outpatient setting with high amount of treatment.

One of the easiest methods of appreciating the model's results is to construct tables of predicted problem rates for various groups represented by the independent variables. Such predicted problem rates are shown in Table 6.18, classified by categories of treatment and by the two most important background characteristics: dependence symptom level and previous treatment. The problem rates represent the percentage of cases in a given cell that the model predicts would experience either symptoms or consequences at the 4-year followup.[6]

The results demonstrate two points. First, the predicted problem rate is uniformly lower for subjects receiving high amounts of outpatient treatment

[6]The problem rates shown in Table 6.18 are estimated by evaluating the logit function at the mean for those variables that are included in the model but not shown in the table.

as compared with those receiving low amounts. The difference is about 16 percentage points. The problem rates predicted for subjects receiving only inpatient treatment are intermediate, and not very different between low- and high-treatment groups. Second, the treatment difference is small compared with the impact of background characteristics. Whatever the treatment, subjects with the most unfavorable background characteristics (high symptom levels and previous treatment) exhibit problem rates in the 60- to 75-percent range, whereas those with the most favorable backgrounds have rates in the 25- to 40-percent range. Moreover, in this table we have, in effect, averaged across other background factors, such as socioeconomic status. If we had compiled a more complex table, disaggregating groups by these other factors, the percentage differences attributable to subject background would be even greater.

Essentially, our results point to a modest role of treatment in the long-term course of alcoholism. They suggest that alcoholics who remain untreated experience more problems than those who get treatment. They also imply that if treatment is begun, the followup status of those who get at least moderate amounts of treatment (in particular, outpatient treatment, in amounts greater than five visits) is likely to be more favorable. However, the strength of these treatment relationships is fairly small, especially compared with the effects of initial subject characteristics. Moreover, no overall difference in followup status is observable between subjects who received inpatient treatment, as opposed to outpatient treatment. These findings are quite consistent with the results of the 18-month followup study. They suggest that very short-term treatments need careful evaluation, and that treatment in inpatient settings, which is much more expensive than in outpatient settings, should be examined for cost-effectiveness. Finally, as we concluded in the 18-month study, the overall results point to a primary role for the characteristics that the alcoholic brings to treatment, and a secondary role for the particular treatment he receives.

SEVEN

Stability and Change
in Drinking Patterns

The analyses in Chapters 3 through 6 focused primarily on the drinking status of our alcoholic sample at the time of the 4-year followup, during the period approximately 6 months before the interview. The various statuses investigated, therefore, represent "snapshots" of current behaviors of interest, including drinking patterns, psychological and social characteristics, and health and mortality status. Chapter 3 showed that the status of the survivor cohort at 4 years is essentially the same as it was at 18 months. Thus the new snapshot of this group of alcoholics replicates the earlier 18-month results (Armor et al., 1978), provided the same definitions are imposed.

The consistent pictures given by the 18-month and 4-year followup snapshots must be interpreted properly. It would be a serious mistake to assume this consistency means that individual members of our alcoholic sample achieved stability by the 18-month followup, or that little change occurred between 18 months and 4 years. On the contrary, as the previous studies of this sample have shown, there can be considerable fluctuation from one status to another over a 1- or 2-year period. Some alcoholics who were abstaining at the 18-month followup may be engaging in alcoholic drinking at 4 years, whereas alcoholics who were unimproved at the 18-month followup may be abstaining at the 4-year point. The net effect of such exchanges can be a series of seemingly constant snapshots that obscure a great deal of switching from favorable to unfavorable statuses. The proper investigation of stability and change requires special analysis that takes us beyond simple snapshot comparisons.

It is the purpose of this chapter to carry out a comprehensive analysis of the stability of drinking patterns over time, and to investigate those factors that are predictive of change. The analysis will be organized according to three major issues: relapse, stability of status, and long-term patterns.

The issue of relapse focuses on one particular type of change. In our terminology, a relapse is a former patient who has improved at one posttreatment followup but who, at a later followup, shows a regression back to an unfavorable status. The phenomenon of relapse is important to our understanding of the natural history of alcoholism, and identification of factors that tend to reduce or exacerbate relapse could be of considerable value in designing or planning a treatment regimen. The analysis will include examination of relapse probabilities between the 18-month and 4-year followups; a replication of the relapse analysis conducted in the 18-month study, using that study's definition of remission (Armor et al., 1978); and a multivariate analysis to specify the correlates of relapse.

Some persons who do not relapse into a clearly unfavorable status can nonetheless change from one improved status to another. Thus, an abstainer at 18 months may be a nonproblem drinker at 4 years, or a nonproblem drinker at 18 months may be abstaining at 4 years. The second area of analysis, which we term "stability," is concerned with this phenomenon. Since a change from one favorable status to another might indicate continuing adjustment difficulties, it appears worthwhile to examine subgroups of persons who were either stable or unstable between the 18-month and 4-year followups. The principal purpose of this stability analysis will be to investigate correlates of stable versus unstable patterns and, among the stable groups, to discover possible factors that could distinguish stable abstainers from stable nonproblem drinkers.

Finally, both the relapse and the stability analyses are turnover analyses that compare an alcoholic's status at one "snapshot" point with his status at a later one. Because of the substantial change in status from one time to another, another purpose of this chapter will be to develop an alternative conception of status that summarizes all the different statuses an alcoholic might occupy at different points in time. In doing this, we will develop a definition of "long-term pattern," taking into account all the drinking and impairment data we have collected on our sample over a 4-year period. This descriptive device will reflect periods of abstention, heavy drinking, and serious alcohol-related incidents that have occurred from treatment admission up to the 4-year followup interview. In effect, the long-term pattern measure will constitute a summary of status that builds long-term stability into the measure itself.

RELAPSE

One of the findings of the 18-month study that prompted a vigorous debate stemmed from an analysis of relapse between a 6-month followup and the 18-month followup (Armor et al., 1978). We concluded that, while the sample was small and the duration of followup fairly short, there were no significant differences in the relapse rates among those who had previously abstained for relatively long periods (6 months or more), those who had abstained for short periods (1 to 5 months), and those who had drunk within "normal" ranges. This finding that some alcoholics can drink moderately, without relapsing, runs directly counter to traditional conceptions of alcoholism. A major goal of the present study, therefore, is to extend that analysis by comparing the relapse rates of abstainers and nonproblem drinkers over the longer four-year followup period.

The traditional conceptions of alcoholism at stake here derive from the "loss of control" theory of alcoholism and its implication for relapse. There are several variations of the loss of control theory, each making somewhat different predictions for the relapse process. According to the classical version, formalized by Jellinek in a widely cited World Health Organization paper (Jellinek, 1952a), the first drink by an alcoholic creates an instantaneous and insatiable demand for more alcohol, which in turn triggers an episode of uncontrolled, excessive drinking. Therefore, this theory predicts that any alcoholic who attempts social drinking will experience an immediate and total relapse. This conception of loss of control and relapse has been popularized by Alcoholics Anonymous as the *sine qua non* of alcoholism, and it is a conception widely accepted among the lay public.

Today there are few scientists or sophisticated clinicians who accept this extreme, deterministic version of loss of control theory. Indeed, Jellinek himself had stated a less deterministic viewpoint in an earlier paper (1946) and even modified his language in a version of the WHO paper reprinted in the Quarterly Journal of Studies on Alcohol (1952b). The deterministic loss of control theory has been repeatedly disconfirmed by experimental studies that have failed to demonstrate uncontrolled drinking following an alcoholic's first or second drink (Lloyd and Salzberg, 1975). Moreover, most followup studies such as the 18-month study of this cohort (Armor et al., 1978) and the present 4-year followup find some alcoholics who are drinking moderately or without alcoholic symptoms for some period of time prior to a followup interview. This type of evidence, along with clinical observations of alcoholics who demonstrate occasional episodes of moderate drinking, is inconsistent with the deterministic view of loss of control, which predicts that an alcoholic's first drink will inevitably lead to immediate relapse.

In recent years, some authors have attempted to formalize a revised loss of control theory consistent with both experimental and practical realities. The most widely accepted versions are the "probabilistic" conceptions represented in the works of Keller (1972) and Ludwig and Wikler (1974). This version can be paraphrased as follows: Many alcoholics can return to social or moderate drinking for a period of time, perhaps for days or even weeks, depending on a variety of circumstances. However, loss of control means that an alcoholic cannot maintain this moderate drinking indefinitely, and consequently the chance of relapse remains very high during this period unless abstention is reestablished. This conception also implies that alcoholics who avoid attempts at moderate drinking and who continue to abstain do not have as high a risk of relapsing as those who do try to drink in moderation.

The empirical deduction that follows from this probabilistic loss of control theory is that at any single point in time one will find some alcoholics drinking moderately or without problems. But the rate of relapse for these nonproblem drinkers (at some future point) will be high, or at least significantly higher than the relapse rate for alcoholics who abstain. Therefore, by finding equal relapse rates for both abstainers and "normal" drinkers, the 18-month study failed to confirm either the classic deterministic loss of control theory or the more recent probabilistic formulation.

There is yet a third conception of loss of control, although it has not been articulated to the degree of the two versions described above. We might call this the "conditional" loss of control theory. It is suggested (rather than formulated) in several works, including those of Glatt (1967) and Ludwig and Wikler (1974). Basically, the conditional theory views loss of control and relapse following onset of drinking as neither immediate nor inevitable, but rather as dependent on a number of physical, psychological, and social characteristics of the alcoholic. Glatt (1967) theorized that loss of control might not take place until a certain blood alcohol level was attained (implying a minimum level of consumption), and even then relapse might depend further upon the alcoholic's state of mind, the setting of the drinking, and one's broader social environment such as marital or employment circumstances. Ludwig and Wikler (1974) invoked a similar conditional loss of control theory to explain why experimental studies have failed to induce the loss of control reaction. These authors contend that the institutional settings of most experiments are artificial and lack key situational determinants of loss of control and relapse.

Another conditional loss of control theory, formulated by Edwards and his colleagues, emphasizes the severity of alcohol dependence symptoms (Edwards, 1976; Edwards and Gross, 1976; Orford et al., 1976; Hodgson et al., 1978). This particular conception posits that the classical loss of control phenomenon is observed mainly in alcoholics who exhibit a very high degree of alcohol dependence, while alcoholics with less frequent or less severe dependence symptoms may be able to drink moderately without relapse.

The 4-year followup study offers a better opportunity to test these alternative conceptions of the relapse process than the 18-month study. The sample is larger, the time span is longer, the response rate is higher, and there are more data—including mortality rates and a continuous record of alcohol-related incidents—with which to formulate multiple criteria for relapse. We will first present the basic patterns of relapse using these criteria, and then carry out multivariate analyses that bear directly on the different loss of control theories.

Relapse: Definitions of Status at Four Years

The definition of a relapse depends on a definition of drinking status that distinguishes between relatively favorable and unfavorable conditions measured by identical means at two different time points. In the 18-month study, the status definition distinguished three favorable conditions of "remission": long-term abstention of 6 months or more, short-term abstention of 1 to 5 months, and "normal" drinking within the past month, with limits placed on both amount of consumption and impairment from drinking. All other persons (i.e., very heavy drinkers and drinkers with serious impairment) were classified as nonremissions. A relapse was defined as a person who was in any of the three remission statuses at the 6-month followup but who fell into nonremission status at the 18-month followup.

For reasons made clear in Chapter 3, the definition of problem drinking used in the present study differs in several respects from the original remission definition. At 4 years, the measure of problem drinking is based on a 6-month window for all subjects, with drinkers during the past 6 months being classified according to drinking behavior during the 30 days before their last drink; hence the category of "short-term abstainer" does not appear. In addition, nonproblem drinkers are distinguished not by the normal drinking criterion, but rather by the absence of *any* symptoms of alcohol dependence and the absence of any serious consequences from drinking, such as medical complications, arrests, or job problems.

Although the problem drinking definition will be tabulated at one point in our discussion of relapse, it is not well adapted to addressing the question of relapse because of several considerations. One reason is substantive. An important purpose of a relapse analysis is to discover the prognosis associated with a given status measured earlier. From this point of view, as explained in Chapter 3, it is of considerable value to know the prognosis of short-term as well as long-term abstention. If short-term abstention has a different prognosis than long-term abstention, then it becomes more complex to specify a proper model for the abstention process and to compare that process with nonproblem drinking.

Another problem is methodological: We cannot construct a classification of drinking behavior at 18 months that is exactly comparable to our measure of status at 4 years. First, no drinking or symptomatology measures are available for persons abstaining 1 to 5 months prior to the 18-month interview. Therefore, not only must the 18-month classification include a short-term abstention category, but also nonsymptom drinking can be defined only for the month prior to the interview. Second, the 18-month interview does not yield a complete set of "adverse consequences" dealing with job, health, and involvement with the law, so we can only distinguish those who drank (in lower or higher amounts) from those with one or more symptoms of alcohol dependence. If we used different measures of status at 18 months and at 4 years, we could confound a true relapse (i.e., a person who experienced a true change in status) with a person who changed status categories artifactually, simply by virtue of the change in definition.

These substantive and methodological reasons lead us to use identical measures at both the 18-month and 4-year followups for the relapse analysis. The measures are designed to come as close as possible to the definition of status at 4 years, while preserving identical measurement procedures at both time points. These comparable classifications of drinking behavior will consist of four categories:

1. Abstained 6 months or more.
2. Abstained 1 to 5 months.
3. Drank in the past month but with no symptoms of alcohol dependence (blackouts, tremors, missing meals, morning drinking, and drinking continuously over 12 hours).
4. Drank with one or more such symptom events in the past month.

It is also possible to distinguish 1-year abstention at both followups, as well as higher and lower levels of consumption among the nonsymptom drinkers. However, we will use the simpler four-category measure except where results show different patterns for the subcategories. This definition will be supplemented by other criteria of drinking behavior, including the regular definition of drinking status at 4 years.

The turnover table showing relapse patterns between 18 months and 4 years is Table 7.1. If we define relapses as persons who were drinking with symptoms during the month before the 4-year followup, but who were not in that status at 18 months, then the relapse rates are the percentages shown in the fourth row in Table 7.1. These relapse rates differ in two important ways from those found in the 18-month study. First, the short-term abstainers have a significantly higher relapse rate than the long-term abstainers (29 percent and 12 percent, respectively). Second, the relapse rate of the nonsymptom drinkers (22 percent) is higher than that of the longer-term abstainers and lower than that of the short-term abstainers, although the former difference is not statistically significant (at the .05 level). Thus, the long-term abstainers at 18 months would appear to have a marginally better prognosis than nonsymptom drinkers, but the short-term abstainers have the worst prognosis. These results are quite consistent with the mortality relapse analysis presented in Chapter 5, particularly regarding the poor prognosis for short-term abstainers.

The quite different results for short- and long-term abstainers again raise the issue of how to evaluate the relative risks of abstention versus nonproblem

Table 7.1 Change in Drinking Status Between 18 Months and Four Years (Percent Distribution of Drinking Status at 4 Years)

Drinking Status at 4 Years (Parallel Definition)[a]	Status at 18 Months				
	Abstained 6 Months or More	Abstained 1-5 Months	Drinking, No Symptoms	Drinking, One or More Symptoms	All Subjects Interviewed at 18 Months
Abstained 6 months	55	35	11	18	29
Abstained 1-5 months	14	17	14	16	15
Drinking, no symptoms	19	19	53	12	23
Drinking, one or more symptoms (relapse)[b]	12*	29*	22*	54	33
(N)	(115)	(99)	(85)	(175)	(474)
Percent of total sample	24	21	18	37	100

[a]Categories directly parallel with those of status at 18 months. That is, drinkers with symptoms and drinkers without symptoms include only persons who drank during the 30 days before the 4-year followup interview.

[b]The rate is 11 percent for 1-year abstainers; 14 percent for 6- to 11-month abstainers; 25 percent for nonsymptom drinkers consuming less than 2 ounces; and 17 percent for nonsymptom drinkers consuming more than 2 ounces.

*Difference between 6-month abstainers and 1- to 5-month abstainers is statistically significant at $p < .005$ ($\chi^2 = 8.67$, 1 df, corrected for continuity); difference between 6-month abstainers and nonsymptom drinkers is not significant at the .05 level ($\chi^2 = 2.97$, 1 df, corrected for continuity).

drinking. Although long-term abstainers have the lowest risk of relapse, a person cannot reach this stage without passing through an early phase of abstention, during which the risk of relapse might be different. The critical question is, Did all persons who started to abstain actually experience a risk of relapse during the early phases, such as that experienced by the short-term abstainers in Table 7.1? To answer this question, we consider two distinct models that could account for the difference between long-term and short-term abstainers.

According to one possible model, at the 18-month followup the long-term abstainers may be identical to the short-term abstainers in all respects except for the length of abstention. In that case, the relapse rate for short-term abstainers would represent the chance of relapse for persons in the early stages of abstention, and the relapse rate for all abstainers would be somewhat higher than that for long-term abstainers alone. A second possibility is that long- and short-term abstainers form two distinct groups with different characteristics that are related to relapse. If this were the case, a causal attribution could not be made for the length of abstention. Although 35 percent of the short-term abstainers at 18 months did become long-term abstainers at 4 years, the short-term abstainers may nevertheless include a disproportionate number of chronic, relapsing alcoholics, whose abstention is only a brief interlude between drinking bouts rather than the beginning of a period of long-term abstention.

We investigated this possibility by using variables measured at admission to treatment, including dependence symptoms, drinking patterns, social impairment, and self-reported intentions for future drinking behavior. We could find no important differences in these variables between those who were classified as long-term abstainers at 4 years and those who were classified as short-term abstainers. For example, among long-term abstainers at 4 years, 95 percent had said at admission that they intended to stop drinking altogether, compared with 90 percent of the short-term abstainers. Also, we could find no important differences on these variables that uniquely identified that subgroup of short-term abstainers at 18 months who made the transition to long-term abstention at 4 years.

Unfortunately, these analyses do not settle the issue, as the two groups could differ on variables that we did not measure. Thus, we cannot be certain that long-term and short-term abstainers constitute comparable groups. Indeed, there is no logical way that this possibility can ever be tested conclusively, even with an experiment, because the two groups represent attained statuses and cannot be randomly assigned.

We must conclude, then, that our data cannot decide on the relative risk of relapse between abstention and nonproblem drinking. We do know that persons who reached long-term abstention had a somewhat lower relapse rate than nonproblem drinkers (though this difference was not statistically significant at the .05 level). The higher relapse rate for short-term abstainers could mean that short-term abstainers constitute a unique group. However, our data did not demonstrate any such unique characteristics, leaving the possibility that the chance of relapse is significantly higher during the early stages of abstention.

Our discussion so far has assumed that a relapse is signaled by a return to drinking accompanied by alcohol dependence symptoms. Actually, other definitions of relapse might be offered. For example, for those schools of thought that recognize only long-term abstention as successful remission, both short-term abstention—which means recent drinking—and nonsymptom drinking can signify relapse from long-term abstention. Such a definition of relapse would mean that long-term abstainers at 18 months show a relapse rate of 45 percent at the 4-year followup.

Finally, we note that the four status categories yield somewhat different patterns of stability. If we define the stable persons as those who occupied the same status at both followups, then three groups have essentially equal stability. Long-term abstainers, nonsymptom drinkers, and drinkers with dependence symptoms all have slightly more than 50 percent remaining in the same category at the 4-year followup.[1] The short-term abstainers, however, have a very low stability rate, with only 17 percent remaining in this status at the 4-year point. Again, this is consistent with the general picture we have formed about short-term abstention, which appears to constitute a state that is both unstable and prognostic of relapse. Interestingly, there are fewer short-term abstainers at 4 years than at 18 months (15 percent versus 21 percent, respectively); this may be a further reflection of the instability of short-term abstention, which tends to resolve itself over time into either long-term abstention or permanent alcoholic drinking (including alcohol-related deaths). We will conduct more detailed analysis of the stable and unstable subgroups in the next section.

There are several questions remaining concerning the robustness of the results in Table 7.1. First, do these patterns hold up for those who are seriously impaired from alcohol at admission? In Chapter 3 we showed that nearly all persons in our sample showed alcohol dependence symptoms at the start of treatment. Nonetheless, we can distinguish 43 cases in Table 7.1 who reported no dependence symptoms prior to admission. Seventeen of these cases fall in the nonsymptom drinking group at 18 months, and 12 of these 17 remain in the nonsymptom drinking group at 4 years; only one case relapsed. There is,

[1]It should be remembered that not all of these "stable" cases were *continuously* stable between 18 months and 4 years. It is possible that some persons were in a different status at some point between 18 months and 4 years.

then, a small group of what appear to be stable drinkers who show no signs of alcohol dependence at admission and who are less likely to relapse. If this group is removed from Table 7.1, the relapse rates become 11 percent for long-term abstainers, 31 percent for short-term abstainers, and 25 percent for nonsymptom drinkers. Although this sensitivity test does not have much effect on the relapse results, it does appear that, among nonsymptom drinkers at 18 months, those who were not alcohol dependent at admission have a lower chance of relapse than those who were dependent.

Second, do these patterns hold up over longer time periods, and with different measures of problem drinking at 4 years? The results presented so far in this section are based on "point" measures of status in the period shortly before each of the followup interviews (except in the case of long-term abstention). A question can be raised as to whether these measures are fair assessments of drinking problems at 4 years, especially for the drinking or short-term abstainer groups, since they assess drinking behaviors only in the 1 to 5 months prior to the 4-year followup. It is quite possible for a person to experience drinking problems several times between 18 months and 4 years, and to experience several relapses, and yet end up in a nonproblem status at the 4-year followup. To test for this possibility, we can tabulate the number of serious alcohol-related incidents that occurred between the 18-month and the 4-year followups. We asked open-ended questions about serious incidents in the areas of family, job, health, and law that occurred during this interval as a result of the respondent's drinking. Only those incidents that are relatively serious were tabulated, such as loss of job, loss (or threat of loss) of spouse, an alcohol-related arrest, and serious alcohol-related illnesses. (See Appendix D for details of the definition of incidents.)

The incident counts are shown in Table 7.2, along with symptoms reported at 4 years. The top row combines all abstention and drinking statuses at 4 years, provided no symptoms or incidents occurred, whereas the last row shows those with symptoms at 4 years regardless of incidents (and hence is identical to the last row in Table 7.1). Overall, about 20 percent of the sample had no dependence symptoms at 4 years but reported one or more serious incidents between the 18-month and 4-year interviews. These reports are fairly evenly spread across the 18-month status groups, with the exception of short-term abstainers, who show a 29 percent rate of incidents without symptoms. If we define subjects with problems as those with 2 or more serious incidents between followups or as those who are drinking with dependence symptoms at 4 years, which means combining the last two rows of Table 7.2, the problem rates at 4 years would be 21 percent for long-term abstainers, 49 percent for short-term abstainers, and 27 percent for nonsymptom drinkers. Such a definition yields a much worse prognosis for short-term abstainers than for others, while diminishing the difference between long-term abstainers and nonsymptom drinkers.

Table 7.2 Symptoms and Alcohol-Related Incidents Between 18 Months and Four Years (Percent Distribution of Symptoms and Incidents)

Symptoms and Incidents Between 18 Months and 4 Years	Status at 18 Months			
	Abstained 6 Months or More	Abstained 1-5 Months	Drinking, No Symptoms	Drinking, Symptoms
No symptoms, no incidents	68	41	57	24
No symptoms, 1 incident[a]	11	9	16	12
No symptoms, 2 or more incidents[a]	9 } 21	20 } 49	5 } 27	10 } 64
Symptoms[b]	12 }	29 }	22 }	54 }
(N)	(115)	(99)	(85)	(175)

[a]Subjects with incidents are those who reported a serious alcohol-related event in the areas of family, job, health, and law enforcement occurring between the 18-month followup and the 4-year followup (see Appendix D for definition).
[b]Subjects with symptoms include only persons who drank during the 30 days before the 4-year followup interview.

Finally, both of the previous tables rely on measures of behavior at 4 years that include a separate category for short-term abstention. As an alternative, we can tabulate the regular 4-year status measure—which classifies short-term abstainers according to their most recent drinking behavior—against the 18-month status measure. Such an analysis is shown in Table 7.3. Note that in this table, as in Table 7.2, the 4-year status measure is not the same as the 18-month status definition. Because of noncomparability of definitions, neither of these latter tables is strictly a relapse analysis. Instead, Table 7.3 tells us the relationship between various 18-month statuses and the regular 4-year status based on a full 6-month period of observation at 4 years. For this analysis, we have subdivided people who drank in the past 6 months into only two groups: those with symptoms or consequences, and those with no symptoms or consequences.

The overall rate of problem drinking at 4 years in Table 7.3 is considerably higher than the rate of drinking with symptoms shown in Table 7.1, primarily because most subjects who were short-term abstainers at 4 years are known to have had drinking problems within the past 6 months. Nonetheless, the relative ranking of 18-month statuses, according to their prognosis for future problems, is about the same as that shown in Table 7.1. Table 7.3 offers a finer breakdown of status at 18 months because of some fairly substantial differences for 1-year abstainers as well as for low-consuming and higher-consuming nonsymptom drinkers.

There appear to be three fairly distinct groupings. First, the persons with the lowest rate of problems at 4 years—25 percent—are those who had abstained 1 year or more at the 18-month followup. This contrasts sharply with the rate of 73 percent among persons with one or more symptoms at 18 months: Those in poor condition at 18 months are highly likely to be in poor condition 2.5 years later. The remaining groups fall in between these extremes: the problem rates for 6- to 11-month abstainers and nonsymptom drinkers with low consumption are near 40 percent; the problem rates for 1- to 5-month abstainers and nonsymptom drinkers with high consumption are near 50 percent. The difference between 1-year abstainers and low consumers is not statistically significant, nor is there a significant difference when the two long-term abstaining groups are combined and compared with the combined drinking groups (30 percent versus 41 percent, respectively).[2] It is important to note that only about one-fourth of the short-term abstainers at 18 months became 1-year abstainers at 4 years, whereas over half developed dependence symptoms or consequences.

---

[2]Tabulating the number of serious alcohol-related incidents between 18 months and 4 years, we find that the percentage with 2 or more incidents in this interval, or with symptoms or consequences at 4 years, is 37 for long-term abstainers, 66 for short-term abstainers, and 41 for nonsymptom drinkers.

Table 7.3 Drinking Status at Four Years, by Status at 18 Months (Percent Distribution of Drinking Status at Four Years)

Drinking Status at 4 Years[a]	Status at 18 Months						All subjects Interviewed at 18 Months
	Abstained 1 Year or More	Abstained 6-11 Months	Abstained 1-5 Months	Drinking, No Symptoms, 0-2 oz.	Drinking, No Symptoms, 3+ oz.	Drinking, Symptoms	
Abstained 1 year or more	52	39	25	5	10	11	22
Abstained 6-11 months	6	8	9	2	7	7	7
Drinking past 6 months, no symptoms or consequences	17	11	13	55	37	9	18
Drinking past 6 months, symptoms or consequences	25 }30*	42	53* }41*	38	46	73	53
(N)	(79)	(36)	(99)	(55)	(30)	(175)	(474)

[a]Drinking status at 4 years is defined by using a full 6-month period of measurement, as described in Chapter 3. All subjects who drank at any time during the 6 months before the 4-year followup interview are classified according to the presence or absence of (a) consequences during that 6-month period and (b) symptoms during the 30 days before the last drink.

*The difference between the 1- to 5-month abstainers and those who abstained for 6 months or more is significant at $p < .005$ ($\chi^2 = 9.26$, 1 df, corrected for continuity); neither difference between nonproblem drinkers combined and the two abstention groups is significant ($\chi^2 = 2.03$ for nonproblem drinkers versus 6-month-or-more abstainers, and 1.97 for nonproblem drinkers versus 1- to 5-month abstainers).

171

The "Remission" Definition

The findings presented so far differ in one important respect from the findings presented in the 18-month study (Armor et al., 1978): The long-term abstainers have many fewer relapses than short-term abstainers and somewhat fewer relapses than drinkers without symptoms (the latter being somewhat analogous to the "normal" drinker category used there). It would be instructive to know the reason for this difference, and, in particular, whether the changes are due to changes in definition, to possible biases in the 18-month samples, to the fact that 4 years represents a long-term followup, or to some combination of these factors.

Table 7.4 shows the relapse rates between 18 months and 4 years, using the same definition of "remission" as that used in the 18-month study except for one variation: normal drinkers with low-frequency symptoms are separated for purpose of clarification. By and large, the relapse results are quite similar to those shown in Tables 7.1 through 7.3, with long-term abstainers (6 months) having a lower rate of relapse than the other two remission groups by a factor of one-half to one-third. Note that the normal drinkers with low-frequency symptoms have a very high relapse rate, thereby confirming the bad prognosis of lower levels of consumption when accompanied by even a few signs of alcohol dependence.

Having shown that definitional changes are not responsible for these different findings, we turn to other possibilities, including sample bias and length of followup. The subsample used in the 18-month study for the 6-month to 18-month relapse analysis was quite small, because of poor response rates at the 6-month followup. It is therefore possible that the subsample represented a biased group with different relapse characteristics from the total 18-month sample. Another possibility, of course, is that the differences are due to the fact that the time between the 18-month and 4-year followups is substantially longer—and more distant from treatment—than the time between the 6-month and 18-month followups.

These two possibilities are evaluated in Table 7.5, which shows both the 18-month and 4-year followup results for 169 persons who are were located and interviewed for the 4-year followup and who can be classified according to their 6-month remission status. The relapse rates at 18 months (in the upper half of the table) are nearly identical to those shown in Armor et al. (1978) for the original relapse sample, thereby suggesting that the sample of 169 is not a seriously biased subset of the original 220. At 18 months, the relapse rates are nearly equal for the three groups in remission at 6 months: long-term abstainers, short-term abstainers, and normal drinkers.

Note, however, that for this same subsample of 169 cases, the relapse rates at 4 years show a different pattern, one that is remarkably similar to the pattern shown in Tables 7.1 through 7.3. The long-term abstainers have a 4-

Table 7.4 Relapse Rates Between 18-Month and Four-Year Followups, Using "Alcoholism and Treatment" Remission Definitions[a] (Percent Distribution of Remission Status at 4 Years)

Remission Status at 4 Years	Abstained 6 Months	Abstained 1-5 Months	Normal Drinking[b]			Nonremissions	All Subjects Interviewed at 18 Months
			Total	No Symptoms	Some Symptoms		
Abstained 6 months	55	34	11	11	9	19	29
Abstained 1-5 months	14	17	15	15	14	17	16
Normal drinking	20	23	46	49	32	17	2[f]
Nonremissions (relapse)	11	25	29	25	45	47	30
(N)	(115)	(99)	(103)	(81)	(22)	(152)	(469)
Percent of total sample	25	21	22	17	5	32	100

[a]Subjects admitted to treatment (Group I).

[b]This set of symptoms includes those that were used in the 18-month study's definition of normal drinking; i.e., one or more instances of shakes, blackouts, morning drinking, missing meals, and missing work, or more than four instances of intoxication, in the 30 days before the followup interview. Drinkers with high rates of alcohol consumption or with frequent episodes of three or more of those symptoms are classified as nonremissions.

Table 7.5 Relapse Rates for the 6-Month "Alcoholism and Treatment" Sample (Percent Distribution of Remission Status at 18-Month and 4-Year Followups)

Remission Status at Followup	Remission Status at 6 Months				
	Abstained 6 Months or More	Abstained 1-5 Months	Normal Drinking	Nonremission	Total
18-Month Followup:					
Abstained 6 months	53	33	12	5	28
Abstained 1-5 months	16	20	25	33	23
Normal drinking	16	31	46	16	27
Nonremission (relapse)	16	16	17	46	23
4-Year Followup:					
Abstained 6 months	44	40	21	21	34
Abstained 1-5 months	22	12	12	24	16
Normal drinking	22	27	46	18	27
Nonremission (relapse)	12	21	21	37	23
(N)	(32)	(75)	(24)	(38)	(169)

year relapse rate of about 12 percent, compared with relapse rates of 21 percent for the other two remission groups. The normal drinking group in this subsample may have some bias, since Table 7.4 shows a total relapse rate of about 29 percent for the full sample between 18 months and 4 years. But this is not a large difference, and in any event the basic pattern of results is still quite similar to relapse results for the full sample.

It would appear, then, that the difference between the new relapse findings and those described in the 18-month study is not due so much to methodological differences between the two studies, but may instead represent a substantive finding. The differential relapse rates in the 4-year study may be explained by the longer time interval. Although the 18-month followup gives the same "snapshot" picture of status as the 4-year followup, the considerable instability of status is such that the time between 6 months and 18 months may be too short to establish long-term relapse patterns.

Correlates of Relapse

While the 4-year measurement shows that long-term abstainers had somewhat lower relapse rates than those who drank without symptoms, there are, nonetheless, a significant number of nonsymptom drinkers who did not relapse, and a significant number of long-term abstainers who did relapse. Given the overall high rates of instability, it is important to know whether there are intervening variables that distinguish nonsymptom drinkers and abstainers who relapse from those who do not. Such relationships, if they exist, may help us to understand the processes that cause relapse.

As a starting point, we examined a number of patient background characteristics for their potential impact on relapse. Table 7.6 summarizes relapse rates by status at 18 months and background characteristics measured at admission. The 4-year measure used is that shown in Table 7.1; it is identical to the measure of status at 18 months. We tabulate the percent of persons in a given status category at 18 months who were drinking with symptoms of alcohol dependence at 4 years.

The patient background characteristics given in Table 7.6 are those shown in this and other studies to be related to improvement. As the column for "all subjects" indicates, some of these measures are indeed related to overall improvement: relationships are clearly demonstrated for level of dependence symptoms, socioeconomic and marital status, and race. These variables were subjected to a multiple regression analysis in Chapter 6, which yielded consistently significant overall coefficients for only three of them: level of dependence symptoms, socioeconomic status, and previous treatment for alcoholism.[3]

---

[3]It should be noted that Table 7.6 uses a different 4-year measure than that used in Chapter 6.

Our primary interest here, however, is in differential relapse rates, given various improved statuses at 18 months. When we consider 18-month status, some of these overall relationships are modified. We note that drinkers with dependence symptoms at 18 months have relatively high relapse rates regardless of background characteristics; in almost all subgroups, 50 percent or more of these persons are drinking with symptoms at 4 years. This suggests that occurrence of serious impairment by the 18-month followup reflects a chronic condition that tends to overshadow any factor at admission that might otherwise promote improvement.

For the other three groups in Table 7.6—those abstaining or drinking with no symptoms at 18 months—the relationships are complex. Some background characteristics appear to increase the differential relapse rates between nonsymptom drinking and long-term abstention at 18 months, or between nonsymptom drinking and all abstainers combined. Thus, among persons who had high levels of dependence symptoms, who were married, or who were over 40 at admission, the relapse rate for previous nonsymptom drinkers was higher than that for long-term abstainers. However, among those who had no symptoms of dependence or low levels of dependence, who were unmarried, or who were under 40 at admission, the relapse rate for nonsymptom drinkers was either equal to or less than that for long-term abstainers. There is a suggestion in these differential relapse rates that both the environment and degree of dependence may affect the probability of relapse associated with nonproblem drinking versus abstention.

Such a conclusion, however, is made tenuous by the complex patterns and the relatively small number of cases in some categories in Table 7.6. We need a more refined analysis to test for significant differences in relapse patterns among these groups. Accordingly, we conducted two dummy-variable logit regression analyses, using the variables in Table 7.6. These two analyses are shown in Table 7.7. The first analysis compares long-term abstainers at 18 months with nonsymptom drinkers at 18 months; short-term abstainers and persons drinking with symptoms are excluded from the analysis. Hence, the first analysis answers the question of differential relapse rates for nonsymptom drinkers versus the long-term abstainers. The second analysis combines short- and long-term abstainers into a category of all abstainers and compares them with nonsymptom drinkers; drinkers with symptoms are excluded. The reason for the second analysis is to provide a test for all abstainers, regardless of the length of abstention.

The independent variables in both analyses are the background characteristics that were listed in Table 7.6 and the interactions involving those characteristics. All of these variables are represented as dummy variables. They include separate dummies for no dependence symptoms and low levels of dependence symptoms; a dichotomy representing the two drinking

Table 7.6 Relapse Rates at Four Years, by Background Characteristics at Admission and by Status at 18 Months

| | | | | | Relapse Rate at 4 Years[a] | | | | | |
| | | | | | Status at 18 Months | | | | | |
Background Characteristics at Admission	Abstained 6 Months or More	(N)	Abstained 1-5 Months	(N)	Drinking, No Symptoms	(N)	Drinking, Symptoms	(N)	All Subjects	(N)
Level of Dependence										
Symptoms										
None	22	(9)	0	(6)	12	(17)	36	(11)	19	(43)
Low	17	(23)	31	(16)	12	(25)	52	(21)	27	(85)
High	10	(83)	31	(77)	33	(43)	55	(143)	36	(346)
Socioeconomic Status										
Low	14	(43)	28	(40)	25	(28)	57	(99)	38	(210)
High	11	(72)	30	(59)	21	(57)	50	(76)	29	(264)
Marital Status										
Married	10	(61)	22	(37)	27	(44)	54	(54)	28	(196)
Unmarried	15	(54)	34	(62)	17	(41)	54	(121)	36	(278)
Employment Status										
Employed, retired	14	(80)	24	(68)	18	(65)	50	(122)	30	(335)
Unemployed, problem[b]	9	(35)	42	(31)	35	(20)	62	(52)	34	(138)
Age										
Under 40	18	(33)	18	(27)	11	(37)	53	(60)	30	(157)
40 or more	10	(82)	33	(72)	31	(48)	54	(109)	34	(317)
Race										
White	11	(90)	29	(73)	23	(66)	51	(33)	30	(342)
Nonwhite	16	(25)	31	(26)	21	(19)	58	(62)	39	(132)
Prior Treatment										
No	11	(70)	29	(55)	18	(63)	55	(95)	31	(283)
Yes	13	(45)	30	(44)	36	(22)	52	(80)	36	(191)

[a]Percentage of cases who drank with symptoms during the 30-day period before the 4-year followup. The measure tabulated here is that used in Table 7.1, which excludes all short-term abstainers from the symptoms category.

[b]Persons out of work because of illness, institutionalization, or drinking problems.

statuses, nonsymptom drinking versus abstaining; and interactions (i.e., products) between the nine background variables and nonsymptom drinking versus abstaining. The interaction terms for drinking versus abstaining are introduced to test for *differential* relapse rates between abstainers and drinkers for the characteristic in question. A positive coefficient for an interaction term means that persons with the characteristic had a higher relapse rate if they were nonsymptom drinkers than if they were abstainers.

The results from these two logit regression analyses predicting relapse at 4 years are shown in Table 7.7.[4] Considering analysis (1)—long-term abstainers (6 months or more) versus nonsymptom drinkers at 18 months—we see that there are, indeed, significant differential relapse rates for several of the background characteristics, controlling for all other characteristics. One of the strongest coefficients is for no dependence symptoms, meaning that such persons had lower relapse rates if they were nonsymptom drinkers at 18 months. The next two strongest coefficients are for age and unemployment, with persons over 40 showing higher relapse rates if they were drinking rather than abstaining at 18 months. Similarly, unemployed persons who drank were more likely to relapse than unemployed abstainers. Finally, there are interactions with marital status and low levels of dependence symptoms, such that less dependent persons and unmarried persons had lower relapse rates if they were drinking rather than abstaining. Notice also that there is no overall main effect for nonsymptom drinking versus long-term abstaining ($t = .59$). Analysis (2) compares nonsymptom drinkers with *all* abstainers (both long-term and short-term). The results are remarkably similar to those of analysis (1).

The regression results in Table 7.7 are fairly difficult to interpret in their present form. A more understandable mode of presentation is to use the coefficients to calculate estimated relapse rates for various subgroups of interest. We have calculated predicted relapse rates for groupings according to age, marital status, level of dependence symptoms, and drinking status. These variables show the strongest and most consistent relationships with relapse at 4 years in both analyses, as well as being the theoretically most important relationships.

The predicted relapse rates for the model comparing long-term abstainers with nonsymptom drinkers are shown in Table 7.8. We note that older men with high levels of dependence symptoms at admission had much lower expected relapse rates if they abstained rather than drank without symptoms at 18 months, regardless of marital status. On the other hand, for younger men with low levels of dependence symptoms, the situation was reversed: abstainers had higher expected relapse rates than nonsymptom drinkers,

---

[4]Both linear and logit regression analyses were calculated, but we shall present and discuss only the logit models, because they are the preferred method of regression for binary variables.

Table 7.7   Logit Regression Analyses Predicting Relapse at 4 Years[a]

Independent Variable[d]	(1) 6-Month Abstainers versus Nonsymptom Drinkers at 18 Months[b]		(2) All Abstainers versus Nonsymptom Drinkers at 18 Months[c]	
	Logit Coefficient	t	Logit Coefficient	t
Main Effects				
Unmarried	.872	1.20	.705	1.76*
Low socioeconomic status	.331	.44	.344	.82
Unemployed (admission)[e]	-.898	-1.09	.094	.24
Unemployed (18 months)[e]	.520	.69	.239	.53
Age 40 or more	-.516	- .81	.176	.43
Nonwhite	.794	.97	.346	.78
Prior treatment	.484	.74	.109	.30
No dependence symptoms	1.313	1.36	-.280	- .35
Low dependence symptoms	.920	1.23	.389	.86
Nonsymptom drinking at 18 months	.887	.59	.374	.30
Interactions with Nonsymptom Drinking				
Unmarried	-1.817	-1.81*	-1.650	-2.07**
Low socioeconomic status	-.073	- .07	-.087	-.10
Unemployed (admission)[e]	2.347	2.00**	1.354	1.47
Unemployed (18 months)[e]	-1.583	-1.24	-1.301	-1.16
Age 40 or more	2.111	2.20**	1.418	1.72*
Nonwhite	-1.040	- .92	-.592	-.67
Prior treatment	.235	.25	.611	.80
No dependence symptoms	-2.749	-2.09**	-1.155	-.96
Low dependence symptoms	-1.891	-1.74*	-1.361	-1.49
Constant	-2.927	-2.85**	-2.414	-3.90**
Linear regression R^2	13.5%		7.2%	

[a]Dependent variable = 1 if the subject had any symptoms during the 30 days before the 4-year followup; 0 otherwise. The logit model is $Y = 1/[1 + \exp(-b'x)]$, where b_i is an element of the vector b.
[b]Model fitted using only the 200 cases who reported either 6 months of abstention or nonsymptom drinking at 18 months.
[c]Model fitted using only the 299 cases who reported 6 months of abstention, 1 to 5 months of abstention, or nonsymptom drinking at 18 months.
[d]Dummy variables, measured at admission to treatment unless otherwise specified.
[e]Unemployed because of disability, institutionalization, or a drinking problem.
*Significant at $p < .10$.
**Significant at $p < .05$.

regardless of martial status. For the other two groups—older men with low dependence symptoms and younger men with high dependence symptoms— the interaction is more complex, with marital status playing an important role: those who were married had lower expected relapse rates if they abstained, whereas the unmarrieds had lower expected relapse rates if they were nonsymptom drinkers.

Do these patterns hold up for all abstainers, including the persons who had just begun to abstain at 18 months? The answer, illustrated in Table 7.9, is a

Table 7.8 Expected Relapse Rates Predicted from the Regression Analysis for 6-Month Abstainers versus Nonsymptom Drinkers at 18 Months

Background Characteristics at Admission	Expected Relapse Rates (Percent Relapsing at 4 Years)[a]			
	Age Under 40 at Admission		Age 40 or Over at Admission	
	Abstaining 6 Months or More at 18 Months	Nonsymptom Drinking at 18 Months	Abstaining 6 Months or More at 18 Months	Nonsymptom Drinking at 18 Months
High Dependence Symptoms[b]				
Married	7	17	4	50
Unmarried	16	7	10	28
Low Dependence Symptoms				
Married	16	7	11	28
Unmarried	32	3	22	13

[a]Relapse rates at four years, based on predictions from a logit regression model fitted using the 200 cases who reported either 6 months of abstention or nonsymptom drinking at 18 months. The model's coefficients are shown in Table 7.7, analysis (1).
[b]High dependence level represents 11 or more symptom events during the 30 days preceding admission to treatment. Low dependence level represents 1 to 10 such events. Subjects with no dependence symptoms at admission are excluded from the table.

180

Table 7.9 Expected Relapse Rates Predicted from the Regression Analysis for All Abstainers versus Nonsymptom Drinkers at 18 Months

| | Expected Relapse Rates (Percent Relapsing at 4 Years)[a] | | | |
| | Age Under 40 at Admission | | Age 40 or Over at Admission | |
Background Characteristics at Admission	Abstaining 1 Month or More at 18 Months	Nonsymptom Drinking at 18 Months	Abstaining 1 Month or More at 18 Months	Nonsymptom Drinking at 18 Months
High Dependence Symptoms[b]				
Married	12	17	14	50
Unmarried	21	7	24	28
Low Dependence Symptoms				
Married	16	7	19	28
Unmarried	29	3	32	13

[a]Relapse rates at four years, based on predictions from a logit regression model fitted using the 299 cases who reported 6 months of abstention, 1 to 5 months of abstention, or nonsymptom drinking at 18 months. The model's coefficients are shown in Table 7.7, analysis (2).
[b]High dependence level represents 11 or more symptom events during the 30 days preceding admission to treatment. Low dependence level represents 1 to 10 such events. Subjects with no dependence symptoms at admission are excluded from the table.

definite *Yes*. In this case, abstention—*including* short-term abstention—has a better prognosis than drinking for older men with high dependence symptoms at admission, but a worse prognosis for younger men with lower dependence symptoms. Likewise, for the other two groups, marital status appears to play a significant role, with abstention yielding a better prognosis for married men but a worse prognosis for unmarried men.

The results in Table 7.9 for all abstainers are important, because they allow a stronger inference about the prognosis for abstention versus nonsymptom drinking; no qualification has to be made regarding attainment of 6 months or more of abstention. Basically, both analyses are consistent in suggesting that older and more dependent men who abstained had lower relapse rates than those who drank with no symptoms. On the other hand, nonsymptom drinking was associated with lower relapse rates among younger and less dependent men, and among most unmarried men as well.

The results of the above analyses are based on a dependent variable at 4 years whose definition is strictly comparable with the definition of status at 18 months. Relapse is therefore indicated by the presence of any dependence symptoms during the month before the followup interview. We also tested the robustness of these findings by using alternative dependent variables that covered the entire 6-month period before the 4-year followup. In such analyses, the dependent variable was defined by the presence of symptoms, or of any drinking problems, among all persons who drank in the 6-month period (thus including short-term abstainers). In various models of that type, significant interactions appeared, involving age and either prior treatment or level of dependence symptoms at admission. Thus, the basic patterns of interaction shown above were confirmed by using a full 6-month period of observation at 4 years.

Theoretical Implications

The results of this new relapse analysis, while different in some respects from the 18-month study, also fail to support the classical deterministic loss of control theory. At best, the newer probabilistic theory receives only scant support from these data. While nonproblem drinkers do have a somewhat higher relapse rate than long-term abstainers, the difference is not statistically significant in most comparisons. Even this modest advantage for long-term abstainers is mitigated if we consider the possibility that the high relapse rate for short-term abstainers could represent the risk of relapse during the early stages of abstention.

These data *are* consistent with a "conditional" loss of control theory, although not one that has appeared in any explicit formulation. First of all, even though certain subject characteristics appear to enhance the risk of relapse for nonproblem drinkers, the rate of relapse is not 100 percent even in the least favorable condition (highly dependent, married, and older). Thus a loss of control theory consistent with these data would have to be both conditional and probabilistic, such that some conditions increase the *probability* of relapse for nonproblem drinkers without making it inevitable.

As to the nature of the conditions, our results are consistent with Edwards' emphasis on alcohol dependence, suggesting that the ability to maintain nonproblem drinking decreases as the severity of dependence increases. The factors of age and marital status may be surrogates for the kinds of mental state or social environment variables cited by Glatt (1967) or Ludwig and Wikler (1974). That is, the chances are that younger and unmarried men are likely to find themselves in milieus where frequent drinking is the norm. The attempt by younger or unmarried alcoholics to maintain abstention in a nonsupportive environment may be sufficiently stressful to make relapse more likely. Moreover, married alcoholics who abstain probably receive considerable support from their spouses; but they may not receive support when they attempt moderate drinking. Because of the widely held belief that alcoholics cannot return to moderate drinking, spouses of alcoholics who try to do so may view them as failures. This attitude may create stress for the alcoholic, eventually contributing to relapse.

While we cannot be certain that our results are explained by these mechanisms, the fact that the prognosis for nonproblem drinking differs among subgroups of alcoholics in our sample suggests important priorities for future research. If the mechanisms that cause differential relapse rates can be identified, or if we can reliably distinguish alcoholics who do adapt better to abstention or to moderate drinking, then the implications for treatment policy could be profound.

STABILITY OF STATUS

The relapse analysis has addressed one particular type of change; namely, a change from a relatively favorable status at one point in time to an unfavorable status at a later time. This does not exhaust all the patterns of change. As Table 7.1 makes clear, many other status changes take place, including changes between two favorable conditions, such as from long-term abstention to nonsymptom drinking, or from an unfavorable status to a more favorable one. Since such changes may be associated with poor adjustment, it seems worthwhile to conduct a brief investigation into the possible determinants of stable versus unstable status. Moreover, there is a certain intuitive appeal in limiting true successes to those alcoholics who not only attain a favorable status, but who remain in that status for long periods of time. Part of our purpose here is to formulate such a classification and to discover whether there are any particular characteristics associated with attainment of a relatively stable status.

Definition of Stable Groups

The turnover table (Table 7.1) forms the basis of our definition of stable status groups. The turnover table is portrayed schematically in Fig. 7.1, along with the identification of the stable and unstable groups to be analyzed in this section. Three stable groups are distinguished. Stable abstainers are persons who have abstained 6 or more months at both the 18-month and 4-year followups. Stable nonsymptom drinkers are those who have occupied that status at both followups. The stable symptom group consists of chronic alcoholics who report drinking with dependence symptoms at both followups.

The three unstable groups are defined somewhat arbitrarily to reflect the potentially more important status they occupied at either followup. Unstable abstainers are those who abstained for 6 months or more at one but not both followups. Unstable nonsymptom drinkers are those who were in that status at one but not both followups, except for long-term abstainers. Short-term

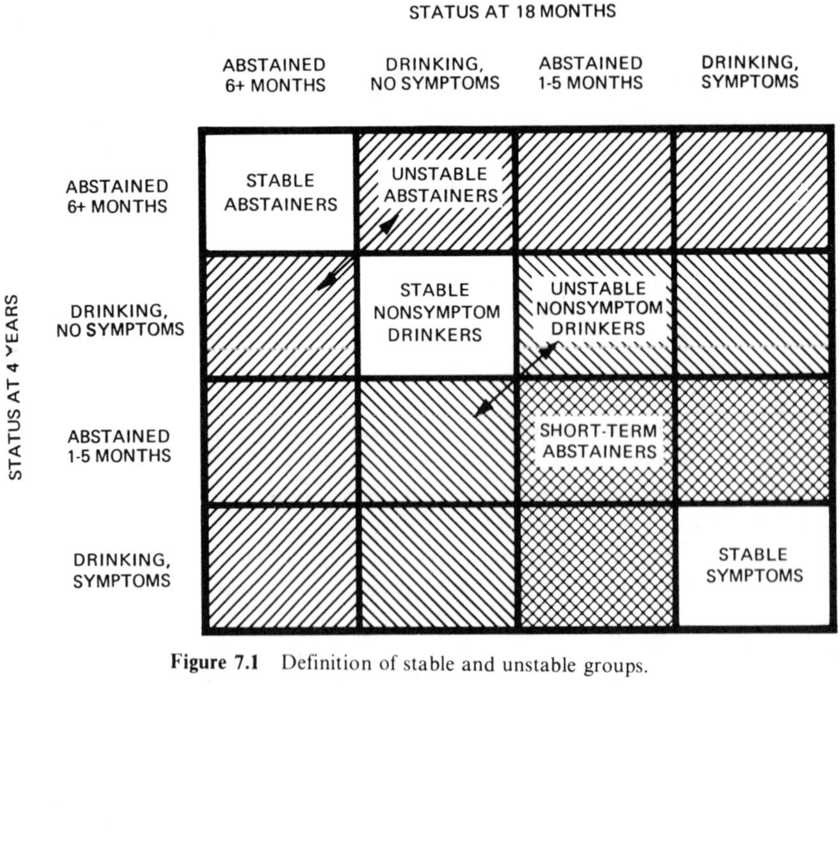

Figure 7.1   Definition of stable and unstable groups.

Table 7.10   Stable and Unstable Groups at the 18-Month and Four-Year Followups

Group	Percent Distribution of Cases	(N)
Stable abstainers	13	(63)
Unstable abstainers		
Abstainers/nonsymptom drinkers[a]	6	(31)
Other unstable abstainers	20	(97)
Stable, nonsymptom drinkers	9	(45)
Unstable, nonsymptom drinkers	15	(75)
Short-term abstainers	16	(75)
Stable, symptom drinkers	20	(94)

[a]Persons classified as long-term abstainers at one point and as nonsymptom drinkers at the other point.

abstainers are those who occupied that status at one or both followups, except for long-term abstainers and nonsymptom drinkers. In view of the seemingly inherent instability of the short-term abstainers, we do not distinguish a stable subgroup for this status.

The number and percentage of persons in each stable and unstable group is given in Table 7.10. One is immediately aware of the relatively small number of persons in the two favorable stable groups. There are only 63 stable abstainers (13 percent of the sample) and 45 stable nonsymptom drinkers (9 percent). A small subgroup of unstable abstainers (6 percent of the sample) shifted from abstaining to nonproblem drinking or vice versa, and thus were in remission at both followups. However, the *form* of remission was not constant for these people, and we found that they were not different from other unstable abstainers on any of our major variables. Therefore, they are not classified as stable according to this definition.

The results in Table 7.10 reemphasize the unstable character of alcoholic remission in this sample. The total number of stable abstainers and stable nonsymptom drinkers barely exceeds the number of chronic alcoholics in the stable symptom group, whereas nearly 60 percent of the sample is in one or another unstable status. Instability of drinking patterns clearly predominates in this cohort.

It must be emphasized that the groups we have labeled "stable" may not have remained in the same status for the entire period between the two followups, since the window of observation at each followup can be as short as 1 month. Nonetheless, we do know that most "stable abstainers," as defined in Table 7.10, in fact abstained most of the time in the full 4-year period; similarly, most of the "stable drinkers" had been drinking throughout the 4 years without serious incidents.[5] Any attempt to refine the groups further would reduce the number of cases to the point where our comparative analysis would be weakened.

Correlates of Stable Status

Although the number of persons with favorable stability patterns is small, it still may be of interest to investigate possible determinants and correlates of these two statuses compared with those of all other groups. We have examined selected characteristics at admission, as well as some physical and psychological characteristics at the 4-year followup.

Those background characteristics that have been used throughout this study in multivariate predictions of favorable status are tabulated in Table 7.11. Two general observations can be made. First, the stable abstainers are not at all distinguishable from the unstable abstainers or from most of the other unstable groups. Second, the stable nonsymptom drinkers do stand out from all other groups in several respects. Although most were heavy drinkers at admission, a lower proportion fell into the very heavy category of 5 or more ounces of ethanol on drinking days (38 percent compared with about 70 for the other groups). Similarly, although most stable nonsymptom drinkers showed signs of alcohol dependence at admission, the number of symptoms was lower than for all other groups. Finally, the stable nonsymptom drinkers showed less unemployment, were somewhat younger, and had less prior treatment than the other groups. Thus, attainment of stable nonsymptom drinking appears to be more likely for the less impaired, less chronic alcoholics in our sample. In this respect, these results are quite consistent with the picture we obtained from the relapse analysis, which suggested that nonsymptom drinking might be more viable for younger or less impaired alcoholics.

We also subjected these variables to regression analysis, first using stable abstainers versus all other groups as the dependent variable, and second using stable nonsymptom drinkers versus all others as the dependent variable. The results generally support the conclusions we have drawn from Table 7.11.

Finally, Table 7.12 presents some relationships with several health variables measured at the 4-year followup. Generally, the two favorable stable groups show somewhat better adjustment and fewer health problems, especially in

---

[5]The long-term pattern definition developed in the next section shows that about 70 percent of the stable abstainers had patterns of predominant abstention over the 4-year period, and 80 percent of the stable nonsymptom drinkers were predominant drinkers without multiple alcohol-related incidents. However, this does not mean that the "stable" groups were *continuously* stable over 4 years. In fact, only 7 percent of the sample abstained throughout the 4-year period from admission to the followup. An additional 7 percent were free of serious alcohol incidents over the 4 years *and* were stable nonproblem drinkers (as defined at both followups).

Table 7.11 Background Characteristics of Stable and Unstable Groups

Background Characteristics at Admission	Percent with the Characteristic					
	Stable Abstainers	Unstable Abstainers	Stable Nonsymptom Drinkers	Unstable Nonsymptom Drinkers	Short-Term Abstainers	Stable Symptom Drinkers
Consumption on drinking days						
2-4.9 oz.	10	11	44	21	11	15
5 oz. or more	71	78	38	65	73	75
Dependence symptom score						
Low (1-10)	22	16	40	19	11	12
High (11 or more)	73	75	33	66	87	84
Over 15 years of heavy drinking	42	40	40	35	40	47
Low socioeconomic status	35	41	31	44	47	60
Unemployed	46	56	27	51	71	63
Divorced or separated	29	39	27	27	51	42
Age 40 or more	79	65	53	65	71	66
Prior treatment	43	43	13	28	65	47
White	78	71	87	70	76	62
(N)	(63)	(128)	(45)	(73)	(75)	(94)

187

Table 7.12 Physical and Psychological Health Characteristics of Stable and Unstable Groups

Health Characteristics at 4 Years	Percent with the Characteristic					
	Stable Abstainers	Unstable Abstainers	Stable Nonsymptom Drinkers	Unstable Nonsymptom Drinkers	Short-Term Abstainers	Stable Symptom Drinkers
Cirrhosis	13	7	4	12	9	7
Two or more health problems[a]	30	29	23	44	60	65
Low life satisfaction	13	21	0	33	35	46
Poor psychiatric functioning[b]	13	24	9	38	45	52

[a]Occurrence in the past 6 months of anemia, weakness in limbs, numbness in legs, dizziness, loss of balance, or fractures.
[b]Based on five psychiatric symptoms: depression, anhedonia (lack of enjoyment), tension or stress, anxiety, and cognitive impairment, as defined in Appendix D.

comparison with the short-term abstainers and the stable symptom group. As such, the results here are really no different from those presented in Chapters 3 and 4 based on an analysis of the 4-year status groups. Long-term abstainers and nonsymptom drinkers at 4 years generally have the most favorable pattern of physical, social, and psychological correlates.

LONG-TERM PATTERN OF DRINKING

The snapshot measurements of drinking status at 4 years and 18 months provide the greatest available detail on drinking behaviors over a limited period of time. It is necessary to examine behavior in such detail in order to obtain useful information about everyday life experiences, using, so to speak, a close-up lens. On the other hand, we must recognize that in so doing we have been focusing on very small samples of time. Even if these time periods are representative of the larger patterns of experience over the 4 years since treatment, the close-up technique may not reveal the outlines of life history in the way that an overall summary would. A broader measure could reveal, for example, the extent to which a subject's "status at 4 years"—his behavior over the 6 months before the followup interview—reflects his total history since admission to treatment. In this section, we report one such summary measure of long-term patterns of drinking among alcoholics.

The four-year followup questionnaire contained three question sequences eliciting information useful for determining long-term drinking patterns. These sequences enquired into the subject's abstention, levels of consumption, and serious incidents related to drinking during the entire period from the approximate date of admission (January 1973) through a point 4 years later (December 1976). The time frame for measurement of long-term patterns thus covered approximately a 4-year period.

In contrast, the period that we have used for our "point assessment" of drinking ("status at 4 years") was the 6 months preceding the followup interview. This 6-month period generally spanned the time frame during the early or middle portion of 1977, because followup interviews were conducted from the middle to the latter part of 1977. Therefore, the 6-month time frame used for assessing status at 4 years was *independent* of the 4-year time frame used for assessing long-term pattern. (This relationship was depicted graphically in Fig. 3.1 in Chapter 3.)[6]

---

[6]Technically, the "4-year period" for assessing long-term pattern, as stated in the questionnaire, covered all dates inclusive from January 1973 through December 1976. This is not quite the same as the period from admission to the end of 1976, because the cohort members were actually admitted to treatment during the 4 months from January through April 1973. Strictly speaking, the "4-year period" actually covers a period of 45 to 48 months, depending on the month in which the particular individual was admitted. Therefore, for those long-term pattern questions in which

Our discussion of long-term patterns of drinking will proceed in three parts. First, we will develop the individual elements of the long-term pattern measure (amount of abstention, alcohol consumption pattern, and alcohol-related incidents over the 4-year period). Second, we will explain a composite measure of a subject's long-term drinking pattern, based on these three elements. Third, we will examine the relationship between the composite measure of long-term pattern and the "point" measure of the subject's drinking status at 4 years.

Amount of Abstention Over Four Years

The first of three elements in a subject's long-term drinking pattern is a classification of abstention periods reported by the subject over the 4-year time frame (1973–1976). Each subject was asked to specify all periods during which he had abstained for *3 months or more* in a row; the beginning and ending month for each such period was obtained. Thus, some subjects reported one long abstention period (occasionally, the entire 4 years); some reported a few shorter ones; and some reported just one short period or none at all.

Table 7.13 shows the distribution of the *total* number of abstaining months reported and the percentage of each abstention group that fell in the most impaired category at 4 years (the group having both symptoms and consequences). The rightmost column shows the distribution of cases, making it clear that most people reported relatively few months of abstaining.[7] In particular, only 48 cases (9 percent of the sample) reported abstaining for all 48 months of the period, although many more reported abstaining between 24 and 47 months. The prognosis for these patterns may be judged by the numbers of each abstention category who were in the symptoms and consequences group at the later point of "status at 4 years." Note that the prognosis is fairly poor for alcoholics abstaining for fewer than 18 months of

---

specific dates were relevant (alcohol incidents and abstention periods), only events occurring after admission were counted.

A second technical complication arises from the fact that some respondents were interviewed in late May or June of 1977. For them, the 6-month period assessing "status at 4 years" included a portion of the months of November and/ or December 1976. For such respondents, this led to a slight overlap in the periods included in the long-term pattern and status at 4 years. However, only two such people reported any relevant events during the last 2 months of 1976, and excluding them from the analysis did not change any of the results significantly. For simplicity, they were included in the tables.

[7]Note that this is not a *complete* count of abstaining months over the 4 years, but rather a count of abstaining months that occurred within a 3-month contiguous period of abstention. Periods of less than 3 months' duration are probably insignificant, since our data show that short-term abstention almost always represents an unstable and unfavorable state.

Table 7.13 Status at Four Years, by Total Amount of
Abstention Over Four-Year Period

Total Months of Abstention During 4 Years[a]	Status at 4 Years[b] (Percent with Symptoms and Consequences)	(N)
0-5	47	(239)
6-11	42	(66)
12-17	47	(58)
18-23	30	(40)
24-35	18	(51)
36-47	11	(46)
48[c]	4	(48)
Total	36	(548)

[a]Counting all periods of abstention lasting at least 3 months between admission to treatment (early 1973) and December 1976.
[b]Drinking status during the 6 months before the 4-year followup interview (1977).
[c]Subjects who abstained during all months between admission to treatment and December 1976. Because some of them drank during 1977, it was possible for them to experience dependence symptoms or consequences in 1977.

the 4-year period (less than 40 percent of the time), and the prognosis improves markedly for alcoholics abstaining for 24 months or more (at least half of the total time).

It is possible that the significant factor in abstention is not the total amount of it in a period, but rather the prolongation of an abstention period. If this hypothesis were correct, a given amount of abstention occurring in a single consecutive set of months should show a better outcome than would two or three shorter abstention periods that sum to the same amount. For example, consider one person who abstains for 18 months consecutively, compared with a second person who abstains for 6 months, then drinks, then abstains for 12 months. The hypothesis would predict that the first individual, having shown the capacity for very long-term abstention, would fare better in later life. Table 7.14 shows that this is generally not so. Both such cases would fall into the 12 to 23 months' category of total abstention; the first would have a "single period" whereas the second would have "broken periods." Yet their probabilities of serious problems at the 4-year followup would be essentially the same (40 versus 39 percent). There is a modest difference between the broken- versus single-period abstainers for those whose total absention time is 24 months or more, but this difference is small compared with the variations due to total amounts of abstention. We conclude, then, that favorable

Table 7.14   Status at Four Years, by Abstention Patterns Over a Four-Year Period

Abstention Pattern	Status at 4 Years (Percent with Symptoms and Consequences)	(N)
0-5 months total	47	(239)
6-11 months total	42	(66)
12-23 months total, broken periods	39	(51)
12-23 months total, single period	40	(47)
24-47 months total, broken periods	19	(47)
24-47 months total, single period	10	(50)
48 months total	4	(48)

prognosis is indicated principally by the attainment of at least 2 years' worth of abstention over the 4-year-period. Whether the total abstention amount comes from a single period or from multiple periods of abstention is relatively unimportant.

Long-Term Consumption Patterns

As we have seen in Chapter 3, measurement of consumption is a highly complex affair. Therefore, summarizing the variation in consumption over 4 years is a formidable task. To attempt such a summary, the followup questionnaire asked about two different types of drinking levels, designated as times "when you were drinking heavily" and times "when you were drinking but *not* heavily" (questions 64 and 65, Client Interview, Appendix E). The respondent was left to define the meaning of "heavily" and "not heavily," but the questionnaire ascertained the quantity per day he meant by those two terms. He was also free to deny that he ever drank heavily or to say that he always drank heavily. As an example, one subject said he drank one fifth of whiskey per day when he was drinking heavily (11 ounces of ethanol) but only a pint (6.9 ounces of ethanol) when he was not drinking heavily. These quantities were recorded and were available to characterize his two differing modes of consumption. Respondents were also asked to describe the length and number of their heavy-drinking periods over the 4 years.

Our analysis showed that valuable information could be gleaned from these questions by classifying the consistency or variation between the "heavy" and "nonheavy" quantities. Each quantity (Heavy Q and Nonheavy Q) was classified according to whether it exceeded the cutoff of 5 ounces or more; if so, that quantity was treated as "heavy" for analysis purposes. The individual's drinking pattern was then classified as follows:

Consistent Nonheavy Pattern.   Both Heavy Q and Nonheavy Q under 5 ounces; i.e., drinking was consistently reported as less than 5 ounces.

Consistent Heavy Pattern.   Both Heavy Q and Nonheavy Q over 5 ounces; i.e., drinking was always reported as more than 5 ounces even when described by the subject as "not heavy."

Mixed Pattern.   One Q over 5 ounces and the other Q under 5 ounces; i.e., some but not all drinking met a 5-ounce limit.

The distribution of these patterns in our sample is shown in Table 7.15. There are relatively few alcoholics who met even the generous limit of 5 ounces for the "consistent nonheavy" pattern over the 4-year period (only 85 cases, or 17 percent of the total sample). However, these people also tend to have fairly low rates of alcohol problems at the point of the 4-year followup. The problem rates at the followup are highest for persons who report *frequent* heavy consumption during the preceding 4 years (i.e., frequently drinking at very high absolute levels). The frequency of heavy-drinking periods also makes a notable difference for those with "mixed" consumption patterns. The people who showed mixed patterns with infrequent heavy periods (less than 90 days over 4 years) had a prognosis almost as favorable as that for people who showed consistently nonheavy drinking. In further analysis, we have therefore combined the "mixed infrequent" category with the "consistent nonheavy"

Table 7.15   Status at Four Years, by Alcohol Consumption Over Four Years

Consumption Over 4 Years (1973-1976)		Status at 4 Years (Percent with Symptoms and Consequences)	(N)
Drinking Pattern	Frequency of Heavy Drinking Periods[a]		
Consistent nonheavy[b]	Infrequent	14	(62)
	Frequent	17	(23)
Mixed	Infrequent	23	(113)
	Frequent	43	(93)
Consistent heavy[c]	Infrequent	36	(80)
	Frequent	57	(139)
Total		37	(510)

[a]"Frequent" = total of 90 or more days in "heavy" drinking periods over the 4 years.
[b]Quantity of ethanol consumed during both "heavy" drinking periods and "nonheavy" drinking periods was less than 5 ounces per drinking day.
[c]Quantity consumed during both "heavy" drinking periods and "nonheavy" drinking periods was 5 ounces or more per drinking day.

group, and the "mixed, frequent" category with the "consistent heavy" group. The two resulting groupings are referred to in the following analysis as "Lower Amount" and "Higher Amount" patterns of consumption.

Alcohol Incidents Over Four Years

A third area of long-term drinking patterns assessed in the 4-year followup instrument was that of serious alcohol-related incidents. Each respondent was asked in the followup interview whether he had experienced any of a series of family, health, work, or job problems because of alcohol between 1973 and 1976. These are *different* from the measures of "adverse consequences" that were used in defining status at 4 years. In our terminology, "adverse consequences" are specific drinking problems enumerated during the 6-month period preceding the followup (1977). "Alcohol incidents" are drinking problems that occurred during the time from 1973 through 1976, as measured from general open-ended questions (Client Interview, questions 66–69, Appendix E).

The month and year of each incident were coded, along with the type of incident. For the analysis of alcohol incidents, only fairly serious events were examined; e.g., we counted an arrest, a spouse's threat to leave, or a dismissal from a job as serious, but we did not count a hangover at work or a series of family arguments as serious. (For scoring details, see Appendix D). Incidents occurring before July 1973 were excluded in order to omit any events that might have been associated with admission to treatment. Provisionally, we adopted the standard of treating two or more such incidents in the 3.5-year period from July 1973 through December 1976 as an indication of chronic problems.

Column (1) of Table 7.16 shows the percentage of the sample experiencing multiple alcohol incidents (two or more) as a function of total abstention and long-term consumption patterns. The relationship is quite strong, showing that both higher-amount consumption patterns and lower total months of abstention are associated with multiple alcohol incidents. Column (2) shows that drinking status at 4 years is also related to the consumption and abstention patterns. Nor is this association simply a result of a possible tendency for some respondents to artifactually report all types of problems with alcohol. That it is not is shown by column (3), which indicates any occurrence of a reentry to inpatient treatment at the ATC during the same 3.5-year period. The data on ATC treatment reentries are *not* derived from self-reports; they come from the monthly treatment records of the ATC monitoring system. Hence, they provide an independent check on our long-term pattern data. (We take the occurrence of reentry into inpatient treatment as an unequivocal indication of relapse.) The data show that treatment

Table 7.16 Characteristics of Abstention and Consumption Patterns Over Four Years

Patterns Over 4 Years: 1973-1976		Characteristics of Patterns			
Abstention, Total Months	Consumption Pattern	(1) Multiple Incidents (Percent with 2 or More)[a]	(2) Status at 4 Years (Percent with Symptoms and Consequences)[b]	(3) Reentry to ATC Treatment (Percent)[c]	(N)
48	None	2	4	6	(48)
24-47	Lower amount	22	18	32	(40)
	Higher amount	26	13	48	(54)
12-23	Lower amount	12	24	32	(34)
	Higher amount	44	50	60	(62)
0-11	Lower amount	21	20	24	(114)
	Higher amount	47	62	40	(177)

[a]Alcohol incidents involving serious family, work, health, or legal problems between July 1973 and December 1976. (See definition in Appendix D).

[b]Subjects reporting symptoms and consequences during the 6-month period before the 4-year followup interview (1977).

[c]Reentry to hospital treatment at the ATC between July 1973 and December 1976, determined from ATC monitoring system data. Reentry is defined as the occurrence of a month with recorded ATC hospital or detoxification treatment preceded by a month with no ATC treatment.

195

reentries over the period are indeed correlated with the abstention and drinking reports given by the respondents.

Definition of Long-Term Pattern of Alcohol Behavior

The preceding elements of drinking behavior over 4 years may be combined into an overall classification of each subject's long-term pattern of alcohol behavior. The classification we employed is shown in Table 7.17. It is a typology based on reasonable breaking-points on the three variables just discussed: abstention, consumption pattern, and alcohol incidents. The two behavior patterns that appear clearest are shown at the top and bottom of the table. Shown at the top is the category of subjects who abstained throughout the 4-year period, designated as "continuous abstainers."[8] Those among the drinkers who reported multiple incidents are segregated from all others in the bottom portion of the table. These people are so classified, regardless of their abstention or consumption amounts, on grounds that multiple incidents indicate a chronic pattern of problems with alcohol. In fact, further subdivisions according to drinking behavior showed that most of these multiple-incident subjects reported higher-amount consumption patterns combined with low amounts of abstention. Among the remainder of the cases, subgroups are disaggregated according to (a) whether they reported 24 months or more of abstention, and (b) whether they reported a lower-amount pattern of consumption as opposed to a higher-amount pattern over the 4-year period.

The percentage distribution demonstrates the high degree of impairment and the chronic character of the alcohol problems suffered by a large part of this sample. Only 9 percent of the treatment admissions reported abstaining for as long as 48 months after admission. An additional 5 percent reported predominant abstention (abstaining at least half of the time) combined with a lower-amount pattern of consumption when drinking. At the other end of the problem continuum, 43 percent reported multiple alcohol incidents during the period. There is, however, a substantial group of cases who reported consumption patterns of lower amounts without repeated incidents, even though they were drinking during most of the 4-year period.

Relationship Between Long-Term Pattern and Status at Four Years

One may wonder, in light of this, how consistent are the long-term patterns compared with the assessments made at the 4-year followup point? Clearly, there is a considerable amount of adverse alcohol-related history in this

---

[8]Note that not all of these "continuous abstainers" in the "long-term pattern" period abstained throughout the entire period from admission through the 4-year followup (a length of 4.5 years). Some of them abstained for 4 years, but drank in 1977 before the followup interview took place.

Table 7.17 Long-Term Pattern of Alcohol Behavior[a]

Term	Definition	Percent Distribution
Continuous abstention over 4 years	Abstained all 48 months	9
Predominant abstention, lower amounts of consumption	Abstained 24-47 months Lower amounts of consumption; 0 or 1 drinking incidents	5
Predominant abstention, higher amounts of consumption	Abstained 24-47 months Higher amounts of consumption; 0 or 1 drinking incidents	5
Predominant drinking, lower amounts of consumption	Abstained less than 24 months Lower amounts of consumption; 0 or 1 drinking incidents	20
Predominant drinking, higher amounts of consumption	Abstained less than 24 months Higher amounts of consumption; 0 or 1 drinking incidents	18
Multiple incidents[b]	2 drinking incidents	13
	3 or more drinking incidents	30
(N)		(537)

[a]Patterns of drinking and alcohol incidents over a 4-year period (1973-1976).
[b]Including both self-reported incidents (see Appendix D) and inpatient treatment reentries.

Table 7.18 Long-Term Pattern, by Drinking Status at Four Years

| | | Percent Distribution of Long-Term Pattern (1973-1976) | | | | | |
| | | Predominant Abstention | | Predominant Drinking | | | |
Drinking Status at 4 Years (1977)	Continuous Abstention	Lower Amounts of Consumption	Higher Amounts of Consumption	Lower Amounts of Consumption	Higher Amounts of Consumption	Multiple Incidents	(N)
Abstention	26	6	15	3	10	40	(154)
Low Q	8	12	0	60	8	12	(40)
High Q	0	6	2	51	16	25	(55)
Consequences	0	7	0	34	7	52	(29)
Symptoms	4	3	3	37	27	26	(67)
Symptoms and consequences	1	2	2	9	25	61	(192)

sample. What does this history tell us about the meaning of the status categories at the time of the 4-year followup? The device of measuring long-term patterns over a time frame that was nonoverlapping with the followup status period allows us to answer these questions. We can classify each case according to the subject's long-term pattern and also according to his status at 4 years. Table 7.18 shows this cross-classification in a way that emphasizes the history of each followup status category. For each drinking-status group defined at the 4-year followup (1977), the table shows the percentage falling in each category of long-term pattern (1973–1976). In this table, we have combined the two subgroups of abstainers that have previously been distinguished in the classification of status at 4 years (6- to 11-month abstainers and 12-month or more abstainers), because the 12-month or more category would have a logical dependency on long-term pattern. In classifying drinking status at 4 years for this analysis, we simply placed anyone abstaining for the whole 6-month period in 1977 in an "abstention" category.

The association between followup status and long-term drinking pattern is notable. There are remarkably different patterns of life history among particular groups that were defined at the 4-year followup. One important finding concerns the history of current abstainers (defined as of 1977). Only 26 percent of them abstained throughout the preceding 4 years; fully 40 percent had a history of multiple incidents during that period. Most of the other abstainers said that although they had fewer than two incidents, when they drank they usually consumed high amounts of alcohol (over 5 ounces per day). This reflects the tendency for many abstainers to oscillate back and forth between abstention on the one hand and very heavy problem drinking on the other.

It is apparent that the Low Q and High Q groups, as defined at 4 years, were disproportionately concentrated in historical patterns of less extreme drinking. These two groups, who reported no concrete problems at the 4-year followup, tended also to show histories of lower drinking levels with fewer incidents. The persons defined as Low Q at 4 years, for example, had a very low historical rate of incidents, and an unusually high number of them drank at levels of less than 5 ounces over the 4-year period. Both the Low Q and High Q groups also reported that most of the 4-year period was taken up by periods of relatively low consumption rather than by abstention periods. At 4 years, then, the current nonproblem drinkers tended toward histories of fairly regular drinking at proportionately lower consumption levels, with fewer cases of oscillation between drinking problems and abstention than were found among current abstainers.

These results are far from definitive, since they rest on retrospective data covering a very long time period. However, given the extent of adverse conditions indicated by these long-term patterns, we are struck by the persistence of alcoholism that these data imply. There appear to be groups within the sample who abstained for several years or who drank for years at nonalcoholic levels with minimal problems. However, those groups do not constitute a majority. These data, by and large, confirm the patterns observed in the point-to-point relapse analysis: although there is frequent improvement, there is also frequent relapse and much instability.

EIGHT

Conclusions

Alcoholism is a multifaceted and highly variable disorder. The results of this study make it clear that the *course* of alcoholism over time is equally variable. There is no single pattern, and no definite path, characterizing the 4-year history of the alcoholics in this study. Instead, we find frequent remission, frequent relapse, and diverse forms of behavior among alcoholics. Our conclusions about the course of alcoholism depend on recognizing these multidimensional and highly diverse features of alcoholic behavior.

The 4-year followup study is well suited, in a number of ways, to address and measure the multiple aspects of alcoholic behavior. First, we have followed a large, nationally representative cohort of alcoholics over 4 years: from admission to treatment, through an 18-month followup, to a 4-year followup. At 4 years, information was obtained from 85 percent of a cohort of 922 male patients randomly drawn from eight Alcoholism Treatment Centers funded by NIAAA. Our conclusions about the course of alcoholism rest on the data available from these two independent followup points.

Second, our picture of alcoholic behavior is rounded out by the presence of systematically collected information on the type, amount, and timing of ATC treatment. These data, coupled with the reports of other treatment obtained from subjects, permit quantitative assessment of the intensity of treatment in an alcoholic population. In addition, we have data on psychological functioning, social adjustment, and mortality, covering a broad range of the phenomena associated with alcoholism.

Our principal purpose has been to trace the "natural history" of an alcoholic cohort over 4 years. Although all of our subjects had some experience with treatment, the particular treatments were not given according to an experimental plan, and the objective was not to evaluate competing treatment methods rigorously. Rather, we are examining the natural sequence of events and experiences that typify the lives of alcoholics who come into contact with treatment institutions. Although we have traced the interplay of treatment experience with other variables, our focus has been on patterns of adjustment and behavior, especially drinking behavior, as they develop over the long term.

201

It is essential to recognize both the strengths and limitations of a natural-history study. Compared with small-scale experimental studies, a longitudinal natural history of a large cohort, such as the present one, has great advantages in generalizability and scope. The data reflect the experiences of a representative group of alcoholics associated with real treatment institutions, without the potentially artificial characteristics that often accompany special experiments. On the other hand, the natural-history framework carries certain limitations. Foremost among them is the need for caution in applying the findings to intervention strategies. Our findings are descriptive statements about how alcoholics behave. They are not prescriptive statements about desirable behavior, nor are they direct guidelines for treatment. Outcomes in a natural history can be affected by various influences—such as a tendency for subjects to select themselves for different treatments or behavior patterns—that might not be present in an actual treatment program. Although a natural history can suggest alternative strategies for intervention or treatment, it cannot show unambiguously what the outcomes of such strategies would be.

There is little question that the study sample was highly impaired by alcohol at the time of admission to treatment. Median alcohol consumption in the group was 8.7 ounces of ethanol (about 17 drinks) per drinking day, and only 8 percent reported drinking without symptoms of alcohol dependence. The adverse effects of alcohol consumption were also evident in the cohort's social characteristics; for example, 37 percent were divorced or separated at admission, and only 40 percent were employed. In this study, we have termed the subjects "alcoholics" because they were admitted to clinical treatment for the disorder. The baseline data also make it clear that this sample was comparable to other groups labeled alcoholic. In particular, the subject's background characteristics were similar to those of patients drawn from a representative sample of alcoholism treatment institutions throughout the United States, both public and private. Nonetheless, the study did not include alcoholics being treated by private physicians, nor did it include any subjects who were entirely untreated. Therefore, generalizations beyond a population of clinically treated alcoholics are not warranted.

In this chapter, we will collect our findings into an overall assessment of the course of alcoholism after treatment. We will present conclusions about drinking behavior at 4 years; the nature of mortality; the character of psychosocial functioning; the extent and impact of treatment; the patterns of stability and relapse; and the implications for further research and policy.

DRINKING BEHAVIOR AT FOUR YEARS

The principal means of assessing alcoholism at the 4-year followup has been our definition of "drinking status at 4 years." This measure classifies the survivors, who constitute 85 percent of the initial cohort, into seven categories of drinking status based on their behavior during the 6 months before the 4-year followup interview. The results showed, first of all, that 21 percent of the survivor sample abstained for 1 year or more at the followup. An additional 7 percent abstained for 6 months or more, but not as long as 1 year. Because our evaluation point was the 6-month period before the followup, these people were not further classified according to drinking behavior. However, it is crucial to note that they are not, for the most part, continuous abstainers. In fact, only one-third of the 1-year abstainers, or 7 percent of the total sample, abstained throughout the period from treatment admission until the 4-year followup.

Among subjects who drank in the 6-month period, drinking patterns were extremely diverse. Our analysis led us to distinguish two principal types of drinkers: those who experienced problems caused by alcohol, and those who did not. Problems were defined as either *symptoms of alcohol dependence* or serious *adverse consequences of drinking.* The alcohol dependence symptoms, which play a central role in much of the history of this cohort, included such events as signs of withdrawal, loss of control over drinking, and alcoholic blackouts. Such symptoms not only signify physical and psychological impairment from alcohol, but also indicate an underlying condition of dependence that resists any improvement in alcoholic drinking patterns. Adverse consequences included such damaging events as alcohol-related illness, medical treatment or hospitalization, arrest, unemployment, and interpersonal problems growing out of present drinking. Thirty-six percent of our sample exhibited dependence symptoms *and* consequences at the followup, thereby constituting our most impaired category. An additional 12 percent showed symptoms without any measured consequences, and 6 percent showed consequences in the absence of symptoms. Altogether, then, the two types of serious alcohol problems characterized 54 percent of the survivors at the 4-year followup.

The remainder of the drinkers, encompassing 18 percent of the survivor sample, were treated as "drinking without problems." These persons were entirely free of any reported dependence symptoms or adverse consequences of drinking during the 6-month period before followup. There was considerable variability in the amount of alcohol consumption in this group. To indicate that variation, we further subclassified nonproblem drinkers into *low consumers,* people consistently drinking less than 2 ounces of ethanol per day (59 ml, about 4 drinks), and *high consumers,* people who exceeded that limit. Limits on the low-consumption group were fairly strict: to be so classified, a subject had to report drinking less than 2 ounces on a typical drinking day, and also report no days on which his consumption exceeded 3 ounces during a representative 30-day sample of recent drinking. By this classification, 8 percent of the sample were classified as consistently low consumers, and 10 percent as high consumers. Among high consumers, the median amount of consumption was about 3 ounces per drinking day (about 6 drinks), with three-fourths of the high consumers drinking between 2 and 5 ounces per drinking day. High consumers thus exhibit some heavy drinking, but not the extreme level of alcohol consumption that characterized this sample at admission. (At that time, median consumption was over 8 ounces of ethanol per day).

Although the rate of drinking problems in this sample was fairly high at the 4-year point, these results nevertheless indicate substantial improvement since the time that the cohort was admitted to treatment. At that time, over 90 percent were drinking with serious problems, compared with 54 percent 4 years later. However, the extent to which this change could be attributed to the ATC treatment regimen is not clear. Groups that had as little as a single contact with the treatment center showed significant amounts of improvement, though not as much as that shown by those more intensively treated. It is possible that the period before admission to treatment was a time of extreme drinking problems for many of the alcoholics in the sample. If so, one would expect those alcoholics to improve substantially at any later followup, simply because of natural fluctuations or statistical "regression to the mean." Therefore, at least part of the improvement of the cohort between admission and followup could be due to nontreatment factors.

Basis of the Classification of Drinking Status

The definitions imposed in measuring drinking status and drinking problems were not arbitrary, nor were they the same as those used in the 18-month studies of this cohort. Many aspects of the new classification were derived from longitudinal analysis of the subsequent risks attached to different drinking patterns at the 18-month followup. This was accomplished by examining the rates of alcohol problems occurring at the 4-year followup among groups classified according to their drinking patterns at the 18-month point. Three significant conclusions can be drawn from those analyses.

First, the longitudinal data clearly indicated that alcohol dependence symptoms after treatment portend an unfavorable prognosis. People with dependence symptoms at 18 months, even those with low levels, were much more likely than others to experience later adverse effects of drinking, including continued dependence, negative consequences of drinking, and alcohol-related death. This finding supports the view of the recent World Health Organization committee (Edwards et al., 1977b) in suggesting that alcohol dependence is of great importance in understanding the persistence of damaging drinking among alcoholics. Dependence symptoms, of course, are widely recognized by research and clinical workers as tools for diagnosis. We found our symptom measures to be highly interrelated empirically, forming a distinct cluster of items signaling an adverse prognosis. Finally, several different analyses imply that even infrequent symptoms represent a heightened risk of future problems. Accordingly, our definition of status at 4 years treated infrequent occurrence of symptoms as evidence of a continuing alcohol problem.

Second, our analyses point to the ambiguity of abstention as a remission pattern, particularly with regard to "short-term abstention." We separated people who were abstaining at the 18-month point into two groups: short-term abstainers, those who were currently abstaining but who had been drinking at some time in the past 6 months; and long-term abstainers, those who had abstained for at least as long as 6 months. The prognosis for these two groups was considerably different. Compared with short-term abstainers, long-term abstainers had much lower rates of future consequences, symptoms, or alcohol-related deaths. In particular, the rate of alcohol-related deaths among short-term abstainers was 9 percent, compared with 1 percent for long-term abstainers. In addition, the recent history of short-term abstainers was marked by frequent and severe alcohol problems. During their last drinking period, short-term abstainers had higher drinking levels and experienced greater problems than current drinkers.

Moreover, short-term and long-term abstainers differed substantially in their stability levels. Fifty-five percent of long-term abstainers at 18 months were also classified as long-term abstainers at the 4-year followup. By contrast, only 35 percent of the short-term abstainers at 18 months were found to be long-term abstainers at 4 years, and only 15 percent had abstained throughout the period from 18 months to 4 years. In short, only a minority of short-term abstainers appeared to be starting a long-term abstention period; by the 4-year point, most of them had relapsed into alcoholic drinking. Given the recent drinking problems, the high mortality rate, and the high degree of instability that characterized this group, it would be inappropriate to regard short-term abstention as a form of remission.

This poses a difficult problem of alternative interpretations. On the one hand, short-term abstainers could constitute a group quite different from long-term abstainers. In that case, short-term abstainers might be seen simply as a special, unstable group alternating between brief periods of abstention and serious drinking episodes. One the other hand, the behavior of short-term abstainers could represent a phase of higher risks that accompany the initial period of abstention. In that case, all abstainers would have to pass through an early phase of abstention, with a relatively poor prognosis, before reaching the long-term phase of abstention, with its relatively good prognosis.

Our data provide little basis for choosing between these two models or among other, alternative models. There were no characteristics among those measured at admission that significantly differentiated the short-term from the long-term abstainers. Nor were there any characteristics that uniquely identified those short-term abstainers at 18 months who were classified as long-term abstainers at 4 years. Therefore, we have no evidence that the short-term and long-term groups were initially different types of persons. However, it is possible that the two groups differed in unmeasured variables, such as commitment or motivation to stop drinking. This ambiguity points to the need for more detailed studies of the actual developmental process of abstention and drinking.

A third conclusion bearing on the drinking status classification concerns the risks of varying consumption levels. There is no question that very high levels of alcohol consumption can be damaging (Lelbach, 1974). However, research that can guide us in determining appropriate or "safe" levels of consumption is very sparse. Some recent evidence suggests that risks of liver disorders rise in a monotonic relationship with consumption level, even at levels of daily consumption lower than 2 ounces (Lieber, 1979). But the effects of consumption level on other aspects of health and behavior are not well specified. Therefore, for our purposes, we adopted the somewhat arbitrary classification of "low" versus "high" consumption described above. However, we did not arbitrarily treat high amounts of high consumption, unaccompanied by any other indications of alcoholism, as an alcohol problem. One reason for not doing so derives from our longitudinal data, which show that the prognosis for 18-month nonproblem drinkers was not affected by amount of consumption *in the absence of dependence symptoms.* By contrast, the presence of symptoms did imply increased risk, regardless of the level of consumption. This is another facet of the 4-year followup data that suggests a central role for dependence, but not for heavy drinking alone, in the alcoholism process.

Comparisons With the 18-Month Study

All of our findings regarding future risks affected the development of the definition of status at 4 years. The results implied a significant departure from the ideas underlying the "remission" definition used in the 18-month study (Armor et al., 1978). In that study, the followup assessment for current drinkers covered only the *30 days* before the interview. Therefore, all persons abstaining for at least 1 month were treated as "abstainers." At that time, we suspected that short periods of abstention might prove less stable. We therefore distinguished between long-term and short-term abstainers, but nonetheless counted short-term abstention as one type of remission. In the 18-month study, there was no indication that short-term abstention would have a less favorable prognosis than long-term abstention.

In contrast, the 4-year followup data not only show a relatively unfavorable prognosis for short-term abstainers, but also indicate serious problem drinking when short-term abstainers last drank. Using data that measured the last drinking episode, at 4 years we were able to classify short-term abstainers according to their behavior during that last drinking period. The result was that in the new definition, 85 percent of them fell into one of the symptom or consequence categories. Compared with the 18-month study, this amounts to a reclassification of almost all short-term abstainers from a "favorable" to an "unfavorable" category. The result is a significant shift between the published rate of nonremission in the 18-month study and the rate of problem drinking in the 4-year study.

A second change between the two definitions occurred because of the importance of dependence symptoms. In the 18-month study, we included people with low levels of certain symptoms in a "normal drinking" category, provided they also met limits on quantity of consumption. At 4 years, we treated even a single occurrence of a symptom as a categorical indication of alcohol problems. The resultant tightening of criteria for nonsymptomatic drinking led to a further difference in definitions, and further changed the percentage distribution of problem and nonproblem categories.

These definitional differences must be sorted out to compare the cohort's status at the two followup points. When the same definitions are applied to survivors at 18 months and 4 years, a nearly identical picture emerges. This is true for both the definition used at 4 years and the one used in the 18-month study. Therefore, there is no evidence that the survivor cohort improved or systematically deteriorated between the two followups. On the contrary, the snapshot picture that one obtains from the 18-month followup is a very good representation of the condition of the survivor cohort at 4 years, using a constant definition. We caution that this does not apply to nonsurvivors, because, as discussed below, there was substantial mortality in the cohort. It is also important to recognize that this does not mean that *individuals* were stable over the period. Rather, it implies that for purposes of assessing the aggregate, a measurement from 18 months after admission would be adequate to predict the future drinking behavior of an alcoholic group, provided the mortality rate is also considered in any long-term projection.

METHODOLOGICAL ANALYSIS

The 4-year followup study contained several components concerned with important methodological issues that affect all alcohol research. First, analyses were conducted to investigate the importance of potential bias arising from nonresponse (i.e., failure to interview all members of the target sample). Since the 4-year followup obtained a response rate of 85 percent, one would expect from the outset that any bias would be small. In fact, comparisons of respondents, both with nonrespondents and with all persons in the original target sample, showed that the groups were very similar in characteristics at admission. There was a slight tendency toward bias among people who were not interviewed at *both* the 18-month followup and the 4-year followup. However, weighted estimates that took all of these factors into account showed that such biases were likely to affect the distribution of status at 4 years by 2 percentage points at most.

More complex analysis of the general relationship between sample bias and response rates was made possible by data on the level of effort required to obtain each respondent interview. Such data permitted us to calculate the 4-year followup characteristics of the sample that would have been obtained had we expended only a given level of effort (implying a particular response rate). This analysis produced models showing the characteristics of obtained samples for various response rates. In general, the results indicated that when response rates are as high as the 60- to 70-percent range, there are only small amounts of bias (5 percentage points or less). Moreover, projections from the models suggest that samples based on response rates of 85 percent or more will have very little bias (2 percentage points or less).

A second major methodological question concerns the reliance that one may place on interview self-reports of drinking behavior. Two separate substudies were made on this issue. First, for a random subsample of subjects, validation interviews were conducted with collaterals (relatives or associates of the subject who were familiar with the subject's drinking). These collateral interviews revealed that, by and large, the collaterals were in agreement with subjects on the subjects' abstention and on major alcohol-related events such as hospitalization or law-enforcement incidents. On other measures, evidence of subject underreporting appeared in fewer than 15 percent of the cases for each item. For several items, the level of collateral underreporting was greater than that of subjects, and the proportion of collaterals who were uncertain exceeded 30 percent for some measures. These findings suggest that collateral interviews alone do not constitute a definitive basis for assessing the validity of subject self-reports.

To complement the collateral data, we also obtained measurements of the subject's blood alcohol concentration through a breath test after the interview. When compared with self-reports of drinking during the previous 24 hours and during the past month, the breath test showed that approximately 25 percent of the drinkers consistently underreported their alcohol consumption (by at least 1 ounce of ethanol per day). Nevertheless, most of the persons who underreported consumption reported other events (symptoms or consequences) that placed them in an alcohol-problem group. Therefore, when we attempted to estimate the impact of underreporting on the distribution of status at 4 years, the results showed that even the most extreme assumptions would lead to a change of only 4 percentage points in the overall distribution.

MORTALITY

A significant proportion of the 4-year followup sample was found to be deceased. When projected to the original admission cohort, the mortality data show that 14.5 percent of the initial cohort of admissions died during the interval covering about four and one-third years since first contact with the treatment facility. This mortality rate is two and one-half times the rate that would be expected in a population of comparable age and racial distribution. Moreover, the absolute rate is high enough that the status of "deceased" at followup must be given due weight in assessing the fate of this or any alcoholic sample when a few years have passed.

As other studies have shown, the deaths disproportionately represent causal categories linked directly to the effects of alcohol: liver disease, accidents, suicide, and chronic alcoholism. The elevated mortality is particularly great among the youngest members of the cohort, although the distribution of causes appears constant across age groups, including both injury and chronic alcoholic diseases. Our data, encompassing both official death certificates and interview information collected from local informants, suggest that almost all the elevated mortality can be accounted for by a classification of individual cases into "alcohol-related" reasons for death. We interpret an alcohol-related death as indicating an alcoholic relapse prior to death. This is suggested by the definite relationship between dependence symptoms measured at the 18-month followup point and later mortality due to alcohol-related causes. Whereas only 1 percent of long-term abstainers and only 3 percent of the drinkers without symptoms at 18 months subsequently died from alcohol-related causes, the rate for symptomatic drinkers was 9 percent. Alcohol-related deaths constitute a majority of deaths, and they clearly reflect a segment of the alcoholic population for whom the chronicity of the condition was too great to be overcome by any of the events occurring after admission. The observation of substantial improvement among survivors, therefore, needs to be balanced by the high rate of alcohol-related mortality.

PSYCHOSOCIAL FUNCTIONING

Our strategy has been to focus on behaviors related to drinking as the criteria most relevant to assessing the alcoholic condition. However, the picture drawn by drinking behavior can be usefully supplemented in several ways by examining social and psychological functioning in relation to drinking behavior. One important finding from the psychosocial analysis is the *lack* of improvement in social adjustment among this cohort. At the time of admission, our sample members were considerably impaired, compared with general male population norms, on numerous standard indices of social adjustment, including marital functioning, employment, earnings, and occupational status. For example, 37 percent were divorced or separated (compared with 8 percent in similar demographic categories of the general population), and only 40 percent were employed (compared with 88 percent of the general population). This lack of social and economic integration in the community generally continued through both followups, with little change occurring. However much their drinking behavior may have improved after treatment, they did not generally achieve rehabilitation, in the sense of full reintegration into normal social roles. There were two exceptions. Constant-dollar earnings increased by a small amount at each followup, and the proportion employed rose slightly between admission and 4 years. However, this rise was counterbalanced by a decrease in labor force participation arising from illness and institutionalization, and the overall employment status of the group at 4 years was considerably less favorable than for men of comparable age in the general United States population. To some extent, this poor adjustment could derive from the low socioeconomic status of the population from which treatment admissions were drawn in the first place. We cannot say with certainty whether their original social problems were derived partly or even primarily from disadvantaged backgrounds, as opposed to their alcoholic behavior. However, their failure to improve on these dimensions is clear.

Psychiatric and psychological functioning were not measured during the interviews at admission and 18 months. Therefore, no trends in such factors can be plotted. At 4 years, though, the sample displayed higher levels of depression, anxiety, and dissatisfaction with life than comparison groups in the general population. Both the psychological and social adjustment measures were significantly correlated with the individual's drinking status at 4 years. Maladjustment was particularly frequent among the problem drinkers (those with symptoms or consequences at followup), and among the abstainers whose duration of abstention was less than 1 year. The nonproblem drinkers and the people who abstained for 1 year or more showed the greatest degrees of positive psychosocial functioning. However, even long-term abstainers and nonproblem drinkers showed more psychosocial impairment than the general population.

A multivariate analysis of group differences reinforced the impression that the nonproblem groups and problems groups are differentiated in psychosocial functioning. The discriminant analysis revealed a general factor of mental health (anchored by psychiatric symptoms, emotional stability, and positive life satisfaction) separating the problem drinkers, on the one hand, from the nonproblem drinkers and abstainers, on the other. But the analysis also revealed an important difference between abstainers and nonproblem drinkers. A second factor, linked to personal beliefs about one's own alcoholic status, sharply differentiated the abstainers from the nonproblem drinkers. The abstainers, in common with the problem drinkers, were much more likely to accept traditional views of alcoholism and, especially, to anticipate great harm or death from future drinking. It appears that the particular mode of behavior that individuals exhibit in dealing with drinking problems is highly related to personal beliefs and ideological factors.

An interesting aspect of this finding is the frequency with which the most impaired group of problem drinkers, those with both dependence symptoms and adverse consequences of drinking, admit, rather than deny, their alcoholism. Most of the subjects in this group acknowledged their problems with alcohol, endorsed traditional statements about alcoholism, and predicted harmful consequences if they continued to drink. The results suggest, therefore, that in the posttreatment environment, refusal to accept one's problems may be less important than is often believed as a factor in the continuance of alcoholic drinking.

TREATMENT

The followup assessments of this cohort, both at 4 years and at 18 months, indicate a substantial reduction in alcohol consumption and alcohol-related problems, compared with their condition at admission to treatment. In the aggregate, the survivor sample experienced a 60- to 80-percent reduction in ethanol intake between admission and the 4-year followup. At admission, more than 90 percent reported alcohol dependence symptoms or serious adverse consequences of drinking; at the 4-year followup, almost half of the sample was not affected by such problems. An important question is: Can some or all of this reduction be attributed to the intervention of treatment?

The 4-year followup study was not designed as an experimental study of alternative treatments. Therefore, our data cannot provide a definitive conclusion about the effects of treatment. Two particular points should be remembered. First, as noted above, a considerable amount of improvement after admission could be expected even without treatment if one accepts the hypothesis that the period immediately preceding admission was a period of unusually severe drinking problems for many alcoholics in the sample. Improvement should therefore be gauged mostly in relative terms, comparing equivalent groups receiving treatment with those not receiving it.

Second, the available data are subject to potential effects arising from nontreatment variables, such as self-selection. If subjects select themselves for a particular treatment regimen, there is a possibility that the subjects receiving that treatment are not truly equivalent to subjects who did not receive it. The possible importance of these effects is difficult to estimate, but they suggest caution in applying our conclusions.

Our main procedure was to conduct correlational analysis and adjust statistically for baseline differences in groups that received different initial treatments. Initial treatment included all treatment received from the NIAAA treatment center during the first year, up to first departure from treatment. The analysis provided two findings that accord with both the 18-month study results and with those of other scientific literature evaluating alcoholism treatment (Baekeland et al., 1975). First, there is a modest correlation between the amount of treatment that a subject received and the subject's condition at followup; and second, there is no correlation favoring one particular type of treatment over another (e.g., outpatient versus inpatient).

The correlation between amount of treatment and favorability of followup status appeared in two contexts. One was the analysis of varying amounts of treatment among ATC admissions. The results showed that the persons who received more treatment had fewer serious alcohol problems at the 4-year followup. This finding held up in several multivariate models when subject characteristics were controlled (in linear regressions, analysis of covariance, and logit regression models). We infer from this that the association of higher amounts of treatment with more favorable followup status is not due to the subject characteristics measured. It is important to note that "high" amounts of treatment, as defined here, represent only modest levels of clinical intensity—more than five outpatient visits or more than seven inpatient days. Our data also showed a correlation between amount of treatment and followup status in the comparison of ATC admissions versus "contact only" cases. The contacts, who made only a single visit to the treatment center, had significantly higher rates of alcohol problems at followup than did people who were admitted to treatment.

It is also important to remember that these correlations are modest. The rate of problems at 4 years was 11 percentage points lower in the group that received high amounts of treatment than in the group that received low amounts of treatment. The difference appears greater among subjects who received high amounts of outpatient treatment, and negligible among those who received inpatient treatment only. Thus, patients who received higher amounts of outpatient treatment were slightly more likely to have a favorable outcome at 4 years, whether or not they received inpatient treatment.

We refer to these findings as documenting "correlations" rather than as causal effects of treatment because of the possibility of selection effects. Since this study did not randomly assign patients to conditions with differing amounts of treatment, patients with better initial prognoses could have remained longer in treatment and could ultimately have received more treatment than others, whether or not the treatment was effective. Or, patients who failed to respond to treatment could have dropped out early, while the more successful patients remained. Such conditions would produce a correlation between amount of treatment and a subject's status at 4 years, even without treatment effects. In at least one well-controlled study, amount of treatment failed to show significant differences (Edwards et al., 1977a). Therefore, the general evidence is mixed. Our data are consistent with a small but positive effect of higher amounts of treatment, but other interpretations are also possible.

The lack of differences between inpatient and outpatient treatment at 4 years suggests that further studies of the cost-effectiveness of inpatient treatment should be made. Our data do not necessarily imply that all inpatient treatment should be deemphasized, because there are considerations other than the long-term effects of treatment. For example, treatment could produce beneficial short-term effects, even if they are not visible 4 years later. In addition, some patients may require 24-hour inpatient treatment because of their physical condition or other characteristics. Ultimately, decisions about where to place treatment resources must be influenced by such factors, as well as by the evidence on the long-term effects of treatment modalities.

A notable finding of our analysis is the amount of continuing treatment in an alcoholic sample. The baseline data showed that about half the sample had received previous treatment before admission. Over the subsequent 4-year period, one-fourth of the admissions (and also one-fourth of the "contact only" group) entered formal treatment at a facility other than the ATC. In addition, about three-fourths of the admissions and half the contacts reported some experience with Alcoholics Anonymous during the 4 years, although few were regular AA participants at the time of the 4-year followup. Finally, numerous subjects left ATC treatment and later reentered. Twenty-eight percent of ATC admissions reentered treatment in an inpatient setting at some point during the 4-year period, and another 23 percent reentered outpatient treatment without inpatient treatment. Clearly, many of our subjects are involved in a recurrent pattern of treatment, remission, and relapse. These results are revealing because of the insight they provide into the chronic character of alcoholism. However, we cannot evaluate these other treatments rigorously because we lack baseline measures on the condition of the patients at the time the treatments were initiated.

The most prevalent form of assistance for alcoholics in our sample was

Alcoholics Anonymous. Although this study was not designed to examine AA intensively, it does indicate certain correlates of AA attendance. We found that those who attended AA regularly at 18 months had about the same problem rates at 4 years as those who had never attended AA. However, the patterns of remission between these two groups were quite different. Previous regular AA attenders were more likely than other groups to be abstaining at 4 years, whereas those who never attended AA were more likely to be nonproblem drinkers. People who attended AA *irregularly* had higher problem rates than all other groups. The cross-sectional data from the 4-year followup show a similar result. Since AA stresses the benefits of abstinence, these patterns could indicate a causal effect. However, although 71 percent of our sample attended AA at some point, only 18 percent attended AA regularly at the 18-month followup, and only 14 percent were doing so at the 4-year point (not necessarily the same individuals). This raises the possibility that regular AA attenders are a highly self-selected group, but with our data it is impossible to sort out the causal and selection effects.

RELAPSE AND STABILITY

Our assessment of alcoholics at the 4-year point after treatment shows adjustment during a relatively short period of time. When we examined longer time periods and multiple points in time, we found a great deal of change in individual status, with some persons continuing to improve, some persons deteriorating, and most moving back and forth between relatively improved and unimproved statuses. Clearly, a complete assessment of the course of alcoholism requires consideration of events that take place throughout the entire 4-year period following treatment.

The amount of change was clearly shown in our investigation of relapse. The relapse analyses at 4 years parallel those carried out in the 18-month study (Armor et al., 1978). In that study, it was found that relapse rates did not differ among three groups with differing modes of remission: long-term abstainers, short-term abstainers, and "normal drinkers," classified according to their drinking behavior at an earlier followup. Using the definition of remission developed at that time, the 18-month study reported that relapse rates in these three groups ranged between 15 and 20 percent.

There are several important differences between the relapse patterns at 4 years and those observed in the 18-month study. At 4 years, relapse rates were evaluated in a survivor analysis, where the criteria for relapse were based on drinking behavior, and in a mortality analysis, where the criterion was an alcohol-related death. According to the definition of problem drinking used at 4 years, the overall *level* of problems was higher than that previously reported. Problem drinking rates among survivors were 30 percent for previous long-term abstainers, 53 percent for short-term abstainers, and 41 percent for previous nonproblem drinkers. This pattern was consistent in analyses using various relapse criteria; the difference between long-term and short-term abstainers was statistically significant in all comparisons, but the difference between nonproblem drinkers and either group of abstainers was generally not significant. The mortality analysis revealed the same pattern: rates of alcohol-related death were 1 percent for long-term abstainers, 9 percent for short-term abstainers, and 3 percent for nonproblem drinkers.

The divergent patterns between long-term and short-term abstainers complicate a direct comparison of relapse rates for abstention and non-problem drinking. Compared with nonproblem drinkers, long-term abstainers have a somewhat better prognosis. But what about people who began abstention without reaching the 6-month point? The short-term abstainers constitute the only group in our sample who fall into that category. However, there is no assurance that they represent the typical person who begins abstaining. As outlined earlier, at least two models of the process could be considered. On the one hand, it is possible that short-term abstainers and long-term abstainers were initially quite different groups of individuals. For example, long-term abstainers could have been initially more stable in their drinking behavior or more committed to abstention, whereas short-term abstainers could have been less stable or less committed. In that case, the relapse rate for short-term abstainers would not accurately represent the rate expected of all abstainers, even during the first few months of abstention. On the other hand, it could be that the two groups were initially no different. In that case, the relapse rate for short-term abstainers would simply represent a high-risk phase through which all alcoholics would pass in the early stages of the process. If this were true, the relapse rate for people beginning abstention would be significantly higher than the relapse rate for long-term abstainers. Our data, unfortunately, are not sufficient to determine whether one of those two models, or some other model, is most appropriate. Clearly, we needed more detailed research into the process of remission.

The complexity of the relapse process was further demonstrated by our multivariate analyses of relapse. These analyses showed that the patterns of relapse were not uniform across different subgroups of alcoholics. In particular, the difference between relapse rates for long-term abstainers and nonproblem drinkers varied substantially according to the subject's initial level of dependence, age, and marital status. The analysis showed that among alcoholics who were 40 or over and who had high levels of alcohol dependence at admission, those who abstained had lower relapse rates than those who engaged in nonproblem drinking. On the other hand, among alcoholics who were under 40 and who had low levels of dependence at admission, those who engaged in nonproblem drinking had lower relapse rates than those who abstained. Marital status had a further effect: most unmarried alcoholics who abstained had higher relapse rates than nonproblem drinkers, with the exception of older men with high dependence levels. For the latter group, the relationship was reversed.

We do not have a complete theoretical explanation for these findings. The finding for older and more dependent alcoholics is consistent with clinical suggestions that highly dependent alcoholics are likely to relapse after attempting nonproblem drinking, whereas less dependent alcoholics may succeed (Edwards and Gross, 1976; Hodgson et al., 1978). We have speculated that other mechanisms may reside in environmental stresses experienced by youthful abstainers and unmarried nonproblem drinkers. A more complete explanation awaits further research.

We also emphasize that these findings represent observations of the behavior of alcoholics in a nonexperimental environment. Thus, they are descriptive statements about how people actually behave, not prescriptive statements about how they should behave. Our data do not show what would happen if patients were advised to abstain or to drink without problems. To address the implications of these results for specific treatment strategies, controlled experimental studies should be conducted. In the meantime, this study does not recommend a particular treatment approach and does not recommend either abstention or controlled drinking as goals for individual alcoholics.

Our other analyses of change, including the description of stable statuses between 18 months and 4 years and the investigation of long-term patterns of drinking over 4 years, revealed considerable instability in all types of remissions. At 4 years, we found 46 percent in remission for at least 6 months: 28 percent abstaining and 18 percent engaging in drinking without problems. However, analysis showed that remissions were generally not lasting. When results of both followups were combined, 13 percent of the sample were classified as long-term abstainers at both followups. Another 9 percent were classified as nonproblem drinkers at both followups, and an additional 6 percent had shifted from abstention to nonproblem drinking or vice versa. Thus, altogether 28 percent of the sample were classified in a remission status at both time points. This is a sizable portion of the sample, and it represents an improvement since the time of admission to treatment. Nevertheless, it also indicates that most sample members did not show stable remission lasting over the entire study period.

IMPLICATIONS FOR POLICY AND RESEARCH

The results of the 4-year followup study contain several implications for our understanding of alcoholism and our policies for dealing with it. Prominent among these are conclusions about the nature of alcoholic remission. In the 18-month followup study of this same cohort, we noted that temporary remission was widespread, but we distinguished the temporary state from a more lasting recovery. We now see, with the passage of several more years, that such a distinction is an essential one. In this cohort, all types of remission were subject to a high probability of relapse. Accordingly, measurements of functioning among alcoholics should distinguish a remission, which may be temporary, from more lasting states. Instead of using long-term continuous remission as the measure of success, we suggest that a more reasonable standard would be the total length of time spent in remission periods.

In addition, although both forms of remission are associated with better mental health compared with nonremissions, even a stable remission is not a guarantee of general rehabilitation. Alcoholics in remission are more likely than nonremissions to possess stable family relationships, adequate incomes, and stable employment. However, even the alcoholic groups whose drinking problems have ceased or abated are considerably lower than the general norm in levels of social adjustment and psychological health. On our measures of social integration and stability, most subjects did not improve substantially after treatment, even when they experienced great reductions in drinking problems per se. Therefore, policies aimed at treating alcoholism should not be based on the premise that present treatment methods will result in full social rehabilitation. Whether alternative treatment methods or rehabilitation services might bring about more improvement in psychosocial functioning is an open question, on which further research is needed.

Our data on treatment are not complete; nevertheless, they point to several relevant policy conclusions. First, the results of the 4-year followup reconfirm those of the 18-month study and several other independent studies on the question of inpatient versus outpatient treatment. No general advantage was demonstrated for either setting of treatment; but increasing amounts of treatment were correlated with better prognosis in the outpatient setting only. As we stated in the 18-month study, this suggests that, other things being equal, it may be feasible to substitute less costly outpatient treatments for more costly inpatient regimens, where other overriding considerations are absent. Further research is needed on this issue; but at present, the cost-effectiveness of inpatient treatments is very much an open question.

Two implications emerge from our analyses of amounts of treatment. First, it appears that substantial resources are invested in provision of short-term treatments, such as occasional outpatient visits. In our data, moderately high amounts of treatment, such as six or more outpatient visits, were associated with more favorable posttreatment functioning. This suggests that very short-term treatments should be deemphasized in favor of somewhat longer treatment periods. However, we recognize that our data are limited and cannot resolve this point definitively. More thorough investigation of the effects of amount of treatment is needed, using randomly assigned control groups and other experimental procedures.

A second implication concerns the substantial number of *reentries* to treatment that we observed over a 4-year period. More than half of our treatment admissions returned after their initial treatment episode and received further treatment at the same facility; of these, half were hospitalized at the return point. Although some of this reentry treatment represented a single detoxification episode, in many instances it embraced much more, including extended hospital stays or extensive outpatient care. Since every such reentry is by definition a case of relapse from previous ATC treatment, this naturally raises a question of treatment effectiveness. The available data do not permit a full assessment of the value of reentry treatment, but there are no indications in this study that it has significant positive effects.

Several important guidelines for future evaluation research emerge from the 4-year followup experience. Both basic research and treatment evaluation would benefit from a more explicit recognition of the unstable character of treatment outcomes. With so much instability evident, followup assessments should concentrate on evaluating patients over longer periods of time, and on measuring the length of time that a patient is without problems rather than assessing his condition over a short interval. Indeed, our findings suggest that at least 6 months of abstention may be required to indicate a relatively good prognosis. Followup assessments before 6 months, therefore, run a serious risk of mistaking short-term abstention for a stable remission pattern, which it manifestly is not.

Some of these points have particular relevance for large-scale state and federal data-collection systems. Existing systems should be modified to concentrate on followup points later than 6 months after admission to treatment; to disaggregate short-term abstainers from abstainers of 6 months or more duration; to show indices of alcohol dependence as well as consumption and general impairment; and to assess adverse consequences of drinking more broadly. The analysis of bias indicates that substantial biases may be present in samples with very low followup rates. Followup efforts should draw a sample of subjects whenever possible, so that resources can be concentrated on locating a sufficient number of cases to obtain at least a 60 percent followup rate. Finally, the collateral and blood alcohol concentration studies imply that reasonable confidence in self-report results is warranted, since the basic assessment of a cohort is not appreciably affected by those reporting errors that the BAC and collaterals revealed.

The 4-year followup results call into question some views of alcoholism that have long been established and that are widely held in the general public. Among these is the idea that alcoholics are a homogeneous group and that alcoholism is a single, undifferentiated "disease" with only one form and only one solution. Such ideas grow out of the traditional Jellinek theory of alcoholism, which postulated that true addicts are marked by "loss of control." According to the theory, loss of control is produced by a physical mechanism: when the alcoholic drinks he feels a demand for more and more alcohol, leading to an uncontrolled drinking bout. Some writers have modified the theory to predict that, on any given drinking occasion, loss of control is only probable rather than certain. However, all such formulations share the basic conception that loss of control renders any form of drinking inherently risky for an alcoholic.

This simple concept has grown to become the basis for an elaborate but nonetheless dogmatic doctrine, which dominates treatment practice and public discussion. Alcoholism is often said to be a physical disease with a definite progressive course, for which abstinence is asserted to be the only known treatment (e.g., Mann, 1958; Gitlow, 1973). Sometimes, after alcoholism is defined as permanent loss of control, the same definition is used tautologically to deny that any "true" alcoholic can control his drinking (Pattison, Sobell, and Sobell, 1977). Thus, the traditional theory, the definition of alcoholism, and the abstinence-drinking issue are bound up together.

Our data are clearly inconsistent with important propositions derived from traditional theory. Manifestly, some persons labeled as alcoholics engage in drinking without problems. Although this result contradicts the loss of control hypothesis, it is now commonly reported in the scientific literature (Pattison, 1976; Pomerleau et al., 1976). Our data also indicate that nonproblem drinkers have levels of social adjustment, mental health, and physical condition that are roughly equivalent to those of long-term abstainers. The weight of this evidence strongly suggests that both nonproblem drinking and abstention should be regarded as forms of remission from alcoholism.

This conclusion is reinforced by our analysis of relapse. Traditional theory argues that all alcoholics tend to lose control when they drink; hence, nonproblem drinkers should have higher relapse rates than abstainers. Our data, however, show that drinking does not inevitably lead to relapse for all alcoholics. Indeed, we found that relapse rates among younger, less dependent alcoholics were lower for nonproblem drinkers than for long-term abstainers. Because the traditional theory is inadequate to explain these empirical phenomena, its predominance as a guide for research and treatment practice must be called into question. A more complex theory is needed, one that recognizes that alcoholic behavior depends upon multiple conditions, including the alcoholic's social environment, previous drinking history, previous level of dependence, and possibly other factors.

We are not, of course, the first researchers to make these points. The weakness of loss of control theory has been cited by numerous investigators. Indeed, a growing sense of unease with the traditional concept of alcoholism was part of the reason for the recent shift toward the use of the term "alcohol dependence" in official definitions of the World Health Organization Committee on Alcohol-Related Disabilities (Edwards et al., 1977b), the International Classification of Diseases (World Health Organization, 1977), and the American Psychiatric Association (1980).

At this point, we do not have a well-developed, alternative theory of alcoholism to offer. Nor do we believe that immediate and sweeping changes in treatment policy would be appropriate because of our findings. Although there is a definite trend toward controlled-drinking methods in the treatment of alcoholism (Sobell and Sobell, 1978a), it appears that most alcoholics in treatment, being older and highly dependent on alcohol, would have a poor prognosis with nonproblem drinking. In addition, attempts at nonproblem drinking are inappropriate for those alcoholics who have physical conditions exacerbated by drinking (e.g., liver disease) and for those who have repeatedly attempted but failed at controlled drinking. Nonetheless, an expansion of treatment approaches, including goals other than the traditional demand for abstinence, might offer advantages for some alcoholics. We recommend that well-controlled experimental studies be undertaken to investigate the efficacy of varying treatment goals.

Finally, our results point to an important area for further research: the developmental processes of alcoholism. Our data suggest that the kind of alcoholism observed in clinics, once established, is unlikely to abate spontaneously. Yet we have little reliable information on the nature of alcoholism among untreated alcoholics, or among alcoholics in the *pretreatment* phase. Such untreated alcoholics are a difficult group to isolate, and research on them is sparse indeed. Invaluable information could be obtained by more research on this part of the course of alcoholism. What little research has been done suggests that "natural" remission, among populations that have never been in treatment, may be quite substantial. This contrasts sharply with our own "contact only" sample of people who visited the treatment facility but never entered treatment; their followup status was even more impaired than that of treatment admissions. This inconsistency implies that at some point in the developmental process, alcoholism takes firm root and becomes more difficult to change. Our data would suggest that the emergence of alcohol dependence is a likely indicator of the beginning of such a stage. But whether this is true or not, the circumstances surrounding the emergence of alcoholism, as opposed to its treatment, constitute a neglected area of research. We would suggest that neither a complete understanding of the course of alcoholism, nor the implementation of effective policies against it, can be achieved without further attention to this crucial area.

APPENDIX A

Followup Rates and Potential Bias Analysis

This appendix reports analyses that examine the factors related to potential bias due to nonfollowup. As noted in Chapter 2, the 4-year followup study attained fairly high completion rates for the target samples (91 percent for Group I and 85 percent overall). These rates imply that any bias due to nonfollowup of the *target sample* is likely to be very small. However, the target sample itself was disproportionately drawn from strata defined partly by whether the subject was followed up or not followed up in the 18-month study. Hence, there is reason to enquire into the possible biases arising from nonfollowup at both 18 months and 4 years. We will examine that question in more detail here than in Chapter 2, and develop a model of status at 4 years that includes nonfollowup variables. This will help us to assess the importance of nonfollowup bias and to develop an overall estimate of the likely distribution of status at 4 years in the original ATC population (all admissions at the eight ATCs in the sampling universe).

BASIC CHARACTERISTICS OF
LOCATED AND UNLOCATED SAMPLE MEMBERS

Table A.1 shows the characteristics of all admissions in the target sample (N = 758) according to several variables that are related to drinking status at 4 years. (We do not attempt to evaluate biases in mortality rates here, but our working assumption is that almost all cases of mortality were uncovered in the fieldwork, so that such mortality bias is likely to be small.) Because most of the target cases were located at 4 years, the differences between the obtained sample and the target sample at admission are very small. The table also disaggregates the members of sampling Groups I and II in order to evaluate possible biases within those groups. By and large, the located and unlocated groups are fairly similar even within Group II, where the differences are greatest. It does seem that the Group II members, in general, had background

222

Table A.1 Characteristics of Located and Unlocated Sampling Groups at Admission to Treatment

				Percent with the Characteristic			
				Sampling Group I (Interviewed at 18 months)		Sampling Group II (Not interviewed at 18 months)	
Characteristic at Admission to Treatment	Target Sample	Located at 4 Years	Not Located at 4 Years	Located at 4 Years	Not Located at 4 Years	Located at 4 Years	Not Located at 4 Years
Age 50 or over	44	43	45	43	49	46	42
3 years or less in community	44	42	56	40	47	57	64
Low SES	45	45	50	45	42	42	58
Low social stability	45	44	50	42	31	50	68
Total consumption (QF) over 5 oz./day	58	58	65	55	55	72	73
2 or more symptoms	78	79	87	77	81	89	92
Previously treated for alcoholism	42	42	46	41	42	47	49
(N)	(758)	(645)	(113)	(540)	(53)	(105)	(60)

223

characteristics that are prognostic of less favorable conditions later (lower socioeconomic status, lower stability, and somewhat more severe problems at admission). It appears, therefore, that some attempt to weight the sample for the disproportionate sampling of Groups I and II might be worthwhile so that we can determine whether the unweighted sample results are reasonably close to properly weighted measures. The closeness of those who were not located to those who were located within each group suggests that a weighting scheme that used the population marginals (63 percent of the population in Group I, 37 percent in Group II) would be reasonably accurate.

Another way to judge the possible bias arising from disproportionate sampling of Group I cases is to examine the 4-year followup status of the two groups, as shown in Table A.2. These data demonstrate that the 4-year status of Group II subjects who were interviewed at 4 years is definitely somewhat poorer than that of Group I subjects. In all, 53 percent of Group I subjects reported experiencing symptoms or consequences compared with 60 percent of the Group II subjects. The last two columns of the table show, however, that weighting for the disproportionate sampling of the two groups does not lead to very much difference in the results; the weighted total shows 56 percent compared with the unweighted total of 54 percent. This is the reason that we

Table A.2   Characteristics of 18-month Interview Groups at Four-Year Followup

Characteristic at 4-Year Interview	Percent of 18-Month Interview Group with Characteristic		Total Unweighted	Total Weighted
	I Interviewed at 18 Months	II Not Interviewed at 18 Months		
Earned income over $7000 in past year	32	31	32	32
Divorced/separated	36	43	37	39
Employed	52	46	51	50
3 years or less in community	40	53	42	45
Status at 4 Years				
Abstained 1 year	22	14	21	19
Abstained 6-11 months	7	10	7	8
Low Q	8	3	8	6
High Q	10	13	10	11
Consequences	6	4	6	5
Symptoms	13	7	12	11
Symptoms and consequences	34	49	36	40
Problem rate (symptoms or consequences)	53	60	54	56
(N)	(478)	(70)	(548)	(548)

have not attempted to weight our sample results in most of the analyses reported in the text.

One reason why weighting for even this minor difference may not be appropriate is that our multivariate models already control for many of the admission characteristics that predisposed Group II members to less favorable outcomes. Table A.3 shows the results of a regression model that tests whether further adjustment for Group I/Group II status would be necessary in a multivariate model that includes admission variables. This model is similar to those reported in Chapter 6 in the analysis of treatment, with a binary variable added to represent Group I/Group II status (being interviewed at 18 months). With the other variables in the model, the indicator for Group I/Group II status does not reach even a borderline level of statistical significance. We conclude, then, that most of the "effect" due to not being interviewed at 18 months is already taken into account by modeling the characteristics that these people had at admission.

Table A.3   Regression Model of Lack of Problems at Four Years[a]

Independent Variable[b]	Coefficient	t
Drinking at Admission		
Severe alcoholism symptoms[c]	−.086	−1.83
Previous treatment	−.150	−3.38
Background		
Social stability (high)	.081	1.80
Socioeconomic status (high)	.104	2.41
Age (40 or over)	.039	(.88)
ATC Treatment		
Outpatient settings[d]	−.115	−1.84
Higher amount of treatment	−.039	(−.52)
Outpatient settings; high amount of treatment	.196	2.19
Interview Status at 18 Months		
Interviewed at 18 months[e]	.034	(.55)

[a]Linear regression predicting lack of problems (1 = abstaining, Low Q, or High Q; 0 = otherwise). R^2 = .083, N = 548 cases. T-values shown in parentheses are not significant at the .10 level; all others are significant at that level.
[b]Binary variables representing the condition named.
[c]Binary variable representing the presence of dependence symptoms at admission.
[d]Binary variable (1 = outpatient or combination setting; 0 = otherwise).
[e]Binary variable (1 = interviewed; 0 = not interviewed).

FOLLOWUP EFFORT AND STATUS AT FOUR YEARS

The analysis of characteristics at admission to treatment suggests that differences between located sample members and nonlocated members will not lead to any substantial bias, and the analysis of 18-month nonfollowup cases seems to indicate the same. Although one can never be completely certain about the characteristics of unmeasured cases, we do have another set of data that is highly relevant to the issue of nonfollowup bias. Because we collected case-by-case information on the amount of effort expended to locate each case, we can construct a model of the relationship between the amount of effort required to locate a case and the status of that case at 4 years. Once this is done, we can determine how much effort would be required to locate the entire sample and then use the model to estimate the resulting status characteristics of the full sample.

Table A.4 shows the distribution of several measures that might serve as indicators of the level of effort required to locate a case. Figures A.1 through A.6 show plots of several such measures of effort against the characteristics of the Group I sample *that would have been obtained if fieldwork had ceased at the given level of effort.* For purposes of interpretation, the effort variables have been rescored to indicate the effective response rate that each level of effort represents. In Fig. A.1, for example, the first point represents a 23-percent response rate, corresponding to the proportion of the Group I sample that would have been obtained if only one person or agency had been contacted for each case. If work had stopped there, about 40 percent of the obtained sample would have been nonabstainers during the past month, and about 54 percent of the obtained sample would have been nonabstainers during the past 6 months. Obviously the curves move upward as response rates increase, although the ascent is very gradual by the time that response rates of 60 to 70 percent are reached.

Other graphs, using different measures of effort or different measures of status at 4 years (e.g., symptoms, consequences, or drinking over 2 ounces per day), show a similar pattern. Often the rise is more attenuated than the rise in Fig. A.1. Figure A.4, for example, shows that the proportion of drinkers consuming more than 2 ounces per day is hardly affected by level of effort; and at a 60-percent response rate, neither the rate of symptoms nor the rate of consequences rises more than 4 or 5 percentage points up to the highest response rate. If these curves are any guide, then, we would see very little change in our sample characterstics by extrapolating to the 100-percent response range (which would correspond to measuring the entire target sample, i.e., no possible nonfollowup bias).

It is instructive to examine level of effort in a somewhat more complex way by including it in an overall model of followup status. If such a model is

Table A.4   Interview Rates, by Level of Effort Expended

Level of Effort Expended	Cumulative Percent of Final Total Interviews Obtained
Time elapsed in study (months):	
1	23
2	60
3	76
4	89
5	96
6	99.7
7	100
Number of persons/agencies contacted:	
1	26
2	42
3	54
4	64
5	72
6-7	82
8-11	90
12 or more	100
Hours spent in locating a case:	
1.0	19
1.5	31
2.0	42
2.5	52
3.0	60
4.0	70
5.0	77
8.0	90
More than 8.0	100
(N)	(668)

developed, one can evaluate the model for higher levels of effort than were obtained to estimate the characteristics of those who were not located in the current followup study. A preliminary look at the importance of level of effort is given by Table A.5, which shows the residuals from the previous regression (that shown in Table A.3), grouped by the level-of-effort variable that we have selected as the best overall measure.[1] The results suggest that there is a regular tendency for higher levels of effort to be associated with slightly lower residuals (more negative), indicating that the model that excludes level of effort as a variable tends to overestimate the "goodness" of followup status

[1]The measure is the "number of persons and agencies contacted," selected because its relationship to 4-year followup status is the most regular of the level-of-effort measures we have examined.

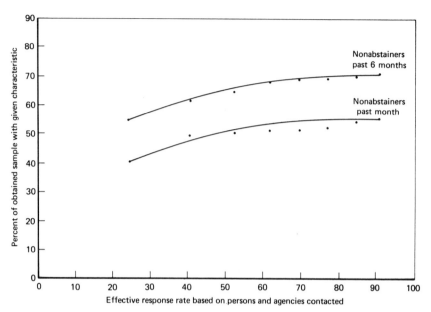

Figure A.1 Estimated percentage of nonabstainers by level of response rate based on number of contacts.

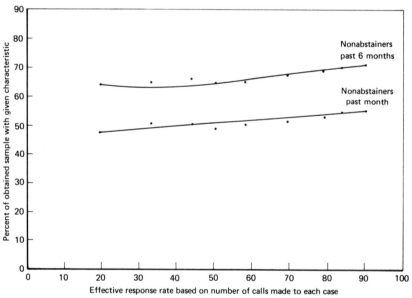

Figure A.2 Estimated percentage of nonabstainers by level of response rate based on number of calls.

228

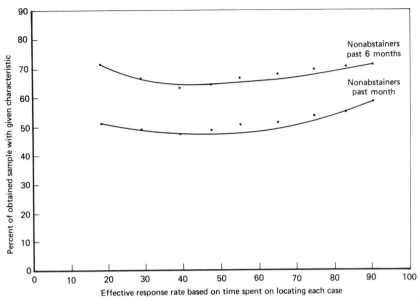

Figure A.3   Estimated percentage of nonabstainers by level of response rate based on locating time.

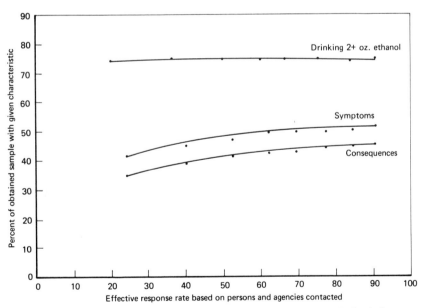

Figure A.4   Estimated rates of consumption, symptoms, and consequences by level of response rate based on number of contacts.

229

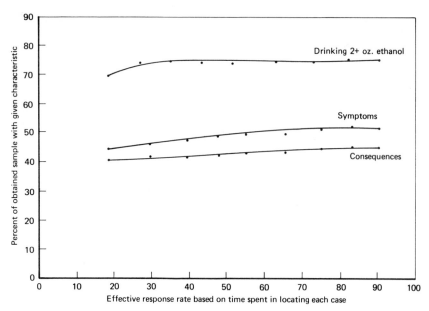

Figure A.5 Estimated rates of consumption, symptoms, and consequences by level of response rate based on locating time.

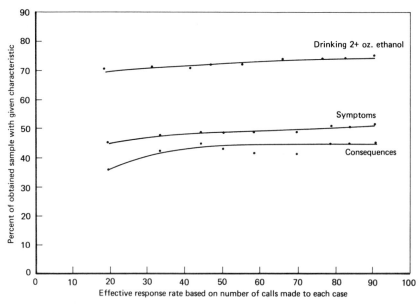

Figure A.6 Estimated rates of consumption, symptoms, and consequences by level of response rate based on number of calls.

Table A.5   Regression Residuals of Lack of Problems at Four Years,[a] by Level of Effort Expended

Level of Effort (Effective Response Rate)	Mean Residual	Percent Distribution of Residuals			(N)
		Under −.4	−.4 to +.4	Over +.4	
8	.081	21	39	40	(57)
21	.089	29	25	46	(87)
34	.014	36	30	34	(94)
44	−.003	32	35	33	(63)
52	−.085	40	35	22	(58)
58	.000	34	34	32	(44)
65	−.033	26	42	32	(19)
80	−.078	22	46	32	(60)

[a]Residuals from model including severity of alcoholism symptoms, previous treatment, social stability, SES, age, outpatient settings, high amount of treatment, interaction of high amount of treatment in outpatient settings, and a dummy variable for being interviewed at 18 months.

when the effort required to locate a case is high. This suggests that level of effort should be included in the model.

Table A.6 shows the results when level of effort is added to the model. The R^2 rises slightly (from .083 to .090) and the effort variable is significant at the .05 level, with higher levels of effort indicating worse problems at 4 years. This confirms the impression in the field that the more difficult-to-locate cases tend to show less favorable outcomes, but it does not by any means suggest that all nonfollowup cases should be regarded as "treatment failures," as some methodological critics have claimed.

We have used this model to estimate what the drinking status of the entire underlying ATC population would be at 4 years if the model properly predicted the characteristics of its members. This estimate was made by computing the mean values on each of the independent variables in Table A.6 over all members of the original target sample (excluding known deaths) separately for Groups I and II.[2] The resulting estimated means produced for the dependent variable were then weighted by a .63/.37 factor for Group I/Group II in order to predict the proportion of the underlying ATC population that would show symptoms or consequences at 4 years if all were included in the correct proportions. The results showed that 43.9 percent would be free of any problems at 4 years. This may be compared with our raw

[2]There are various methods one could use to select the mean that should be used for the level of effort required to obtain the entire target sample. As a first approximation, we have simply made a separate computation of the median response rate level (as gauged by "persons and agencies contacted") for the unlocated cases in Group I and Group II. This response rate was assumed to be the necessary one for all unlocated cases, and the total mean for the target sample was computed by weighting the assumed rate for unlocated cases and the actual rate for located ones.

Table A.6   Regression Model of Drinking Status at Four Years[a]

Independent Variable[b]	Coefficient	t
Drinking at Admission		
Severe alcoholism symptoms[c]	−.085	−1.81
Previous treatment	−.150	−3.38
Background		
Social stability	.076	1.69
Socioeconomic status	.101	2.34
Age	.035	(.79)
ATC Treatment		
Outpatient settings[d]	−.112	−1.80
High amount of treatment	−.050	(0.67)
Outpatient settings; high amount of treatment	.201	2.25
Interview Status at 18 Months		
Interviewed at 18 months[e]	.006	(.10)
Effort Expended in Locating Case		
Effective response rate[f]	−.002	−2.08

[a]Linear regression predicting lack of problems (1 = abstaining, Low Q, or High Q; 0 = otherwise). $R^2 = .090$, N = 548 cases. T-values shown in parentheses are not significant at the .10 level; all others are significant at that level.
[b]Binary variables representing the condition named.
[c]Binary variable representing presence of dependence symptoms at admission.
[d]Binary variable (1 = outpatient or combination setting; 0 = otherwise).
[e]Binary variable (1 = interviewed; 0 = not interviewed).
[f]Effort expended, recoded to the response rate that would be obtained if all cases requiring greater effort were excluded from the obtained sample.

sample figure of 46.5 percent for the unweighted combined Group I / Group II sample, as shown in Table 3.20.

These estimating methods clearly include only some of the procedures that could be followed in assessing bias, but they demonstrate the likely magnitude of biases arising from nonresponse. It should be remembered that the estimates from this model include not only admission characteristics, but also the extra difficulties involved in finding Group II subjects and the additional unfavorable followup cases that would be present among the most difficult-to-locate subjects. We conclude, then, that although the actual characteristics of an unmeasured population are always unknown, there is little evidence to suggest significant biases in our sample, or indeed in any sample with a fairly high response rate.

Validity of Self-Reported
Drinking Behaviors

Like most behavioral research in the alcoholism field, this study has relied on self-reported drinking behaviors for assessing the status of an alcoholic sample 4 years after treatment. In spite of the widespread use of self-report data, however, the validity of self-reports remains a continuing source of concern to alcoholism researchers. Accordingly, this study was designed to include a special investigation of self-report validity. An overview of this investigation and its main conclusions were presented in Chapters 2 and 3; the purpose of this appendix is to provide the detailed analysis and findings that form the basis of these conclusions.

We pointed out in a literature review in our last report (Armor et al., 1978) that there are only a relatively small number of well-designed validity studies. This comes as a surprise, given the controversy regarding the validity of self-reports. As yet, there is no strong consensus among the findings of these studies; some have found relatively good agreement between self-reports and other validating sources (such as official records or collateral reports) and others have not. We will not review this literature again here, except to say that there are some new studies by Linda and Mark Sobell of Vanderbilt University whose findings are relevant to our own validity study. We will cite the results of the Sobell studies at the appropriate place in the discussion of our results.

As described in Chapter 2, we conducted two separate validity studies. First, all the subjects in the interviewed sample were asked to take breath tests; this provided objective physiological data for investigating the validity of self-reported alcohol consumption. A randomly drawn subsample of 193 subjects was reinterviewed about their recent alcohol consumption; they were then asked to take another breath test. Second, another randomly drawn subsample of subjects formed a group for whom collateral interviews were sought; interviews were subsequently obtained for 128 of these subjects. The results of the breath test and collateral studies will be presented separately.

THE BREATH TEST VALIDITY STUDY

Of the 659 subjects interviewed in the 4-year followup study for whom we had usable consumption data, all but 27 agreed to a breath test for determining blood alcohol concentration (BAC). Since we have BAC determinations for over 95 percent of the sample, the issue of possible sample bias is clearly not a serious one. The analysis results presented in the following subsections are based on a total of 632 cases who have usable self-report data and a completed BAC test.

Breath-Test Procedures

Following the interview portion of the study, breath samples were obtained by using the SM-7, a portable breath-testing device.[1] The basic procedures for the breath tests have already been described in Chapter 2. Since we are using the breath tests to validate self-reports, it is clearly important to establish the validity of the breath test itself.

Even though the theoretical relationship between breath and blood samples is well established, and the SM-7 samples were subjected to careful laboratory procedures, nevertheless the fundamental issue is whether the SM-7, as used in the field, gives accurate results when compared with actual blood samples. For this reason we obtained simultaneous blood samples and breath samples from nine volunteer subjects who had been drinking. The subjects were briefly instructed in the use of of the SM-7 device, and they then employed it to give a breath sample.

Figure B.1 shows a scatterplot of the breath and blood sample estimates of BAC from this special study. The values plotted are the averages of the two blood estimates and the two breath estimates for each subject.[2] The plot shown in Figure B.1 makes it clear that the relationship is very strong, with no blood-breath difference exceeding .01 percent. The product-moment correlation between the two sets of values is .996, and the average difference is .005, with a standard error (of differences) of .0039. Therefore, the differences between the blood and breath estimates are not statistically significant. Moreover, since for a male subject of average weight (165 lb) a difference of .01 in two BAC values represents about one-fourth of an ounce of ethanol, or about one-half of a standard-sized drink, even the largest discrepancies in the plot would not significantly affect estimates of total ethanol consumption.

---

[1]Manufactured by Luckey Laboratories, San Bernardino, California.

[2]The BAC levels are derived by first averaging the two estimates and then truncating the third digit (rather than rounding). This procedure corresponds to practices mandated by the California Department of Health.

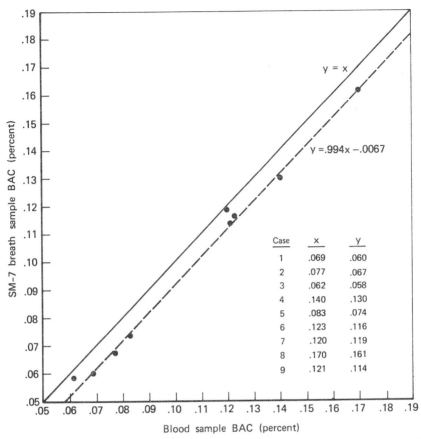

Figure B.1   Relationship between BAC levels determined by blood samples and SM-7 breath samples.

Comparing Self-Reports with BAC Results

The types of self-reported consumption behavior used in this study normally involve fairly long time periods, such as abstention for the past 6 months or amount of consumption in the 30 days before a person's last drink. Ideally, the validity of these longer-term behavioral reports requires a true criterion measure that covers the same time periods. Unfortunately, at the present time, there is no established physiological testing procedure that can measure total alcohol consumption over such long intervals. A BAC procedure can only establish the amount of ethanol in the bloodstream at the instant of testing. Given the fact that ethanol is metabolized (eliminated) at the average rate of about one drink (or one-half ounce of ethanol) per hour, a BAC can establish with certainty only the lower limit of total consumption within the past 24 hours or so.

These inherent time limitations affect the type of validity tests that can be made with BAC estimates. The most definitive type of validity test that can be made is the *disconfirmation* of a report of abstention or of an amount of drinking. That is to say, if a subject says that he has been abstaining for a month or more, a positive BAC is definitive evidence for a false report. Likewise, if a BAC estimate shows more alcohol in his bloodstream than the total amount he claims to have consumed in the past 24 hours or so, we can be certain that the claimed amount was underreported. As to amounts consumed over longer periods, however, the BAC can only be used as a "consistency" check and not as a true validity criterion. Both the disconfirmation approach and the consistency approach will be investigated in this analysis.

The first disconfirmation test is carried out for reports of abstention. Table B.1 shows the actual BAC level cross-tabulated by the time of last drink as reported by subjects. For the purpose of interpretation, a BAC of .02 for an average-weight male is the equivalent of about one-half ounce of ethanol or one average-sized drink (e.g., one can of beer or one shot of distilled spirits) in the bloodstream.

The results in the table show that very few reports of abstention are disconfirmed by a positive BAC in our sample. Only 4 percent of persons who say they abstained for 2 days to 1 year or more before the interview have nonzero BACs. There is a small difference in the percentage of disconfirmed abstention reports between those abstaining for 2 to 181 days and those

Table B.1   Relationship Between BAC Level and Time of Last Drink

Actual BAC Level[a]	Percent Distribution of Cases by Time of Last Drink					
	Past 12 Hours	13 to 24 Hours Ago	2 to 30 Days Ago	31 to 180 Days Ago	6 Months to 1 Year Ago	1 Year or More Ago
0	27.4	76.2	94.6	94.0	97.6	99.2
.001–.01	3.2	3.2				
.01–.05	17.8	7.9	3.4	3.0		
.05–.10	18.5	9.5	2.0	2.0		
.10–.15	15.3	1.6		1.0	2.4	
.15–.20	8.3	1.6				.8
.20–.25	5.7					
.25–.30	3.8					
(N)	(157)	(63)	(148)	(100)	(42)	(122)

[a]Percentage of alcohol in bloodstream, by weight.

abstaining for 6 months or more (5.6 percent versus 1.2 percent), but the size of the difference renders it negligible. Although the BAC does not tell us how long a person has been abstaining—only that he has not been drinking in the past 24 hours or so—the very low rate of disconfirmation among abstainers strongly suggests that reports of abstention are quite valid.

Among persons drinking within the past 24 hours, a substantial number have positive BACs, as one would expect. About 73 percent of those drinking in the past 12 hours and 24 percent of those drinking 13 to 24 hours ago have positive BACs. Since both of these groups reported drinking recently, the relevant validity question for these 220 subjects is whether the *amount* they report is disconfirmed by their BAC level. The interview schedule included detailed questions on the amount of alcohol consumed on the day of the interview and on the day before it; these questions were asked before the subject knew that a BAC test would be requested. The amounts can be compared with the amount of alcohol (ethanol) implied by their BAC readings for a disconfirmation test of the amount of recent consumption.

The amount of ethanol in the bloodstream, as implied by a given BAC level for men, can be given by the formula

$$Q = .14 \times W \times BAC,$$

where Q is fluid ounces of ethanol, BAC is in percent, and W is the person's weight in pounds. The constant .14 reflects the specific gravity of alcohol (.8), the proportion of body weight capable of absorbing alcohol, and a constant for converting pounds to ounces.[3]

The relationship between ethanol in the bloodstream, as determined by the BAC, and self-report consumption today or yesterday is shown in Table B.2. Today's self-report is always used if a subject reported drinking on the day of the interview, and yesterday's report is used if he did not drink today but drank yesterday within 24 hours of the BAC test. Those drinking more than 24 hours ago are excluded from the analysis.

Persons whose bloodstream ethanol exceeds their self-reported amounts are those below the circled numbers in the table. These persons are definitely underreporting, since they had to drink at least as much ethanol as is indicated by their BAC. We note that there are many such cases, particularly at the lower levels of self-reported consumption. The underreporting is most serious for self-reports of .001 to 1 oz. of ethanol (one or two standard drinks), where 27 out of 83 subjects, or nearly one-third, show bloodstream alcohol

---

[3]Since BAC is the ratio 100 × (ounces of alcohol by weight)/(ounces of body fluid), a BAC can be expressed as BAC = (100 × .8 × Q)/(.7 × 16 × W). The .8 is the specific gravity (weight) of alcohol, and .7 is a standard constant for converting body weight to fluid capable of absorbing alcohol (Wallgren and Barry, 1970). A constant of .6 would be more appropriate for women.

Table B.2 Relationship Between Ethanol in the Bloodstream and Self-Reported Consumption, for Persons Drinking in the Past 24 Hours

Ethanol from BAC[b]	Number of Cases Reporting Ethanol Consumption Today or Yesterday[a]								Total
	.001–1 oz.	1–2 oz.	2–3 oz.	3–4 oz.	4–5 oz.	5–6 oz.	6–7 oz.	7+ oz.	
0 oz.	45	17	5	5	4	3		12	91
.001–1 oz.	(11)	12	7	2	1	1		3	37
1–2 oz.	14	(12)	4	2	1			1	34
2–3 oz.	6	4	(2)	4	2	2		1	21
3–4 oz.	4	2	3	(3)	2			2	16
4–5 oz.		4		1	(O)	1	1	1	8
5–6 oz.	1	2		2	2	(O)	1	1	9
6–7 oz.	1				2		(O)		3
7+ oz.	1							(O)	1
Total	83	53	21	19	14	7	2	21	220
Percent definitely underreporting	33	23	14	16	29	0	0	0	

[a]Today's report (or yesterday's report if subject did not drink today).
[b]Ethanol from BAC is calculated as .14 × BAC (%) × weight (lb).

exceeding 1 ounce. For about half of these subjects, the discrepancy is not great, with the BAC reflecting 1 to 2 ounces of ethanol. Somewhat lower underreporting rates are shown for persons reporting consumption from 1 to 5 ounces of ethanol (over 2 to 10 standard drinks), with 22 out of 107 subjects, or 20 percent, definitely underreporting.

It must be stressed that these rates of underreporting are *lower bounds* of total underreporting. The reason, of course, has to do with the metabolic elimination of alcohol. According to laboratory studies, alcohol is eliminated at rates ranging from .010 to .025 BAC % per hour for most persons, the average being around .02 for alcoholics (Wallgren and Barry, 1970). This means that if a sufficient period of time has passed since the drinking started, a BAC level will show less alcohol than the total actually consumed. For example, if a male of average weight drank 2.5 ounces of ethanol in a half-hour period, his BAC should rise to about .11 within another half-hour or so. If the BAC test was then taken 3 hours later, an average alcoholic would register a BAC of about .05, which reflects only about 1.2 ounces of ethanol remaining in the bloodstream. Clearly, some of the people who are on or above the diagonal in Table B.2 may also be underreporting, if their drinking started and ended more than an hour or two before the BAC test. The analysis of validity can be refined and expanded somewhat by taking into account the metabolic elimination of alcohol.

Self-Reports and Estimated Total Consumption from the BAC

Before describing our procedure for estimating total consumption from the BAC, we should note one other limitation of the data in Table B.2. The relationship described there is, of necessity, between *recent* drinking today or yesterday and BAC levels. However, all the analyses in this study have relied on self-reported consumption during the 30 days before a subject's last drink. By establishing the underreporting rate for drinking in the past 24 hours, we are not necessarily establishing the underreporting rate for the main criterion of interest, which is typical consumption over the past 30 days. It is possible, for example, that underreporting is worse for the 30-day criterion than for today's drinking. This is a reasonable hypothesis if one believes it is easier for a subject to misrecall or misrepresent his "typical" drinking over a 1-month period than his total drinking on the day of the interview.

Another way to consider this potential problem is to raise the question of whether today's and yesterday's alcohol consumption resembles typical consumption on drinking days last month. The answer to this question is provided in Table B.3, where typical consumption is compared with both yesterday's and today's consumption. For yesterday's consumption, the relationship to typical consumption is quite strong, with a product-moment

Table B.3 Relationship Between Ethanol Consumption Reported Today or Yesterday and Consumption Reported on Typical Drinking Days Last Month

Reported Ethanol Consumption on Day Specified	Number of Cases Reporting Typical Daily Ethanol Consumption Last Month								Total
	0–1 oz.	1–2 oz.	2–3 oz.	3–4 oz.	4–5 oz.	5–6 oz.	6–7 oz.	7+ oz.	
Yesterday									
0–1 oz.	⑩	8	8	2	1	1		3	33
1–2 oz.	2	⑲	9	3	2	4	2	1	42
2–3 oz.		3	⑪	3	2		1	1	21
3–4 oz.			2	⑥		1		2	11
4–5 oz.	1		1	3	④	3		4	16
5–6 oz.			1	3		③	2	5	14
6–7 oz.					1		⑦	1	9
7+ oz.		1	1	2	4		4	㊺	57
Total	13	31	33	22	14	12	16	62	203
Today									
0–1 oz.	⑪	17	12	6	4	5	3	9	67
1–2 oz.	2	⑨	7	8		3	6	9	44
2–3 oz.	1	1	①	1	3	1	1	5	13
3–4 oz.	1	1		②			3	6	13
4–5 oz.				1	○			8	11
5–6 oz.						①	1	3	5
6–7 oz.							○	2	2
7+ oz.			1					④	5
Total	14	28	22	18	7	10	14	46	159

Correlations and Statistics

	Correlation, r	Means			(N)
		Typical	Yesterday	Today	
Typical, Yesterday:	.70	6.1	5.0	—	(203)
Typical, Today:	.40	6.2	—	2.1	(159)

240

correlation of .70. Nevertheless, there are more people whose typical consumption exceeds yesterday's consumption than vice-versa, so that the mean typical consumption is 1 ounce higher than yesterday's (6.1 compared with 5.0).

A more serious discrepancy occurs for today's alcohol consumption, which is correlated only .40 with typical consumption last month. The low correlation is caused by a large number of persons who report high typical consumption but low consumption today; thus, today's consumption averages only 2.1 ounces compared with a typical mean (for this subgroup) of 6.2 ounces. Naturally, some of this discrepancy can be explained by the fact that most interviews took place during the daytime, so that subjects had not completed a full day of drinking. But the fact that yesterday's consumption is also lower than typical amounts consumed raises the possibility that recent drinking may be underreported to a greater extent than typical drinking. For this reason, our consistency analysis will compare estimated total consumption from the BAC with self-reports of both today's consumption and typical consumption.

Estimated total consumption can be derived for a given subject with a positive BAC by taking into account his elimination rate and the elapsed time between the onset of drinking (less the time for absorption) and the time of the BAC test. Since it is well established that the decline in BAC level is approximately linear over time, once drinking has stopped, a reasonable formula for a given subject would be

$$\text{Estimated Total } Q = .14W(BAC + EH),$$

where E is the elimination rate in BAC percent and H is the elapsed hours between the start of drinking today (or yesterday if no drinking occurred today) and the BAC test less 1 (to allow for ethanol absorption).

This estimating procedure has three major limitations. First, there is no way to apply it to persons whose BAC is zero, because the number of hours since it became zero is unknown. Thus, by definition, a recent drinker with a zero BAC cannot underreport his consumption. This problem can be overcome to some extent by varying the "window" of evaluation, e.g., 12 hours versus 24 hours. Second, the number of hours since drinking started must be estimated by using self-reports, which may also be subject to error, although on the surface it seems unlikely that a subject would intentionally distort the time when he began drinking. In any event, we can conduct a sensitivity analysis by adding or subtracting a given number of hours to or from the self-reported drinking start-times to see if varying time periods have any substantial effects on underreporting rates.

The third and most difficult limitation concerns estimates for the elimination rate E. This value is known to vary from person to person, and even for the same person at different times. The average value for most samples of the general male population is about .015 percent per hour, with a standard deviation of about .004; the average value for alcoholics or heavy drinkers is normally higher, with many studies showing a mean value of about .020 and a standard deviation of about .005 (Wallgren and Barry, 1970). Since our main interest is in determining the rate of underreporting for our sample as a whole, rather than for separate individuals, our approach will be to rely on a mean value of .020 for E, and then to conduct sensitivity tests by substituting values one standard deviation above or below this mean (i.e., assuming that the mean values for our sample are .015 or .025). The sensitivity test will tell us whether the underreporting rate is robust under different assumptions about average elimination rates.

Using the estimating formula and comparing the estimate with self-reports of both today's consumption and typical consumption, Table B.4 shows the number of persons whose self-report of typical consumption or today's consumption is less than their estimate from the BAC. Only those persons drinking in the past 24 hours are included, and as a starting point we have assumed that the average elimination rate is .020 percent per hour. In effect, these comparisons test the consistency between self-reports and an estimate of total consumption from the BAC.

Considering the last two columns first, we see that 96 out of 220 persons, or 44 percent, have BAC estimates that exceed their today's self-report by 1 ounce or more. This rate is remarkably close to an underreporting rate in a recent BAC study (Sobell, Sobell, and VanderSpek, 1979). Thus, by taking elimination rate into account, albeit by a rough approximation, we have increased the figure for the rate of underreporting of recent drinking by a substantial percentage. Note, however, that a considerable number of those underreporting today's consumption (46) report consistent *typical* consumption during the past month. On the other hand, only three cases show a consistent report of their today's drinking but an inconsistent report of their typical drinking.

Altogether we have only 50 out of 220, or 25 percent, who consistently underreport both today's consumption and typical consumption, based on their actual consumption estimated from the BAC. Contrary to the hypothesis offered earlier, it appears that in our sample, recent drinking episodes are more subject to underreporting than episodes in the past month or so. This is an important finding, because our study relies on typical drinking measures and not on drinking in the past day or two.

Since most of those persons consistently underreporting do so by considerable margins (over 2 ounces or 4 drinks), in the remainder of this analysis we shall treat underreporting of typical consumption over 1 ounce as serious. Further, we shall create a four-category consistency typology corresponding to the dotted lines in Table B.4:

Table B.4 Consistency Between Self-Reported Ethanol Consumption and Actual Consumption Estimated from BAC,[a] for Persons Drinking in the Past 24 Hours

Self-Report of Today's Ethanol Consumption[b]	Number of Cases Reporting Typical Ethanol Consumption on Drinking Days Last Month			Total	
	Not Exceeded by BAC	Exceeded by BAC by 1–2 oz.	Exceeded by BAC by 2 or more oz.	Number	Percent
Not exceeded by BAC	121	0	3	124	56
Exceeded by BAC by 1–2 oz.	19	4	1	24	11
Exceeded by BAC by 2 or more oz.	27	4	41	72	33
Total number	167	8	45	220	
Total percent	76	4	20		100

[a]Using mean elimination rate of .02 percent/hour.
[b]Yesterday's report if person did not drink today but drank yesterday less than 24 hours ago.

1. *Consistent underreporters:* Reports of both today's consumption and typical consumption last month are exceeded by the BAC estimate.
2. *Typical underreported:* Report of typical consumption is exceeded, but not of today's consumption.
3. *Today's underreported:* Report of today's consumption is exceeded, but not of typical consumption.
4. *No underreporting:* Neither the report of today's consumption nor that of typical consumption is exceeded by the BAC estimate.

Given that our main drinking-status criterion is typical consumption, the first two categories form the underreporting rate of major interest.

Using this summary measure of consistency, Tables B.5a and B.5b show the results of some sensitivity analyses designed to demonstrate the impact of varying assumptions about elimination rates and errors in self-reported

Table B.5a   Consistency Between Self-Reported Ethanol Consumption and Actual Estimate from BAC, for Differing Elimination Rates[a]

Consistency Pattern	Assumed Elimination Rate		
	.02 Percent/Hour (Mean for Alcoholics)	.015 Percent/Hour (Mean for General Population)	.025 Percent/Hour (1 Standard Deviation Above Alcoholic Mean)
Consistent underreporters	23	20	26
Typical underreported	1	2	1
Today's underreported	21	19	21
No underreporting	55	60	52
(N)	(220)	(220)	(220)

[a]For persons drinking in past 24 hours.

Table B.5b   Consistency Between Self-Reported Ethanol Consumption and Actual Estimate from BAC, for Varying Estimates of the Time That Drinking Started[a]

Consistency Pattern	Time Assumption (Assuming .020 Elimination Rate)	
	2 Hours Later Than Self-report	2 Hours Earlier Than Self-report
Consistent underreporters	19	30
Typical underreported	2	1
Today's underreported	14	20
No underreporting	64	48
(N)	(220)	(220)

[a]For persons drinking in past 24 hours.

drinking times. Table B.5a shows that increasing the mean elimination rate by one standard deviation above the alcoholic mean, to .025, increases the serious underreporting rate by only 3 percent (from 24 to 27 percent). Likewise, reducing the elapsed time since the start of drinking by 2 hours has only negligible effects. Increasing the elapsed time has a stronger effect, raising the underreporting rate to 31 percent. However, all of these underreporting rates are of the same general magnitude, so that varying the assumptions about the estimating procedure does not change the overall conclusion: Between 20 and 30 percent of the sample of recent drinkers, and more likely 25 percent, are found to be seriously underrepresenting their true consumption. For the remainder of these analyses, therefore, we will assume a mean elimination rate of .02 and accept the subject's own estimate of drinking time.

Variations in Underreporting Rates

Having established that typical consumption has an underreporting rate of around 25 percent, we now evaluate the possible variations in underreporting rates and the effect that underreporting might have on our overall drinking status measures. Is underreporting uniform at all consumption levels? or is it concentrated among lighter or heavier drinkers? How does the under-reporting rate affect the proportion of subjects who have been classified as drinkers without serious problems?

The first question is answered in Table B.6, which breaks down the consistency categories by level of typical consumption on drinking days last month. Note that the highest rate of serious underreporting (42 percent) occurs among persons who report typical amounts of two or fewer drinks on drinking days. The rate falls off to about 30 percent for persons whose typical quantities range from 1 to 4 ounces of ethanol (over 2 to 8 drinks), and declines further to about 10 percent for persons whose typical quantities exceed 4 ounces. Thus, underreporting is clearly concentrated among those drinking lower amounts. Note also that nearly half of the persons whose BAC disconfirmed today's report (but not the typical report) usually consume more than 7 ounces. The very heavy drinkers seem quite ready to admit their typical consumption patterns but deny the amount they drank over the past day or two.

Up to this point we have been analyzing the group of persons who drank in the past 24 hours. Since zero BACs cannot be adjusted to reflect total actual consumption, and since the longer a person has stopped drinking the more likely he is to have a zero BAC, it is possible that the 24-hour window reduces the underreporting rate. We can carry out yet another sensitivity analysis by using only those persons who drank within the past 12 hours. Those who have

Table B.6 Consistency Between Self-Reported Ethanol Consumption and Actual Estimate from BAC,[a] by Typical Consumption Last Month, for Persons Drinking in the Past 24 Hours

Typical Ethanol Consumption on Drinking Days Last Month	Number of Cases in Each Consistency Pattern						
	Consistent Underreporters	%	Typical Underreported	%	Today's Underreported	No Underreporting	Total
0–1 oz.	8	42			1	10	19
1–2 oz.	11	31			5	20	36
2–3 oz.	11	30	1	3	4	21	37
3–4 oz.	8	31	2	7	3	13	26
4–5 0z.	1	7			3	10	14
5–6 oz.	4	31			2	7	13
6–7 oz.	3	18			6	8	17
7+ oz.	4	7			22	32	58
Total	50	23	3	1	47	129	220

[a]Using elimination rate of .02 percent/hour.

been drinking during this shorter window are more likely to still have a positive BAC (in fact, as shown in Table B.1, 73 percent do).[4]

The underreporting results for a 12-hour window are shown in Table B.7. Overall the results are quite similar to those in Table B.6, with a total serious underreporting rate of 26 percent. The distribution of underreporting by typical consumption is also about the same as for the 24-hour window sample, except that the 0-1 category now has a 57 percent underreporting rate (but it is based on only 14 persons). In general, the length of the window for recent drinking does not have any substantial effect on the degree of serious underreporting.

Finally, Tables B.6 and B.7 both use our measure of typical consumption last month, as does the comparison with the BAC estimate shown in previous tables. It is possible that persons underreport both their typical consumption and their consumption today but admit to drinking very heavily on certain days during the past month. Since our final drinking status measure in Chapter 3 takes into account self-reported days of very heavy drinking, we need to investigate the possibility that underreporters admit to atypical heavy drinking.

Table B.8 breaks down typical consumption of alcohol into three additional categories: 3 or more days of very heavy drinking (10 drinks or more) in the past month; 1 or 2 days; and no days. As the table makes clear, the underreporting rates in Table B.6 are largely unaffected. Of the 42 subjects who say they drink less than 5 ounces of ethanol and who are serious underreporters, only nine are found to report 3 or more atypical days on which they consumed more than 10 drinks. Three more report 1 or 2 days of heavy drinking; but considering they underreported both today's and typical drinking, it would not be reasonable to consider their self-reports consistent with the BAC. Therefore, the majority of subjects who underreport both today's and typical consumption appear to underreport other drinking measures as well.

Given the degreee of underreporting documented here, what is the impact on our overall measure of status at 4 years? If persons who underreport their consumption are reclassified, is the rate of poor adjustment at 4 years seriously affected?

A preliminary answer to these questions is shown in Table B.9, which tabulates 4-year status by underreporting status. Interestingly, at 4 years, the rate of serious underreporting is relatively constant across both nonproblem drinking groups and the problem group. Thus, underreporting of alcohol

---

[4]Some analysts who have used BAC reports calculate underreporting only for the subgroup with positive BACs. This seems inappropriately restrictive, however, because such a subgroup excludes, by definition, light drinkers for whom a zero BAC reflects a consistent self-report.

Table B.7 Consistency Between Self-Reported Ethanol Consumption and Actual Estimate from BAC, by Typical Consumption Last Month for Persons Drinking in the Past 12 Hours

Typical Ethanol Consumption on Drinking Days Last Month	Number of Cases in Each Consistency Pattern						
	Consistent Underreporters	%	Typical Underreported	%	Today's Underreported	No Underreporting	Total
0–1 oz.	8	57	—	—	1	5	14
1–2 oz.	8	31	—	—	5	13	26
2–3 oz.	5	23	1	4	4	12	22
3–4 oz.	6	30	2	10	3	9	20
4–5 oz.	—	0	—	—	3	5	8
5–6 oz.	4	40	—	—	2	4	10
6–7 oz.	2	14	—	—	6	6	14
7+ oz.	3	7	—	—	22	18	43
Total	36	24	3	2	46	72	157

Table B.8

Consistency Between Self-Reported Ethanol Consumption and Actual Estimate from BAC[a] by Typical Consumption and Number of Days of Drinking More Than 10 Drinks, for Persons Drinking in the Past 24 Hours

Typical Consumption	Days Drank 10+ Drinks	Number of Cases in Each Consistency Pattern						
		Consistent Underreporters	%	Typical Underreported	%	Today's Underreported	No Underreporting	Total
0–2 oz.	None	16	34	—	—	4	27	47
	1 or 2	—	—	—	—	1	3	4
	3 or more	3	75	—	—	1	—	4
2–5 oz.	None	14	34	—	—	6	21	41
	1 or 2	2	25	1	11	1	4	8
	3 or more	4	14	2	7	3	19	28
5+ oz.	None	1	9	—	—	5	6	12
	1 or 2	2	29	—	—	1	4	7
	3 or more	8	13	—	—	19	33	60

[a]Using elimination rate of .02 percent/hour.

Table B.9 Self-Report Consistency Pattern, by Drinking Status at Four Years, for Persons Drinking in the Past 24 Hours

Drinking Status at 4 Years	Number of Cases in Each Consistency Pattern							
	Consistent Underreporters	%	Typical Underreported	%	Today's Underreported	No Underreporting	Total	%
Consumption under 2 oz; no problem	4	25			3	9	16	7
Consumption over 2 oz; no problem	9	24			3	26	38	17
Symptoms or consequences	37	22	3	2	40	86	166	75
Total	50	23	3	1	46	121	220	100

consumption is not related to the existence of symptoms or consequences, which were also based on self-reports. This suggests that the nonproblem drinking groups are not especially prone to underreporting, at least compared with the group that has reported serious problems in connection with alcohol.

The difficulty in adjusting our total 4-year-status measure for under-reporting is that we have a consistency measure only for the 220 persons who drank in the past 24 hours. The consistency of self-reports for the 265 persons who drank in the past 6 months but not in the past 24 hours cannot be assessed with the BAC measure. Given this situation, it seems to us that the most conservative procedure is to assume that the 25-percent rate of serious underreporting applies to the other 265 persons who drank in the past 6 months. (Persons who abstain for 6 months or more have already been shown to have a negligible percent with positive BAC.) It seems unlikely that these persons would underreport at a higher rate, since we showed in Chapter 3 that, if anything, short-term abstainers report even higher rates of consumption than current drinkers. Indeed, their underreporting rate may be lower, given the very low rate of disconfirmation (of abstention) for the short-term abstainers. Persons who have been abstaining for some time may feel more inclined to be truthful about their consumption than those who have been drinking very recently.

The results of two sensitivity analyses for consumption underreporting are given in Table B.10. Column (1) shows the 4-year drinking status of the total sample. Column (2) shows an adjustment assuming that consumption underreporters are truthful about symptoms and consequences; this means that the only effect is to move 25 percent of the low consumers into the high-consumption group. A more conservative assumption is that 25 percent of

Table B.10   Sensitivity Analysis for Inconsistent Self-Reports of Alcohol Consumption

	Percent Distribution of Cases		
Drinking Status at 4 Years	(1) Consumption as Reported[a]	(2) Consumption Adjustment[b]	(3) Consumption Adjustment[c]
Abstained 1 year	21	21	21
Abstained 6-11 months	7	7	7
Consumption under 2 oz.	8	6	6
Consumption over 2 oz.; no consequences or symptoms	10	12	8
Symptoms or consequences	54	54	58

[a]Total sample.
[b]Adjustment for inconsistent low reports: 25 percent of the low consumers moved to high-consumption group.
[c]Adjustment for inconsistent low and high reports: 25 percent of the low and high consumers shifted to "symptoms or consequences" group.

both low- and high-consumption groups have underreported not only their consumption, but their symptoms or consequences as well; i.e., they are general deniers, and must be reclassified into the "symptoms or consequences" group. This adjustment is shown in Column (3) of Table B.10.

It is readily apparent that even the most conservative adjustment procedure affects the final status measure by only a small degree. Instead of 18 percent nonproblem drinkers we have 14 percent, and instead of a problem rate of 54 percent we have a problem rate of 58 percent. The status of our sample at 4 years is quite robust, given the degree of underreporting we have observed by using BAC procedures.

THE COLLATERAL VALIDITY STUDY

The collateral validity study is based on interviews with 128 persons who, by virtue of acquaintance or kinship, were in a position to corroborate the subject's status on a number of concrete measures. Since both an overview of this study and its major conclusions have been presented in Chapters 2 and 3, this subsection will present only the more detailed analyses.

The relationship of collaterals to subjects is shown in Table B.11. Most of the collaterals are about evenly divided among "wife," "close friend," and "other relative" (usually a parent or child of the subject). Theoretically, then, the collaterals are in a fairly good position to evaluate the subject's drinking behavior.

The collateral interview did not attempt to evaluate all aspects of a subject's drinking status and impairment. Moreover, many of the areas covered in the interview schedule are either too subjective or did not find their way into our most important measures of subject status. Accordingly, the analysis presented here focuses on eight measures deemed crucial to an evaluation of the 4-year status of our alcoholic sample:

> *Drinking:* Abstention
> Amount of consumption

> *Consequences:* Jailed due to drinking problem
> Hospitalized due to drinking problem
> Missing work due to drinking problem

> *Symptoms:* Morning drinking
> Tremors
> Missing meals

Table B.11   Relationship of Collaterals to Subjects

Relationship	*Percent*
Wife	32
Friend	33
Other relative	24
Coworker	4
Alcoholism counselor/social worker	4
Landlord	3
(N)	(128)

Although a number of others measures could also be investigated, these variables are among the most important and most susceptible to corroboration by a collateral observer. Moreover, the results for these items are representative of the results for other measures assessed in the collateral interviews.

Table B.12 shows the results for abstention, categorized according to the important distinction in our 4-year status measure: abstention for 6 months or more. Significantly, there is very strong agreement between collateral and subject on this item, with only six discrepant pairs (5 percent). More important, only *one* subject report of 6-month abstention is disconfirmed by a collateral, whereas five collateral reports of subjects' abstention were disconfirmed by subjects and six collaterals were unsure. Consistent with the BAC validity test, self-reports of abstention appear to be quite valid.

A different story emerges for amount of consumption among the 92 persons drinking in the past 6 months, as shown in Table B.13 (all the remaining analyses are carried out for the drinking subsample). There are 21 discrepant pairs (23 percent), but in this case there are as many subject underreports as collateral underreports. More important, 24 of the collaterals are not sure about amount, which raises the question of whether the collateral is an adequate validating source, given the number of underreports due to

Table B.12   Subject-Collateral Agreement: Abstained or Drank in Past Six Months

	Collateral Report: Number of Cases			
Subject Self-Report	Abstained 6 Months or More	Drank Past 6 Months	Unsure	Total
Abstained 6 months or more	35	1	0	36
Drank past 6 months	5	81	6	92
Total	40	82	6	128

Table B.13 Subject-Collateral Agreement: Drank More Than 2 Ounces of Ethanol Per Day in Past Six Months

	Collateral Report: Number of Cases			
Subject Self-Report	Yes	No	Unsure	Total
Yes	14	10	19	43
No	11	33	5	49
Total	25	43	24	92

collateral misjudgments. In any event, the rate of subject underreporting (11 of 92, or 12 percent) is less than what we found in the BAC test.

The results shown in Tables B.14 and B.15 are for far more observable behavioral events: being jailed or hospitalized for a drinking problem. Accordingly, the collateral unsureness rate drops considerably. Also, the self-reports of jailing or hospitalization are fairly valid, with only five and four cases of subject underreporting, respectively. Since collateral underreporting occurs at about the same rate, the aggregate percentage with a drinking problem is nearly identical for both sources.

Table B.14 Subject-Collateral Agreement: Jailed Due to Drinking in Past Six Months

	Collateral Report: Number of Cases			
Subject Self-Report	Yes	No	Unsure	Total
Yes	10	5	0	15
No	5	66	4	75
Total	15	71	4	90

Table B.15 Subject-Collateral Agreement: Hospitalized Due to Drinking in Past Six Months

	Collateral Report: Number of Cases			
Subject Self-Report	Yes	No	Unsure	Total
Yes	20	6	1	27
No	4	55	6	65
Total	24	61	7	92

For the remaining measures—missing work, morning drinking, tremors, and missing meals—shown in Tables B.16 through B.19—the results are confounded by the relatively high rates of collateral uncertainty, ranging from 22 percent to nearly 40 percent of all pairs. Also, as with amount of alcohol consumption, there is as much or more collateral underreporting as subject underreporting (with one exception: tremors, with 9 and 14, respectively).

Table B.16   Subject-Collateral Agreement: Missing Work

Subject Self-Report	Collateral Report: Number of Cases			Total
	Missed Work Twice or More Often in 1 Month	Did Not Miss Work Twice or More Often in 1 Month	Unsure	
Missed work twice or more often in 1 month	2	8	7	17
Did not miss work twice or more often in 1 month	7	53	15	75
Total	9	61	22	92

Table B.17   Subject-Collateral Agreement: Morning Drinking

Subject Self-Report	Collateral Report: Number of Cases				Total
	Yes, Frequent[a]	Yes, Infrequent	No	Unsure	
Yes, frequent	8	1	13	25	47
Yes, infrequent	0	0	2	1	3
No	5	2	25	10	42
Total	13	3	40	36	92

[a]Frequent = 3 or more times in 30 days before last drink; infrequent = 1 or 2 times.

Table B.18   Subject-Collateral Agreement: Tremors

Subject Self-Report	Collateral Report: Number of Cases				Total
	Yes, Frequent[a]	Yes, Infrequent	No	Unsure	
Yes, frequent	11	2	6	17	36
Yes, infrequent	0	1	3	1	5
No	10	4	26	11	51
Total	21	7	35	29	92

[a]Frequent = 3 or more times in 30 days before last drink; infrequent = 1 or 2 times.

Table B.19   Subject-Collateral Agreement: Missing Meals

Subject Self-Report	Collateral Report: Number of Cases				Total
	Yes, Frequent[a]	Yes, Infrequent	No	Unsure	
Yes, frequent	18	0	6	24	48
Yes, infrequent	1	0	2	2	5
No	7	0	22	10	39
Total	26	0	30	36	92

[a]Frequent = 3 or more times in 30 days before last drink; infrequent = 1 or 2 times.

Thus, although the subject underreporting rates range from 8 to 15 percent, depending on the drinking problem, it is not clear that we should accept the collateral report as the true state of affairs. For the sample as a whole, the total rate of every drinking problem is higher when estimated from self-reports than when estimated from collateral reports.

In many respects, the results of the collateral study are disappointing. When the status measure is fairly observable, as with abstention or being jailed or hospitalized, we find self-reports to be quite valid. In this regard, our results parallel those reported in a major new validity study (Sobell and Sobell, 1978b). But for less observable—though no less important—measures of impairment and alcohol dependence symptoms, we find that the level of uncertainty and underreporting by collaterals raises serious questions about using collaterals as validation sources. Our results indicate that other sources will have to be investigated in order to validate self-reports of alcoholic symptomatology. Until that source is discovered and verified, we will have to be content with self-reports.

Supplemental Analyses

This appendix presents a variety of tabulations and analyses, addressed principally to methodological questions. They concern the basic characteristics of the sample; measures of drinking behavior at 4 years; results for individual treatment centers; and data on psychosocial characteristics.

BASIC CHARACTERISTICS OF THE SAMPLE

Table C.1 shows the frequency distributions (in percent) for background characteristics of the sample of subjects admitted to treatment. These distributions may be used to compare the present sample with samples used in similar studies.

MEASURES OF DRINKING BEHAVIOR

This section discusses the interrelationships of the components of drinking behavior (consumption, symptoms, and consequences), in order to provide additional data supporting the approach to measuring drinking status described in Chapter 3.

Factor Analysis of Drinking Behavior

Table C.2 shows the results of a principal components factor analysis including our basic measures of symptoms, consequences, and consumption quantity. The principal components extraction shows that most of the common variance is dominated by a factor composed of the symptom and consumption measures. Because the second and third components have such weak eigenvalues, a case could be made that only one factor should be recognized. The varimax rotation of all three factors scarcely changes the pattern, but it does clarify the multifactorial character of consequences. Factor II is defined principally by law enforcement incidents, while Factor III

Table C.1 Background Characteristics of Sample, Measured at Admission to Treatment

	Percent Distribution	
Characteristic	All Subjects[a]	Interviewed Subjects[b]
Ethnicity		
White	76	72
Black	15	18
Mexican-American	7	8
American Indian	2	1
Other	1	1
Marital Status		
Never married	17	17
Married	38	40
Widowed	6	5
Divorced	26	25
Separated	13	13

	Percent Distribution	
Characteristic	All Subjects[a]	Interviewed Subjects[b]
Occupation of Training		
Professional, technical	11	10
Manager	3	4
Sales	7	7
Clerical	4	3
Craftsmen	27	27
Operatives	16	16
Laborer, service	28	30
Farm	4	3
Living Quarters		
Group quarters	15	14
Private	85	86

	Percent Distribution	
Characteristic	All Subjects[a]	Interviewed Subjects[b]
Number of Times Treated for Alcoholism		
None	58	58
1	18	18
2	8	7
3 or more	17	18
Hospitalized for Reasons Related to Alcohol Past Year		
Yes	32	32
No	68	68
Years of "Heavy"		

	All subjects admitted to treatment (N = 758)[a]	Subjects admitted to treatment and interviewed (N = 548)[b]
Employment Status		
Employed		
Full time	34	37
Part time	3	3
Looking for work	23	24
No job due to drinking	21	21
Ill, institutionalized	10	9
Retired	8	5
Education (Years)		
1–8	27	25
9–11	22	22
12	32	31
13–15	13	16
16 or more	6	6
Household Income ($)		
0–2999	32	30
3000–5999	24	24
6000–9999	22	23
10000–13999	12	12
14000 or more	11	11
Age		
20–29	9	10
30–39	21	24
40–49	26	27
50–59	30	28
60–69	11	9
70 or over	3	2
Mean age	46.4	45.2
Years in Community		
Less than 1	25	23
1	7	7
2	7	7
3	5	5
4	5	5
5–9	14	15
10–19	17	17
20 or more	20	21
Drinking		
1–4	16	15
5–9	20	20
10–14	18	18
15–19	14	15
20–24	12	12
25 or more	20	21
Arrests for DWI Past Year		
Yes	20	21
No	80	79
Other Drinking-Related Arrests Past Year		
None	68	66
1	13	13
2 or more	19	21
Ever Attended AA		
Yes	56	57
No	44	43

[a] All subjects admitted to treatment (N = 758), including those interviewed, deceased, and not located at the 4-year followup.
[b] Subjects admitted to treatment and interviewed at the 4-year followup (N = 548).

Table C.2   Factor Analysis of Drinking Behavior Measures[a]

Drinking Behavior Measures	Principal Components			Varimax Rotation		
	I	II	III	I	II	III
Symptoms						
Tremors	.657	−.243	.122	.610	−.070	.360
Morning drinking	.771	−.169	−.129	.787	−.011	.144
Loss of control	.519	−.254	.055	.505	−.121	.260
Blackouts	.697	−.130	−.097	.701	.015	.144
Missing meals	.779	−.042	−.129	.773	.113	.120
Continuous drinking	.563	.276	−.256	.564	.352	−.130
Consequences						
Liver disease	.416	−.074	.548	.216	.104	.650
Physician visits	.176	−.217	.707	−.037	−.064	.756
Nonliver alcohol-related disease	.578	.068	.351	.409	.246	.484
Hospitalization	.607	.236	.110	.488	.379	.232
DWI arrest	.090	.784	.253	−.128	.814	.095
Jail	.352	.686	.028	.206	.743	−.016
Work impairment	.607	.062	−.151	.605	.172	.026
Fights	.340	−.040	.067	.300	.047	.172
Consumption						
Typical quantity	.751	.047	−.172	.747	.186	.053
Total consumption (QF)	.839	−.113	−.183	.858	.050	.103
Eigenvalues/sum of squares	5.496	1.466	1.217	4.915	1.659	1.605

[a]Base $N = 393$ (all persons drinking in past 6 months).

reflects diseases and physician visits. Most of the other consequences (except work impairment) are split across several factors.

It appears that the principal domain measured by these items is one common to alcohol dependence and heavy consumption. There may be other domains tapped by the measures of adverse consequences, but there does not seem to be any internal coherence among them. These findings suggest that consequences are diverse, fragmented, and only weakly related to the more integrated phenomena of dependence and consumption patterns. The results support our contention that dependence is central to alcohol problems, whereas consequences are more a by-product of the process.

Behavioral Impairment Measures

The six dependence symptoms were selected from a larger set of items representing impairment or dysfunction caused by heavy or deviant drinking. Table C.3 shows a factor analysis of all such "behavioral impairment" measures available in the 4-year followup interview (question 25). All of them except "inability to stop" and "drinking more than intended" are used in the NIAAA monitoring system as components of an overall index of impairment.

Table C.3   Factor Analysis of Behavioral Impairment Measures

Impairment Measure[a]	Principal Component		
	I	II	III
Tremors	.695	.149	−.053
Morning drinking	.813	−.059	.046
Blackouts	.637	.106	−.030
Being "drunk"	.731	−.123	.343
Missing meals	.778	−.006	.224
Missing work/activities	.628	.084	.374
Inability to stop	.595	−.098	−.500
Drinking more than intended	.639	−.250	−.290
Fighting while drinking	.445	−.406	.031
Difficulty sleeping	.427	.527	−.159
Longest continuous drinking period	.375	.123	.183
Longest dry period	−.464	.372	.018
Drinking on job	.339	.665	−.068
Drinking alone	.238	−.029	−.596
Eigenvalue	4.754	1.170	1.068

[a]30 days before the last drink among drinkers during the past 6 months. N = 393. Except for "inability to stop" and "drinking more than intended," the items are those appearing in the NIAAA "impairment index," which is used for the ATC monitoring system.

There is apparently one principal factor representing the domain sampled by these behavioral measures, but many of the measures are only weakly related to that factor. Basically, the first eight measures ("shakes" through "drinking more than intended") exhibit a strong relation to the factor. The others appear to reflect miscellaneous phenomena, not the type of impairment represented by shakes, morning drinking, blackouts, etc. This constitutes further evidence that our six dependence symptoms form a coherent entity. It also implies that the dependence symptoms, possibly augmented by a few other measures from the set that are highly loaded on the first component, would make a better index of alcohol impairment than the current miscellaneous list does.

Symptom Levels and Consequences

Despite the evidence of coherence among the dependence symptoms, one may question the decision, discussed in Chapter 3, to differentiate symptomatology by splitting cases with zero symptoms from those with one or more. Our principal reasons for making that split are explained in Chapter 3. Here we present additional supporting data showing that the threshold between

Table C.4   Reported Rates of Drinking Consequences at Four Years, by Type of Consequence and Levels of Symptoms

Consequence at 4 Years	Symptom Level[a] at 4 Years					
	0	1–2	3–5	6–10	11–20	Over 20
	Percent Reporting Consequences					
Any health consequence	15	31	32	39	50	67
Any law enforcement consequence	8	13	18	21	33	29
Any work consequence	3	9	12	25	21	52
Interpersonal consequence	1	13	15	18	33	29
Any of the above	23	47	53	68	88	89
(N)	(129)	(45)	(34)	(28)	(24)	(132)

Consequence at 4 Years	"Classical" Symptom Level[b] at 4 Years					
	0	1–2	3–5	6–10	11–20	Over 20
	Percent Reporting Consequences					
Any health consequence	18	32	35	72	61	67
Any law enforcement consequence	10	29	15	20	29	29
Any work consequence	4	21	18	36	52	51
Interpersonal consequence	4	18	21	40	29	25
Any of the above	29	65	62	92	87	87
(N)	(171)	(34)	(34)	(25)	(31)	(97)

[a]Symptom score (sum of frequencies during the 30 days before the last drink) based on six symptoms: tremors, morning drinking, loss of control, missing meals, blackouts, and continuous drinking.
[b]Symptom score (sum of frequencies during the 30 days before the last drink) based on three symptoms: tremors, morning drinking, and loss of control.

zero symptoms and one or more symptoms holds up when a number of different measures are used.

Table C.4 shows rates of reported consequences at 4 years by levels of symptoms. In the top panel, symptoms are measured by the six-item dependence scale and in the bottom panel, by the more restrictive "classical" symptom scale (tremors, morning drinking, and loss of control). Consequences are measured in five ways: separately by each of the four types of consequences, and by total consequences ("any of the above"). In every case, the threshold between zero symptoms and one or more symptoms is obvious.

Table C.5 shows that symptoms are also likely to be perpetuated from the 18-month point to the 4-year point. This is true even for subjects who report just one or two symptoms. The same pattern appears if the criterion is defined as the appearance of "classical" symptoms at 4 years. Again the threshold is suggested by the discontinuous rise in the rates between zero symptoms and one or more symptoms.

Table C.5   Symptom Level Carryover: 18 Months to Four Years

	Symptom Level at 18 Months[a]					
	0	1- 2	3- 5	6- 10	11- 20	Over 20
Type of Symptoms at 4 Years	Percent with Symptoms at 4 Years					
Any symptom at 4 years[b]	33	59	52	58	80	83
Any "classical" symptom at 4 Years[c]	26	44	40	47	76	75
(N)	(87)	(34)	(25)	(19)	(25)	(72)

[a]Symptom score (sum of frequencies during the past 30 days) based on 5 items: tremors, morning drinking, missing meals, blackouts, and continuous drinking.
[b]Symptom score (sum of frequencies during the 30 days before the last drink) based on six symptoms: tremors, morning drinking, loss of control, missing meals, blackouts, and continuous drinking.
[c]Symptom score based on three symptoms: tremors, morning drinking, and loss of control.

TREATMENT CENTER DIFFERENCES

Table C.6 shows the distribution of drinking status at 4 years across treatment centers. In the 18-month study, it was found that the remission rates were not significantly different among treatment centers after background characteristics of the client population were controlled, and the same is true at the 4-year point (see footnote b of Table C.6). Thus, it appears that whatever differences exist among treatment centers at the 4-year followup may be explained by the background characteristics of the subjects at the centers, rather than by the unique characteristics of the centers themselves. For this reason, we have not analyzed treatment-center characteristics in detail in this study.

Variations in problem rates across different treatment centers at 4 years are not explained by variations in the field followup completion rates. (Completion rates for individual centers varied between 72 and 96 percent.) The rank-order correlation between the completion rate for a center and the percentage of the center's subjects without problems at 4 years is not significant at the .05 level ($\rho = -.151$). A similar result appears if the subject's condition at 4 years is measured by the "remission" definition that was used in the 18-month study.

PSYCHOSOCIAL MEASURES

Tables C.7 through C.10 provide detailed backup data for the discussion in Chapter 4. The results document, in particular, the highly impaired psychosocial functioning in Group 7 (and to a lesser extent, Groups 5 and 6).

Table C.6 Drinking Status at Four Years, by Treatment Center

Treatment Center	Drinking Status at Four Years:[a] Percent Distribution of Cases							Problem Rate[b]	(N)
	Abstained 1 Year	Abstained 6-11 Months	Low Q	High Q	Consequences	Symptoms	Symptoms and Consequences		
A	18	6	6	9	4	17	39	60	99
B	15	8	22	21	11	8	14	33	72
C	19	4	6	2	8	13	49	70	53
D	19	14	5	10	5	10	38	53	42
E	31	8	4	6	4	8	38	50	133
F	20	10	5	12	2	22	29	53	41
G	27	4	4	27	0	14	23	37	22
H	17	4	8	10	6	12	43	61	86

[a]All admissions (Groups I and II).

[b]Percentage with symptoms or consequences. Differences in problem rates across treatment centers were compared by analysis of covariance, adjusting for background characteristics of subjects measured at admission to treatment. The unadjusted problem rates (coded as a zero-one indicator variable for problem versus nonproblem) were significantly different across treatment centers (F = 3.22, $p < .01$). However, when subject background characteristics were included as covariates (symptom level, previous treatment, social stability, socioeconomic status, ethnicity, and age), the adjusted problem rates were not significantly different across treatment centers (F = 1.53, $p > .10$). The covariates were highly significant (F = 4.73, $p < .001$).

Table C.7 Marital Status, by Drinking Status at Four Years

		Percent of Respondents Reporting Current Marital Status				
Group No.	Drinking Status at 4 Years	Married[a]	Widowed	Divorced or Separated	Never Married	(N)
1	Abstained 1 year	54	3	31	12	(117)
2	Abstained 6-11 months	56	5	28	10	(39)
3	Low Q	48	7	31	14	(42)
4	High Q	56	2	30	12	(57)
5	Consequences	45	7	34	14	(29)
6	Symptoms	49	6	30	15	(67)
7	Symptoms and consequences	30	3	47	20	(196)

[a]Includes commonlaw spouse.

Table C.8 Employment, by Drinking Status at Four Years

Group No.	Drinking Status at 4 Years	Percent Distribution of Respondent's Current Employment Status							
		Employed		Unemployed[a]	Not Employed[b]				(N)
		Full Time	Part Time		Not in Force[c]	Drinking Problem[d]	Ill or Institutionalized[e]	Other	
1	Abstained 1 year	58	4	10	8	3	14	3	(117)
2	Abstained 6-11 months	59	0	3	8	0	23	8	(39)
3	Low Q	52	14	7	10	0	17	0	(42)
4	High Q	61	7	7	11	0	12	2	(57)
5	Consequences	27	3	20	17	7	17	10	(30)
6	Symptoms	48	10	16	6	0	18	2	(67)
7	Symptoms and consequences	29	6	22	2	11	27	3	(196)

[a]Not employed but currently looking for work; or laid off temporarily.
[b]Not employed, not looking for work, and not laid off temporarily.
[c]Retired or student.
[d]Not looking for work because of a drinking problem.
[e]Not looking for work because of illness not related to alcohol, or because of being institutionalized.

Table C.9 Respondent's Own Income, by Drinking Status at Four Years

Group No.	Drinking Status at 4 Years	Percent Distribution of Respondent's Own Income in Past Year						
		$0–$999	$1000–$3999	$4000–$6999	$7000–$9999	$10,000–$13,999	$14,000 or more	(N)
1	Abstained 1 year	34	10	16	11	11	18	(117)
2	Abstained 6-11 months	29	11	18	11	18	13	(39)
3	Low Q	38	8	15	8	20	12	(42)
4	High Q	27	7	14	18	20	14	(57)
5	Consequences	50	14	11	11	0	14	(30)
6	Symptoms	37	12	20	9	15	6	(67)
7	Symptoms and consequences	49	20	11	6	6	7	(196)

Table C.10 Respondent's Household Income, by Drinking Status at Four Years

Group No.	Drinking Status at 4 Years	Percent Distribution of Total Household Income in Past Year						
		$0–$999	$1000–$3999	$4000–$6999	$7000–$9999	$10,000–$13,999	$14,000 or more	(N)
1	Abstained 1 year	6	25	12	8	12	38	(117)
2	Abstained 6-11 months	5	19	14	11	22	30	(39)
3	Low Q	0	18	26	3	21	32	(42)
4	High Q	4	15	7	19	20	35	(57)
5	Consequences	14	31	14	10	14	17	(30)
6	Symptoms	3	26	26	8	15	21	(67)
7	Symptoms and consequences	14	38	17	10	7	14	(196)

Table C.7 shows the distribution of marital status at 4 years. As discussed in the section on "Social Adjustment" in Chapter 4, Table C.7 reveals that Group 7 respondents are especially likely to be living without a spouse (30 percent are currently married, whereas 47 percent are currently divorced or separated). The tendency toward being unmarried is not counterbalanced by the presence of stable nonmarital living arrangements; very few members of any sample group reported having a girl friend with whom they lived at the time of the followup.

Tables C.8 through C.10 provide detailed distributions of employment and income variables, by category of drinking status at 4 years. These data supplement the summary tables for the same variables shown in the section on "Social Adjustment" in Chapter 4. Table C.8 indicates that high rates of unemployment characterize not only Group 7, but also Groups 5 and 6. Moreover, a substantial proportion of alcoholics in every drinking-status category report that they are not employed either because of institutionalization or because of illness *not* related to drinking. Likewise, Tables C.9 and C.10 show that substantial proportions of every drinking-status category have low incomes (compared with the general-population figures cited in Chapter 4), although Groups 5, 6, and 7 are considerably lower than the other groups.

APPENDIX D

Index Construction

This appendix describes the logic and procedures for defining multiple-item indices. Unless otherwise specified, all question numbers refer to questions in the Client Interview form (reproduced as Appendix E).

QUANTITY OF ALCOHOL CONSUMPTION

An index of the typical quantity consumed on a drinking day was derived from the questions that asked for the subject's frequency of drinking and typical amount of consumption on drinking days during the 30 days before the last drink. The following notation was adopted:

$$D = \text{total days when any beverage was drunk (question 19)}$$

$DB, DW, DL =$ days when beer, wine, or liquor was drunk (questions 20A, 21A, and 22A)

$QB, QW, QL =$ typical quantity of beer, wine, or liquor consumed on days when each was drunk (questions 20B, 21B, and 22B), multiplied by the appropriate ethanol content factor (.04 for beer, .12 for table wine, .18 for fortified wine, and .43 for distilled liquor).

Typical quantity per drinking day, in ounces of ethanol, was estimated by the following formula:

$$Q \text{ (typical quantity)} = (QB \cdot DB + QW \cdot DW + QL \cdot DL)/D$$

Each subject was also asked how often, during the 30-day period before his last drink, he consumed quantities approximating 3 ounces of ethanol (6 or more cans of beer, one or more fifths of wine, or one-half or more pints of distilled liquor: Questions 20D, 20E, 21F, 21G, 22E, and 22F). A subject who reported a typical quantity under two ounces per day and no days consuming 3 ounces or more was classified as having "low consumption;" others were classified as having "high consumption."

269

DEPENDENCE SYMPTOM SCALE

The scale of dependence symptoms, as described in Chapter 3, was constructed by taking the sum of the six symptom items: tremors, morning drinking, loss of control, blackouts, missing meals, and continuous drinking (questions 25E, 25D, 25K, 25B, 25C, and 25M). The first five items were scored as 0 through 30, representing the number of days when the symptom occurred during the 30 days before the last drink. The sixth item, continuous drinking, was scored only as 1 or 0, indicating whether or not the longest period of uninterrupted drinking lasted 12 hours or more.

Similar scales were developed for symptoms at 18 months and at admission. However, the 18-month and admission interviews did not measure loss of control, so the symptom scales for those time points include only the other five items.

ADVERSE CONSEQUENCES INDEX

The index of adverse consequences of drinking was constructed by scoring any instance of the following events during the past 6 months as a consequence.

Health Problems

1. Liver disease diagnosed by a physician in the past 6 months (question 44B); or liver disease treated by a physician in the past 6 months (question 44C); or liver disease reported by the subject as "still" present (question 44D), provided a physician had diagnosed a liver disease before the past 6 months (question 44); or an episode of "hepatitis or yellow jaundice" reported by the subject in the past 6 months (question 46C).
2. Medically advised to stop drinking in the past 6 months (question 48B).
3. Hospitalized because of drinking in the past 6 months (question 49B).
4. Episode of an alcohol-related disease reported in the past 6 months (pancreatitis, DTs, or bleeding, questions 46 and 47).

Law Enforcement Problems

5. Arrest for drinking and driving in the past 6 months (question 58).
6. In jail for something connected with drinking in the past 6 months (question 59B).

Work and Interpersonal Problems

7. Currently not employed because of a drinking problem (question 8B).
8. Missed work on 2 or more days because of drinking during the 30 days before the last drink (question 25I).
9. Had arguments or fights while drinking on 2 or more days during the 30 days before the last drink (question 25F).

A score of "number of consequences" was computed by scoring each of the above nine variables as a zero-one indicator (having a consequence versus not having one) and taking the sum of the nine variables.

SERIOUS ALCOHOL-RELATED INCIDENTS

Chapters 6 and 7 present analysis of an index of "serious alcohol-related incidents" experienced by the subject over the period from 1973 to 1976. To ensure that incidents directly related to admission to treatment were excluded, only those incidents occurring in July 1973 or later were counted.

In the 4-year followup questionnaire, each subject was asked to report the date (month and year) when he had experienced any family, health, job, or police problems *because of drinking* (questions 66 to 69). Examples of responses that were treated as serious incidents are listed below.

Family problems.   Wife or girl friend left or threatened to leave; subject hit or physically harmed family; subject left home or was evicted from home.

Health problems.   Subject had hepatitis, "yellow jaundice," other liver problems, diabetes, numbness or tingling in limbs, dizziness, pancreatitis, vitamin deficiency, anemia, bleeding, or other serious alcohol-related disorders.

Job problems.   Subject was fired, quit job, lost a promotion, was demoted or suspended, or could not hold a job because of drinking.

Police problems.   Subject was arrested or convicted for driving while intoxicated, driving under the influence of alcohol, public intoxication, disorderly conduct, disturbing the peace, assault, or other felony.

We also distinguished two types of entries to treatment that were counted as alcohol-related incidents.

ATC reentry.   An inpatient reentry to any ATC, defined as the occurrence of one or more days of detoxification or hospital treatment, provided the subject did not receive treatment of any kind at the ATC during the preceding month.

Other treatment entry.   Any entry to treatment reported by the subject in answer to question 73 (any time between 1973 and 1976 when the subject received help for a drinking problem from a "hospital, mental health clinic, or alcohol counseling center").

INDICES OF SUBJECT CHARACTERISTICS AT ADMISSION TO TREATMENT

Socioeconomic Status

The index of socioeconomic status (SES) at admission to treatment, which was also used in the 18-month study (Armor et al., 1978), was computed by taking the mean of scores for occupation of training, annual household income, and education. The three measures were scored on similar scales, each ranging between 1 and 14 points. A similar index of SES at 4 years was defined in Chapter 4, based on the subject's 4-year followup measures. It included only measures of occupation and income, because education is usually constant over time and was not determined in the 4-year interview.

Social Stability

A two-point index of the subject's general social stability at admission to treatment was defined as follows: (1) subjects who lived in group quarters, or who were both unmarried and unemployed, were classified as "unstable"; (2) all other subjects were classified as "stable." A similar index of social stability at 4 years was defined in Chapter 4, based on the subject's measures of these variables at the 4-year followup.

NIAAA Quantity-Frequency Index of Daily Consumption

Previous studies on this cohort measured alcohol consumption principally according to the Quantity-Frequency Index of Average Daily Consumption (QF). This index, also used in several places in this report (Chapter 2, Chapter 3, and Appendix A), estimates the total volume of ethanol consumed per day by the subject during a specified period (generally 30 days). The QF Index is computed according to the following formula:

$$QF = \sum_{i=1}^{3} F_i \, Q_i \, C_i,$$

where $F =$ the fraction of days in the period when beverage i was consumed,

$Q =$ the quantity of beverage i consumed (in fluid ounces) on a typical day when the subject drank beverage i,

$C =$ the estimated proportion of ethanol content (by volume) in beverage i.

Behavioral Impairment Index

A general index of behavioral impairment from alcohol is used principally in government data systems and is also reported in Chapter 2. The standard index, as defined by NIAAA, is composed of the following 12 items representing symptoms and functional impairment arising from alcohol abuse. The index score is computed by taking the mean of the 12 item scores and multiplying that sum by 10. The resulting score ranges from 0 to 30.

Components of the NIAAA Behavioral Impairment Index

Item	Scoring Scheme	Question Number
1. Had difficulty sleeping	None = 0; 1-2 = 1; 3-5 = 2; 6 or more = 3	25A
2. Had memory lapses or "blackouts"	None = 0; 1-2 = 1; 3-5 = 2; 6 or more = 3	25B
3. Had the "shakes"	None = 0; 1-2 = 1; 3-5 = 2; 6 or more = 3	25E
4. Had arguments or fights with others while drinking	None = 0; 1-2 = 1; 3-5 = 2; 6 or more = 3	25F
5. Missed work or other activities because of drinking	None = 0; 1-2 = 1; 3-5 = 2; 6 or more = 3	25I
6. Missed a meal because of drinking	None = 0; 1-4 = 1; 5-10 = 2; 11 or more = 3	25C
7. Had a drink as soon as you woke up	None = 0; 1-4 = 1; 5-10 = 2; 11 or more = 3	25D
8. Were "drunk"	None = 0; 1-4 = 1; 5-10 = 2; 11 or more = 3	25G
9. Longest period without drinking	12 hours or more = 0; less than 12 hours = 2	25L
10. Drank alone or with others	Always with others = 0; usually with others =1; usually alone = 2; always alone = 3	25N
11. Longest period of continuous drinking	Less than 6 hours = 0; 6 to 12 hours = 2; 12 hours or more = 3	25M
12. Drank while on the job	Never = 0; 1 day or more = 2	25H

PSYCHIATRIC SYMPTOMATOLOGY SCALE

The psychiatric symptomatology scale discussed in Chapter 4 included items measuring anhedonia, tension and stress, cognitive impairment, depression, and anxiety (questions 52 through 56 in the Client Interview form, Appendix E). Each item was rescored as follows: "none of the time" = 1; "some of the time" = 2; "most of the time" = 3; "all of the time" = 4. The total psychiatric symptomatology scale was then computed as the sum of the five item scores.

APPENDIX E

Client Interview Form

ATC FOUR-YEAR FOLLOWUP STUDY
CLIENT INTERVIEW FORM

CASE # ☐☐☐☐

TIME STARTED _____ a.m.

_____ p.m.

DATE: _____ _____ _____
      Month   Day   Year

1. First, where do you live—in what city and state?

    _____ _____
    City   State

    And what is your zipcode?

    _____
    Zipcode

2. How long have you lived in this (city/town)?

    No. of years _____
    and
    No. of months _____

3. During the past 12 months how many different addresses have you lived at—including your current address?

    PROBE FOR NUMBER OF DIFFERENT ADDRESSES.

    No. of addresses _____

4. **CIRCLE ONE CODE; ASK IF NECESSARY:**

    In what type of residence are you living now?

    Apartment 01

    Private house 02

    Mobile home (trailer) 03

    Hotel 04

    Rooming house 05

    Halfway house, or recovery home . 06 ⎫

    Other group quarters (Salvation   ⎬ Go to Q. 6
    Army/ dormitory, etc.) . . . . . . 07 ⎪

    Street. . . . . 08 ⎭

    Other **(SPECIFY** _____

    _____) 09

275

5. How many people do you live with, including children?

No. of people _____

IF OTHER THAN RESPONDENT ASK:

A. I would like to know the age of each of the other people in your household and their relationship to you.

Age	Relationship
____	_____
____	_____
____	_____
____	_____
____	_____
____	_____

6. What is your date of birth?

Month _____

Day _____

Year _____

7. How much do you weigh?

PROBE FOR BEST ESTIMATE

Lbs. _____

8. At the present time do you have a full-time job, part-time job, do you work at odd jobs, or are you not employed?

Full-time job **(GO TO C)** 1

Part-time job 2

Work at odd jobs **(ASK A)** 3

Not employed 4

A. Have you been looking for (work/full-time work) during the past 30 days?

Yes **(GO TO C)** 1

No **(ASK B)** 2

276

B.   What is the main reason you haven't been looking for work?
     RECORD VERBATIM AND CODE

                                          Homemaker 01

                                          Student 02

                                          Retired/too old 03

                                          Illness or disability *not* related
                                               to alcohol 04

                                          Drinking problem (including
                                               illness related to alcohol) . . , . . 05

                                          Institutionalized 06

                                          Don't want a job/more work 07

                                          No job available 08

                                          In this location only temporarily/
                                               intend to move on 09

                                          Have independent income/no
                                               need to work 10

                                          Seasonal worker 11

                                          Temporarily laid off 12

                                          Other **(SPECIFY**_____

                                          _____) 13

C.   How many months were you employed during the past 12 months?

                                          No. of months   _____

     IF DID NOT WORK DURING THE PAST 12 MONTHS, SKIP TO Q. 10.

D.   What kind of place (do/did) you work for (most recently in the past 12 months)?

     (PROBE: What do they make or do?)   _____
                                                Industry

E.   What kind of work (do/did) you do?

     (PROBE: What (is/was) your job called?)   _____
                                                Occupation

     IF NOT ALREADY ANSWERED, ASK:

F.   What (do/did) you actually do in that job?

     (PROBE: What (are/were) some of your main duties?)

9. How many days did you work during the past 30 days?

    USE CALENDAR   No. of days worked _____

    A.   How many paid vacation days, if any, did you take in the past 30 days?

                    No. of paid vacation days _____

10. Are you now legally married, widowed, divorced, separated, do you have a common-law wife, or have you never been married?

        Married [**ASK A, B, & E**] 1

        Common-law wife [**ASK A, B, & E**] 2

        Widowed [**ASK A–E**] 3

        Divorced [**ASK A–E**] 4

        Separated [**ASK A–E**] 5

        Never married [**ASK D**] 6

    A.   How many times have you been married? [**INCLUDES COMMON-LAW SPOUSE**]   No. of times _____

    B.   In what month and year did you get married (the last time)?   Month _____
        [**INCLUDES COMMON-LAW SPOUSE**]
        Year _____

        IF CURRENTLY WIDOWED, DIVORCED, OR SEPARATED:

    C.   How long have you been (widowed/living apart)?   No. of years _____
        [**INCLUDES COMMON-LAW SPOUSE**]   and
        No. of months _____

    D.   Do you have a steady girlfriend now?   Yes 1

                  No [**GO TO Q. 11**] 2

    E.   Are you living with your (wife/girlfriend) now?   Yes 1

                  No 2

11. How many children do you have, whether or not they live with you?   No. of children _____

    Now I have some questions about how things are going for you right now.

12. Taking all things together, how would you say things are these days—would you say you are very happy, pretty happy, or not too happy, these days?

Very happy   1

Pretty happy   2

Not too happy   3

13. Now I'm going to ask you about how things are going in various areas of your life at the present time. As I ask about each area, just tell me whether things are going very well, fairly well, or not very well.

How about:	Very well	Fairly well	Not very well
a. your friendships and social life— would you say things are going very well, fairly well, or not very well?	1	2	3
b. your home life or marriage?	1	2	3
c. your relationship with your children? does not have contact with children. . . . 4 does not have children. 5	1	2	3
d. your work or employment opportunities?	1	2	3
e. your money or finances?	1	2	3
f. your health in general?	1	2	3

14. How do you think things will go for you in the next few years? Do you think your life will get better, get worse, or stay about the same?

Get better. 1

Get worse 2

Stay about the same 3

15. About how many _close_ friends do you have—people you feel at ease with and can talk with about what is on your mind? You may include people who live with you or relatives.

No. of close friends _____

IF ANSWER IS "0", GO TO Q. 17

A. How many of these close friends are heavy drinkers at the present time?

No. of heavy drinkers_____

B. How many of these close friends do not drink at all at the present time?

No. who do not drink_____

C. How many of these close friends would you say are recovered or recovering alcoholics at the present time?

No. of recovered or recovering alcoholics

_____

279

16. Think about the close friend you see most often. About how frequently do you get together? Would you say . . .

Every day 1

Several times a week 2

Once a week 3

2 or 3 times a month 4

Once a month. 5

Less than once a month. . . . 6

or, Never 7

17. **IF CURRENTLY LIVING WITH SPOUSE/GIRLFRIEND:**

Do you think of your (wife/girlfriend) as drinking occasionally, drinking frequently, having a drinking problem, or doesn't she drink?

Drinks occasionally 1

Drinks frequently. 2

Has a drinking problem 3

Doesn't drink 4

18. What was the approximate date of your last drink—the last time you had any alcoholic beverage like beer, wine, or liquor, even if it was only a little?

Month _____

Day _____

Year _____

IF DATE OF LAST DRINK IS MORE THAN 1 YEAR AGO, SKIP TO QUESTION 34.

19. Let's talk about the 30 days before your last drink, including the day of your last drink. Let's see—that would be

from _____ to _____.

On about how many days would you say you drank any alcoholic beverage during that 30-day period?

IF RESPONDENT *CANNOT* ESTIMATE NUMBER OF DAYS, HAND ORANGE CARD AND SAY:
I know it's hard to remember—just look at this card and give me your best guess.

No. of days _____

20. Did you drink beer, ale, or any other malt beverage, such as malt liquor, during that 30-day period?

                                                Yes [ASK A-G] 1

                                                No [GO TO Q. 21] 2

A. During those 30 days, on about how many days did you drink beer or any other malt beverage?

IF RESPONDENT *CANNOT* **ESTIMATE NUMBER OF DAYS, HAND ORANGE CARD AND SAY:**
I know it's hard to remember—just look at this card and give me your best guess.

                                                No. of days _____

B. On a *typical* day when you drank beer or any other malt beverage, about how much did you drink?

**RECORD VERBATIM AND FILL IN NO. OF UNITS
IN COLUMN 1 AT RIGHT.**

1. Number of Units	2. Ounces in Container
_____ Cans ⟶	_____ oz. per can
_____ Bottles ⟶	_____ oz. per bottle
_____ Six packs ⟶	_____ oz. per can
_____ Glasses ⟶	_____ oz. per glass
_____ Quarts ⟶	32 oz. per quart
_____ Other (SPECIFY	
_____) ⟶	_____ oz. per unit

**IF RESPONDENT ANSWERS IN TERMS OF CANS,
BOTTLES, GLASSES, OR OTHER UNITS:**

C. About how many ounces are there in the (cans/bottles/glasses/other units) you *usually* drink? (For example: Are they standard 12-ounce cans, half-quart cans, or what?)

**RECORD VERBATIM AND RECORD NUMBER OF
OF OUNCES IN COLUMN 2 ABOVE.**

D. On how many days (if any) during that period did you drink

$\left\{\begin{array}{l}\text{10 cans}\\ \text{10 bottles}\\ \text{10 glasses}\\ \text{4 quarts}\end{array}\right\}$ or more? No. of days _____

E. On how many days (if any) during that period did you drink

$\left\{\begin{array}{l}\text{6 to 9 cans}\\ \text{6 to 9 glasses}\\ \text{6 to 9 bottles}\\ \text{2 to 3 quarts}\end{array}\right\}$ but not more?

No. of days _____

F. What did you drink most often during that 30-day period? Was it *usually* . . .

Beer 1

Ale 2

Malt liquor 3

or, Another malt beverage

(SPECIFY_____

_____) 4

G. What is the name of the brand, or brands, you usually drink?

RECORD VERBATIM _____

_____

21. Did you drink wine during that 30-day period?

YES (ASK A-G) 1

NO (GO TO Q. 22) 2

A. During those 30 days, on about how many days did you drink wine?

IF RESPONDENT *CANNOT* ESTIMATE NUMBER OF DAYS, HAND ORANGE CARD AND SAY:
I know it's hard to remember—just look at this card and give me your best guess.

No. of days _____

B. On a <u>typical</u> day when you drank wine, about how much wine did you drink?

**RECORD VERBATIM AND FILL IN COLUMN
1 AT RIGHT**

| | 1. Number of Units | 2. Ounces in Container |

_____Quarts ➤ 32 oz. per quart

_____Fifths ➤ 26 oz. per fifth

_____Glasses➤ ____ oz. per glass

_____Other **(SPECIFY**

_____)➤ _____oz. per unit

**IF ANSWER IS IN TERMS OF WINE GLASSES,
WATER GLASSES OR OTHER UNITS:**
C. About how many ounces are there in the (glasses/
other units) you usually drink?

RECORD VERBATIM AND RECORD NUMBER OF OUNCES IN COLUMN 2 ABOVE.

IF RESPONDENT CANNOT ANSWER HOW MANY OUNCES ARE IN A GLASS ASK:

[1] Are they wine or water glasses?

Wine glasses. 1

Water glasses 2

D. Do you usually drink a fortified wine such as sherry or port?

Yes 1

No. 2

E. What is the type or brand you usually drink?

_____

F. On how many days during that 30-day period, if any, did you drink
two fifths of wine or more?

No. of days _____

G. On how many days during that period, if any, did you drink as much
as a fifth of wine but less than two fifths?

No. of days _____

22. Did you drink any whiskey, gin, or other hard liquor during that 30-day period?

Yes [ASK A-H] 1

No [GO TO Q. 23] 2

A. During those 30 days, about how many days did you drink liquor?

IF RESPONDENT *CANNOT* **ESTIMATE THE NUMBER OF DAYS, HAND ORANGE CARD AND SAY:**

I know it's hard to remember—just look at this card and give me your best guess.

No. of days _____

B. On a *typical* day when you drank liquor, about how much liquor did you drink?

RECORD VERBATIM AND CODE

No. of pints _____

No. of fifths _____

No. of quarts_____

No. of shots _____

No. of drinks _____

IF ANSWER IS IN TERMS OF SHOTS:

C. About how many ounces are there in the shots you drink?

No. of ounces _____

IF ANSWER IS IN TERMS OF DRINKS:

D. About how much liquor (do/did) you usually have in a drink?

RECORD VERBATIM AND PROBE FOR OUNCES IF POSSIBLE.

No. of ounces _____

E. On how many days during that 30-day period, if any, did you drink a full pint of liquor or more? That would be about 16 ounces.

No. of days _____

F. On how many days during that period, if any, did you drink as much as a half-pint of liquor but less than a pint? That would be between 8 and 15 ounces.

No. of days _____

284

G. How (do/did) you usually drink liquor—straight or with water or a mixer?

NOTE: CODE NON-MIXER COCKTAILS SUCH AS MARTINIS,
MANHATTANS AS "1"

Straight 1

With water or mixer 2

H. What is the type or brand of liquor you usually drink?

RECORD VERBATIM

_____

_____

ASK 23 AND 24 ONLY IF DATE OF LAST DRINK WAS _YESTERDAY_ OR _TODAY_

IF DATE OF LAST DRINK WAS TODAY, ASK:

23. Did you have anything to drink yesterday?

Yes [ASK A] 1

No [GO TO Q. 24] 2

IF DATE OF LAST DRINK WAS YESTERDAY, ASK:

A. When you drank yesterday, what time did you have your first drink?

_____ _____ a.m.

_____ p.m.

B. What time did you finish your last drink before going to bed (include today's time if necessary)?

_____ a.m.

_____ p.m.

C. Including all beer, wine, and liquor, how much did you drink between these two times?

RECORD ALL BEER, WINE, AND LIQUOR

BEER	WINE	LIQUOR
_____ Cans	_____ Quarts	_____ Pints
(_____ oz. per can)	_____ Fifths	_____ Fifths
_____ Bottles	_____ Glasses	_____ Quarts
(_____ oz. per bottle)	(_____ oz. per glass)	_____ Shots
_____ Six Packs	_____ Other	(_____ oz. per shot)
(_____ oz. per can)	(SPECIFY_____	_____ Drinks
_____ Glasses	_____)	(_____ oz. per drink)
(_____ oz. per glass)		
_____ Quarts		
_____ Other		
(SPECIFY _____		
_____)		

IF CLIENT DID NOT DRINK TODAY, SKIP TO Q. 25.

24. What time did you have your first drink today?   _____ a.m.

                                                           _____ p.m.

    A. What time did you finish your *last* drink?   _____ a.m.

                                                            _____ p.m.

    B. Including all beer, wine, and liquor, how much did you drink between these two times?

        RECORD ALL BEER, WINE, AND LIQUOR

BEER

_____ Cans

(_____ oz. per can)

_____ Bottles

(_____ oz. per bottle)

_____ Six Packs

(_____ oz. per can)

_____ Glasses

(_____ oz. per glass)

_____ Quarts

_____ Other

(SPECIFY _____
_____)

WINE

_____ Quarts

_____ Fifths

_____ Glasses

(_____ oz. per glass)

_____ Other

(SPECIFY _____
_____

LIQUOR

_____ Pints

_____ Fifths

_____ Quarts

_____ Shots

(_____ oz. per shot)

_____ Drinks

(_____ oz. per drink)

25. These next few questions have to do with things that may have happened to you during the 30 days we've been talking about—that is, from _____ to _____ . Just tell me how many days these things happened.

USE ORANGE CARD, IF NECESSARY, AND SAY: I know it's hard to remember— just look at this card and give me your best guess.

A. First, during that period how often did you have difficulty sleeping at night?

No. of days _____

B. During that period, how many days did you have memory lapses or "blackouts"?

No. of days_____

C. How many days did you miss a meal because of drinking?

No. of days _____

D. During that period, how many days did you have a drink as soon as you woke up?

No. of days _____

E. How many days did you have the "shakes"?

No. of days _____

F. How many days did you have arguments or fights with others while drinking?

No. of days _____

G. During that period, how many days were you drunk?

No. of days _____

H. How many days did you drink while on the job?

No. of days _____
Not working 77

I. During that period, how many days did you miss work or other activities because of drinking?

No. of days _____

J. How many days did you drink more than you really wanted to?

No. of days _____

K. How many days did you try to stop drinking but couldn't?

No. of days _____

L. What was the longest period you went without drinking during those 30 days?

No. of hours _____
OR
No. of days _____

M. What was your longest continuous period of drinking?

No. of hours _____
OR
No. of days _____

N. When you drank during that 30-day period, did you . . .

Always drink with others. 1

Usually drink with others 2

Usually drink alone 3

or, Always drink alone. 4

IF DATE OF LAST DRINK WAS MORE THAN 6 MONTHS AGO, SKIP TO QUESTION 33.

TAKE OUT BLUE CARD AND MARK 30-DAY PERIOD ON IT.

26. Now I'd like to ask you generally about your drinking over the past 6 months, going back to ___(date 6 months ago)___. Here is a card showing that 6-month period. (HAND BLUE CARD). We've just been talking about your drinking during this period here (POINT TO 30-DAY PERIOD AND MARK ON CARD). Were there any other times during this 6-month period when you were drinking, even if it was only a small amount?

Yes [ASK A-C] 1

No [GO TO Q. 28] 2

IF YES:

A. What other times were you drinking anything, even when you were drinking only a small amount? Just tell me the name of each month when you drank anything.

WRITE NAMES OF ALL MONTHS ON CHART BELOW AND RECORD WHETHER CLIENT DID DRINK OR DID NOT DRINK IN EACH MONTH.

B. FOR EACH MONTH CLIENT DRANK ANYTHING, ASK:

Now during the month of _____, was your drinking about the same, more, or less than the 30-day period we have been talking about?

CODE "SAME," "MORE," OR "LESS" ON CHART BELOW FOR EACH MONTH WHEN CLIENT DRANK ANYTHING.

[WRITE NAME OF MONTH BELOW]	A. Did Drink	Did Not Drink	B. Same	More	Less
This month	1	2	1	2	3
One month ago	1	2	1	2	3
2 months ago	1	2	1	2	3
3 months ago	1	2	1	2	3
4 months ago	1	2	1	2	2
5 months ago	1	2	1	2	3
6 months ago	1	2	1	2	3

C. IF "MORE" OR "LESS" FOR ANY MONTH IN B, ASK FOR EACH MONTH IT WAS MORE OR LESS.

During those times when you were drinking (more/less)—that is, during ___(name of month)___ —about how many days did you drink and about how much on a *typical* day?

[NO. OF DAYS] C. How Often	[AMOUNT IN OUNCES OR OTHER UNITS—REFER TO BACK OF CALENDAR CARD]		
	How Much BEER	How much WINE	How much LIQUOR

289

27. Now, thinking of this earlier period [POINT TO PERIOD ON BLUE CARD *BEFORE 30-DAY WINDOW*] —tell me how many times each of these things happened to you, if at all.

USE ORANGE CARD, IF NECESSARY, AND SAY: I know it's hard to remember— just look at this card and give me your best guess.

		Total Number OR of Days	Number of Days per Month
A.	How many days did you have the "shakes" during this period?	_____	_____
B.	How many days did you have memory lapses or "blackouts" during this period?	_____	_____
C.	How many days did you miss a meal because of drinking during this period?	_____	_____
D.	How many days did you miss work or other activities because of drinking during this period?	_____	_____
	Not working 1		
E.	How many days did you have a drink as soon as you woke up during this period?	_____	_____
F.	How many days were you drunk during this period?	_____	_____

28. Now I'd like to ask some questions about the *whole period* of the past 6 months— going all the way from _____(date of 6 months ago)_____ to today. [POINT TO ENTIRE 6-MONTH PERIOD ON BLUE CARD.] When I say "the past 6 months," I mean this whole period.

Which answer on this card best fits your own pattern of drinking during that 6-month period?

HAND TAN CARD.

Drinking every day or almost every day [ASK A] 1

Drinking mainly on weekends or days off [ASK A] . . 2

Drinking only a few days a week [ASK A] 3

Going on binges [SKIP TO B-C] 4

Some other pattern? **RECORD VERBATIM**

_____

_____ [ASK A] 5

290

A. During that 6-month period would you say you *ever* went on a binge?

Yes [**ASK B & C**] 1

No [**GO TO Q. 29**] 2

B. How many binges did you go on in that 6-month period?

No. of binges _____

C. How long did the average binge last?

No. of days _____

29. What was the *most* you drank on any single day during the whole 6-month period?
RECORD ALL BEER, WINE, AND LIQUOR

BEER

_____ Cans

(_____ oz. per can)

_____ Bottles

(_____ oz. per bottle)

_____ Six Packs

(_____ oz. per can)

_____ Glasses

(_____ oz. per glass)

_____ Quarts

_____ Other

(SPECIFY _____
_____)

WINE

_____ Quarts

_____ Fifths

_____ Glasses

(_____ oz. per glass)

_____ Other

(SPECIFY _____
_____)

LIQUOR

_____ Pints

_____ Fifths

_____ Quarts

_____ Shots

(_____ oz. per shot)

_____ Drinks

(_____ oz. per drink)

A. How many days during these 6 months did you drink that much or nearly that much?

No. of days _____

30. When you drank, during the past 6 months, where did you do most of your drinking?

RECORD VERBATIM AND CODE

At home. 1

At other persons' homes 2

At bars or restaurants 3

On the street/alley/hallway 4

Other (**SPECIFY** _____) 5

---

31. Did you usually drink all day or only at certain times?

All day [**GO TO Q. 32**] 1

Certain times [**ASK A**] 2

IF CERTAIN TIMES:

A. What time of day—usually?

Mornings 1

Afternoons 2

Evening/night 3

Mornings & afternoons 4

Afternoons & evenings/nights 5

Evenings/nights & mornings 6

Other (**SPECIFY**_____) 7

32. Overall, which choice on this card best fits your drinking over the past 6 months? Choose the answer you feel comes closest.

HAND GOLD CARD

A. Abstaining 1

B. Almost abstaining, rarely drinking 2

C. Social or moderate drinking . . 3

D. Fairly heavy drinking 4

E. Very heavy drinking 5

F. Problem drinking 6

G. Alcoholic drinking 7

33. People drink alcoholic beverages for different reasons. I am going to read some statements that people have made about why they drink. As I read each statement, just tell me how often you drink for each reason—most of the time, some of the time, or rarely or never. If you don't drink now, answer for when you *were* drinking. **REPEAT CATEGORIES AFTER EACH STATEMENT.**

		Most of the time	Some of the time	Rarely or never
A.	I drink to be sociable	1	2	3
B.	I drink because I like the taste	1	2	3
C.	I drink to forget my worries	1	2	3
D.	I drink to relax	1	2	3
E.	A drink helps cheer me up when I am in a bad mood	1	2	3
F.	A drink helps me when I am depressed or nervous	1	2	3
G.	I drink when I am bored and have nothing to do	1	2	3
H.	I drink when I am thirsty	1	2	3
I.	I drink to increase my self-confidence	1	2	3

34. Do you feel you have ever been an alcoholic?

Yes [ASK A] . . . 1

No 2

A. Do you feel you are an alcoholic at the present time?

Yes 1

No 2

IF DATE OF LAST DRINK WAS WITHIN THE PAST 30 DAYS ASK Q. 35. OTHERWISE, GO TO Q. 36.

35. Would you say that, right now, you can control the amount you drink when you start drinking, or do you usually lose control and drink too much?

Can control the amount [GO TO Q. 37] 1

Usually lose control 2

Don't know. 3

36. Would you say there was ever a time when you were drinking that you were able to control the amount you drank?

Yes [ASK A] 1

No 2

Don't know 3

A. When was the last time?

_____

(Month/Year)

37. If you drink in the future, how do you think it would affect you— do you think it wouldn't hurt you at all, would it hurt you only a little, or would it hurt you very much?

Wouldn't hurt at all [GO TO Q. 38] . . 1

Would hurt a little [ASK A]. 2

Would hurt very much [ASK A] 3

    A. In what ways would it hurt you the most?

RECORD VERBATIM AND CODE *ALL* **THAT APPLY**

Death 01

Physical health 02

Mental health/emotionally 03

Marriage and family 04

Friends 05

Job or career 06

Finances. 07

Nerves 08

Jail/problems with the law 09

Other (SPECIFY _____

_____) . . 10

38. How would it affect your life if you never took another drink again—do you think your life would be better, worse, or about the same?

Better 1

Worse 2

About the same 3

39. I'd like to know how you feel about your drinking now. Would you say that your drinking . . .

Never was a problem 1

Is under control 2

Has improved, but is still a problem . . 3

or, Continues to be a serious problem. . . 4

40. Do you think there are some people who are so sensitive to alcohol that they can't stop drinking after just one or two drinks?

Yes 1

No 2

41. Do you think that alcoholism is a disease from which a person can never completely recover?

Yes 1

No 2

42. Do you think that a person who was once an alcoholic will always be an alcoholic?

Yes 1

No 2

43. Do you think that an alcoholic can ever go back to _moderate_ drinking and not start drinking too much?

Yes 1

No 2

44. Now I have some questions about some medical conditions you may have had. Has a doctor _ever_ told you that you had cirrhosis of the liver, alcoholic liver disease, an enlarged liver, or something called "fatty liver?"

Yes [ASK A-D] 1

No 2

A. Which condition did he say you had?

CODE ALL THAT APPLY

Cirrhosis of the liver 1

Alcoholic liver disease 2

Enlarged liver 3

Fatty liver 4

B. When did he tell you this, approximately?

_____ _____
Month   Year

C. When was the last time you saw a doctor about your liver problem?

_____ _____
Month   Year

D. Do you still have this problem?

Yes 1

No. 2

Don't know 3

45. The next set of questions are about your physical health during the past 6 months—since _____(date 6 months ago)_____ .

How often in the past six months did you take antacids for stomach pain or heartburn, such as tablets like _Tums_ or _Rolaids_ or white liquid medicine like _Maalox_ or _Gelusil?_

RECORD VERBATIM AND CODE

Several times a day 1

Once a day 2

Several times a week 3

Several times a month 4

Once a month or less. 5

Never. 6

46. Now, I'm goint to read you a list of some other medical conditions you might have had in the past 6 months. As far as you know, have you had any of these during that period?

Have you had . . . READ EACH ITEM	Yes	No
A. Colds	1	2
B. The flu	1	2
C. Hepatitis or yellow jaundice	1	2
D. Ulcers	1	2
E. Stomach pain or stomach ache not caused by overeating	1	2
F. High blood pressure	1	2
G. Heart disease—heart failure, heart attack, or chest pains	1	2
H. High blood cholesterol, high blood fat, or high lipid content	1	2
I. Arthritis, rheumatism	1	2
J. Headaches	1	2
K. Diabetes	1	2
L. Gout	1	2
M. Numbness, tingling, or burning in legs and feet	1	2
N. Episodes of dizziness, lightheadedness, or vertigo	1	2
O. Fractures or broken bones	1	2
P. Pancreatitis	1	2
Q. Loss of balance or trouble walking straight when not under the influence of alcohol	1	2
R. Vitamin deficiencies or anemia	1	2
S. Trouble focusing eyes when not under the influence of alcohol	1	2
T. Weakness in muscles and limbs	1	2
U. D.T.s, convulsions, or hallucinations related to alcohol	1	2

47. Have you had any other serious physical problems, or problems with your health *during the past 6 months*?

Yes [ASK A]. 1

No. 2

Don't know. 3

A. What were they?

_____

_____

_____

48. Has a doctor *ever* told you that you had a particular physical problem that required you to stop drinking altogether—other than alcoholism?

Yes [ASK A-B] 1

No. 2

    A.   What was this problem?

             _____

             _____

             _____

    B.   When was this?

             _____   _____

             Month   Year

49. During the past 6 months, did you stay overnight in a hospital, nursing home, or other medical facility?

Yes [ASK A-B] 1

No. 2

    A.   In the past 6 months, how many nights altogether did you stay overnight in places like that?

No. of nights _____

    B.   (Was that time/were any of those times) because of something connected with drinking?

Yes 1

No 2

50. Have you ever taken Antabuse?

Yes [ASK A] 1

No 2

IF YES:

    A.   Are you now taking Antabuse?

Yes 1

No [ASK B] 2

    B.   When did you stop taking it?

Month _____

Year _____

51. In the past 6 months, have you taken any medicine or drugs other than Antabuse?

Yes [ASK A-C] 1

No [GO TO Q. 52] 2

A. What (are/were) you taking and what (do/did) you take it for?

RECORD ANSWERS IN COLUMNS 1 AND 2 BELOW

ASK FOR EACH MEDICINE OR DRUG:

B. How much did you take per day or per week?

RECORD ANSWERS IN COLUMN 3 BELOW

C. For how many weeks or months, did you take it? **TOTAL FOR 6-MONTH PERIOD**

RECORD ANSWERS IN COLUMN 4 BELOW

1. Name of drug	2. Taken for (tension, sleep, pain, etc.)	3. How much		4. How long

1. _____ _____ _____ per day } for { _____ weeks
   _____ _____ or _____ or
   _____ _____ _____ per week _____ months

2. _____ _____ _____ per day } for { _____ weeks
   _____ _____ or _____ or
   _____ _____ _____ per week _____ months

3. _____ _____ _____ per day } for { _____ weeks
   _____ _____ or _____ or
   _____ _____ _____ per week _____ months

4. _____ _____ _____ per day } for { _____ weeks
   _____ _____ or _____ or
   _____ _____ _____ per week _____ months

The next set of questions are about your general well-being over the past 6 months. Here is a card with a list of answers; just tell me for each question which answer comes closest to how you feel.
HAND YELLOW CARD

52. How much of the time during the past 6 months would you say you have enjoyed the things you do?

    READ CATEGORIES

        A. All of the time 1

        B. Most of the time 2

        C. Some of the time 3

        D. None of the time 4

53. During the past 6 months, how much of the time have you felt tense or "high-strung?"

        A. All of the time 1

        B. Most of the time 2

        C. Some of the time 3

        D. None of the time 4

54. During the past 6 months, how often have you been bothered by problems with your memory or by problems concentrating?

        A. All of the time 1

        B. Most of the time 2

        C. Some of the time 3

        D. None of the time 4

55. During the past 6 months, how much of the time have you felt downhearted, blue, or depressed?

        A. All of the time 1

        B. Most of the time 2

        C. Some of the time 3

        D. None of the time 4

56. During the past 6 months, how much of the time have you felt anxious, worried, or upset?

    A. All of the time 1

    B. Most of the time 2

    C. Some of the time 3

TAKE BACK CARD   D. None of the time 4

---

57. During the past 6 months, have you consulted a professional for any personal problems (other than drinking)?

    Yes [**ASK A**] 1

    No 2

A.   Who did you see? Was it a:

    Psychiatrist 1

    Psychologist 2

    Medical Doctor 3

    Brain or nerve specialist 4

    Marriage or family counselor . 5

    Social worker 6

    or, Someone else (**SPECIFY** _____

    _____) 7

---

58. During the past 6 months, have you been arrested for drinking and driving?

    Yes [**ASK A**] 1

    No 2

A.   How many times during the past 6 months?

    No. of times _____

---

59. During the past 6 months, have you been in jail?

    Yes [**ASK A-C**] 1

    No [**ASK C**] 2

A.   How many days have you been in jail during that period?

    No. of days _____

B.   (Was that time/were any of those times) because of something connected with drinking?

    Yes 1

    No 2

C.   How many days were you in jail during the 6 months _before_ that, that is from _____ to _____ ?

    No. of days _____

60. Now, I'd like to ask some general questions about how you've been doing over the past *four years.* Here is a card showing that period, going back from now to 1973.

HAND GRAY CARD

First, I am going to ask you about some experiences you may have had in the past four years. Just tell me whether or not you have had the experience and, if so, when it happened to you.

In the past four years . . .

	YES [ASK A]⟶	NO	A. In what month and year did it happen to you?

A. Did your last child leave home—including going away to college or into the service?

            1   2   _____ _____
                          Month Year

B. Were you discharged from military service?   1   2   _____ _____
                          Month Year

C. Did you get married or remarried?   1   2   _____ _____
                          Month Year

                          _____ _____
                          Month Year

D. Did you get divorced or separated?   1   2   _____ _____
                          Month Year

                          _____ _____
                          Month Year

E. Were you widowed?   1   2   _____ _____
                          Month Year

F. Was a child added to your household?   1   2   _____ _____
                          Month Year

                          _____ _____
                          Month Year

                          _____ _____
                          Month Year

G. Did a close friend or family member die?   1   2   _____ _____
                          Month Year

                          _____ _____
                          Month Year

                          _____ _____
                          Month Year

| | | YES | NO | A. In what month and year did it happen to you? |
| | | | [ASK A]→ | |

H. Did you have a serious illness?   1   2

_____ _____
Month   Year

_____ _____
Month   Year

_____ _____
Month   Year

I. Did you change jobs?   1   2

_____ _____
Month   Year

_____ _____
Month   Year

_____ _____
Month   Year

J. Were you out of work?   1   2

_____ _____
Month   Year

_____ _____
Month   Year

_____ _____
Month   Year

IF DATE OF LAST DRINK WAS WITHIN THE PAST YEAR, READ THIS:

We've talked in some detail about your drinking in the past few months; now we'd like to ask a few questions about your drinking at other times since 1973.

61. Let's consider the period from the beginning of 1973 to the end of 1976. What were the times during this four-year period when you were abstaining for 3 months or more?

RECORD VERBATIM   From   To

_____   _____
Month/Year   Month/Year

_____   _____
Month/Year   Month/Year

_____   _____
Month/Year   Month/Year

_____   _____
Month/Year   Month/Year

_____   _____
Month/Year   Month/Year

None 1

62   The last time you stopped drinking, what were the main reasons you stopped?

RECORD VERBATIM

63.   The last time you started drinking, what were the main reasons you started?

RECORD VERBATIM

64.   During this 4 year period from 1973 to 1976, what about the times when you were drinking heavily-- about how much beer, wine, or liquor did you drink on a *typical* day?

RECORD VERBATIM, INCLUDING ALL BEER, WINE, AND LIQUOR. IF RESPONDENT WAS NOT DRINKING HEAVILY SKIP TO Q. 65.

BEER

_____ Cans

(_____ oz. per can)

_____ Bottles

(_____ oz. per bottle)

_____ Six Packs

(_____ oz. per can)

_____ Glasses

(_____ oz. per glass)

_____ Quarts

_____ Other

(SPECIFY _____
_____)

WINE

_____ Quarts

_____ Fifths

_____ Glasses

(_____ oz. per glass)

_____ Other

(SPECIFY _____
_____)

LIQUOR

_____ Pints

_____ Fifths

_____ Quarts

_____ Shots

(_____ oz. per shot)

_____ Drinks

(_____ oz. per drink)

302

A. About how long would a period *last* when you drank heavily—I mean, on the *average*, how many days, months, or years?

No. of days _____
or
No. of months _____
or
No. of years _____

B. About *how many times* during the four years did you have a period of heavy drinking— even if it was longer or shorter than that average time?

No. of times_____

65. What about the times during these 4 years when you were drinking but *not* drinking heavily— about how much beer, wine, or liquor did you drink on a *typical* day?

RECORD ALL BEER, WINE, AND LIQUOR

BEER

_____ Cans

(_____ oz. per can)

_____ Bottles

(_____ oz. per bottle)

_____ Six Packs

(_____ oz. per can)

_____ Glasses

(_____ oz. per glass)

_____ Quarts

_____ Other

(SPECIFY _____
_____)

WINE

_____ Quarts

_____ Fifths

_____ Glasses

(_____ oz. per glass)

_____ Other

(SPECIFY_____
_____)

LIQUOR

_____ Pints

_____ Fifths

_____ Quarts

_____ Shots

(_____ oz. per shot)

_____ Drinks

(_____ oz. per drink)

66. Often people report that drinking has created serious problems in their lives. During any of these periods when you were drinking, did your drinking have a harmful effect on your family or home life?

Yes [ASK A] 1

No 2

A. What exactly happened, and when? Did your wife leave you or threaten to leave you? Did you have a lot of fights or arguments, or what?

RECORD VERBATIM

_____ From _____ _____
                                                     Month   Year

                                                    To   _____ _____
                                                     Month   Year

_____ From _____ _____
                                                     Month   Year

                                                    To   _____ _____
                                                     Month   Year

_____ From _____ _____
                                                     Month   Year

                                                    To   _____ _____
                                                     Month   Year

67. During (that/any of the) period(s) when you were drinking in those 4 years, did drinking have a harmful effect on your health? That is, did you have any illnesses or accidents that were related to drinking?

Yes [ASK A] 1

No. 2

A. What exactly were the problems and when did they happen?

RECORD VERBATIM

_____ From _____ _____
                                                    Month   Year

                                                 To   _____ _____
                                                   Month   Year

_____ From _____ _____
                                                    Month   Year

                                                 To   _____ _____
                                                   Month   Year

_____ From _____ _____
                                                    Month   Year

                                                 To   _____ _____
                                                   Month   Year

68. During (that/any of the) period(s) when you were drinking, did drinking have a harmful effect on your job—things like missing work because of drinking, getting fired, or losing out on a job opportunity or a raise?

Yes [ASK A] 1

No 2

Didn't work 3

A. What exactly happened and when?

RECORD VERBATIM

_____ From _____ _____
                                                  Month   Year

                                            To   _____ _____
                                                  Month   Year

_____ From _____ _____
                                                  Month   Year

                                            To   _____ _____
                                                  Month   Year

_____ From _____ _____
                                                  Month   Year

                                            To   _____ _____
                                                  Month   Year

69. Were there any times during the period from 1973 to 1976 when you were arrested or got into trouble with the law because of drinking?

Yes [ASK A] 1

No 2

A. What exactly happened and when?

RECORD VERBATIM. IF MORE THAN 3, LIST THE MOST RECENT.

_____ From _____ _____
                                                  Month   Year

                                            To   _____ _____
                                                  Month   Year

_____ From _____ _____
                                                  Month   Year

                                            To   _____ _____
                                                  Month   Year

_____ From _____ _____
                                                  Month   Year

                                            To   _____ _____
                                                  Month   Year

70. Have you ever attended any AA meetings?

Yes [ASK A & B] 1

No 2

A. About how long ago did you last attend an AA meeting?

Today 1

Days _____

Weeks _____

Months_____

Years _____

B. How often (do/did) you attend AA meetings (when you were going)— would you say ...

Regularly 1

or, Occasionally 2

71. You'll recall I said we're talking to people like yourself who've had some contact with programs like ___(Name of ATC)___. When you were there in 1973, did you receive any of the following kinds of help?

READ EACH ONE AND CODE ALL THAT APPLY   Yes   No

A. Individual counseling or therapy—where you talked with a therapist one-on-one alone 1   2

B. Group counseling or therapy 1   2

C. Family therapy—where you were seen together with your wife or other family members 1   2

D. Lectures or educational sessions 1   2

E. Antabuse 1   2

F. Other medications 1   2

G AA meetings 1   2

H. Recreational therapy—things like sports, games, or field trips 1   2

I. Occupational therapy—learning skills, trades, crafts, or hobbies 1   2

J. Relaxation therapy—where they taught you ways to relax or relieve tension without using drugs or alcohol 1   2

K. Counseling on getting jobs 1   2

L. Counseling or advice on healthy diet and eating habits 1   2

M. Did you stay overnight in the hospital or ward? 1   2

N. Were you referred to another facility for help or treatment? 1   2

O. Was there anything else? (SPECIFY _____

_____) 1   2

72. How much would you say the _____ (Name of ATC) _____ helped you— did it help
you very much, somewhat, only a little, or didn't it help you at all?

Helped very much . . . . 1 ⎫
Helped somewhat . . . . . 2 ⎬ ASK A
Helped only a little. . . . . 3 ⎭
Didn't help at all 4

A. In what ways was the _____ (Name of ATC) _____ most helpful?

RECORD VERBATIM

---

73. Have you gotten any help to stop or cut down your drinking besides help you may have gotten from
_____ (Name of ATC) _____ or AA?

Yes [**ASK A-B**] 1
No [**GO TO Q. 74**] 2

A. How long ago was the last time?

_____   _____
Month   Year

B. What type of place was that—was it a . . .

Hospital, mental health clinic, or
alcohol counseling center 1
A private physician 2
A boarding home or mission . . . 3
Or, some other place (**SPECIFY**
_____) 4

IF YEAR GIVEN IN 'A' WAS 1972 OR EARLIER, SKIP TO 'D'

C. Have you gotten any other help since the beginning of 1973 besides that?

Yes [**ASK 1 and 2**] 1
No [**GO TO D**] 2

[1] How many other places? No. of places_____

[2] What type of (place was that/places were those)?

CODE ALL THAT APPLY

A hospital, mental health clinic, or
alcohol counseling center 1
A private physician 2
A boarding home or mission 3
Or, some other place (**SPECIFY**
_____) 4

D. What about before 1973—did you ever get any other help?

Yes [ASK 1 and 2] 1

No. 2

[1] How many other places?   No. of places _____

[2] What type of (place was that/places were those)?

CODE ALL THAT APPLY

A hospital, mental health clinic, or
alcohol counseling center 1

A private physician 2

A boarding home or mission 3

Or, some other place (**SPECIFY**

_____) 4

---

74. What was your one *major* source of financial support last month, that is the
month of _____?

RECORD VERBATIM AND CODE ONE

Job(s) 01

Spouse 02

Alimony/child support 03

Family or friends 04

Public assistance (welfare/SSI) . . . 05

Pension (include Social Security) . 06

Insurance (include Workman's
Compensation, Unemployment
Insurance) 07

Savings/investments 08

Other (**SPECIFY**_____

_____) 09

---

75. What was the total income before taxes that *you earned* from your job(s) in the last month?

Amount $_____

None 1

76. What was the approximate total income you _earned_ from jobs during 1976, before taxes? Just look at this card and tell me.

   USE GREEN CARD

A.	Less than $1,000	01
B.	$1,000-$1,999	02
C.	$2,000-$2,999	03
D.	$3,000-$3,999	04
E.	$4,000-$4,999	05
F.	$5,000-$5,999	06
G.	$6,000-$6,999	07
H.	$7,000-$7,999	08
I.	$8,000-$8,999	09
J.	$9,000-$9,999	10
K.	$10,000-$11,999	11
L.	$12,000-$13,999	12
M.	$14,000-$15,999	13
N.	$16,000-$18,999	14
O.	$19,000-25,999	15
P.	$26,000-$50,000	16
Q.	Over $50,000	17

77. What was the approximate _total_ income of your _household_ in 1976, before taxes? I mean income from _all_ sources—including social security, family or friends, public assistance, or any other source.

   INCLUDE INCOME FROM ALL SOURCES

   USE GREEN CARD

A.	Less than $1,000	01
B.	$1,000-$1,999	02
C.	$2,000-$2,999	03
D.	$3,000-$3,999	04
E.	$4,000-$4,999	05
F.	$5,000-$5,999	06
G.	$6,000-$6,999	07
H.	$7,000-$7,999	08
I.	$8,000-$8,999	09
J.	$9,000-$9,999	10
K.	$10,000-$11,999	11
L.	$12,000-$13,999	12
M.	$14,000-$15,999	13
N.	$16,000-$18,999	14
O.	$19,000-25,999	15
P.	$26,000-$50,000	16
Q.	Over $50,000	17

78. How often do you attend religious services—would you say . . .

Regularly 1

Occasionally 2

Rarely 3

or, Never 4

79. What is your religious preference?

Protestant [ASK A] 1

Catholic 2

Jewish 3

Other (SPECIFY_____

_____) [ASK A]   4

None 5

A.   Which denomination or group is that?

RECORD VERBATIM AND CODE

Methodist 01

Presbyterian 02

Lutheran 03

Baptist 04

Episcopalian 05

Congregationalist 06

Jehovah's Witness 07

Seventh-Day Adventist . . . 08

Disciple of Christ 09

Church of Christ 10

Latter-Day Saints, Mormon 11

Pentecostal 12

Unitarian 13

Black Muslim 14

Other (SPECIFY _____

_____) 15

No specific denomination   16

80. What do you consider to be your main racial or ethnic group?

RECORD VERBATIM AND CODE.

White 1

Black 2

Asian-American 3

Mexican-American 4

Puerto Rican 5

Other Spanish-American 6

American Indian/Alaskan
Native 7

Other (SPECIFY _____) 8

Now I would like you to answer some questions by yourself about your general attitudes and interests. Here they are. Please read the written instructions carefully and circle the answers you feel come closest to you.

GIVE THE RESPONDENT THE SELF-ADMINISTERED FORM

RECORD TIME INTERVIEW ENDED

TIME ENDED _____ a.m.

_____ p.m.

CHECK THE FRONT COVER AND INDICATE BELOW IF RESPONDENT IS IN GROUP A OR B.

Group A. . . . 1 → READ CONSENT FORM A AND ADMINISTER SM-7 BREATH TEST

Group B. . . . 2 → READ CONSENT FORM B AND ADMINISTER SM-7 BREATH TEST

RECORD CASE NUMBER AND EXACT TIME OF BREATH TEST, BELOW, AND ON THE SM-7 BOX.

TIME BREATH TEST WAS ADMINISTERED _____ a.m.

_____ p.m.

References

American Psychiatric Association. *Diagnostic and Statistical Manual of Mental Disorders,* 3rd edition. Washington, D.C.: American Psychiatric Association, 1980.

Armor, David J., J. Michael Polich, and Harriet B. Stambul. *Alcoholism and Treatment.* The Rand Corporation, R-1739-NIAAA, 1976.

Armor, David J., J. Michael Polich, and Harriet B. Stambul. *Alcoholism and Treatment.* New York: Wiley, 1978.

Bacon, M. K., H. Barry, and I. L. Child. "A Cross-Cultural Study of Drinking. II. Relations to Other Features of Culture." *Quarterly Journal of Studies on Alcohol,* Supplement No. 2: 29, 1965.

Baekeland, Frederick, Lawrence Lundwall, and Benjamin Kissin. "Methods for the Treatment of Chronic Alcoholism: A Critical Appraisal." In Robert J. Gibbins et al. (eds.), *Research Advances in Drug and Alcohol Problems,* Vol. 2. New York: Wiley, 1975.

Baekeland, Frederick, Lawrence Lundwall, Benjamin Kissin, and Thomas Shanahan. "Correlates of Outcome in Disulfiram Treatment of Alcoholism." *Journal of Nervous and Mental Disease,* 153: 1-9, 1971.

Baekeland, F., L. Lundwall, and T. Shanahan. "Correlates of Patient Attrition in the Outpatient Treatment of Alcoholism." *Journal of Nervous and Mental Disease,* 157: 99-107, 1973.

Barchha, Ramnik, Mark A. Stewart, and Samuel B. Guze. "The Prevalence of Alcoholism Among General Hospital Ward Patients." *American Journal of Psychiatry,* 125: 133-136, 1968.

Beigel, Allan, E. James Hunter, John S. Tamerin, Edwin H. Chapin, and Mary J. Lowery. "Planning for the Development of Comprehensive Community Alcoholism Services. I. The Prevalence Survey." *American Journal of Psychiatry,* 131: 1112-1133, 1974.

Berry, Ralph E., and James P. Boland. *The Economic Cost of Alcohol Abuse.* New York: Free Press, 1977.

Blane, H. T. *The Personality of the Alcoholic: Guises of Dependency.* New York: Harper & Row, 1968.

Brandsma, Jeffrey M. "Alcoholismic Dysbehaviorism Revisited: A Reply to Keller." *Journal of Studies on Alcohol,* 38: 1838-1842, 1977.

Brenner, B. "Alcoholism and Fatal Accidents." *Quarterly Journal of Studies on Alcohol,* 28: 517–528, 1967.

Bruun, Kettil, Griffith Edwards, Martti Lumio, Klaus Mäkelä, Lynn Pan, Robert E. Popham, Robin Room, Wolfgang Schmidt, Ole-Jørgen Skog, Pekka Sulkunen, and Esa Österberg. *Alcohol Control Policies in Public Health Perspective.* Helsinki: Finnish Foundation for Alcohol Studies, 1975.

Cahalan, Don. *Problem Drinkers.* San Francisco: Jossey-Bass, 1970.

Cahalan, Don, and Ira H. Cisin. "American Drinking Practices: Summary of Findings from a National Probability Sample." *Quarterly Journal of Studies on Alcohol,* 29: 642–656, 1968.

Cahalan, Don, and Ira Cisin. "Drinking Behavior and Drinking Problems in the United States." In *The Biology of Alcoholism,* Vol. 5: *Treatment and Rehabilitation of the Chronic Alcoholic.* New York: Plenum Press, 1977.

Cahalan, Don, Ira H. Cisin, and Helen M. Crossley. *American Drinking Practices.* New Brunswick, N.J.: Rutgers Center of Alcohol Studies, 1969.

Cahalan, Don, and Robin Room. "Problem Drinking Among American Men Aged 21–59." *American Journal of Public Health,* 62, 1473–1482, 1972.

Cahalan, Don, and Robin Room. *Problem Drinking Among American Men.* New Brunswick, N.J.: Rutgers Center of Alcohol Studies, 1974.

Campbell, A., P. E. Converse and W. L. Rodgers. *The Quality of American Life.* New York: Russell Sage, 1976.

Cartwright, A. K. J., S. J. Shaw, and T. A. Spratley. "The Validity of Per Capita Alcohol Consumption as an Indicator of the Prevalence of Alcohol Related Problems: An Evaluation Based on National Statistics and Survey Data." In J. S. Madden, Robin Walker, and W. H. Kenyon (eds.), *Alcoholism and Drug Dependence: A Multidisciplinary Approach.* New York: Plenum Press, 1977.

Caster, David U., and Oscar A. Parsons. "Locus of Control in Alcoholics and Treatment Outcome." *Journal of Studies on Alcohol,* 38: 2087–2095, 1977.

Celentano, David D., and David V. McQueen. "Comparison of Alcoholism Prevalence Rates Obtained by Survey and Indirect Estimators." *Journal of Studies on Alcohol,* 39: 420–434, 1978.

Chandler, Jane, Celia Hensman, and Griffith Edwards. "Determinants of What Happens to Alcoholics." *Quarterly Journal of Studies on Alcohol,* 32: 349–363, 1971.

Clare, Anthony. "How Good is Treatment?" In Griffith Edwards and Marcus Grant (eds.), *Alcoholism: New Knowledge and New Responses,* Baltimore: University Park Press, 1976.

Clark, Walter. "Operational Definition of Drinking Problems and Associated Prevalence Rates." *Quarterly Journal of Studies on Alcohol,* 27: 648–668, 1966.

Clark, Walter, B. "Conceptions of Alcoholism: Consequences for Research." *Addictive Diseases,* 1: 395–430, 1975.

Clark, Walter B. "Loss of Control, Heavy Drinking and Drinking Problems in a Longitudinal Study." *Journal of Studies on Alcohol,* 37: 1256–1290. 1976.

Clark, Walter, B., and Don Cahalan. "Changes in Problem Drinking Over a Four-Year Span." *Addictive Behaviors,* 1: 251–259, 1976.

Coleman, J. *Abnormal Psychology and Modern Life,* 4th edition. Glenview, Illinois: Scott, Foresman & Company, 1972.

Comrey, A. L. *Comrey Personality Scales.* San Diego: Educational and Industrial Testing Service, 1970.

Cox, D. R. *Analysis of Binary Data.* London: Methuen, 1970.

Davies, David L. "Definitional Issues in Alcoholism." In Ralph E. Tarter and A. Arthur Sugerman (eds.), *Alcoholism: Interdisciplinary Approaches to an Enduring Problem.* Reading, Mass.: Addison-Wesley, 1976.

Davis, D. "Mood Changes in Alcoholic Subjects with Programmed and Free-Choice Experimental Drinking." In *Recent Advances in Studies in Alcoholism.* Washington, D.C.: U.S. Government Printing Office, 1971.

de Lint, Jan, and Wolfgang Schmidt. "The Epidemiology of Alcoholism." In Yedy Israel and Jorge Mardones (eds.), *The Biological Basis of Alcoholism.* New York: Wiley, 1971.

de Lint, Jan, and Wolfgang Schmidt. "Alcoholism and Mortality." In Benjamin Kissin and Henri Begleiter (eds.), *The Biology of Alcoholism,* Vol. 4: *Social Aspects of Alcoholism,* New York: Plenum Press, 1976.

Drew, Leslie R. H. "Alcoholism as a Self-Limiting Disease." *Quarterly Journal of Studies on Alcohol,* 29: 956–967, 1968.

Dunning, Bruce, and Don Cahalan. "By-Mail vs. Field Self-Administered Questionnaires: An Armed Forces Survey." *Public Opinion Quarterly,* 37: 618–624, 1974.

Edwards, Griffith. "The Status of Alcoholism as a Disease." In Richard Phillipson (ed.), *Modern Trends in Drug Dependence.* London: Butterworths, 1970.

Edwards, Griffith. "Drugs, Dependence, and the Concept of Plasticity." *Quarterly Journal of Studies on Alcohol,* 35: 176–195, 1974.

Edwards, Griffith. "The Alcohol Dependence Syndrome: Usefulness of an Idea." In Griffith Edwards and Marcus Grant (eds.), *Alcoholism: New Knowledge and New Responses.* Baltimore: University Press, 1976.

Edwards, Griffith, et al. "Drinking in a London Suburb. I. Correlates of Normal Drinking." *Quarterly Journal of Studies on Alcohol,* Supplement 6: 69–93, 1962.

Edwards, Griffith, and Milton M. Gross. "Alcohol Dependence: Provisional Description of a Clinical Syndrome." *British Medical Journal,* 1, 1058–1061, 1976.

Edwards, G., M. M. Gross, M. Keller, J. Moser, and R. Room. *Alcohol-Related Disabilities.* Geneva: World Health Organization, Offset Publication Number 32, 1977b.

Edwards, G., Celia Hensman, Ann Hawker, and Valerie Williamson. "Who Goes to Alcoholics Anonymous?" *The Lancet,* 382–384, August 13, 1966.

Edwards, Griffith, Jim Orford, Stella Egert, Sally Guthrie, Ann Hawker, Celia Hensman, Martin Mitcheson, Edna Oppenheimer, and Colin Taylor. "Alcoholism: A Controlled Trial of 'Treatment' and 'Advice'." *Journal of Studies on Alcohol,* 38: 1004–1031, 1977a.

Einstein, Stanley, Edward Wolfson, and Diana Gecht. "What Matters in Treatment: Relevant Variables in Alcoholism." *International Journal of the Addictions,* 5: 43–67, 1970.

Emrick, Chad D. "A Review of Psychologically Oriented Treatment of Alcoholism. I. The Use and Interrelationships of Outcome Criteria and Drinking Behavior Following Treatment." *Quarterly Journal of Studies on Alcohol.* 35: 523–549, 1974.

Emrick, Chad D. "A Review of Psychologically Oriented Treatment of Alcoholism. II. The Relative Effectiveness of Treatment versus No Treatment." *Journal of Studies on Alcohol,* 36: 88–108, 1975.

Emrick, Chad D. "Relative Effectiveness of Alcohol Abuse Treatment."Unpublished manuscript, 1978.

Filstead, William J., Marshall J. Goby, and Nelson J. Bradley. "Critical Elements in the Diagnosis of Alcoholism: A National Survey of Physicians." *Journal of the American Medical Association,* 236: 2767–2769, 1976.

Fine, Eric W., Robert A. Steer, and Pascal E. Scoles. "Relationship Between Blood Alcohol Concentration and Self-Reported Drinking Behavior." *Journal of Studies on Alcohol,* 39: 466–472, 1978.

Fisher, Joseph C., Robert L. Mason, and Joseph V. Fisher. "A Diagnostic Formula for Alcoholism." *Journal of Studies on Alcohol,* 37: 1247–1255, 1976.

Fisher, S., H. P. Swan, and M. A. Rozalla. "Morbidity Monitoring in General Practice: A Pilot Scheme in Central New South Wales." *Medical Journal of Australia,* 1: 207–213, 1975.

Fitzgerald, Bernard J., Richard A. Pasewark, and Robert Clark. "Four-Year Follow-up of Alcoholics at a Rural State Hospital." *Quarterly Journal of Studies on Alcohol,* 32: 636–642, 1971.

Foster, F. Mark, John L. Horn, and Kenneth W. Wanberg. "Dimensions of Treatment Outcome: A Factor-Analytic Study of Alcoholics' Responses to a Follow-up Questionnaire." *Quarterly Journal of Studies on Alcohol,* 33, 1079–1098, 1972.

Gerard, Donald L., and Gerhart Saenger. "Interval Between Intake and Follow-Up as a Factor in the Evaluation of Patients with a Drinking Problem." *Quarterly Journal of Studies on Alcohol,* 20: 620–630, 1959.

Gerard, Donald L., and Gerhart Saenger. *Out-Patient Treatment of Alcoholism.* Toronto: University of Toronto Press, 1966.

Gerard, Donald L., Gerhart Saenger, and Renee Wile. "The Abstinent Alcoholic." *Archives of General Psychiatry,* 6: 83–95, 1962.

Gerrein, John R., Chaim M. Rosenberg, and Velandy Manohar. "Disulfiram Maintenance in Outpatient Treatment of Alcoholism." *Archives of General Psychiatry,* 28: 798–802, 1973.

Gibbins, Robert J., Yedy Israel, Harold Kalant, Robert E., Popham, Wolfgang Schmidt, and Reginald G. Smart (eds.). *Research Advances in Alcohol and Drug Problems,* Vol. 1. New York: Wiley, 1974.

Gibbins, Robert J., Yedy Israel, Harold Kalant, Robert E. Popham, Wolfgang Schmidt, and Reginald G. Smart (eds.). *Research Advances in Alcohol and Drug Problems*, Vol. 2. New York: Wiley, 1975.

Gillis, L. S., and M. Keet. "Prognostic Factors and Treatment Results in Hospitalized Alcoholics." *Quarterly Journal of Studies on Alcohol*, 30: 426–437, 1969.

Gitlow, Stanley E. "Alcoholism: A Disease." In Peter Bourne and Ruth Fox (eds.), *Alcoholism: Progress in Research and Treatment*, New York: Academic Press, 1973.

Glatt, M. M. "Alcoholism Disease Concept and Loss of Control Revisited." *British Journal of Addiction*, 71: 134–144, 1976.

Glatt, M. M. "Alcoholism Disease concept and Loss of Control Revisited." *British Journal of Addiction*, 71: 134–144, 1976.

Glendening, Blaine L., Allen C. Rush, and Nicholas D. Duffett. "The Use of Small Gas Chromatographs for Breath Testing of Drunken Drivers by the Highway Patrol Utilizing the Public Health Laboratory (Kansas)." *Health Laboratory Science*, 8: 131–141, 1971.

Goodwin, Donald W., J. Bruce Crane, and Samuel B. Guze. "Felons Who Drink: An 8-Year Follow-Up." *Quarterly Journal of Studies on Alcohol*, 32: 136–147, 1971.

Gross, Milton M. "Psychobiological Contributions to the Alcohol Dependence Syndrome: A Selective Review of the Recent Evidence." In G. Edwards, et al. (eds.), *Alcohol-Related Disabilities*. Geneva: World Health Organization, Offset Publication Number 32, 1977.

Guze, Samuel, and Donald Goodwin, "Consistency of Drinking History and Diagnosis of Alcoholism." *Quarterly Journal of Studies on Alcohol*, 33: 111–116, 1972.

Guze, Samuel, B., Vincent B. Tuason, Paul D. Gatfied, Mark A. Stewart, and Bruce Picken. "Psychiatric Illness and Crime, with Particular Reference to Alcoholism: A study of 223 Criminals." *Journal of Nervous and Mental Disease*, 134: 512–521, 1962.

Guze, Samuel B., Vincent B. Tuason, Mark A. Stewart, and Bruce Picken. "The Drinking History: A Comparison of Reports by Subjects and Their Relatives." *Quarterly Journal of Studies on Alcohol*, 24: 249–260, 1963.

Haglund, R., and Marc Schuckit. "The Epidemiology of Alcoholism." In N. Estes and E. Heinemann (eds.), *Alcoholism: Psychological and Physiological Bases*. St. Louis: Mosby, 1977.

Harford, Thomas C., and George S. Mills. "Age-Related Trends in Alcohol Consumption." *Journal of Studies on Alcohol*, 39: 207–210, 1978.

Hershon, Howard I. "Alcohol Withdrawal Symptoms and Drinking Behavior." *Journal of Studies on Alcohol*, 38: 953–971, 1977.

Hill, Marjorie A., and Howard T. Blane. "Evaluation of Psychotherapy with Alcoholics." *Quarterly Journal of Studies on Alcohol*, 28: 76–104, 1967.

Hingson, Ralph, Norman Scotch, and Eli Goldman. "Impact of the 'Rand Report' on Alcoholics, Treatment Personnel, and Boston Residents." *Journal of Studies on Alcohol*, 38: 2065–2076, 1977.

Hodgson, Ray, Tim Stockwell, Howard Rankin, and Griffith Edwards. "Alcohol Dependence: The Concept, Its Utility, and Measurement." *British Journal of Addiction,* 73, 339–342, 1978.

Hoffman, H. "Personality Measurement for the Evaluation and Prediction of Alcoholism." In R. E. Tarter and A. A. Sugerman (eds.), *Alcoholism: Interdisciplinary Approaches to an Enduring Problem.* Reading, Mass.: Addison-Wesley, 1976.

Horn, John L., and Kenneth W. Wanberg. "Symptom Patterns Related to Excessive Use of Alcohol." *Quarterly Journal of Studies on Alcohol,* 30: 35–58, 1969.

Imber, S., E. Schultz, F. Funderburk, R. Allen, and R. Flamer. "The Fate of the Untreated Alcoholic." *Journal of Nervous and Mental Disease,* 162: 238–247, 1976.

Irwin, T. "Attacking Alcohol as a Disease." *Today's Health,* 46: 21–23, 72–74, 1968.

Jackson, D. N. *Personality Research Form Manual.* New York: Research Psychologists Press, Inc., 1974.

Jackson, Joan K. "Definition and Measurement of Alcoholism." *Quarterly Journal of Studies on Alcohol,* 18: 240–262, 1957.

Jellinek, E. M. "Phases in the Drinking History of Alcoholics." *Quarterly Journal of Studies on Alcohol,* 7: 1–88, 1946.

Jellinek, E. M. "Phases of Alcohol Addiction." In *Expert Committee on Mental Health, Alcoholism Subcommitee, Second Report.* Geneva: World Health Organization, Technical Report Number 48, 1952a.

Jellinek, E. M. "Phases of Alcohol Addiction."*Quarterly Journal of Studies on Alcohol,* 13: 673–684, 1952b.

Jellinek, E. M. *The Disease Concept of Alcoholism.* New Brunswick, N.J.: Hillhouse Press, 1960.

Jessor, Richard, and Shirley Jessor. *Problem Behavior and Psychosocial Development.* New York: Academic Press, 1977.

Jessor, R., T. D. Graves, R. C. Hanson, and S. L. Jessor. *Society, Personality, and Deviant Behavior: A Study of a Tri-Ethnic Community.* New York: Holt, Rinehart, and Winston, 1968.

Keller, Mark. "The Definition of Alcoholism and the Estimation of Its Prevalence." In D. J. Pittman and C. R. Snyder (eds.), *Society, Culture, and Drinking Patterns.* New York: Wiley, 1962.

Keller, Mark. "On the Loss-of-Control Phenomenon in Alcoholism." *British Journal of Addiction,* 67: 153–166, 1972.

Keller, Mark. "Problems of Epidemiology in Alcohol Problems." *Journal of Studies on Alcohol,* 36: 1442–1451, 1975.

Keller, Mark. "The Disease Concept of Alcoholism Revisited." *Journal of Studies on Alcohol,* 37: 1694–1717, 1976.

Keller, Mark, and M. McCormack. *A Dictionary of Words About Alcohol.* New Brunswick, N.J.: Rutgers Center of Alcohol Studies, 1968.

Kendell, R. E., and M. C. Staton. "The Fate of Untreated Alcoholics." *Quarterly Journal of Studies on Alcohol,* 27: 30–44, 1966.

Kish, George B., and Harlan T. Hermann. "The Fort Meade Alcoholism Treatment Program: A Follow-up Study." *Quarterly Journal of Studies on Alcohol*, 32: 628–635, 1971.

Kissin, Benjamin, Arthur Platz, and Wen Huey Su. "Social and Psychological Factors in the Treatment of Chronic Alcoholism." *Journal of Psychiatric Research*, 8: 13–27, 1970.

Kissin, Benjamin, Sidney M. Rosenblatt, and Solomon Machover. "Prognostic Factors in Alcoholism." *Psychiatric Research Report*, 48: 22–43, 1968.

Kittredge, Lee D., Jack L. Franklin, Jean H. Thrasher, Harold A. Berdiansky. "Estimating a Population in Need of Alcoholism Services: A New Approach." *The International Journal of the Addictions*, 12: 205–226, 1977.

Kreitman, Norman. "Three Themes in the Epidemiology of Alcoholism." In Griffith Edwards and Marcus Grant (eds.), *Alcoholism: New Knowledge and New Responses*. Baltimore: University Park Press, 1976.

Lelbach, Werner. "Organic Pathology Related to Volume and Pattern of Alcohol Use." In Robert J. Gibbins et al. (eds.), *Research Advances in Alcohol and Drug Problems*, Vol. 1. New York: Wiley, 1974.

Lemere, Frederick. "What Happens to Alcoholics?" *American Journal of Psychiatry*, 109, 674–676, 1953.

Lieber, C. S. "Ethanol and the Liver: A Decreasing 'Threshold' of Toxicity." *American Journal of Clinical Nutrition*, 32: 1177–1180, 1979.

Lipscomb, Wendell R. "Mortality Among Treated Alcoholics: A Three-Year Followup Study." *Quarterly Journal of Studies on Alcohol*, 20: 596–603, 1959.

Lisansky, E. S. "The Etiology of Alcoholism: The Role of Psychological Predisposition." *Quarterly Journal of Studies on Alcohol*, 21: 314–343, 1960.

Little, Ruth E., Francia A. Schultz, and Wallace Mandell. "Describing Alcohol Consumption: A Comparison of Three Methods and a New Approach." *Journal of Studies on Alcohol*, 38: 554–562, 1977.

Lloyd, Richard W., Jr., and Herman C. Salzberg. "Controlled Social Drinking: An Alternative to Abstinence as a Treatment Goal for Some Alcohol Abusers." *Psychological Bulletin*, 82: 815–842, 1975.

Lowe, George D., and Alan L. Ziglin. "Social Class and the Treatment of Alcoholic Patients." *Quarterly Journal of Studies on Alcohol*, 34: 173–184, 1973.

Ludwig, A. M. "On and Off the Wagon." *Quarterly Journal of Studies on Alcohol*, 33: 91–96, 1972.

Ludwig, Arnold M., and Abraham Wikler. "'Craving' and Relapse to Drink." *Quarterly Journal of Studies on Alcohol*, 35: 108–130, 1974.

Lundquist, G. A. R. "Alcohol Dependence." *Acta Psychiatrica Scandinavica*, 49: 332–340, 1973.

Mann, Marty. *New Primer on Alcoholism*. New York: Holt, Rinehart, and Winston, 1958.

Marlatt, G. Alan, Barbara Demming, and John B. Reid. "Loss of Control Drinking in Alcoholics: An Experimental Analogue." *Journal of Abnormal Psychology*, 81: 233–241, 1973.

Maxwell, Milton A. "Alcoholics Anonymous: An Interpretation." In David J. Pittman and Charles R. Snyder (eds.), *Society, Culture, and Drinking Patterns.* New York: Wiley, 1962.

McClelland, D. C., W. N. Davis, R. Kalin, and E. Wanner. *The Drinking Man: Alcohol and Human Motivation.* New York: Free Press, 1972.

McCord, W., J. McCord, and J. Gudeman. *Origins of Alcoholism.* Stanford University Press, 1960.

Medical Services Study Group. "Death Certification and Epidemiological Research." *British Medical Journal,* October 14, 1978.

Miller, Byron, A., Alex D. Pokorny, Jorge Valles, and Sidney E. Cleveland. "Biased Sampling in Alcoholism Treatment Research." *Quarterly Journal of Studies on Alcohol,* 31: 97-107, 1970.

Miller, William R., and Glenn R. Caddy. "Abstinence and Controlled Drinking in the Treatment of Problem Drinkers." *Journal of Studies on Alcohol,* 38: 986-1003, 1977.

Mindlin, Dorothee F. "The Characteristics of Alcoholics as Related to Prediction of Therapeutic Outcome." *Quarterly Journal of Studies on Alcohol,* 20: 604-619, 1959.

Moos, Rudolf, and Frederic Bliss. "Difficulty of Follow-up and Outcome of Alcoholism Treatment." *Journal of Studies on Alcohol,* 39: 473-490, 1978.

Mules, Janet E., William H. Hague, and Donald L. Dudley. "Life Change, Its Perception, and Alcohol Addiction." *Journal of Studies on Alcohol,* 38: 487-493, 1977.

Mulford, Harold A. *Identifying Problem Drinkers.* Washington, D.C.: U.S. Public Health Service Publication 1000, 1966.

Mulford, Harold A. "Stages in the Alcoholic Process: Toward a Cumulative, Nonsequential Index." *Journal of Studies on Alcohol,* 38: 563-583, 1977.

National Center for Health Statistics, *United States Life Tables: 1969-1971,* Vol. 1, No. 1. Washington, D.C.: U.S. Government Printing Office, 1978.

National Center for Health Statistics, *United States Life Tables by Causes of Death: 1969-1971,* Vol. 1, No. 5. Washington, D.C.: U.S. Government Printing Office, 1975.

National Center for Health Statistics. *U.S. Vital Statistics, 1971.* Washington, D.C.: U.S. Government Printing Office, 1975.

National Center for Health Statistics. *Vital Statistics Instructions for Classifying the Underlying Cause of Death, 1976-1978,* Part 2a. Research Triangle Park, North Carolina, 1976.

National Council on Alcoholism [U.S.]. "Criteria for the Diagnosis of Alcoholism." *Annals of Internal Medicine,* 77: 249-258, 1972.

National Council on Alcoholism [U.S.]. "Definition of Alcoholism." *Annals of Internal Medicine,* 85: 764, 1976.

National Institute on Alcohol Abuse and Alcoholism. *Alcohol and Health: Second Special Report to the U.S. Congress.* Washington, D.C.: U.S. Government Printing Office, 1974.

National Institute on Alcohol Abuse and Alcoholism. *Alcohol and Health: Third Special Report to the U.S. Congress.* Washington, D.C.: U.S. Government Printing Office, 1978.

Nicholls, P., G. Edwards, and E. Kyle. "Alcoholics Admitted to Four Hospitals in England. II. General and Cause-Specific Mortality." *Quarterly Journal of Studies on Alcohol,* 35: 841–855, 1974.

Ogborne, A. C. "Patient Characteristics as Predictors of Treatment Outcomes for Alcohol and Drug Abusers." In Yedy Israel et al. (eds.), *Research Advances in Alcohol and Drug Problems,* Vol. 4. New York: Plenum Press, 1978.

Orford, Jim. "Alcoholism: What Psychology Offers." In Griffith Edwards and Marcus Grant (eds.), *Alcoholism: New Knowledge and New Responses.* Baltimore: University Park Press, 1976.

Orford, Jim, Edna Oppenheimer, and Griffith Edwards. "Abstinence or Control: The Outcome for Excessive Drinkers Two Years after Consultation." *Behavioral Research and Therapy,* 14: 409–418, 1976.

Owens, D., "Physical Complications of Alcohol Excess—Metabolism of Alcohol." In J. S. Madden, Robin Walker, and W. H. Kenyon (eds.), *Alcoholism and Drug Dependence: A Multidisciplinary Approach.* New York: Plenum Press, 1977.

Paredes, Alfonso. "The History of the Concept of Alcoholism." In Ralph E. Tarter and A. Arthur Sugerman (eds.), *Alcoholism: Interdisciplinary Approaches to an Enduring Problem.* Reading, Mass.: Addison-Wesley, 1976.

Paredes, Alfonso, William R. Hood, Harry Seymour, and Maury Gollob. "Loss of Control in Alcoholism: An Investigation of the Hypothesis, with Experimental Findings." *Quarterly Journal of Studies on Alcohol,* 34: 1146–1161, 1973.

Park, Peter. "Developmental Ordering of Experiences in Alcoholism." *Quarterly Journal of Studies on Alcohol,* 34: 473–488, 1973.

Parker, Douglas A., and Marsha S. Harman. "The Distribution of Consumption Model of Prevention of Alcohol Problems: A Critical Assessment." *Journal of Studies on Alcohol,* 39: 377–399, 1978.

Pattison, E. Mansell. "Rehabilitation of the Chronic Alcoholic." In Benjamin Kissin and Henri Begleiter (eds.), *The Biology of Alcoholism,* Vol. 3. New York: Plenum Press, 1974.

Pattison, E. Mansell. "A Conceptual Approach to Alcoholism Treatment Goals." *Addictive Behaviors,* 1: 177–192, 1976.

Pattison, E. Mansell, Ronald Coe, and Hans O. Doerr. "Population Variation Among Alcoholism Treatment Facilities." *International Journal of the Addictions,* 8: 199–299, 1973.

Pattison, E. Mansell, Ronald Coe, and Robert J. Rhodes. "Evaluation of Alcoholism Treatment: A Comparison of Three Facilities." *Archives of General Psychiatry,* 20, 478–488, 1969.

Pattison, E. Mansell, E. B. Headley, G. C. Gleser, and L. A. Gottschalk. "Abstinence and Normal Drinking: An Assessment of Changes in Drinking Patterns in Alcoholics After Treatment." *Quarterly Journal of Studies on Alcohol,* 29: 610–633, 1968.

Pattison, E. Mansell, Mark B. Sobell, and Linda C. Sobell. *Emerging Concepts of Alcohol Dependence*. New York: Springer, 1977.

Pell, S., and C. A. D'Alonzo. "A Five-Year Mortality Study of Alcoholics." *Journal of Occupational Medicine*, 15: 120–125, February, 1973.

Pequignot, G., A. J. Tuyns, and J. L. Berta. "Ascitic Cirrhosis in Relation to Alcohol Consumption." *International Journal of Epidemiology*, 7: 113–120, 1978.

Pernanen, Kai. "Validity of Survey Data on Alcohol Use." In Robert J. Gibbins et al. (eds.), *Research Advances in Alcohol and Drug Problems*, Vol. 1. New York: Wiley, 1974.

Pfeffer, Arnold Z., and Stanley Berger. "A Follow-up Study of Treated Alcoholics." *Quarterly Journal of Studies on Alcohol*, 18: 624–648, 1957.

Phillipson, Richard. *Modern Trends in Drug Dependence*. London: Butterworths, 1970.

Pittman, David J., and Robert L. Tate. "A Comparison of Two Treatment Programs for Alcoholics." *Quarterly Journal of Studies on Alcohol*, 30: 888–899, 1969.

Plaut, T. F. *Alcohol Problems: A Report to the Nation by the Cooperative Commission on the Study of Alcoholism*. New York: Oxford University Press, 1967.

Pokorny, Alex D., Byron A. Miller, and Sidney E. Cleveland. "Response to Treatment of Alcoholism: A Follow-up Study." *Quarterly Journal of Studies on Alcohol*, 29: 364–381, 1968.

Polich, J. Michael, and Bruce R. Orvis. *Alcohol Problems: Patterns and Prevalence in the U.S. Air Force*. The Rand Corporation, R-2308-AF, June 1979.

Pomerleau, Ovide, Michael Pertschuk, and James Stinnett. "A Critical Examination of Some Current Assumptions in the Treatment of Alcoholism." *Journal of Studies on Alcohol*, 37: 849–867, 1976.

Popham, R. E. "Indirect Methods of Alcoholism Prevalence Estimation: A Critical Evaluation." In R. E. Popham (ed.), *Alcohol and Alcoholism*. Toronto: University Press, 1970.

Price, Richard H., and Joan Curlee-Salisbury. "Patient-Treatment Interactions Among Alcoholics." *Journal of Studies on Alcohol*, 36: 659–669, 1975.

Rathod, N. H., E. Gregory, Derek Blows, and G. H. Thomas. "A Two-Year Follow-up Study of Alcoholic Patients." *British Journal of Psychiatry*, 112: 683–692, 1966.

Ringer, C., H. Kufner, K. Antons, and W. Feuerlein. "The N.C.A. Criteria for the Diagnosis of Alcoholism." *Journal of Studies on Alcohol*, 38: 1259–1273, 1977.

Robinson, David. "The Alcohologist's Addiction: Some Implications of Losing Control Over the Disease Concept of Alcoholism." *Quarterly Journal of Studies on Alcohol*, 33: 1028–1042, 1972.

Rohan, William P. "Comment on 'The N.C.A. Criteria for the Diagnosis of Alcoholism; an Empirical Evaluation Study'." *Journal of Studies on Alcohol*, 39: 211–218, 1978.

Roizen, Ron. "The 'Rand Report': Some Comments." *Journal of Studies on Alcohol,* 38: 170–178, 1977.

Roizen, Ron, Don Cahalan, and Patricia Shanks. "Spontaneous Remission Among Untreated Problem Drinkers." In Denise B. Kandel (ed.), *Longitudinal Research in Drug Use: Empirical Findings and Methodological Issues.* New York: Wiley, 1978.

Room, Robin. "Survey vs. Sales Data for the U.S." *Drinking and Drug Practices Surveyor,* 3: 15–16, 1971.

Room, Robin. "Comment on 'The Alcohologist's Addiction'." *Journal of Studies on Alcohol,* 33: 1049–1059, 1972.

Room, Robin. "Measurement and Distribution of Drinking Patterns and Problems in General Populations." In G. Edwards, M. Gross, M. Keller, J. Moser, and R. Room (eds.), *Alcohol-Related Disabilities.* Geneva: World Health Organization, Offset Publication 32, 1977.

Rosenberg, Chaim M., and Maryann Amodeo. "Long-Term Patients Seen in an Alcoholism Clinic." *Quarterly Journal of Studies on Alcohol,* 35: 660–666, 1974.

Rossi, Jean J., Alex Stach, and Nelson J. Bradley. "Effect of Treatment of Male Alcoholics in a Mental Hospital: A Follow-up Study." *Quarterly Journal of Studies on Alcohol,* 24: 91–108, 1963.

Rotter, J. B. "Generalized Expectancies for Internal versus External Control of Reinforcement." *Psychological Monographs,* 80 (Whole No. 609), 1966.

Rubin, E., and C. S. Lieber. "Fatty Liver, Alcoholic Hepatitis, and Cirrhosis Produced by Alcohol in Primates." *New England Journal of Medicine,* 290: 128–135, 1974.

Ruggels, W. Lee, David J. Armor, J. Michael Polich, Ann Mothershead, and Mae Stephen. *A Follow-up Study of Clients at Selected Alcoholism Treatment Centers Funded by NIAAA.* Menlo Park, Calif.: Stanford Research Institute, 1975.

Saunders, W. M., and P. W. Kershaw. "Spontaneous Remission from Alcoholism: A Community Study." *British Journal of Addiction,* 74: 251–265, 1979.

Schmidt, Wolfgang. "Cirrhosis and Alcohol Consumption: An Epidemiological Perspective." In Griffith Edwards and Marcus Grant (eds.), *Alcoholism: New Knowledge and New Responses.* Baltimore: University Park Press, 1976.

Schmidt, Wolfgang, and Jan de Lint. "Estimating the Prevalence of Alcoholism from Alcohol Consumption and Mortality Data." *Quarterly Journal of Studies on Alcohol,* 31: 957–964, 1970.

Schmidt, Wolfgang, and Jan de Lint. "Causes of Death in Alcoholics." *Quarterly Journal of Studies on Alcohol,* 33: 171–185, 1972.

Schmidt, Wolfgang, and Robert E. Popham. "The Single Distribution Theory of Alcohol Consumption." *Journal of Studies on Alcohol,* 39: 400–419, 1978.

Selzer, Melvin L., Amiram Vinokur, and Timothy D. Wilson. "A Psychosocial Comparison of Drunken Drivers and Alcoholics." *Journal of Studies on Alcohol,* 38: 1294–1312, 1977.

Smart, Reginald, "Spontaneous Recovery in Alcoholics: A Review and Analysis of the Available Research." *Drug and Alcohol Dependence,* 1: 277–285, 1975.

Smart, R., W. Schmidt, and M. K. Moss. "Social Class as a Determinant of the Type and Duration of Therapy Received by Alcoholics." *International Journal of the Addictions,* 4: 453–543, 1969.

Sobell, Linda C., and Mark B. Sobell. "Outpatient Alcoholics Give Valid Self-Reports." *Journal of Nervous and Mental Disease,* 161: 32–41, 1975.

Sobell, Linda C., and Mark B. Sobell. "Validity of Self-Reports in Three Populations of Alcoholics." *Journal of Consulting and Clinical Psychology,* 46: 901–907, 1978b.

Sobell, Mark B., and Linda C. Sobell. *Behavioral Treatment of Alcohol Problems: Individualized Therapy and Controlled Drinking.* New York: Plenum, 1978a.

Sobell, Mark B., Linda C. Sobell, and Fred H. Samuels. "Validity of Self-Reports of Alcohol-Related Arrests by Alcoholics." *Quarterly Journal of Studies on Alcohol,* 35: 276–280, 1974.

Sobell, Mark B., Linda C. Sobell, and Robert VanderSpek. "Relationship Among Clinical Judgment, Self-Report, and Breath Analysis Measures of Intoxication in Alcoholics." *Journal of Consulting and Clinical Psychology,* 47: 204–206, 1979.

Stein, Leonard, Dolores Niles, and Arnold M. Ludwig. "The Loss of Control Phenomenon in Alcoholics." *Quarterly Journal of Studies on Alcohol,* 29: 598–602, 1968.

Sundby, P. *Alcoholism and Mortality.* Oslo: Universitetsforlaget, 1967.

Tatsuoka, Maurice M. *Multivariate Analysis: Techniques for Educational and Psychological Research.* New York: Wiley, 1971.

Trice, Harrison M., and Paul M. Roman. "Sociopsychological Predictors of Affiliation with Alcoholics Anonymous." *Social Psychiatry,* 5: 51–59, 1970.

Trice, H. M., P. M. Roman, and J. A. Belasco. "Selection for Treatment: A Predictive Evaluation of an Alcoholism Treatment Regimen." *International Journal of the Addictions,* 4: 303–317, 1969.

Trice, Harrison M., and J. Richard Wahl. "A Rank Order Analysis of the Symptoms of Alcoholism." *Quarterly Journal of Studies on Alcohol,* 19: 638–648, 1958.

Tuchfeld, Barry, J. B. Simuel, M. L. Schmitt, J. L. Ries, D. L. Kay, and G. T. Waterhouse. *Changes in Patterns of Alcohol Use Without the Aid of Formal Treatment.* Final Report prepared for the National Institute on Alcohol Abuse and Alcoholism. North Carolina: Research Triangle Institute, 1976.

U.S. Bureau of the Census. *Population Characteristics: Marriage, Divorce, Widowhood and Remarriage by Family Characteristics.* Series P-20, No 312. Washington, D.C.: U.S. Government Printing Office, August 1977.

U.S. Bureau of the Census. *Population Characteristics: Population Profile of the United States.* Series P-20, No. 324, Washington, D.C.: U.S. Government Printing Office, April 1978a.

U.S. Bureau of the Census. *Consumer Income.* Series P-60, No. 116. Washington, D.C.: U.S. Government Printing Office, July 1978b.

Vannicelli, Marsha, Bruce Pfau, and Ralph S. Ryback. "Data Attrition in Follow-up Studies of Alcoholics." *Journal of Studies on Alcohol,* 37: 1325–1330, 1976.

Wallgren, Henrik, and Herbert Barry. *Actions of Alcohol,* Vols. 1 and 2. Amsterdam: Elsevier, 1970.

Walsh, Brendan M., and Dermot Walsh. "Validity of Indices of Alcoholism—A Comment from Irish Experience." *British Journal of Preventive Social Medicine,* 27: 18–26, 1973.

Wanberg, Kenneth W., John L. Horn, and F. Mark Foster. "A Differential Assessment Model for Alcoholism." *Journal of Studies on Alcohol,* 38: 512–543, 1977.

Westermeyer, Joseph, and Jacob Bearman. "A Proposed Social Indicator System for Alcohol-Related Problems." *Preventive Medicine,* 2: 438–444, 1973.

Williams, A. F. "The Alcoholic Personality." In Benjamin Kissin and Henri Begleiter (eds.), *The Biology of Alcoholism,* Vol. 4: *Social Aspects of Alcoholism.* New York: Plenum Press, 1976.

Witkin, H. A., S. A. Karp, and D. R. Goodenough. "Dependence in Alcoholics," *Quarterly Journal of Studies on Alcohol,* 20: 493–504, 1959.

Wolff, Sulammith, and Lydia Holland. "A Questionnaire Follow-up of Alcoholic Patients." *Quarterly Journal of Studies on Alcohol,* 25: 108–118, 1964.

Wood, H. P., and E. L. Duffy, "Psychological Factors in Alcoholic Women." *American Journal of Psychiatry,* 123: 341–345, 1966.

World Health Organization. *Expert Committee on Mental Health, Alcoholism Subcommittee, Second Report.* Technical Report Number 48. Geneva, 1952.

World Health Organization. *International Classification of Diseases,* 1965 revision. Geneva: World Health Organization, 1967.

World Health Organization. *International Classification of Diseases,* 9th revision. Geneva: World Health Organization, 1977.

"W.H.O. and a New Perspective on Alcoholism," *The Lancet,* 1087–1088, May 21, 1977.

Zax, Melvin, Elmer A. Gardner, and William T. Hart. "A Survey of the Prevalence of Alcoholism in Monroe County, N.Y., 1961." *Quarterly Journal of Studies on Alcohol,* 28: 316–327, 1967.

Zung, Burton J. "Factor Structure of the Michigan Alcoholism Screening Test." *Journal of Studies on Alcohol,* 39: 56–67, 1978.

Index

Abstention:
  Alcoholics Anonymous and, 150-152,
    214
  alcoholic self-concept and, 99-100
  continuous, 196
  at four years, 61, 203, 205-206
    amount of, 190-192
    characteristics of, 195
    length of, 36-39
      during 30-day period, 39
      during past 6 months, 37-38
    long-term, 8-9
      alcohol-related mortality and,
        128, 215
      background characteristics and,
        135
      prognosis of, 57, 164-168, 205
      relapse rate in, 164-168, 178-179,
        180-182, 185, 205
    nonabstainers, estimated percentage of,
      228-229
    problem rates, relation to, 168, 215
    psychosocial functioning in, 211
    short-term:
      alcohol-related mortality and, 124-125,
        128, 215
      at 18-month vs. four years followup,
        75, 205
      prognosis of, 57-58, 205-207
      relapse rate in, 164-168, 178-179,
        180-182, 185, 205
    6-month, 180-181
  social adjustment and, 82, 84
  subject-collateral agreement on,
    253
  see also Validity, of self-reports
Accidents, 105, 110, 113
Addiction, to ethanol, phases in, 4-6

Admission:
  sample, see Subject, characteristics, at
    admission to treatment
  to treatment, see Treatment, admission
    to
Age factors:
  in mortality:
    alcohol-related, 122
    due to selected causes, 114-115
  in relapse rate, 178-179, 182-183, 216
Alcohol:
  behavior:
    long-term pattern, 196-200
      definition of, 196
      -status relationship, 196-200
    personality theories of, see Personality,
      theories
  blood level of, see Blood alcohol con-
    centration
  consumption:
    over four years, 193, 195
    in past 24 hours, BAC measurements
      and, 238, 243, 246
    patterns:
      distribution of, 45
      long-term, 192-194
      problem rates at four years and,
        193
      see also Drinking, patterns
    quantity of (Q), 39-46, 77, 269
      atypical, 40
      classification of, 43-44, 192
      drinking status at four years and, 65
      at 18-month, alcohol problems at
        four years, 59
      estimated rates of, 229-230
      high, and very high Q, 44, 63, 65,
        199

low Q, 63, 65, 68, 199
  prognosis and, 58
quantity-frequency index (QF), 44-46,
    272-273
symptoms, adverse consequences of
    drinking and, 58
  typical, 41-43, 240, 245-249, 269
  today, vs. typical day last month,
    240
  see also Self-reports
dependence symptoms, 4-5, 13-14, 39,
    46-50, 203-204, 261-263
  at admission to treatment, 73
  alcohol-related mortality and,
    122-123
  relapse rate and, 168
  alcohol consumption patterns and,
    58
  alcohol-related incidents and, 169
  blackouts, 5, 47
  continuous drinking, 38-39, 48
  correlational analysis of, 49
  at 18-month followup, 207, 263
  alcohol problems at four years and,
    56, 58, 131, 204-205
  alcohol-related mortality and, 124,
    204
  estimated rates for, number of contacts
    and, 229-230
  index, 46, 50, 270
  loss of control, 4, 47, 161-162
  "missing meals," 47
  in nonproblem drinkers, 73-75, 206
  prognosis of patient with, 57, 128,
    172, 204-205
  psychiatric symptomatology and, 93
  relation to adverse consequences of
    drinking, 53-57, 262
  relation to drinking at admission to
    treatment, 71-73
  relation to relapse, 162, 168, 178-179
  reported by collaterals, validity study
    on, 255
  risk patterns of drinking behaviors
    and, 53-57
  symptom level carryover, 18 months to
    4 years, 263
  elimination rate for, 235-236, 239, 241-
    242, 244
problems, see Problem drinking

-related:
  incidents, 169, 194-196, 271-272
  medical conditions, see Drinking,
    adverse consequences of
  mortality, see Mortality, alcohol-related
Alcohol and Drug Problems Association of
    North America, 18
Alcoholics Anonymous (AA):
  attendance to, 146, 214
  drinking status and, 148-152
  problem rates at four years and,
    214
Alcoholic self-concept, 98-100
Alcoholism:
  addictive form of, 4-6
  beliefs about, 4-7, 97-100
    alcoholic self-concept, 98-100
    traditional disease concept, 97-99
  classical conception of, implications
    of, 4-6, 39, 219
    alternative conceptions, 6-7
  delta species of, 5
  evidence of change in, 7-9
    see also Stability, of status
  gamma species of, 4
  nonaddictive forms of, 5
  research background in, 4-14
  "spontaneous recovery" in, 9
  World Health Organization Committee
    definition of, 5-6
  see also Drinking
Alcoholism Treatment Centers (ATCs),
    NIAAA-funded, 15-16
  client interview form for, 275-311
  monitoring system, 135-137
  population, 17-20
  see also Treatment
Anhedonia, 91
Anxiety, 91-92
Arteriosclerosis, 113
Autonomy, as personality trait, 93,
    96

Background characteristics:
  of cohort, 15-20, 202
  long-term abstention and, 135
  relapse and, 175-177
  of sample at admission to treatment,
    258-259
  of stable and unstable groups, 187

Behavior(s):
  alcohol, see Alcohol, behavior
  deviant, 97
  drinking, see Drinking, behavior
Behavioral impairment index, 273
Behavioral impairment measures, 260-261
Beliefs, about alcoholism, see Alcoholism,
    beliefs about
Bias, potential, analysis of, 31-34, 222-225
Blackouts, 5, 47
Bleeding, gastrointestinal, 118-119
Blood alcohol concentration (BAC):
  formula for, 237
  measurement of:
    instruments for, 28-29, 234
    procedures for, 234-235
    vs. self-reports, 27-31, 69, 235-252
      consistency approach, 236-237,
        246
      consistency typology and, 242-243,
        250
      consumption in the past 24 hours and,
        238, 243, 246
      disconfirmation approach, 236-237
      estimated total consumption and,
        239-245
      underreporting rates, variations in,
        245-252
    subject knowledge prior to, 28
    time of last drink and, 236
    validity of, status classification and,
      67-68
    validity study of, 234-252
Brain syndrome, chronic, 91
Breath test, see Blood alcohol concentra-
    tion

Cancer, death rate from, 110, 112-113,
    116
Chronic brain syndrome, 91
Chronology, of data collection procedures,
    25-26
Cirrhosis, of liver, 51, 65, 113
Client interview form, 275-311
Coding, of underlying cause of death,
    109
Cognitive impairment, 91
Cohort:
  background characteristics of, 15-20, 202
  origination of, 16-18

study, representativeness of, 18-20
Collateral(s):
  interview, 27, 117-119, 208-209, 252
  measures, drinking status validity and,
    68-71
  -subject agreement, see Subject-collateral
    agreement
  -subject relationship, 253
  validity study, 252-256
Conceptions, on alcoholism, 4-7, 39,
    97-100, 219
Conclusions, see Followup, four years
    study
Consent forms, 25-28
Consistency typology, and alcohol consum-
    tion reporting, 242-243, 250
Contact(s):
  defined, 11
  drinking status of, treatment and,
    148
  estimated rates of consumption,
    symptoms and consequences in,
    229
  followup status in, 139-140
  treatment of, 146-148, 212
Continuous abstention, 196
Continuous drinking pattern, 38-39, 48
Control:
  of impulse, as personality trait, 93-96
  internal locus of, 95
  loss of, 4, 47, 161-162, 219
Convulsions, 52
Coronary heart disease, 113
Correlational analysis:
  of alcohol dependence symptoms,
    49
  of treatment, 212-214

Data collection procedures, 25-27,
    106-107
  chronology, 25-26
  on mortality, 106-107
  subject interviews, 26-27
Data coordinator, 17
Death:
  certificate, 105-107
  underlying cause of, 107-111
  see also Mortality
Delta species, of alcoholism,
    5

Dependency theory, of alcoholic behavior, 96-97
Depression, 91-92
Design, of four years study, *see* Study design and methods
Deviant behavior, 97
  see also Alcohol, behavior; Drinking, behavior
Discriminant analysis, 100-101
Discriminant function coefficients, 101-102
Disease concept, of alcoholism, 97
Drinking:
  adverse consequences of, 50-53, 202-204, 261-263
    alcohol consumption patterns and, 58
    distribution of, 52
    estimated rates of, number of contacts and, 229-230
    health-related, 51-52, 270
    index for, 270-271
    law enforcement incidents, 52, 270
    psychiatric symptomatology and, 93
    relation to alcohol dependence symptoms, 53-57, 262
    social effects, 52, 81-84, 271
  behavior:
    classification of, 164
    at 18-month, alcohol problems at four years, 56
    factor analysis of, 257-263
    measures of, 257-263
      behavioral impairment measures, 260-261
      symptom levels and consequences, 261-263
    risk patterns of, 53-60
    self-reported, validity of, 27-31, 69, 234-256
      breath test validity study, 234-252
      collateral validity study, 252-256
      see also Blood alcohol concentration
    treatment and, 129, 131-137, 152-158
  categories, psychosocial profile of, 100-104
  "escape" reasons for, 92-93
  jailing caused by, 254
    see also Incidents, alcohol-related
  nonproblem, 163
    alcohol dependence symptoms, 73-75

alcohol-related mortality and, 128, 215
  drinking status at four years and, 231
  at 18-month, prognosis of, 206
  high consumers, low consumers, 203-204
  psychosocial functioning and, 211
  relapse rate in, 164-168, 180-182, 215-216
  stability of status in, 185-186
patterns:
  at admission to treatment, status and, 71-75
  from admission to four years, 77-79
    aggregate changes in, 78
  at four years, 35-79
    abstention, *see* Abstention, at four years
    adverse consequences of drinking, *see* Drinking, adverse consequences of
    alcohol dependence symptoms, *see* Alcohol, dependence symptoms
    continuous drinking pattern, 38-39, 48
    vs. 18-month followup, 77-79
    group changes over time, assessment of, 77-79
    intermittent drinking pattern, 38-39
    period of last drink, problem assessment and, 40
    quantity of alcohol consumption, *see* Alcohol, consumption, quantity of
    risk patterns of drinking behavior, 53-60
    status, assessment of, *see* Drinking status; Status
  long-term, 189-200
    abstention, amount of, 190-192
    alcohol consumption pattern, 192-194
    alcohol-related incidents and, 194-196
    drinking status at four years and, 198
  at 6-month, 63
  stability and change in, 159-200
    long-term patterns, 189-200
    relapse, *see* Relapse
    stability of status, 183-189
  problems, *see* Problem drinking
status:
  at admission, mortality and, 122

alcoholic self-concept and, 98
change in, 18-month to four years
  period, 165
at four years, 62
  Alcoholics Anonymous and, 149,
  151
  by amount of initial treatment, 137-
  139, 142
  assessment of, 60-78
  beliefs about alcoholism and, 98
  category discrimination, 103-104
  classification, 67-71, 204-206
  consistency of, with 6-month drinking
  patterns, 63
  for contact an admission samples,
  139-140, 148
  definitions of, 75-76, 163-171
  distributions of, 64, 146
  drinking patterns at admission and,
  71-75
  income and occupational level and,
  84, 266-267
  life satisfaction and, 86-87
  long-term pattern of drinking and,
  198
  marital status and, 265
  for nonproblem drinkers, 231
  psychiatric symptoms and, 92
  psychological traits and, 94
  regression models of, 133, 154,
  232
  self-reports consistency pattern
  and, 250
  by setting and amount of initial treatment, 71-75, 137-139, 142, 212,
  217-218, 263-264
  social stability and, 82
  by status at 18-month, 171
  stressful life events and, 88
  by subject characteristics at admission,
  132
at 18-month, 171
  Alcoholics Anonymous and,
  150-151
  alcohol-related mortality and, 123-
  128
  for contact and admission samples,
  140
Driving while intoxicated (DWI),
  16-17

Elimination rate, for alcohol, 235-236,
  239, 241-242, 244
Emotional adjustment, 89-91
Emotional stability, 93-97
  scale score, 100-101
Employment status, 83-86
  alcohol-related mortality and, 121
  -drinking status relationship, 266
  time trends in, 85-86
"Escape" reasons, for drinking, 92-93
Ethanol, see Alcohol
Ethanol poisoning, 117

Factor analysis:
  of behavioral impairment measures,
  261
  of drinking behavior, 257-263
Fieldwork results, 23-25
  validity samples and, 29-31
Followup:
  effort, status at four years and,
  226-232
  18-month study, 12-13, 17-18, 206-
  207
  see also specific followup problem
  four years study, conclusions of, 201-
  221
  comparisons with 18-month study,
  206-207
  drinking behavior, 202-204
  drinking status, basis of classification
  of, 204-206
  implications for policy and research,
  217-221
  methodological analysis, 207-209
  mortality, 209
  psychosocial functioning, 209-211
  relapse and stability, 214-216
  treatment, 211-214
  6-month study, 11-12
  nonfollowup, bias due to, 31-34
  rates, and potential bias analysis, 222-
  225

Gamma species, of alcoholism, 4
Gastrointestinal bleeding,
  118-119
Gastrointestinal ulcer, 114

Hallucinations, 52

Health:
-related problems of drinking, 51-52, 270
in stable and unstable groups, 188
Heart disease, 113-114, 116
Hospitalization, 144-145, 158, 254

Impulse control, as personality trait, 93-96
Incidents:
alcohol-related, 169, 194-196, 271-272
counts, 168
Income, 84, 267
Index (indices):
construction, 269-274
dependence symptoms, 46, 50, 270
mental health, 100-101
quantity-frequency (QF), 44-46, 272-273
of subject characteristics at admission, 272-274
Inpatient care, 144-145, 158, 254
see also Treatment
Instruments, for BAC measurements, 28-29, 234
Intermittent drinking pattern, 38-39
International Classification of Diseases Adapted for United States, 108
Interview:
collateral, 27, 68-71, 208-209, 252
form, 275-311
rates, by level of effort expended, 227
subject, 26-27, 29

Jailing, 254
Jellinek model, of alcoholism, 4-6, 39, 219

Law enforcement incidents, 52, 254
see also Incidents, alcohol-related
Life events, stressful, 87-90
Life satisfaction, 86-87
Linear regression models, 154
Liver disease, 51-52, 65
consumption level and, 206
mortality due to, 105, 110, 113
Located and unlocated sampling groups, characteristics of, 222-225
Logit model, problems prediction by, 156

Logit regression analyses, of relapse patterns, 176-181
Loss of control, 4, 47, 161-162, 219
Lung cancer, 112-113

Marital status, 82-83
alcohol-related mortality and, 121
relapse rate and, 176, 182-183, 216
Mental health index, 100-101
Methodological analysis, of four years study, 207-209
Methodological issues in alcoholism research, 9-11
Methodology, in alcoholism research, 4
see also Study design and methods
"Missing meals," 47-48
"Morning drinking," 47, 255
Mortality, 105-128, 209.
actual and expected, 111-114
after admission to treatment, 121-123
by age groups, 114-115, 122
alcohol-related, 117-128, 215
in abstainers, 124-125, 128, 215
background characteristics at admission, role in, 122
correlates of, 121-128
determination of, methods for, 126-127
by drinking and symptomatology:
at admission, 122-123
at 18-month, 123-128
in nonproblem drinkers, 128, 215
by underlying cause, 120
data, 31, 106-107
after 18-month, 115-116, 123-128
probably alcohol-related, 118
socioeconomic status and, 121-122
underlying cause of death, 107-111, 120

National Center for Health Statistics (NCHS), 105-107
National Institute on Alcohol Abuse and Alcoholism (NIAAA):
Alcoholism Treatment Centers of, see Alcoholism Treatment Centers, NIAAA-funded; Treatment
behavioral impairment index of, 273
monitoring system of, 15-16

quantity-frequency index of, 44-46,
272-273

Objectives, in alcoholism research, 2-4
see also Research, questions
Outpatient care, 141-145, 153, 158,
217-218

Pancreatitis, 52
Personal resources, emotional stability
and, 93-97
Personality:
"high risk," 89-91
theories of alcoholic behavior, 95-97
dependency theory, 96-97
power theory, 96
social psychological theory of deviance,
97
see also Psychological traits
Physical dependence, to alcohol, 4, 39
see also Alcohol, dependence symptoms
Physical health, in stable and unstable
groups, 188
Poisoning, ethanol, 117
Policy, in dealing with alcoholism,
217-221
Posttreatment assessments, 3
Power theory, of alcoholic behavior,
96
Problem drinking, defined, 163
see also Alcohol, dependence symptoms;
Drinking, adverse consequences of
Problem rate, at four years, 170-171
for abstainers, 168, 215
Alcoholics Anonymous and, 214
by 18-month drinking behavior, 56
by18-month symptom level, 56
logit model and, 156
long-term patterns of alcohol consumption and, 193
for nonproblem drinkers, 168, 215
regression model and, 225
treatment and, 157-158, 212
Prognosis, 3-4
for abstainers:
amount of abstention and,
190-191
long-term, 57, 128, 164-168
short-term, 57-58, 125, 164-168,
205-207

factors in:
alcohol consumption, 58
alcohol dependence symptoms, 57,
128, 172, 204-205
personality, 89-90
socioeconomic status, 131, 154
treatment, 12, 153
for nonproblem drinkers, 206
see also Relapse
Psychiatric symptomatology, 91-97
anhedonia, 91
anxiety, 91-92
cognitive impairment, 91
depression, 91-92
drinking status and, 92
emotional stability, personal resources
and, 93-97
scale, 274
tension, 91
Psychological health, in stable and unstable
groups, 188
Psychological traits, 93-96
see also Personality
Psychosocial functioning, 80-104, 209-
211
emotional adjustment, 89-91
life satisfaction and, 86-87
personality, "high risk," 89-91
psychiatric symptomatology, 91-97
psychosocial profile, of drinking
categories, 100-104
social adjustment, 81-86, 210
stressful life events and, 87-90
Psychosocial measures, 263-268
Psychosocial profile, of drinking categories,
100-104

Quantity (Q), of alcohol consumption,
see Alcohol, consumption,
quantity of
Quantity-frequency index (QF), 44-46,
272-273

Race, alcohol-related mortality, role in,
122
"Rand Report," 12
Recovery, spontaneous, 9
Reentry, *see* Treatment, reentries to
Regression models, 133, 154, 225,
232

Regression residuals, nonproblem drinking
  and, 231
Relapse, 159-183
  correlates of, 175-183
    background characteristics, 175-177
    theoretical implications, 182-183
  loss of control theory and, 161-162
  rates:
    during 18-month and four years, 173-
      174
    at four years, 172-175, 214-216
    in abstainers, 164-168, 178-179,
      180-182, 185, 205
    age, as a factor in, 178-179, 182-183,
      216
    alcohol-dependence symptoms and,
      162, 168, 178-179
    background characteristics at
      admission and, 177
    logit regression analyses of, 176-
      181
    marital status and, 176, 182-183,
      216
    in nonproblem drinkers, 164-168,
      178-179, 180-182, 215-216
    in 6-month abstainers, 180-181
  status at four years, definition of,
    163-171
Remission, 216-217
  abstention and nonproblem drinking
    as forms of, 219
  definition of, 75-76, 172-175
  stability of, 3, 8-9
  see also Relapse
Research:
  background, 4-14
    change in alcoholism, evidence for,
      7-9
    classical conception of alcoholism,
      implications of, 4-6
    alternative conceptions, 6-7
    methodological issues, 9-11
    see also Study design and methods
  four years study results, implications
    for, 217-221
  questions, 2-4
    methodology, 4
    posttreatment assessments, 3
    prognosis and intervention, 3-4
    stability and change, 3

Residential stability, of alcoholic, 83
Respiratory disease, nonmalignant,
  113
Risk patterns, of drinking behavior,
  53-60
  adverse consequences of drinking and,
    53-57
  alcohol dependence symptoms and,
    53-57
  short-term abstention as, 57-59

Sample, admission, see Subject characteristics, at admission to treatment
Sampling:
  adequacy of, 9
  for four years study, 20-24
Selected Underlying Causes of Death,
  110
  see also Mortality
Self-administered form, 27
Self-concept, alcoholic, 98-100
Self-reports, 70
  vs. BAC, see Blood alcohol concentration,
    measurement of
  consistency patterns in, 242-243, 250
  inconsistent, sensitivity analysis for,
    251
  validity, 10-11, 70-71, 233-256
    procedures for assessment of, see
      Validity, procedures
Sensitivity analysis, for inconsistent self-
  reports, 251
Smoking, 113
SM-7 device, for breath-testing, 28-29,
  234
Social adjustment, 81-86, 210
  at 18-month, 85-86
  at four years, 81-84
Social effects, of drinking, 52, 81-84,
  271
Social psychological theory, of deviance,
  97
Social stability index, 272
Socioeconomic status (SES):
  index of, 272
  mortality and, 121-122
  prognosis and, 131, 154
  relapse and, 175, 177
Stability:
  emotional, 93-97, 100-101

of remission, 3, 8-9
  see also Relapse
residential, 83
social, index for, 272
of status, at four years, 159, 183-189,
    214-216
Stable groups:
  definition of, 184-186
  and unstable groups, 185-188
    background characteristics of, 187
    physical and psychological health
      characteristics of, 188
Stanford Research Institute, report of,
    12
Status:
  drinking, see Drinking, status
  employment, see Employment status
  at four years:
    by alcohol consumption over four years,
      193
    definitions of, relapse and, 163-171
    followup effort and, 226-232
    long-term patterns of alcohol behavior
      and, 196-200
    measure of, 60-61
    stability of, 159, 183-189, 214-216
    treatment, amount of, 212
  marital, see Marital status
  socioeconomic, see Socioeconomic
    status
Stress, 5, 81, 87-90
Study design and methods, 15-34
  cohort, background characteristics of,
    15-20, 202
  data collection procedures, 25-27
  four years followup sampling, 20-24
    sampling frame, defined, 20-23
    sample results, 23-24
  mortality data collection, 31, 106-107
  nonfollowup, bias due to, 31-34, 222-
    225
  validity procedures, 27-31
Subject:
  characteristics:
    at admission to treatment, 32, 77-79
      see also Treatment, admission samples
    of ATC population, 18-20
    of background, 258-259
    drinking status at four years and, 132
    indices for, 272-274

of located and unlocated groups, 223
  treatment, effect on, 131-135
-collaterals agreement, 69
  abstained or drunk, 253
  drank more than 2 oz. ethanol per day,
    254
  hospitalization, alcohol-related, 254
  jailed, due to drinking, 254
  "missing meals," 256
  missing work, 255
  morning drinking, 255
  tremors, 255
-collaterals relationship, 253
  interviews, 26-27, 29
Suicide, 105, 111, 113
Symptoms, of alcohol dependence, see
    Alcohol, dependence symptoms

Tension, 91
Theory, on alcoholic behavior:
  dependency theory, 96-97
  loss of control theory, 161-162
  power theory, 96
  social psychological theory of
    deviance, 97
  see also Alcoholism, beliefs about
Time trends, in social adjustment, 85-86
Treatment, 211-214
  admission to:
    drinking patterns at, 71-75
    estimated problem rate at four years
      and, 157
    mortality after, 121-123
    social adjustment at, 85-86
    subject characteristics at, see Subject
      characteristics, at admission to
      treatment
  admission samples:
    drinking status in, by type of treatment,
      148
    status at four years in, 139-140
  Alcoholism Treatment Centers (ATCs),
      NIAAA-funded:
    center differences, drinking status and,
      263-264
    population, characteristics of, 18-20
    reentry to, 136-137, 141-146, 153,
      158, 271-272
  amount of, 137-142, 212, 217-218
  of contacts, 146-148, 212

at four years:
  correlational analysis of, 212-214
  drinking behavior and, 129, 131-137,
    152-158
  drinking status and, 71-75, 137-139,
    142, 212, 217-218, 263-264
  models of, drinking behavior and, 152-
    158
  non-ATC, 146-152
    Alcoholics Anonymous, 148-152
    formal, 147
  patterns, measuring of, 135-137
  previous, prognosis and, 153
  prognosis in relation to, 12, 153
  reentries to, 136-137, 141-146, 153,
    158, 194-195, 271-272
    inpatient care, 144-145, 158
    number of, drinking status and,
      146
    outpatient care, 141-145, 153, 158,
      217-218
  setting of, followup status and, 140-
    141
  subject characteristics, effect on, 131-135
  type of, 137-141, 212
Tremors, 70, 255
Typical quantity, of alcohol consumption:
  defined, 41-43

distribution of, 41-43
formula for estimation of, 269
underreporting of, 245-249

Ulcer, gastrointestinal, 114
United States Life Tables, 107
  by causes of death, 107
Unlocated sampling groups, characteristics
  of, 222-225
Unstable groups, *see* Stable groups, and
  unstable groups

Validity:
  procedures:
    blood alcohol concentration measure-
      ments, 27-31, 69, 235-252
    collateral interview, 27, 68-71, 208-
      209
    completion rates for, 30
  samples, fieldwork results and, 29-31
  of self-reports, 10-11, 70-71, 233-256
    procedures for, *see* Validity, procedures
  of status classification, 67-71
  study, of breath test, 234-252

Withdrawal symptoms, 47
World Health Organization Committee,
  alcoholism definition by, 5-6

Psychology and Psychiatry in Courts and Corrections: Controversy and Change
  by Ellsworth A. Fersch, Jr.
Restricted Environmental Stimulation: Research and Clinical Applications
  by Peter Suedfeld
Personal Construct Psychology: Psychotherapy and Personality
  edited by Alvin W. Landfield and Larry M. Leitner
Mothers, Grandmothers, and Daughters: Personality and Child Care in
Three-Generation Families
  by Bertram J. Cohler and Henry U. Grunebaum
Further Explorations in Personality
  edited by A. I. Rabin, Joel Aronoff, Andrew M. Barclay, and Robert A. Zucker
Hypnosis and Relaxation: Modern Verification of an Old Equation
  by William E. Edmonston, Jr.
Handbook of Clinical Behavior Therapy
  edited by Samuel M. Turner, Karen S. Calhoun, and Henry E. Adams
Handbook of Clinical Neuropsychology
  edited by Susan B. Filskov and Thomas J. Boll
The Course of Alcoholism: Four Years After Treatment
  by J. Michael Polich, David J. Armor, and Harriet B. Braiker